ORAL INTERPRETATION

ORAL INTERPRETATION

EIGHTH EDITION

Charlotte I. Lee

Professor Emeritus, Northwestern University

Timothy Gura

Professor, Brooklyn College,
City University of New York

Houghton Mifflin Company   Boston

Dallas   Geneva, Illinois   Palo Alto   Princeton, New Jersey

Cover: "Two Dancers" 1980
       Oil on canvas, 48″ × 72″
       © David Hockney
Part openers: "Dancer" 1980
       Oil, 48″ × 36″
       © David Hockney

Chapter openers and selection illustrations by Michael Crawford.

Acknowledgments begin on page 499.

Printed in the U.S.A.

Library of Congress Catalog Card Number: 91-71976
ISBN: 0-395-59329-8

BCDEFGHIJ-D-998765432

CONTENTS

Part III   THE INTERPRETATION OF DRAMA

Appendix A

Appendix B

TO THE STUDENT

At first this book — and the course of study we propose — may strike you as strange. For most of our lives we have been taught to read silently, not to move our lips, and to get through the material as rapidly as possible. Moreover, we have been asked to look at poems, plays, or stories much as we look at rocks in the geology laboratory or dissect frogs in biology. We are frequently encouraged to point out metaphors, tragic flaws, or third-person narrators, as if literature were aggregates of those items. Too often this approach leads to study *around* the work. When finished, we are left with masses of facts about the text but not much of the excitement or delight we felt when we enjoyed the reading itself.

Interpretation, on the other hand, asks you to speak up, move your lips, respond to the fullness of the story, and take time to experience what the characters are undergoing. All those "facts" you discovered about literature in other courses can finally be put to use! They refine and clarify your own performance because interpretation goes several steps beyond the mere vocalization of silent reading. It requires that you appreciate a work of literary art, and it demands that you communicate that work of art with your voice and body. Interpretation is built on scholarship, technical know-how, sensitivity, and the desire to share. You cannot skimp on any of these.

Like any other art, interpretation requires practice and study. A musician translates written notes into sounds and thus conveys the composer's achievement. An interpreter brings to life the printed words that preserve the ideas and experiences of humankind. Your instruments are your voice and your body and, as musicians, using these instruments requires skill developed by rehearsal. You'll have rocky patches at first because learning to read aloud requires care and effort. You might be wondering, as do many students, how this course can be of use to you. We believe that it can change your life.

Many people, as we all know, spend their most prized hours outside of their jobs. Even the most ambitious of us is unlikely to spend more than a third of a week pursuing commercial success. On the weekends, on vacations, and during free time, many people feel a desire for something more out of life and themselves than another beer and a video. They want something that enhances their sense of being human. The oral interpretation of literature is not only the fullest way to enjoy stories and poems and plays: it also allows us to share our experiences and our pleasures with people who care about literature as we do.

This book can teach you ways to embrace literature and give life to its performance. In Part I we describe a method of detailed analysis that helps you develop your own responses to literature you have chosen and provides the foundation on which you can build your performance. In Part II, we apply these principles of analysis to prose. We guide you through each step of your first performance. Drama is the focus in Part III, where we suggest ways of character and scene analysis and offer helpful tips about creating characters and scenes vividly in the minds of your audience. Part IV deals with poetry. Group performance is discussed last — in Part V — because it includes poetry, prose, and drama and because the success of any group depends on the preparation and technical skill of every individual involved in it.

If you are already a performer, you will find that the method we encourage increases your flexibility in handling various kinds of material. If you are new to performing — perhaps you have spent time studying literature by other methods — you will find that performance before an intelligent audience is a valuable test of your thoroughness and accuracy. You will also discover why others find performing so challenging and enjoyable. Whatever your previous experience in performance, this book asks intriguing questions. In chapters 2, 4, 6, 8, 10, and 11 we ask a series of questions to help you both analyze your own performance and the performances of your classmates. These questions are not rules or recipes; they are ways to help you think carefully and precisely about all the choices that made your performance uniquely yours. Additionally, each of the selections is followed by one or two questions that ask you to consider a central performance problem in that text. Thus, *Oral Interpretation* offers both practical suggestions for solving specific problems and a wide choice of literary selections at various levels of sophistication and degrees of difficulty.

One final word about the selections at the ends of the chapters: each is substantial and challenging and each contains clear clues to help you embody that special experience. Some may even "remind you of something you did not know you knew," as Robert Frost has written. But if one selection seems difficult, don't give up on it right away: walk around a bit in its shoes before dismissing it. You may be surprised at how much you discover about yourself as you reach out to understand the literature. In that respect (as in many others), what you derive from *Oral Interpretation* will depend on how much of yourself you are willing to invest. Let us know how you make out.

TO THE INSTRUCTOR

Four decades have passed since the first edition of this book appeared, and much has changed in the field of oral interpretation since 1952. Most obviously, many courses and programs that were called "oral interpretation" (or something similar) now use "performance studies." These changes have not been simple onomastic exercises, but genuine attempts to reflect a wider focus and broader scope. We applaud these efforts to expand the field because we have always been convinced that the rich rewards performance offers ought not to be limited solely to traditional literary texts. Indeed, as you examine this eighth edition, you will note many references to this new order.

At the same time, we remain *Oral Interpretation*. Our title is unchanged not because we are divorced in spirit from the broad scope of the field, but because we remain committed to the firmest possible foundation for students beginning to perform literature. For us, that foundation remains the oral interpretation of literature, which is equally concerned with the analysis and appreciation of a work of literary art and with the requirements and preparations of a performing art. Art, for us, continues to unify our concern. Literary works of art and works of performance are always in part the result of the sociological, political, and anthropological forces that shape them, but they are not, for us, chiefly sociological, political, or anthropological works. We have often in these pages referred to the ways in which the texts we study — and even the nature of "text" itself — can be viewed through various, but rewarding, spectacles, but we remain focused on the student whose early experiences with performing literature will prepare him or her for the wonders open to all who study performance and literature.

The fundamental theory of the book remains the same: only when a student fully understands a literary selection can any reliable performance preparation begin. Thus, we continue to emphasize the analysis of literary selections as a guide to their appreciation and, more immediately, as the indispensable first step of any rehearsal. The process of analysis described here emphasizes the writer's relationship with the reader and thus the position the interpreter takes in re-creating the experience, whether that experience is an author's personal discovery or the sensibilities of a created character. In addition to an awareness of the work's complexities, oral performance demands a flexible voice and body able to suggest all the subtleties discovered through close analysis. Throughout the process, the only reliable yardstick of the success of performance remains the text itself. Thus, interpreters and critics have as their ultimate recourse that with which they began: the literature being performed.

These principles, of course, have characterized the previous editions of this book. From the seventh edition, we have retained the six sections called "Analyzing the Performance," which appear in chapters 2, 4, 6, 8, 10, and 11. Each of the sections contains practical hints for describing and evaluating student performances and concludes with several general questions we have found useful in guiding students to analyze both their own performances and those of classmates. These questions are not check lists, rating sheets, or score cards. Rather, they are suggestions that probe the concerns raised in the preceding pages. As well, the headnotes to each selection for oral interpretation and the specific questions that address problems most often encountered by performers of the work direct students to consider what we believe to be the most important post-performance question: How fully did *this* reader communicate *this* selection to *this* audience?

In addition to repeated references to topics or issues that can profitably be explored from other perspectives within the field of performance studies, new to this edition are a reorganized and broader discussion of the fundamental aesthetic principles explored in Chapter 1 and the substantively reorganized Chapter 2, which accompanies students through each step of preparing their first performance. In both chapters we use stories and poems as examples, and the works we explore range from classic to modern, simple to complex, apparent to richly suggestive. The chapters on prose now explore a broader sampling of texts and the performance problems they entail, including a discussion of second-person narration. The drama chapters continue to focus on the ways in which the solo performer can create believable character and interaction. The poetry chapters directly explore the structural and experiential foundations of poetry in classic and contemporary forms. A chapter on group performance again concludes the book, exploring the explosion of interest in these forms and providing some useful suggestions to beginning students who are tempted by the performance opportunities groups provide. In two appendixes we look at ways to build programs and at a new review of the history of interpretation. Pruned and updated bibliographies again follow most chapters.

These changes mean that there may be more material here than can be covered comfortably in a single term, but the general format of this edition will be familiar to readers of earlier editions. We suggest beginning with the introductory material of Part I. Here we examine the fundamental principles of analysis, selection, and evaluation of literature and apply these principles to a brief story and a poem. We then look at the ways interpreters can use their bodies and their voices. The early chapters establish the basic principles common to all kinds of literature and complement the modal, rhetorical, or dramatistic approaches. Then the course may either concentrate on one or two areas or briefly survey all genres in the parts that follow. Part II, devoted to the interpretation of prose, pays particular attention both to the embodiment and evocation of prose style and to the problems inherent in narration. Part III deals with drama, with specific attention given to the structure of a play, character analysis, and style in dialogue, in addition to practical advice about technique. Although many poems appear in earlier parts of the book, as well as some selections from verse drama and epic poetry, the interpretation of poetry *per se* is not discussed until Part IV, where the analysis is as detailed as befits the condensation and complexity of a successful poem, no matter how brief. Part V concerns group interpretation and makes a basic distinction between Readers Theatre and Chamber Theatre as a guide to preparing scripts and implementing production and performance.

New selections in this edition have been chosen, in part, by their relationship to other selections. In this light, we continue to value the intertextuality of literary works, and our questions often encourage students to focus on the dialogue of one text with another, to probe the ways in which the interpretation of one text relates to other, often quite diverse, texts. Particularly in the discussion of group performances and of planning programs, we encourage students to explore the broad range of possibilities inherent in the "conversation" that occurs when one work of art confronts another. The new selections reflect as well that broad range of interest, topics, and levels of sophistication that marked prior editions. Among the new selections are stories by David Leavitt, Ann Beattie, and Toni Cade Bambara; reportage from H. G. Bissinger and a memoir from Jay Allison; poetry from Garret Kaoru Hongo, Judith Baumel, and Cynthia Macdonald. Performing any of the selections in this edition

is richly rewarding — in different ways with different students, of
course. None of the selections is simple because we are convinced
of the superior educational benefit of the gallant struggle over the
easy victory. We encourage you to use the selections in the text
whenever possible because it is important that students have a copy
of the literature to consult *after* — not during — the reading as a
guide to their criticism. We have found it valuable and expeditious
to hold all critiques until the performers scheduled for a given day
have finished. There are usually some common problems, and students find it agonizing to analyze others' readings when they are
still concentrating on their own. Criticism of material about which
we know nothing tends to focus on technical proficiencies that can
obscure or even obliterate the very work we seek to enjoy.

The success of this edition depends in large measure on two
intangibles that have contributed to earlier editions: the interest and
enthusiasm of the individual student and the spark that only a dedicated teacher can give any body of knowledge. We have tried to
create a book that can guide, encourage, and challenge its readers in
the hope that if our suggestions seem inadequate, students and
teacher together will discover a fuller, richer response.

By their questions and responses to previous editions, our colleagues and their students have substantially improved this edition.
Lee Beltzer and Leland Croghan continue to excite new ways to solve
perennial performance problems. John Anderson, with his voracious
appetite for reading and viewing, has suggested many works that
appear in this edition. Other colleagues — Beverly Whitaker Long,
Martha Nell Hardy, Mary Frances HopKins, Annette Martin, and
Judith Espinola come immediately to mind — will find in these pages
theories or practices we discovered together. In their admirable re-
fusal to accept easy answers, students across the country challenged
us to refine our thinking on the practical application of several theories we *thought* were crystal clear. We are grateful to the following
colleagues who reviewed the seventh edition and whose suggestions
helped to improve the eighth:

William Alfred Boyce, *Wayne State University*
Helen Cermak, *Concordia College (Moorhead, Minnesota)*
Katie Damp, *West Virginia University*
Christie Logan, *California State University Northridge*
J. Paul Marcoux, *Boston College*
Jeanette S. Myers, *Maryville College (St. Louis)*
Aileen Sundstrom, *Henry Ford Community College*
Abanne Waters, *Brevard Community College.*

We proudly note that the high esteem in which we held — and hold — Frank Galati's contributions is shared now by other professional communities, as evidenced by his 1989 Oscar nomination for the screenplay for *An Accidental Tourist* and a pair of 1990 Tony awards (scripting and directing) for *The Grapes of Wrath*. Eleanor Huff endured still another edition — practically. Finally, we note that all of the eight editions have subtly (and, sometimes, not so subtly) been enriched, improved, deepened by nearly fifty years of exemplary effort in the study of literature and performance undertaken by two men we are honored to describe as colleagues and friends: Wallace A. Bacon and the late Robert S. Breen.

I

Basic Principles

The sense of danger must not disappear:
The way is certainly both short and steep,
However gradual it looks from here;
Look if you like, but you will have to leap.

W. H. Auden, "Leap Before You Look"

A BEGINNING AND AN END

1

INTERPRETATION IS THE ART OF COMMUNICATING TO AN AUDIENCE A WORK OF LITERARY ART IN ITS INTELLECTUAL, EMOTIONAL, AND AESTHETIC ENTIRETY.

Interpretation is the art of communicating . . . By its very definition, art implies skill in performance. No sooner have we used the word "performance" — and suggested the study of it — than a constellation of allied concerns and interlocking interests emerge. "Performance" itself is broadly understood, meaning different but related things in different contexts. Actors and actresses and singers give performances, of course, but we speak as well of how politicians performed during a debate, how we performed on a test, how a car performs more efficiently after a tune-up, how a surgeon performs an appendectomy, and how well a friend performs under pressure. Performance surrounds us, encloses us, and is as natural as breathing; society would not exist were performance banished from it. We perform everyday: as student, parent, child, roommate, romantic partner, short-order cook, waitress, and swimmer. From among the vast array of performance activities you will have already obtained both expertise and vital experience that will help you in this course.

   We focus here on a special kind of performance that moves beyond the performance of living: we focus on the performance of literature. We don't suggest that this is the only performance useful or desirable for study. On the contrary, we refer often to other kinds of performances — performance art, performance as argument, political performance, ethnographic performance, and storytelling — as we discuss the skill you will need and acquire for the performance of literature. Studying all the kinds of performance enables us to more fully engage in the performance of literature, just as performing itself alerts us in new and vital ways to the kinds of performance that surrounds our daily lives.

Every art requires discipline and training in the use of the appropriate tools, as well as intelligence, experience, and the ability to order both experience and response into meaningful form. The writer of a literary selection is a creative artist who orders ideas, words, sounds, and rhythms into a particular form, putting them into written symbols. The interpreter, in turn, takes these symbols printed on a page and brings personal experience and insight to bear on the clues the author has given. He or she then submits subjective experience and responses to the order imposed by the creative artist and assumes the responsibility of re-creating the literary entity. This process demands thorough analysis, painstaking rehearsal, and strict discipline in the use of voice and body.

The writer is the creative artist; you, the interpreter, are also a creative artist. You have the privilege of choosing a meaningful example of literary art and bringing it, with its aesthetic qualities intact, to an audience. The introduction, transitions, and program arrangement become part of a *new* artistic product, which, though it owes its first responsibility to the creative artist, in fact becomes a creative act of the interpreter. You are director, arranger, and performer, all in one. The oral interpreter's art is comparable to the art of a musician playing the work of an artist-composer.

The truest and finest art is disarming in its seeming simplicity. Observers are aware of the result, not of the means used to attain the result. Technical display is not art. Art implies the systematic application of knowledge and skill in effecting a desired result, and the desired result in interpretation is in part precisely the same as that in any other phase of speech: communication. In your case communication includes communion, the *sharing* of an *experience*, first with the work performed and then with an audience.

It is the perfect tribute when the members of the audience are captured so thoroughly by the experience of the material that they cannot immediately break the spell to applaud. If an audience says, "What a beautiful voice!" or "What graceful gestures!", the interpreter has failed. When the audience's attention is held by the effect of the material presented, the interpreter has succeeded. But this unobtrusiveness on your part does not result from casual preparation or from a feeling that because the literature is the important thing, you need do no more than face the audience, open the book, and open your mouth. On the contrary, your effectiveness is the result of a preparation so thorough and a technique so perfectly coordinated that the audience cannot see the wheels go around.

. . . *communicating to an audience* . . .   An audience may consist of one person or several thousand. No matter what the size or nature of the audience, your responsibilities are the same. You should communicate as skillfully as possible what is on the printed page, making intelligent use of every detail to achieve the organic whole. The listeners' understanding, their mental and emotional responses to the content and to the form in which it is presented, depend to a large degree on your ability to discover these elements and to project them satisfactorily in their proper relationship.

How do you communicate these elements to the audience? You use your voice and body, which work together and are controlled by an alert and informed mind. Interpreters train their voices and bodies to respond to the particular requirements of a work of literature. They strive to eliminate mannerisms that may distract the audience; they are aware of the effect of posture, muscle tone, and general platform presence; and they try to devise physical action that aids communication and in no way calls attention to itself. Interpreters work with their voices during practice periods so that they may be heard and understood. They are aware of the need for flexibility in range, force, stress, and volume, if they are to do justice to the writing and bring out whatever strength and beauty the author has achieved through the sounds and relationships of the words. Their concentration on communicating, on sharing, the material at hand must be strong and continuous. During early rehearsals, interpreters stop to work on difficult segments, as pianists repeatedly finger complicated passages or dancers work a complicated series of steps in slow motion. In later rehearsals, when the selection is thoroughly in mind and has indeed become a part of them, interpreters turn their attention out to an imagined audience, being careful not to become distracted from the essense of the material that they wish to share with that audience.

Sometimes an interpreter chooses not to memorize selections completely. The time it would take to commit the words to memory might be better spent in studying the material and in perfecting the techniques of communication. Technically, it does not matter in the least whether the material is completely memorized. If you choose to memorize, you must concentrate on embodying and sharing the literature rather than on the act of remembering. If you choose not to memorize completely, you must be free enough of the text to concentrate on communicating with the audience rather than on reading. By the time you have analyzed the material in detail, put it back together again, and practiced conscientiously, you will have your selection so firmly implanted in your mind that you will need to glance at the page only occasionally.

Whether the selection is memorized or not, many interpreters have the book or a typescript of the selection with them during performance. Its presence serves two important purposes. First, it establishes the interpreter as the intermediary between the author and the audience. The printed page is a tool, a medium. Neither the pages in a book nor the words on the page constitute a literary work of art. Printed words are merely a record, a way to preserve word symbols through which an author has set down certain thoughts, emotions, and attitudes. Through the interpreter's voice and body the symbols on the page come alive, and the ideas and experience they symbolize are created anew.

Second, the presence of the book or manuscript serves an aesthetic purpose. It lets the audience know that the emotions and concepts presented belong to the author, the speaker, or the characters in the writing. Thus, the book allows the audience to respond to the literature out of their own experience. As an interpreter, you should respond thoroughly to the emotions evident in the selection; when your own personal experience is substituted for the experience conveyed by the literature, however, an audience may become uncomfortable. The presence of the book or manuscript can help avoid this problem.

. . . *a work of literary art in its intellectual, emotional, and aesthetic entirety* . . .   Your concern is to communicate the total effect of the literary work of art. This does not mean that you should present only complete works, or that you cannot use excerpts. Neither does it mean that the listeners will always receive the full impact of the author's achievement. For instance, they may be able to respond to a complex poem in only a general way. How fully they respond depends in part on their backgrounds and their familiarity with the work. You should always strive to present the literature in its "intellectual, emotional, and aesthetic entirety." The elements of good writing work so interdependently that to ignore or eliminate any one element is to misread the work.

Listening is a wholly time-bound activity. You, the interpreter, are able to go back and reread certain passages in rehearsal to clarify their relationship with the whole. You know where the entire selection is going and how it gets there. Your audience, however, has only the fraction of a second to hear words, to translate them into ideas, and to add associations and responses, which are guided by your skillful suggestion in voice and body. Thus, if you understand only half of what you hope to share with the members of your audience, their chances of comprehension and response become minimal. All the various qualities that contribute to the total effect of a selection must be held in their proper relation to the whole.

For purposes of analysis, it is convenient to break a work down into its parts. You should always remember, however, that such arbitrary division is only a device to facilitate your understanding. We may conveniently speak of content and structure, of logical meaning, and of emotive quality. But separating literature into these elements is useful *only* as a way of getting at full understanding. Content and structure do not exist as separate entities; they work together to form one organic whole. You should always examine them in relation to each other as you attempt to arrive at the writer's total achievement, which is undeniably more than the sum of its various parts. You should always put the material back together after each step in your analysis of it.

Analysis is one of the most difficult aspects of interpretation, but also one of the most rewarding. We refer to it frequently in the chapters that follow. As soon as you have discovered one or more clues given by the author, reread the entire selection aloud, seeing how what you have just discovered works within the whole. You should always rehearse aloud even before you are ready to pay particular attention to vocal techniques. Then go back to your analysis and repeat the reading aloud of the entire selection each time you discover more and more helpful details.

Although it is difficult to isolate and separately discuss certain aspects of a work of art, a full appreciation of the whole is enhanced by careful analysis of the particulars. To begin, you should distinguish the content from the structure of a piece of literature. In the broadest sense, *content* has to do with what is being said, *structure* with the way it is said. Content has two aspects. The first is the *intellectual* or *logical* aspect, which is simply what the material says. It involves an intellectual understanding of the meanings of the words and the relationships between words and groups of words. The other aspect of content is its *emotive* quality, the capacity of both meaning and sound to arouse pleasure or pain, to stimulate the reader and listeners to activity or repose through association. Words seldom have meaning independent of association or have emotion-arousing qualities without meaning. Consequently, for all purposes except analysis the logical and emotive qualities of a work of art can never be divorced. Since understanding takes place simultaneously on the intellectual and emotional levels, you must find out exactly what the author is saying, experience emotionally what is said, and communicate the total response — intellectual and emotional — to the audience.

Structure involves the way a writer has organized the expression of ideas, his or her choice of words, and the relationship of the parts to each other and to the whole. Structure is concerned with the manner of expression, ranging from simple lucidity to the most complex ornamentations of language. The structure of prose, for instance, includes the patterns of phrases and individual sentences, as well as the effect created by several sentences in combination. The structure of drama involves the rhythm of the characters' speeches, their choice of words, the structure of the sentences, and the interrelationship of the speeches, scenes, and acts of the entire play. The structure of poetry includes all the contributions to the sound patterns, the sounds of words in combination, stanzaic structure, scansion, rhyme, and length of line. These elements are examined in more detail as these types of writing are discussed in later chapters.

. . . aesthetic entirety . . .   The phrase "aesthetic entirety" embraces all the qualities that must be considered to appreciate a piece of writing as a successful work of literary art. These elements should always be evaluated in relation to each other and to the whole.

Aesthetics deals with the theory of the fine arts and the individual's response to the arts. Although the field of aesthetics includes all areas of art, our primary concern in this book is literary art. As a study, aesthetics concerns itself with the ordering of the parts of a work of art, as well as with the response of the beholder. In our case, the interpreter and the listeners are the beholders. Some books for further reading about the topic of aesthetics are listed in the bibliography at the end of this chapter. At the moment, we need to be aware only that there are aesthetic standards for the way that parts work together to create a literary whole. It is this whole, with all its elements intact and correlated, that is to be shared with the audience.

Sources of Material

Interpreters can choose from an almost unlimited range of material. They may use traditional literary forms such as prose, poetry, or drama in epic, lyric, or dramatic modes. Major considerations are the literary value of the selection, its suitability for the audience, and personal interests. Alternatively, they may choose to perform works that do not fit easy or traditional classification: autobiography, diaries, oral history, interviews, personal narrative, ethnographic research, concrete poetry, and even conversation. This freedom of choice is a distinct advantage for an experienced interpreter, but it may present the beginning student with a problem. From the wealth of available material, where does one begin to select something?

The first question, obviously, is where to look. The selections at the ends of chapters in this book offer a wide variety of material and should be helpful. However, part of your assignment may be to find your own material, and literary anthologies are a good place to begin your search.

Anthologies are especially valuable to the beginning student of interpretation because they offer a wide selection in a single volume. You will find collections of all types of prose: essays, short stories, humorous and satirical pieces, biographies, letters, diaries, and even novels. You will find poetry classified by kind, such as lyric, narrative, humorous, or didactic; by period or nation, such as Elizabethan, Russian, or contemporary American; and by subject or spirit, such as poems about nature, love, religion, Christmas, protest, or patriotism. If you decide to try drama, you will find many volumes that include either entire plays, both one-act and full-length, or selected scenes. Other anthologies cut across these classifications, presenting, for example, chronological surveys of a particular type of literature or examples of regional writing. Of course, there are volumes of selected works by individual authors. Dozens of useful anthologies are available in inexpensive editions in any bookstore or in hardback editions in any library.

After your first few assignments, you will have a better idea of the kind of material that appeals to you and where to look for it. You might begin by asking yourself, "What am I most interested in?" Is it the city or the country? Is it some exotic part of the world or your own home state? Perhaps you are much more interested in people than in places. What kind of people? In what circumstances?

Choosing the Selection: Three Touchstones

To choose material because of its interesting subject matter does not imply that you should make no effort to evaluate its literary worth. On the contrary, throughout this book there is constant concern with evaluation of material through analysis.

Most of us are attracted first to a piece of writing by what it says — its content. As we become more sophisticated, we appreciate more fully the complex relationship between meaning and structure. Although there are numerous ways to treat any subject, some ways are more effective than others. You are probably quite fond of certain poems, plays, or stories because of early associations. You are not expected to give up those feelings, but you should not impose them on an audience that does not share your associations, unless your selections are also successful as works of literary art. Neither, of course, should you reject a piece of writing as "bad" because the author did not write what you wish you had written. If you do not enjoy a selection, do not choose to read it. Be careful, though, not to limit yourself to what you have always liked and known. Be willing to broaden your horizons. The important thing is not so much to know what you like as to establish criteria for evaluating a literary artist's success or failure. It is important to understand why you do or do not wish to study a certain selection. Even though you may not come to like it, you may learn to respect its qualities as good literature.

Let us assume that you have made a tentative choice of material, or have narrowed down the possibilities to two or three selections that are equally appealing as far as content is concerned. Before making a final decision, you wish to evaluate the choices as literature. You will do well to consider three factors as touchstones: universality, individuality, and suggestion.

Universality does not mean that the material will immediately appeal to all persons regardless of their intellectual or cultural backgrounds. It means, rather, that the idea expressed is potentially interesting to all people because it touches on a common experience. The emotional response it evokes is one that most readers (and listeners) have felt at one time or another: love or hate, hope or fear, joy or despair, confronting death or reclaiming life.

Literature draws its material from life, but literature is not exactly like life. A writer endeavors to select and control attitudes and motivations, to impose order on the flux and change of human existence, and to give us clues that direct us in relating our own experiences to the order he or she has chosen. Even deliberately distorted events can have relevance to our existence. When writing has universality, you will respond to it, using your background and experience. When you communicate all the levels of meaning to an audience, they in turn will have a basis for identification with their own experiences.

However, you need not have undergone an event to test your own experience against that recorded by the author. Even without an identical experience, you certainly have known, to at least some degree, the emotions of joy or sorrow, fear or yearning, hope or love that the experience recorded calls forth. Although your own reaction to the specific situation might not be the same as the author's, strive to identify with the literature to broaden and open yourself; adapt your own remembered event to make your response relevant to that which the author has recorded.

The second touchstone of good writing is *individuality* — the writer's own fresh approach to a universal subject. This quality is revealed in choice of words, images, and method of organization. You cannot decide whether the author has handled the subject with individuality unless you have had some acquaintance with a wide variety of literature. After some time and experience, you will be able to recognize that individuality results in large part from the author's selectivity and control and is reflected in both content and structure. We take a closer look at the element of individuality when we compare three works later in the chapter.

The subtlest and most rewarding writing is characterized by *suggestion*. The readers are left with something to do: they are not told everything on an immediate, purely logical level. This does not mean that the writing is obscure. It means, rather, that the author has chosen references and words that allow the readers to enrich the subject matter from their own backgrounds. There must be, however, enough clear signals for the readers' imaginations to follow. Frequently, considerable analysis is necessary to find and use these signals properly. But once the possibilities for relevant association are realized, the writing continues to grow in meaning and in emotional impact for both the reader-interpreter and the audience. We touch on this aspect, too, in our later comparison.

It is obvious, of course, that these three touchstones — universality, individuality, and suggestion — are closely related and serve to enhance and balance each other in effective writing. The author's idea has been drawn from an experience that all people are able to share; the method of expressing that idea is different from the method used by other authors; and the suggestion of associated ideas and responses points the way for the reader's imagination to follow and allows for continuing enrichment through the various levels of meaning. Sometimes these three qualities are not present in equal force in a selection, nor is it necessary for them to be. But if any one quality is totally absent or patently weak, you will do well to look elsewhere for material that interests and moves your audience.

To illustrate, let us look at two brief poems, one by Helen Hoyt and one by Emily Dickinson, and a short story by Deborah Sherman. Each work contains an intensely personal experience and is written in the first person.

The Sense of Death

HELEN HOYT

Since I have felt the sense of death,
Since I have borne its dread, its fear —
Oh, how my life has grown more dear
Since I have felt the sense of death!
Sorrows are good, and cares are small,
Since I have known the loss of all.

Since I have felt the sense of death,
And death forever at my side —
Oh, how the world has opened wide
Since I have felt the sense of death!
My hours are jewels that I spend,
For I have seen the hours end.

Since I have felt the sense of death,
Since I have looked on that black night —
My inmost brain is fierce with light
Since I have felt the sense of death.
O dark, that made my eyes to see!
O death, that gave my life to me!

Before we look at the second poem, a word of explanation may
be in order. Emily Dickinson did not give her poems titles and in
fact never readied them for publication. Consequently, some of the
poems have several versions, each differing in punctuation and even
in word choice. Dickinson's use of capital letters and dashes is
unique. She frequently capitalizes all the nouns and sometimes uses
dashes instead of commas. The dashes seem compatible with interrupted or suspended thought units.

I Felt a Funeral

EMILY DICKINSON

I felt a Funeral, in my Brain,
And Mourners to and fro
Kept treading — treading — till it seemed
That Sense was breaking through —

And when they all were seated,
A Service, like a Drum —

Kept beating — beating — till I thought
My Mind was going numb —

And then I heard them lift a Box
And creak across my Soul
With those same Boots of Lead, again,
Then Space — began to toll,

As all the Heavens were a Bell,
And Being, but an Ear,
And I, and Silence, some strange Race
Wrecked, solitary, here —

And then a Plank in Reason, broke,
And I dropped down, and down —
And hit a World, at every Crash,
And Got through knowing — then — [1]

The three touchstones we have been discussing do not occur solely in poetry. Many obvious differences distinguish the two poems from the story that follows: length of sentences or, indeed, of the selection itself; arrangement by stanza or by paragraph; very different word choice among the works. More telling are the similarities they share. This story — as concerned with death and its impact as are the prior two poems — is very tightly controlled by its first-person narrator. There is no doubt that the story demonstrates a sense of death, no doubt that it's narrator feels a funeral quite keenly. Can you decide why the author chose such a simple title?

Dulce

DEBORAH SHERMAN

I can still hear the pick hitting the caliche, Lambert breathing hard, sweat at the edge of his gray hair. I knew that the difficulty in breathing wasn't just from the steady swinging of the heavy pick, nor was it because of his age. He said later that he couldn't cry and yet his eyes were red and I could see the tears.

When I saw Dulce lying there, the blood still wet, a small pool on the pavement, I couldn't touch her or move her. I ran to get Lambert, the one person who Dulce would never leave. "Damn it," he said. "Son of a bitches." Slowly, with Paula Sue at his side, bowlegged and tired,

1. Dickinson's manuscript shows an earlier version in which the last line reads "And Finished knowing—then—"

he walked down to the highway. I didn't have to watch him to know
that he touched every part of Dulce to make sure that it was really true.
He came so quietly up the driveway, carrying Dulce the way one carries
a butchered lamb, holding the front paws in one hand and the back in
the other, her head hanging by his legs. Gently, caressing her, he laid
her on the grass by the ditch where he had buried Trixie a few years
ago, then he went to put on his boots and get the pick and shovel.
When he came back he looked at me. "Do you think that animals do
things like this because they don't want to live?"

"No, Lambert," I said, "it was just an accident, a stupid accident."

"Maybe they're unhappy and don't want to live."

"No, Lambert."

"When Barbara and I first lived here, the house was right over
there, and this tree was our tree." He kept digging. "When I put Trixie
here I told Trixie this is your tree now. Now it's Duls' too." He got on
his hands and knees, loosening a big rock. "Do you think this is wide
enough? Enough room for her feet?"

"Ya, I think so Lambert."

But he widened it anyway.

"Do you think this is deep enough? I made it deeper than this for
Trixie."

"Ya, I think so Lambert."

But he made it deeper anyway.

"Paula Sue," he said, "go get the hoe, the little one, in the shed."

His breathing was becoming labored, strained. Dulce was lying
beside him. It was almost as if she were asleep, out in the pasture
keeping him within view at all times even if she dozed off, waiting for
him to finish whatever little chore he was occupied with. He looked
down at her. "Do you think those who are supposed to die suffer later
for being kept alive past their time?" The pick stopped. "When it's your
time it's your time."

"I don't know, Lambert," I said, watching him climb slowly out of
the hole.

When Paula Sue came back with the hoe he got in the hole again
and carefully scraped the earth from the corners, making the surface
flat and smooth. "Go ask Barbara for some rags, I know she has some,"
he said quietly, so slowly, so gently.

Paula Sue walked up with an old blanket. "It has pee on it though."

I looked at the blanket. "That's okay."

"No, that's not good for Duls. Barbara has other ones. Go ask her."

"It's okay, Lambert," I said. But Paula Sue had already dropped the
blanket and was walking toward the house.

This time when Paula Sue came back, she brought the old patch-
work quilt that used to be her bedspread. Lambert put down his hoe
and looked at the quilt. A neighbor had made it. "It's too good."

"No," said Paula Sue, "it's got lots of tears in it."

I smiled, watching her pointing out each tear. "It's okay, Lambert."

He took the quilt and laid it in the hole, smoothing out each wrinkle.

And then he went to Dulce, his hand petting her, automatically. He picked her up gently, as if afraid of disturbing her, and lowered her onto the blanket. "Let's clean up your nose, Duls," he said, as he took his glove and wiped the blood from her face. He wrapped her in the blanket.

"Are you ready, Lambert?" I said. He just nodded, and I started shoveling the dirt over her as fast as I could. Ma had come out to see her lowered into the hole and as the colors disappeared she said that it was only right that Dulce have that quilt.

Lambert bent down and laid his hand on the earth, "Bye Duls, bye Duls." He picked up his worn tools and, dragging the old blanket that Canoncito had peed on, he walked back up to the house.

When I came around the corner, he was on the portal, sitting on the bench, his head bent down, his hands holding Dulce's white bowl. He just sat there, not moving. All the other dogs were at his feet, as if they knew that something had happened.

"Just a few minutes ago. We were in the shop and Duls was lying there on the chair, the old chair from Denver. We shared a cheese, what do you call it, a cheese ball. We ate together, Duls and me. Just a few minutes ago."

Neither the fact nor the effect of death can be denied, but these works present this universal experience in markedly different ways. In her poem, Hoyt is talking about the aftermath of having *sensed* death, probably physical death. Dickinson is talking about the *period* of the *sensing*. She probably is also talking about despair, a kind of spiritual death so numbing and soul shattering that it became a "funeral" in her brain. Sherman partakes of and observes the impact of death. All three women use straightforward language and sentences. Hoyt draws definite, even moralistic, conclusions; Dickinson merely describes the experience and draws no conclusions. Sherman recounts events and lets us create the impact.

Hoyt obviously wishes to place death in sharp contrast to a resulting acute appreciation of life. Half of the lines are concerned with death and half with life, and this comfortable balance belies the distinct impression that this poem is more about death than life.

She asks us to take "Since" in the sense of "after," as well as in the sense of cause and effect. She repeats her title in six of the eighteen lines of the poem, and approximates it by parallel construction in three more. Such repetition could be most effective in creating a driving, insistent impact. The phrase "felt the sense of death," however, does not cut into our consciousness with much force. The word "sense" implies recognition or perception. It is quite possible to "feel" a "perception," and Hoyt's perception of death is characterized by "dread," "fear," "forever at my side," "the hours end," "black night," and "O dark." None of these references is fresh or individual. Each has been used in the same connection for so many centuries that it has become trite. Taken separately and skillfully developed, each could carry a wealth of suggestion, but Hoyt gives us no time or incentive to establish an individual identification with what the "sense" of death was for her, or indeed might be for us.

Admittedly, Hoyt tells us that the experience of sensing death led her to a new awareness of the value of life. Unfortunately, her references to life are equally vague and familiar. Life is referred to in "grown more dear," "Sorrows are good," "cares are small," "world has opened wide," "hours are jewels that I spend," "inmost brain is fierce with light," "eyes to see," and "gave my life to me." "Sorrows" is so inclusive and allows for such a weight of personal association that we cannot fix on the paradox of sorrows being "good" before we are whisked on to "cares" that are "small." Presumably, this line is intended to set up a balance, but it is not entirely successful, partly because of the inclusiveness and permissiveness of "sorrows" and "cares," and partly because even small cares are not "good," as she asks us to believe sorrows have become. Even the singular form of "sorrow" and "care" would at least have allowed us to accept these terms in a more abstract sense and hence to identify more easily with the emotional implication. There is, too, a disturbingly familiar ring in the phrase "hours are jewels" and in the verb "spend." It may be quibbling to say that one does not "spend" jewels unless one lives in a medieval economy; nevertheless, the association here is strained. The phrase "inmost brain is fierce with light" is probably the strongest line of the poem, particularly since the poet has set it carefully against "black night." But, again, it goes nowhere — except back to the already quite familiar refrain.

With little individuality, in either the selection of details or the way they are expressed, suggestion is also poorly established beyond the poem's basic premise. After one comes close to death, whether in the actual physical sense or in having been made aware of its omnipresence, life becomes more precious. The words and figures of speech chosen to develop this premise lack the force, freshness, sharpness of focus, and emotive quality that would make us feel that the poet has made us think about something important in an entirely new way, or even permitted us much room to enter her world.

Dickinson also begins her poem with "I felt," but the clear positioning of the event in time past and its implied completion put it firmly in perspective. She introduces the extended metaphor of a funeral service, and since a funeral carries a complex weight of values and images, we are bombarded by associations of grief, dignity, ritual, the presence of the body, and a mixture of respect and grim, formal, finality. To "feel" a funeral goes beyond merely attending one, and a funeral *in the brain* goes still further. We immediately are aware of a new and individual approach to the universal subject of death, of spiritual death that destroys the life of the senses, crushes hope, and even denies the power of the soul.

We are given time to develop associations suggested here, and our focus is sharpened by the mourners going to and fro and by the sound they make "treading — treading." We then are returned to sensation in the last line of the first stanza. Two suggested interpretations of this line, rather than being contradictory, provide a thin thread of suspense, strengthened by "till it seemed." On one level, "Sense" may be taken to mean the mind bending under the strain of the "treading." This interpretation is strongly suggested by the word "Brain" in the opening line. But Dickinson may also mean that awareness — "Sense" — had become so acute that the sensation was unbearable. These two interpretations are not mutually exclusive, and both can operate well here in a deliberate, disturbing, but highly functional ambiguity.

The balancing of the concrete elements of a funeral service with the sensation felt in the brain continues to the last line of the third stanza. It is held together and kept vivid by a strict chronological progression, as well as by constant references to sound, already prepared for by "treading — treading." Sound reaches an almost unbearable intensity as "Space — began to toll," and it becomes overwhelming in the opening lines of the next stanza. Our attention is snatched from this climax of sound by "and Silence," which by its very contrast is equally deafening.

At the same time, the mourners and the pallbearers disappear abruptly, leaving the senses "solitary." But the experience does not stop there. It continues in a swift downward pattern, suggesting a lowering into the grave and much more. The breaking "Plank in Reason" suggests a wealth of associations and adds still another dimension to the horror of the drop "down, and down — ," which culminates in the highly graphic "hit" and "Crash" in the next-to-last line. The repeated use of "and" involves us in this swift and helpless dropping.

The last line, like several of the others, carries deliberate ambiguity and moves on more than one level. "Got through" may mean "finished" with a mortal type of knowledge. It also may imply having "broken through" into a superhuman, mystical type of knowledge that is possible only after death or a great spiritual crisis. The " — then — " also functions on more than one level. It completes the chronological progression; it terminates the immediate recorded experience; it teases us with a hint that there was more. A skilled interpreter can convey this multiplicity of meanings to the audience.

Hoyt's poem only weakly balances life and death. Dickinson is not talking about life and death as contrasting states, but she manages skillfully to keep us aware of the world of the living. The reference to those who are attending the "funeral" that she felt in her brain is strong through the first three stanzas, but it is held constantly within the framework of her point of view. Even in the sensation responses there is a quality of living awareness. "Sense," "Mind," "Soul," "Being," "Ear," "Race," and "Reason" all relate to but do not parallel "knowing" in the final line. There is also an alive, human quality in "hit a World," and "every Crash," because they are so essentially physical.

Thus, from the opening line we are aware of a fresh, individual approach to the sensation that Dickinson is writing about. It catches and holds our interest, because it is an unusual but certainly acceptable way of talking about a subject whose universality cannot be denied. It is a succinct, compressed statement that cuts into our awareness and increases our understanding.

During the discussion of Dickinson's poem we mentioned the term "deliberate ambiguity." *Ambiguity* is sometimes confused with lack of clarity, but the term as it is used today in literary criticism means "having more than one possible meaning, all of which are relevant and congruent within the organic whole of the piece of writing." Ambiguity may result in some obscurity, but it must not defy careful study or split the literary selection into incompatible segments. The kind of ambiguity we have been discussing is one of the richest sources of suggestion for the very reason that it does not narrowly circumscribe the experience of the poem.

Hoyt uses outworn and too-familiar references to suggest the terror of death and the glory of life. Dickinson uses images that stir the senses and cause us to respond both emotionally and physically. At the same time, she engages our minds by juxtaposing unexpected and strongly suggestive words. Almost any line serves as an example, but two of the most striking are the opening line and the reference to "a Plank in Reason." Much more can be said about Dickinson's poem — and we say some of it in the next chapter. At its best, then, suggestion takes us beyond the poem without taking us out of the poem. Suggestion and individuality go hand in hand.

Deborah Sherman's short tale is small without being little. In simple, raw, unembroidered language — no jewel-like hours here — she explores the ways in which four persons have been affected by the death of a pet. Elaborate language is not needed to elevate this event for its participants, and descriptive language is not needed for those of us who watch and finally partake of it. In coming to understand the relationship of the narrator, Lambert, Paula Sue, and Ma we understand not only how much Dulce affected their lives, but how much they rely on each other. The decisions each person makes are made with the help of the others, and all decisions are directed not to the dead animal Dulce is now but to the world they shared when Dulce was alive, when even something as insignificant as a "cheese ball" could be meaningful because of its being shared. Thus, this short story phrases big questions in small ways.

One need not have lost a dog to recognize the *universality* of this tale. Dulce's death — or the death of any well-loved pet — leads us to consider questions not easily phrased. Lambert has difficulty phrasing his fears, but it is clear that these questions are on the minds of all the family. Similarly, they all search for the best way to remember their dead, and their joining together in this effort to survive Dulce's death suggests some of the ways that they will undertake life after Dulce. This sentiment seems to fill their little community, for by the end of the story, "All the other dogs were at his feet, as if they knew that something had happened." Generations and communities joining to bury their dead and beginning to live again is, sadly but splendidly, one of the oldest stories told. It is a story told as often to mark a group's having "Got through knowing" as to survive a present moment of pain. Universal is a small word to describe the tale.

Yet this is a striking family group, and their lives are probably not like yours. The setting on a farm in the southwest suggests a location urban dwellers or coastal residents might find unfamiliar. And that setting is crucial in establishing the *individuality* of the family: note the images of Lambert in the fields with Dulce "out in the pasture keeping him within view at all times even if she dozed off . . ." and Lambert's carrying the dead body "the way one carries a butchered lamb." Even on this ranch, where deaths commonly occur, this death is different. What would suffice will not do: Lambert makes the grave wider, though it need not be, and deeper, though it is big enough. He dedicates the tree to Dulce, as he also dedicated it to a predecessor, Trixie. In each event, in detail after detail, Sherman shows us how this death uniquely affects these lives — and, in its small way, us.

As these issues confront us, we see how this simple story can, in its decidedly simple way, raise complicated and complex questions, so that what unfolds before us *suggests* echoes and shadows much larger than a dead dog on a ranch. It begins with the sounds of the pick hitting the caliche — that hard, striking sound with a rhythm like a heartbeat. That sound echoes Lambert's breath, and tantalizingly contrasts with Dulce's silence. And consider what we learn about the relationship between master and pet when Lambert picks the dead Dulce up, "his hand petting her, automatically." Or watch his hands, again, "holding Dulce's white bowl" and remembering the simple sharing moments before her death. In these glimpses of the fleeting moments of life — what Hoyt describes so broadly as "Sorrows are good, and cares are small" (although Lambert and Paula Sue are not likely to consider this loss either good or small) — we understand the ways in which death interrupts, startles, wrecks, and isolates those who live on.

There are numerous matters that we have not even touched on in our evaluation of these three works, such as rhythm, sound patterns, the structural complexities of verse, and narrative strategies. We refer to these matters in succeeding chapters when we work with analysis. It was not our intention here — although it was a temptation — to do more than illustrate how the three touchstones of universality, individuality, and suggestion can operate within a piece of literature.

Bibliography

As we mention in the chapter, a wide range of anthologies, many of them in inexpensive editions, contain a wealth of material. Also, most current textbooks in interpretation include a large variety of selections. The following books will help you in clarifying terms and in understanding the various approaches to criticism and analysis. Each provides an extensive bibliography.

Abrams, M. H. *The Mirror and the Lamp: Romantic Theory and the Critical Tradition.* New York: Oxford University Press, 1953.
A classic in the expressive theory of criticism, most often remembered for its model whereby all critical theories can be classified according to their primary focus.

Barnet, Sylvan, Morton Berman, and William Burto. *A Dictionary of Literary Terms.* Boston: Little, Brown and Company, 1960.
A paperback of brief definitions with cross-references.

Booth, Wayne C. *Critical Understanding: The Powers and Limits of Pluralism.* Chicago: University of Chicago Press, 1979.
An examination of M. H. Abrams, Kenneth Burke, and R. S. Crane as pluralist critics and an attempt to formulate an overarching pluralism.

An important work in that it argues the significance of all forms of literary criticism and calls for understanding rather than warfare among critics.

Gardner, Helen. *The Business of Criticism*. New York: Oxford University Press, 1963.
A good defense of the historical method of criticism and a plea for the re-alliance of criticism with scholarship.

Gilbert, Allan H., ed. *Literary Criticism*. Vol. 1, *Plato to Dryden*; Vol. 2, *Pope to Croce*. Detroit: Wayne State University Press, 1962.
Brief, helpful comments on excerpts from the great critics. Extended bibliographies for each period plus a general bibliography. Carefully indexed for cross-reference.

Grambs, David. *Words About Words*. New York: McGraw-Hill Book Company, 1984.
A dictionary of prose terminology containing entries not often found in traditional literary handbooks. Although many of the entries are technical, this dictionary is a helpful companion to *A Dictionary of Literary Terms*.

Hoffman, Daniel, ed. *Harvard Guide to Contemporary American Writing*. Cambridge, Mass.: Harvard University Press, 1979.
An outstanding critical survey of trends in American prose, poetry, and drama from the 1940s through the 1970s.

Kaplan, Charles, ed. *Criticism: The Major Statements*. 2nd ed. New York: St. Martin's Press, 1985.
Representative essays on criticism from Plato to Barthes.

McGuire, Richard. *Passionate Attention: An Introduction to Literary Study*. New York: W. W. Norton and Company, 1973.
A clear discussion of four approaches to literary criticism based on the first chapter of M. H. Abrams's *The Mirror and the Lamp*.

Shipley, Joseph T., ed. *Dictionary of World Literature: Criticism-Form-Techniques*. 2nd ed. New York: Philosophical Library, 1945.
A complete, scholarly sourcebook of literary terms and genres.

Tomkins, Jane, ed. *Reader-Response Criticism: From Formalism to Post-Structuralism*. Baltimore: Johns Hopkins University Press, 1980.
A collection of essays that traces the re-emergence of the reader in critical theory since 1950.

Wimsatt, W. K., Jr., and Cleanth Brooks. *Literary Criticism: A Short History*. New York: Alfred A. Knopf, 1957.
A clearly presented, succinct account of the development of the field of literary criticism.

It may be the case that you expected what you are hearing now. But even in that case you expected something different.

Peter Handke, "Offending the Audience"

ANALYZING THE SELECTION

2

IN CHAPTER 1 WE USE the three touchstones of universality, individuality, and suggestion to examine two short poems and a story that appear on their surfaces to be about the same thing. Our discussion reveals many differences among the selections. It also presents a starting point for interpreters to learn how to choose a selection to which they can respond and that will interest any audience.

Preparing the First Performance

Two tasks now confront you: discovering the architecture of the work you have chosen to perform and discovering how it manifests its aesthetic foundations. Both of these tasks are essential because, as we consistently maintain, you cannot perform what you do not know, and you cannot shape your rehearsal until you understand the shape of what you are rehearsing. This chapter, then, will help you along the way. First, we explore the major structural components of a work of literary art: the denotative and connotative meanings of the words, the ways in which the words are put together to achieve their central purpose, the agents of speaking, and the relationship between the speaker and the world of the work. Next, we look at how the major aesthetic components of a work of literature operate together to enrich the experience of the performer and the audience. To help you through this segment, we explore a story you may not know and a poem we briefly examined in Chapter 1. Your selection will probably have many different features, but you should by then have the experience of knowing what to look for and where to find it. Finally, we apply all we have discovered by carefully rehearsing the selection. Synthesis sometimes seems more difficult than analysis, but the real challenge is to embody and evoke all that you have discovered, and to be open and ready to discover during the rehearsal process itself.

Major Structural Components

Once you've selected the poem or story that most interests you, thoroughly investigate everything within that particular piece of literature. You should know precisely what the author has given you to work with, accepting responsibility for discovering and making proper use of the author's organization and method of presentation. Only when you fully understand the author's achievement can you decide how to use your own technique to create the experience for the audience.

Denotative and Connotative Meanings

First, of course, you should try to find out precisely what the literature is saying. You may easily understand the general meaning of a selection and yet find some specific lines or phrases that are not entirely clear. If so, look up the unfamiliar words and references. You cannot afford to gloss over them. The word or allusion is there because the author felt that it expresses exactly what he or she wished to say. For the author, it is not *almost* the right word; it is *precisely* the right word. Consequently, you cannot hope to achieve the author's full purpose with only a vague idea of the definitions or connotations of the words. In fact, an idea may be distorted if you mistake the full meaning of a word or phrase.

The dictionary is, of course, the first source to consult. The dictionary gives primarily *denotative* meanings — what a word means *explicitly.* For example, it defines "funeral" as "the ceremonies held in connection with the burial or cremation of the dead." But, of course, we all know perfectly well what the denotative meaning of "funeral" is. As we look at the word in Emily Dickinson's poem in

Chapter 1, however, a cluster of associations grows out of our experience with "funeral." Gradually, the word begins to mean more than its bare dictionary definition. The "more" is the *connotative* meaning: suggestions of associations and overtones that go beyond the explicit, or denotative, meaning. Connotative meaning is an associated meaning and often is partially based on subjective values. But successful writers give the reader enough clues to the way the word should be taken so that the connotative meaning is not entirely subjective. We should remember that connotation suggests *"in addition* to," not "instead of."

Connotation is most important when we consider the emotive quality of content, but it must not be overlooked or misunderstood when determining logical content. When a writer selects a particular word from several possible choices, it is because that word conveys something over and above what it "means." What that something else is, what special flavor it adds to the whole, is for you to ferret out and convey to the audience. We have more to say about connotation when we examine the various ways in which it operates in the major types of literature.

Closely allied with connotative meaning is the function of allusions. Allusions are references to persons, places, or events, real or mythological, that call up relevant associations. Allusions are useful because in a word or phrase they can establish an entire complex of connotations. Tennyson's "Ulysses" (Chapter 4), for example, is based on allusion. The name Ulysses immediately brings to mind the great adventurer and leader in *The Odyssey* by Homer.

Our primary concern in this text is the words of the literature and their "messages," which become complex appeals to our own universal experiences. The individuality in an author's choice of "signals" gives us a basis for making our responses relevant to the experiences the author is sharing. After making sure of the full meaning of the words, the interpreter must examine the organization of ideas. Most material divides rather easily into three parts: the introduction or lead-in portion, the body of the material, and the conclusion or tying-up unit. Usually, the body of the material contains the author's main point. However, it is important to make careful use of the selection and arrangement of details and ideas in each unit if the listeners are to perceive each section in its proper relation to the whole.

Within each unit there are key sentences or phrases on which the logical and emotional progression depends. They may contain a new idea or another aspect of an idea introduced previously. The interpreter should know the position and function of each key so that it can be clearly established in the minds of the audience in its proper relationship to all the other phrases and sentences and to the whole unit.

Climax

As you discover the key details within the introduction, body, and conclusion of the selection and evaluate each one in its relationship to the whole, you will find that they vary in importance. Occasionally they merely implant an idea or clue that becomes important later in the development of plot or action. Frequently, however, they indicate a high point of logical development or emotional impact and may be considered *climaxes*. Often several minor climaxes lead up to and/or follow the major climax. A climax may be the culmination of the logical content, the high point of emotional impact, or a combination of both. Thus, we may speak of *logical climax* and *emotional climax*, remembering that this separation is only for convenience in analysis and that ultimately we will put them back together as they operate within the whole.

In a play or story, the logical climax is often called the *crisis*. The crisis is the point at which the conflict becomes so intense that a resolution must occur and after which only one outcome is possible. In an essay, the logical climax occurs when the writer makes the main point with such clarity that the conclusion is inevitable. In a poem, it is the point at which the author completes the logical development on which the emotional content is based.

The emotional climax is the moment of highest emotional impact and involvement for the reader. If this seems to be a completely subjective matter, we should remember that the writer gives us clues to follow. If our analysis is careful and we let the author lead the way, we generally are moved most strongly at the point of emotional climax. It is important to ensure that we take into account the *whole* selection in our response. Because there are many degrees of emotion, the emotional climax may be as gentle as that in Hopkins's "The Starlight Night" at the end of this chapter or as dramatic as that in Sophocles' *Oedipus the King* (Chapter 8). If you use only part of a long selection, locating the climax or climaxes within that unit is especially important in making the audience feel that they have received a complete, unified, and fulfilling experience.

Sometimes the highest emotional intensity coincides with the logical climax. Often, however, this is not the case. The logical climax may precede and prepare for the emotional high point. This happens when the emotional climax depends on a character's or speaker's response to a completed cycle of events. On the other hand, if the outcome of events depends on an emotional reaction, the emotional climax precedes the logical climax, as it does in Dickinson's poem in Chapter 1. Here the impact of space, silence, and solitude precedes the completion of the fall. In "Dulce" the logical climax occurs when Lambert places the dog in the grave he so carefully prepared, and the emotional climax occurs as he sits contemplating her white bowl.

You may find this dual aspect of climax difficult to convey, but understanding and experience will help you cope with the problem. The logical climax, for instance, probably needs a particularly high degree of definition on the part of the interpreter. If you drive too hard at your listeners with this concept, however, the impact of the emotional climax may suffer. The audience will receive the full emotional impact only if you respond personally while reading. This does not mean that you should pull out all the stops and burst into tears or shake your fists in fury. You should, however, train yourself to respond in such a way that your nonverbal communication (or body signals) is in harmony with what the words are saying. It is important to be aware that literature moves on several levels and consequently may achieve its high point of logical development in one place and its emotional climax in another, although neither climax may be said to occur independently of the other. After each step in analysis, remember to put the material back together so that you may look again at the selection in its entirety as a guide to the use of performance techniques.

Persona

Once you know how a work is built, you can begin to discover who speaks it. *Personae,* the plural form of *persona,* has traditionally meant the characters in a piece of fictional writing such as a narrative or a play. Recently the singular, *persona,* has been used to indicate the speaker, the one who relates the experience in a piece of literature, whether it is fictional or true, poetry or prose, dramatic or nondramatic. The speaker may be someone who closely resembles the author in thoughts and attitudes, as in Capote's *A Christmas Memory* (at the end of this chapter), or the character may be quite different from the author, as in Browning's "Soliloquy of the Spanish Cloister" (Chapter 9). In our everyday lives, when we function naturally as performers, we assume the persona of student, child, parent, or lover. Although these personae obviously share some characteristics, we highlight some elements at the expense of others.

In drama, obviously, there may be many speakers, and although all are under the control of the author, the speaking character's motivation and reactions will arise from the dramatic situation and from his or her relationships with other characters. In some cases, one or more of these characters may seem to speak directly for the playwright, indicating a particular attitude toward the world, human nature, or the events of the play. Such a character may even resemble the playwright in biographical details or may share an immediate concern or a general interest with the playwright. For example, Stephen Sondheim is not a painter, but he, too, must "finish the hat" — because it's what all artists do (see the end of Chapter 8).

In narratives, the narrator is clearly the controlling voice that tells us what we need to know about background and plot progression. The narrator may be a character in the story and involved directly in the events; in this case he or she speaks in his or her own person as that character, as in Sherman's "Dulce" (Chapter 1) or in Cameron's "Homework" (at the end of this chapter). Or the speaker may be a benevolently objective reporter, as Morrill is in "Miss Lizzie" (Chapter 11).

In lyric poetry the persona is often the poet speaking. Of course, authors change their minds and their moods. We have only to compare two sonnets by Shakespeare to be aware that they exhibit quite different attitudes. There can be no doubt that Dickinson, Hoyt, and Sherman (in Chapter 1) are sharing their own highly personal experiences, as are Whitman, Keats, and Hopkins in the three poems about stars that appear at the end of this chapter. It is not unusual, however, for a poet to create a thinly veiled mouthpiece to express ideas and reactions. This is certainly the case with Frost's "Wild Grapes" (at the end of this chapter), where the speaker is a woman "grown to wisdom": one critic has said of her, "She speaks in Robert Frost's tone of voice." In Roethke's "Child on Top of a Greenhouse" (Chapter 10), Roethke is recalling an experience out of his own childhood. The speaker is not the little boy who got himself into such an exciting predicament; rather, it is the poet, who remembers how it felt. The language and images are not a child's. In Roethke's "Old Lady's Winter Words" (Chapter 4), however, the persona is the old lady, as Roethke carefully indicates in the title.

Locus

Now you must discover *where* the persona speaks and the relationship between the speaker and the world of the literature, or the locus of the piece. *Locus*, which is closely allied to the concept of persona, is the physical and psychological position of the persona in relation to the experience. The speaker in "The .38" is glued to his room — in part because he *can't* venture out and in part because it isn't safe to leave (Chapter 4). Locus encompasses both time and space. It refers, initially, to place, deriving from the Latin root that underlies our words *location*, *locale*, and *locate*. Actors and directors who refer to shooting films "on location," or writers who speak of searching for a "new locale" for a story, are concerned with locus. In the term's broadest sense, then, the locus of a work of literature is the place where the action of the story occurs. In Tennyson's "Ulysses," the locus is the hearthside at which the hero muses about his past and future. In "Dulce," the locus is sharply focused on the grave during most of the story. The locus affects and is reflected in the mood and attitude of the speaker.

Locus includes more than simply the locale or setting for the action. It also involves the relationship between the speaker of a given line and all the surrounding world — not just the physical world of trees or hills or country, but also the audience to whom that speaker addresses that line and the relationship that speaker enjoys with that audience. In *Romeo and Juliet* (Chapter 8), when Juliet addresses her mother, it should be clear that she has a definite established relationship with her, a relationship that is very different from the ones she has established with the Nurse and with Romeo. She addresses her mother in a way appropriate to their particular relationship.

Less immediately obvious, on the other hand, is the situation of the speaker in Roethke's "Old Lady's Winter Words." What is her environment? Is she speaking these words to herself or to someone else? Where is this person who is being addressed? What would an audience at your performance of this poem see and hear as your relationship with the world of the poem?

Locus also addresses the relationship between the speaker and the audience. Is the audience overhearing what the character says? Is the character talking directly to them? Is the character speaking directly to an audience in the story — to one other person or several? If so, what will the audience at the performance see and hear? Each of these questions presumes a different environment and a different attitude, because each question demonstrates a different locus. These examples (and those given earlier from *Romeo and Juliet* and Roethke's "Old Lady's Winter Words") all involve questions of locus. These questions all explore the relationship between the speaker and his or her surroundings. If the persona addresses another character, the performer envisions that character slightly above and beyond the heads of the audience. If the persona is speaking or musing to himself or herself, the performer may keep the scene and surrounding environment out front, in the audience area, without, of course, singling out any specific audience members as the object of these words.[1] Obviously, other choices can be made, but the questions we ask at the beginning of this paragraph should be answered for every text you undertake.

Finally, for some interpreters, locus refers to the story's attitude about the events it describes. Just as a camera describes the point of view of the action, either from a sweeping panorama or focusing closely on a specific detail, so does a story, poem, or play evoke an attitude toward the events it recounts. This attitude is not simply the same perspective as the point of view of the narrator, although the narrator's position is a part of it. We may feel some revulsion at an incident or character attribute within a selection, but perhaps no such revulsion is expressed by any of the characters or even by the narrator. In this, its fullest sense, locus includes the relationship between the entire tale and the world it inhabits and describes. Only when the locus of the line or speech or scene is clear in your mind can you make those performance choices that convey most fully the literature you have chosen.

Major Aesthetic Components

At this point you are well on your way to your first performance. (You will survive!) Now you can see more clearly how your selection depends on denotative and connotative meanings in the words, emotional and logical climaxes, the personae who speak the words, and locus. But your selection also depends on many more subtle components to sustain its life as a work of art. Literary works of art share common traits, however different their content or form may be. These factors, which we call *intrinsic factors*, are found in varying degrees in all successful writing.

The intrinsic factors are unity and harmony, variety and contrast, balance and proportion, and rhythm. We call them intrinsic because they are clearly discernible within the printed selection and because all reasonably qualified readers recognize them. To appreciate the

1. For some interpreters, when a character directly addresses an audience, the situation is "open," and when the character addresses another character or muses to himself, the situation is "closed." For further examples and discussion, see Wallace Bacon, *The Art of Interpretation*, 3rd ed. (New York: Holt, Rinehart and Winston, 1979), p. 74, and Alethea Smith Mattingly and Wilma Grimes, *Interpretation: Writer, Reader, Audience*, 2nd ed. (Belmont, Calif.: Wadsworth, 1970), pp. 18–19.

intrinsic factors, one does not depend on the uniqueness and range of one's personal experience, but rather on the scrutiny and evaluation of the selection itself.

The intrinsic factors should not be thought of as separate entities. They have bearing on and are affected by both the arrangement and organization of the material, and also by its logical meaning and emotive quality. As a matter of fact, analysis will show that no one factor can be completely separated from the others. They overlap, correlate with, and affect each other. Many elements in the writing may contribute to more than one of these factors within a single selection. Yet each makes its own subtle contribution to the whole. We discuss the intrinsic factors briefly and then identify and examine them in both a story and a poem.

Unity and Harmony

Unity is the combining and ordering of all the parts that make up the whole. It consists of those elements of content and form that hold the writing together and keep the readers' and listeners' minds focused on the total effect.

Unity may be achieved in any number of ways. The persona is a strong unifying factor, as is locus. The setting and time may change within a piece of narrative, but the locus — the physical and psychological relationship of the persona to the events that control the persona's point of view — usually remains constant. Sometimes the persona or the characters go through a clear and unmistakable process of development, which in its progression unifies the material. As you look at a selection, you should observe all of the details that help accomplish this unification. Connectives, such as "and," "then," "next," "a few hours later," and "after this," are important. Approach each selection as a new problem and analyze it carefully to find everything that holds the material together.

Harmony is the appropriate adjustment of parts to one another to form a satisfying whole. In literature it is the concord between the idea and the way that idea is expressed. Harmony is achieved in part through the author's choice of words, the sentence structure, and the relationship of phrases and clauses within the sentences. Obviously, then, it depends to a large extent on elements of style. In poetry, rhythmic elements serve to enhance harmony. Another important source of harmony is the selection of details that set up associations in the readers' minds. Thus, harmony is paired with unity. Although these two factors differ in definition, they are clearly interdependent and must function together if the writing is to achieve its intended effect.

Variety and Contrast

A picture painted in only one color or a musical composition with only one repeated melody is generally dull and uninteresting. In the same way, a piece of literature that lacks variety and contrast is not likely to hold a reader's attention for long.

Variety is provided when two things of the same general kind differ from each other in one or more details. For example, several characters of the same age, sex, and social background essentially may agree but express themselves differently. Or one character, at two or more points of his or her development, may retain unifying qualities but may demonstrate reactions in varying ways.

Contrast implies a sharper differentiation. It is concerned with the opposition or differences between associated things. Two characters may be set against each other by their opposing responses to a situation, or by different actions and motivations. Characters may be contrasted in appearance, age, wisdom, emotion, or any number of other attributes. One place or time may be contrasted with another. Quiet may be set against noise, dark against light, hope against despair, positive elements against negative.

Thus, variety and contrast function together to provide a change of emphasis or to heighten an effect. They are extremely effective in holding attention. You will find them invaluable in the clues they give for vocal and physical vividness. At no time, however, should these two factors exceed the bounds of unity and harmony.

Balance and Proportion

Balance and *proportion* are difficult to evaluate. The test to apply is how well they implement the other factors and contribute to the effect of the whole.

Because proportion provides balance, the two factors should be considered together. A seesaw balances when the fulcrum is exactly the same distance from each end of the board. When equal weights are placed at each end, that balance is retained. But when a heavier weight is placed on one end of the board, the balance is destroyed. Balance can be restored by an adjustment of proportions, either by moving the fulcrum toward the end on which the heavier weight rests or by moving the heavier object closer to the fulcrum.

When equal weights or quantities lie at equal distances from a central point (or fulcrum), the balance is said to be symmetrical. For example, identical candlesticks placed equidistant from the center of a mantelpiece provide a symmetrical balance. Perfect balance is satisfying to the senses, but sometimes the asymmetrical or unequal balance achieved by an adjustment of distance, weights, and masses may be more interesting and effective. Instead of the candlesticks on the mantel, there may be a tall plant at one end and a low, bright-colored bowl at the other. These two objects do not agree in size and shape, but the bulk, height, or weight of the one is somehow balanced by the intensity of color in the other.

Balance also exists within a piece of literature. It is brought about by the intensity or the proportion of content on either side of the point at which the entire selection seems to pivot and change direction. This point of balance occurs at the *crisis* in a story or a play. In a poem, as on a seesaw, it is called the *fulcrum.* The fulcrum or point of balance may or may not coincide with either the logical or the emotional climax.

The principle of point of balance is more important in the consideration of brief, compact selections than of longer units, and you will find it particularly helpful when you analyze poetry. As we mention in Chapter 1, in the twelfth line of Dickinson's "I Felt a Funeral," attention shifts from the funeral and things of the earth to "Space." This, then, is the fulcrum of the poem.

Some selections seem to reach a balance point almost exactly in the middle: there is about the same amount of material leading up to and following the fulcrum. This is clearly the case with Chopin's "The Story of an Hour" (analyzed later in this chapter) or Alice Walker's untitled poem from *Horses Make a Landscape Look More Beautiful* (Chapter 10). Such symmetrical balance gives the interpreter a fairly easy task. You need only to be sure to build to the proper point and not to allow the audience's interest to wane thereafter. If the author has arranged the material so that such handling is achieved without too much difficulty, he or she may be considered successful in the use of symmetrical balance.

Frequently, however, the balance is off center, especially in contemporary writing. In many cases, the greater proportion of the total material precedes the fulcrum. For example, Roethke's "Child on Top of a Greenhouse" (Chapter 10) turns on the last line.

Asymmetrical balance is effective in producing sudden shock, or a feeling of unrest, or a spark of humor. It is effective, however, only when the author has been careful to weight the smaller proportion of material with enough vividness and emotional intensity to enable it to hold its own against the greater number of words it must balance. When this has been taken care of in the writing, you need only to make use of the author's clues and add the proper amount of emotional intensity, emphasis, and stress to the smaller unit to achieve perfect balance in your performance.

Rhythm

In literature *rhythm* is usually thought of as an element of poetic structure, such as the relationship between stressed and unstressed syllables. But rhythm is an important aspect of content as well. Rhythm of content is found in both logical and emotional content as they operate together. We discuss structural rhythm in the later chapters on prose style and poetic structure.

Rhythm of content may be established in many ways in both prose and poetry, and it will begin to emerge as you study details of organization and style. For example, in Dickinson's "I Felt a Funeral," there is a steady alternation between references to the speaker in the poem and to "them." The briefer the selection, the more important this factor is likely to be.

A rhythm of content can be set up by the recurrent shift of attention from one character to another or from one place or time to another, or by the alternation of description and narration or dialogue and exposition. The rhythm of emotional quality can be measured by the increased and decreased intensity of the reader's response, and it becomes evident as the minor climaxes are discovered. As we analyze more deeply, we will discover many more ways of identifying and expressing this factor.

Rhythm of content is important to an interpreter, because it is closely related to holding an audience's attention. Most people are able to concentrate fully and exclusively on an idea for only a brief time. The skillful writer allows for this fatigue or wavering of attention and permits the reader to relax from time to time. By understanding and conveying this rhythm of concentration, you can do the same for your audience.

Furthermore, listeners cannot be held at a high emotional pitch for long periods of time. In spite of themselves, and in spite of the interpreter's best efforts, they experience a sense of relaxation after high points of emotional response. The wise writer and the informed interpreter will provide for this relaxation so that the emotional climaxes may be more effective, especially if they depend on accumulation of feeling. Be careful, however, not to break your own concentration. As we have seen, rhythm is also an excellent device for keeping variety and contrast in control within the essential frame of unity.

You will receive a great deal of help from the intrinsic factors within a piece of literature. The problem is how to go about finding

them and using the understanding gained from this analysis in preparation and performance. Each selection differs from every other in
the degree of importance that should be attached to the various
factors. You should let the author lead the way, using what is actually
in the writing rather than trying to fit the selection to a preconceived
pattern. Look at the selection carefully. Try to discover everything
that the author has given you to work with. Then, and only then,
should you be concerned specifically with unity and harmony, variety
and contrast, balance and proportion, and rhythm. A careful consideration of these intrinsic factors will help you to put the piece of
literature back together so that all the elements operate within the
organic whole.

Using the Tools

So far we have described a process; now let's see it work with two
different texts — a story that may be new to you and a poem with
which you have become familiar. Those devices of analysis we spoke
of thus far are really only tools to help you understand both what
the author wrote and how it was written. Do not allow yourself to
pass by the analysis stage, however. You wouldn't begin a long car
journey to a place you've never been without carefully consulting a
reliable map. Literary analysis, as we have said, is not an end in
itself for interpreters; analysis is the way interpreters achieve an
informed and rich rehearsal period that alone can guarantee the
fullest possible performance.

   The analyses of a story and of a poem that follow differ in several
respects, in part, obviously, because poems and stories differ. These
works, again about superficially similar topics, present different performance problems and suggest different solutions. Do not be concerned that any other selection you make — another poem or another
story — may not demonstrate exactly the same relationships between
variety and contrast or the same use of balance and proportion as
these do. These works are *examples.* You may discover aspects of the
literature we have not mentioned, or you may emphasize something
we have only touched on. Remember: informed discussion requires
information. Look carefully, gauge cautiously; an exciting journey is
about to begin.

A Sample Analysis of a Story

"The Story of an Hour" was written around the turn of the century
by the American author Kate Chopin. Read it carefully once or twice

before reading the analysis. (We have numbered the paragraphs for easy reference.)

The Story of an Hour

KATE CHOPIN

1   Knowing that Mrs. Mallard was afflicted with a heart trouble, great care was taken to break to her as gently as possible the news of her husband's death.

2   It was her sister Josephine who told her, in broken sentences, veiled hints that revealed in half concealing. Her husband's friend Richards was there, too, near her. It was he who had been in the newspaper office when intelligence of the railroad disaster was received, with Brently Mallard's name leading the list of "killed." He had only taken the time to assure himself of its truth by a second telegram, and had hastened to forestall any less careful, less tender friend in bearing the sad message.

3   She did not hear the story as many women have heard the same, with a paralyzed inability to accept its significance. She wept at once, with sudden, wild abandonment, in her sister's arms. When the storm of grief had spent itself she went away to her room alone. She would have no one follow her.

4   There stood, facing the open window, a comfortable, roomy armchair. Into this she sank, pressed down by a physical exhaustion that haunted her body and seemed to reach into her soul.

5   She could see in the open square before her house the tops of trees that were all aquiver with the new spring life. The delicious breath of rain was in the air. In the street below a peddler was crying his wares. The notes of a distant song which some one was singing reached her faintly, and countless sparrows were twittering in the eaves.

6   There were patches of blue sky showing here and there through the clouds that had met and piled above the other in the west facing her window.

7   She sat with her head thrown back upon the cushion of the chair quite motionless, except when a sob came up into her throat and shook her, as a child who has cried itself to sleep continues to sob in its dreams.

8   She was young, with a fair, calm face, whose lines bespoke repression and even a certain strength. But now there was a dull stare in her eyes, whose gaze was fixed away off yonder on one of those patches of blue sky. It was not a glance of reflection, but rather indicated a suspension of intelligent thought.

9   There was something coming to her and she was waiting for it, fearfully. What was it? She did not know; it was too subtle and elusive to name. But she felt it, creeping out of the sky, reaching toward her through the sounds, the scents, the color that filled the air.

10   Now her bosom rose and fell tumultuously. She was beginning to recognize this thing that was approaching to possess her, and she was striving to beat it back with her will — as powerless as her two white slender hands would have been.

11   When she abandoned herself a little whispered word escaped her slightly parted lips. She said it over and over under her breath: "Free, free, free!" The vacant stare and the look of terror that had followed it went from her eyes. They stayed keen and bright. Her pulses beat fast, and the coursing blood warmed and relaxed every inch of her body.

12   She did not stop to ask if it were not a monstrous joy that held her. A clear and exalted perception enabled her to dismiss the suggestion as trivial.

13   She knew that she would weep again when she saw the kind, tender hands folded in death; the face that had never looked save with love upon her, fixed and gray and dead. But she saw beyond that bitter moment a long procession of years to come that would belong to her absolutely. And she opened and spread her arms out to them in welcome.

14   There would be no one to live for during those coming years; she would live for herself. There would be no powerful will bending her in that blind persistence with which men and women believe they have a right to impose a private will upon a fellow-creature. A kind intention or a cruel intention made the act seem no less a crime as she looked upon it in that brief moment of illumination.

15   And yet she had loved him — sometimes. Often she had not. What did it matter! What could love, the unsolved mystery, count for in face of this possession of self-assertion which she suddenly recognized as the strongest impulse of her being.

16   "Free! Body and soul free!" she kept whispering.

17   Josephine was kneeling before the closed door with her lips to the keyhole, imploring for admission. "Louise, open the door! I beg; open the door — you will make yourself ill. What are you doing, Louise? For heaven's sake open the door."

18   "Go away. I am not making myself ill." No; she was drinking in a very elixir of life through that open window.

19   Her fancy was running riot along those days ahead of her. Spring days, and summer days, and all sorts of days that would be her own. She breathed a quick prayer that life might be long. It was only yesterday she had thought with a shudder that life might be long.

20   She arose at length and opened the door to her sister's importunities. There was a feverish triumph in her eyes, and she carried herself unwittingly like a goddess of Victory. She clasped her sister's waist, and together they descended the stairs. Richards stood waiting for them at the bottom.

21   Some one was opening the front door with a latchkey. It was Brently Mallard who entered, a little travel-stained, composedly

carrying his grip-sack and umbrella. He had been far from the scene of accident, and did not even know there had been one. He stood amazed at Josephine's piercing cry; at Richards' quick motion to screen him from the view of his wife.

22   But Richards was too late.

23   When the doctors came they said she had died of heart disease — of joy that kills.

The most important questions an interpreter confronts when studying a story are "Who is telling this story?" and "What is happening during the story?" All of the devices of structure we have mentioned, all of the intrinsic factors, all of the author's skill, give clues to help you discover the answer to these questions. "The Story of an Hour" provides a rich opportunity to examine the ways in which an author creates a storyteller and a story to tell.

Often, the best way to understand the nature of the narrator and the tale being told is to examine the story very closely. First, of course, we have to be sure we understand the dictionary meanings of all of the words. Are you sure that "elixir" (paragraph 18) refers to a cure-all? Are Josephine's "importunities" (paragraph 20) requests or demands or both? Have you ever seen a picture of a "goddess of Victory"? There are several famous sculptures on this theme. How does Mrs. Mallard carry herself to look like such a figure? Once these questions are answered, we can investigate the story in more depth.

In the space of this hour (although performing the story takes little more than eight minutes), Mrs. Mallard undergoes an extraordinary change. On one hand, the characters in the story see only a woman distraught with grief who appears to die from joy at the appearance of the husband she thought dead. *Balancing* that view, we know that within this hour Mrs. Mallard begins to live another, richer, more fearful life of independence, a life of her own. When her old life returns (in the person of her husband), she knows that the rich new life she had embraced will never be possible, and she dies from a "joy that kills." The narrator lets us imagine what pained disappointment goes through her mind when she sees her husband again. But just as we did not share her thoughts when she learned of her husband's death, we do not share her thoughts when she sees he lives. Because we were with her only for the time she began to live, we know Mrs. Mallard better than any of her family or friends.

"Who is telling this story?" The storyteller is unnamed but clearly knows all the people in the tale. For all of them — storyteller and characters — Mrs. Mallard is the center of the tale, from the first paragraph to the last. The other characters — Josephine, Richards, and Brently — exist only as agents in her life. The narrator describes

Mrs. Mallard's grief over her husband's presumed death, notes carefully her fears and concerns, and dwells at length on the impending changes his death carries. In so brief a story, her victory is scrupulously described. Clearly, the narrator has a close, sensitive relationship with Mrs. Mallard.

We understand this relationship more fully when the narrator tells us of Mrs. Mallard's change. After having expended "the storm of grief," Mrs. Mallard "went away to her room alone. She would have no one follow her" (paragraph 3). But *we* follow her closely, guided by the narrator, who describes for us the furnishings of this room barred to everyone else (paragraph 4), the view only Mrs. Mallard can see (paragraphs 5–6), Mrs. Mallard's very private behavior (paragraph 7), and her physical features as she is experiencing the change (paragraph 8). Because of the narrator's special access to Mrs. Mallard, we are privileged to know her in complex ways others cannot. And our view gets richer. We move from the world outside Mrs. Mallard to the world inside her. In *contrast* to what others hear through the doors, we see a woman confronting independence. Thus, by varying the ways in which the narrator reveals Mrs. Mallard to us, the author contrasts her inner and outer worlds, and the *locus* of the story moves from the hallway into Mrs. Mallard's mind.

As Mrs. Mallard begins to consider life without her husband, the narrator carefully describes the internal turmoil Mrs. Mallard experiences — how she feels, what she thinks, how her body throbs with anxiety and fear (paragraphs 9 and 10). Only because the narrator tells us are we permitted to hear her whispered cries (paragraph 11). Solely because the narrator shows us do we see how she starts to live without a husband (paragraphs 12–14). Her new status both dismays and exhilarates her. It seems to have rushed in on her after the stately opening paragraphs, but there is something splendid about it all the same. Dauntless, she continues to repeat the exhilarating word "Free!" (paragraph 16).

To balance this internal view, at this point the narrator returns us to the world outside the bedroom. Josephine's concern about Mrs. Mallard and her fear that she will make herself ill contrast sharply with what we know about how exciting these glimpses of freedom have been. Given just these few moments of freedom, Mrs. Mallard now sees an extraordinary life ahead of her, eagerly anticipates what her own life might become, and remembers how little she had to look forward to only yesterday (paragraph 19). With this realization of her future she rises to confront at last the old world she inhabited. Triumphing over her past, she now sees the future she had never even been able to hope for (paragraph 20). And, just as at the beginning of the story, she again receives news about her husband.

The final scene moves quickly. Note that the narrator tells us that "some one" opens the front door (paragraph 21). In suspense, we join the world of the story for a moment, not knowing who will appear. All in the hall turn to see who is intruding on this scene of grief (or, in Mrs. Mallard's case, joy), only to discover Brently's return. Richards again tries to help but is too late (just as earlier he had been too hasty). The doctors diagnose Mrs. Mallard's death of a heart overjoyed. We know better.

The language the narrator chooses describes both Mrs. Mallard and the narrator. The opening paragraphs of the story contain formal, rather stilted grammar and vocabulary: the passive voice ("was afflicted," "was taken") and the legalistic "It was" introducing the summarized action of the story. Such forms tend to remove action from immediate experience, making it seem something that happened to someone else. The *rhythm* is stately and gradual. The Mrs. Mallard of the opening paragraphs is thus different from the rejuvenated woman who emerges ready to face a new life. In paragraphs 9 through 13, colorful language conveys the terror of her acceptance. "Powerful will bending" and "blind persistence" describe the relationship between men and women (paragraph 14). The forces of life seem to rush in on her. Love is characterized as "an unsolved mystery" that pales in front of the "possession of self-assertion," which becomes "the strongest impulse of her being," an "elixir" transforming her into a "goddess of Victory" over the past she has known (paragraphs 15–20). But as the story concludes, the language returns to its placid depiction of the opening, and the tempo resumes its slow, stately progress. The events again seem to happen to someone we do not know. Brently Mallard's appearance and the subsequent events are narrated from afar. He "stood amazed" at the cry of his sister-in-law and at his partner's attempt to "screen him from the view of his wife" (a tantalizingly rich phrase). All the narrator tells us about Mrs. Mallard's death is in one paragraph of six syllables. Only afterward does the word "died" appear, placed in the mouths of the doctors who, like everyone else in Mrs. Mallard's world, misunderstood her life.

Several other clues inform us about this narrator. He or she is sensitive to the natural world as the appropriate order of things, relies on the good sense and the justness of personal integrity, is sympathetic, and clearly understands what living in the world requires. Josephine and Richards are compassionate characters who care deeply about Mrs. Mallard. Her husband is kindly and enjoys his wife's affection. But this narrator knows that none of them understand who *she* is. Ironically, her family's loving concern simply reinforces her sense of living the trapped, airless life. With her discovery that she can — and must — live her own life, she also sees how she could no longer live any other way. And she doesn't.

Finally, of course, this narrator is supremely interested in life's ironies. Little ironies abound. The sad message of Brently Mallard's death actually brings a kind of joy to his wife. Richards's haste at the beginning to protect Mrs. Mallard and his tardiness at the end eventually contribute to her death. The doctors' diagnosis is true, but not at all in the way they mean or everyone else believes. Mrs. Mallard begins to live after years of marriage have been violently ended. In the springtime of the year she, too, comes to a new life, but she dies just as she is beginning to know what her new life is like.

Variety and contrast in tempo and character, balance and proportion in narrative and scene, unity and harmony of theme and incident, rendered with delicate but clear changes of rhythm that seem almost effortless: these have been the characteristics of successful storytelling for centuries. This story, then, is built in a classic form: an opening scene summarized initiates the rising action leading to the carefully described scene at the emotional fulcrum of the story. The moment of self-discovery leads inevitably to the emotional and thematic climax of the story in the last two paragraphs. By using suspense, surprise, understatement, and irony, the storyteller captures in a brief moment a story to resonate beyond an hour.

Mrs. Mallard's life and death — the story the narrator wants us to understand — causes us to wonder about what it means to be a human being living with other human beings, how love can both free and imprison, how human freedom is essential to happiness. To understand the story of Mrs. Mallard's last — and first — hour of life is to understand something about human integrity and human need. To tell such a story, then, becomes a profound act of sharing truth.

A Sample Analysis of a Poem

In Chapter 1 we valued Dickinson's poem when measured against the touchstones of universality, individuality, and suggestion. Let us look again at Dickinson's "I Felt a Funeral" to discover how the details of the intrinsic factors work together as well. Since the poem is brief, it is repeated here, and the lines are numbered for easier reference.

I Felt a Funeral

EMILY DICKINSON

1   I felt a Funeral, in my Brain,
2   And Mourners to and fro

3   Kept treading — treading — till it seemed
4   That Sense was breaking through —

5   And when they all were seated,
6   A Service, like a Drum —
7   Kept beating — beating — till I thought
8   My Mind was going numb —

9   And then I heard them lift a Box
10 And creak across my Soul
11 With those same Boots of Lead, again,
12 Then Space — began to toll,

13 As all the Heavens were a Bell,
14 And Being, but an Ear,
15 And I, and Silence, some strange Race
16 Wrecked, solitary, here —

17 And then a Plank in Reason, broke,
18 And I dropped down, and down —
19 And hit a World, at every Crash,
20 And Got through knowing — then —

There are probably no words in this poem that you need to look up in the dictionary. In our earlier discussion, we touched briefly on the connotation of some of the words. We come back to this matter later, for it is impossible to avoid it in a selection so filled with suggestion. For the moment let us move on to organization.

The first line gives the complete opening situation. We know that she "felt" rather than saw a funeral, and that she felt it in her brain. Immediately the possibility opens up that this poem is not about an actual funeral but about a sensation and thus is, in a highly poetic way, an analogy. It may be about the sense of death, or despair, or both. In any case, it is about sensation within the rational part of one's body. That is a paradox in itself. To establish this essential paradox, Dickinson uses two stanzas, which we may consider as the introduction. The third and fourth stanzas take us from the tightly enclosed earthly place to "Space" and the almost intolerable tolling followed by silence. In the opening line of the final stanza, we begin the descent and the conclusion of the experience. Thus, the organization is really very simple and unified. The logical climax is located in the last line, where the experience reaches its only possible outcome.

Although each stanza has its own emotional build-up, the major emotional climax coincides with the fulcrum, where heaviness is suddenly replaced by space and sound swells to sudden silence. In the final line of the middle stanza, the poem turns from earth and people, in a sense, to space and solitude. After the weight of the box, the "creak across my Soul," which strongly suggests a creak across a floor, and the "Boots of Lead," we are suddenly confronted with the sharply contrasting vast and empty expanse of space. This is, as we have said, the fulcrum. It is approximately in the center of the poem and causes no trouble as far as balance and proportion of stanzas is concerned.

The poem gives us a sense of continuing development, and yet without real speed except for lines 19 and 20, where the drop occurs. This is achieved in part by the structure. The effect of steady continuation first suggested in "to and fro" is strengthened by the connectives "and," "till," "and when," and "and then." It is interesting that the use of the word "and" increases sharply in the last stanza so that the drop picks up speed, and the experience is terminated with the final "then."

The verb forms also help create this effect. Although the entire poem is in the past tense, there is a subtle variation within it. The repetition in "Kept treading — treading," "Kept beating — beating," and "down, and down," combined with the imperfect tense of "was breaking," and "was going," gives a feeling of action continuing over a period of time. It is interesting to notice, however, that at the fulcrum there is a shift into the infinitive with "began to toll," followed immediately by a subjunctive form throughout the entire fourth stanza ("As" in line 13 implies "as if"). The subjunctive is used to speak of a hypothesis or a condition contrary to fact. The final stanza returns to the simple past with "broke," "dropped," "hit," and "Got through" — about as completed a past as one can have!

We have already mentioned the use of "I felt" in the opening line. Taking the first person singular *I*, we find that the poem moves from "I felt" to "I thought," "I heard," "And I, and Silence" to "I dropped," "[I] hit," and "[I] Got through." Although the first four *I*'s are evenly spaced one to a stanza, the last three occur in quick succession in the last three lines. Our attention is focused on the *I* at the opening of the poem, and then we are quickly introduced to the mourners. The rhythm of attention alternates, although not with perfect regularity, until line 12, when "Space" is introduced. We have no references to the mourners or to the funeral after that, and the next reference to *I* is "I, and Silence." A look at the funeral references reveals that they continue at least by implication through line 13 with "toll" and "Bell," but it is really "Space" that begins to toll and "the Heavens" that are a bell.

A specific set of references that a writer returns to often is called a *motif*. A motif in music, design, or literature is any detail repeated often enough to become important. In music, it may be a phrase of melody or a set of chords. In design, it may be a leaf, a flower, or any particular element used in a pattern. In literature, the repeated reference need not be an *exact* repetition of images or ideas. It may present recurring references to a concept like the elements: storms, clouds, or sunshine. It may refer repeatedly to things related to each other, such as colors, nature, or animals.

The first line of Dickinson's poem refers to "my Brain," and this reference is strengthened and at the same time is made more specific three lines later by "Sense," which we discussed in Chapter 1 when we talked about suggestion. Thus, we move from "my Brain" to "it seemed," "Sense," "I thought," and "My Mind." This mental motif does not reappear until the final stanza, which opens with a reference to "Reason" and closes with "knowing." We are very carefully returned to the poet with "I" in line 15; "Reason" and "knowing" are in identical positions with "Brain" and "Sense" in the opening stanza. Although psychologists might disagree, "heard" in line 9 appears to be more physical than emotional. The next reference is to "Soul," then to "Being," and then to "Race," a large, general, abstract category rather than a specific personal reference. Moreover, the race is "strange," "Wrecked," and, most important, "solitary." Even more subtle is the use of "Ear" with "Being." Thus, lines 9 through 16 form a unit that differs from the rest of the poem in motif. As we have remarked, there is also a shift in verb form, and this is the only place in the poem where a sentence continues past the stanza break without being broken by a dash.

A simple listing by line in the table that follows makes this discussion more graphic. Remember, however, that a list is not a poem. It is useful only as a step in analysis. In the interest of clarity we do not follow Dickinson's use of capital letters.

Remembering that the intrinsic factors are closely related and that a detail may contribute to more than one of them, let us see how what we have found relates to unity and harmony, variety and contrast, balance and proportion, and rhythm.

The use of "I" and "my" is a strong *unifying* factor. It is clearly established in the first ten lines and returned to in line 15 and throughout the final stanza. The connectives and the simple progression of events also help hold the poem together. The psychological motif opens and closes the poem and is constant throughout, except in the middle portion, where it is weaker but still operating in "heard" and "as [if]." The sound motif with the contrasting silence is heavy in the beginning, reaches a high level at the fulcrum, is somehow strengthened by the sudden silence, and returns with force in the final stanza. A feeling of weight and heaviness begins in the first stanza, reaches its peak in "lift a Box" and "Boots of Lead," and recurs in "Plank . . . broke" in line 17.

We cannot fully appreciate *harmony* until we have examined poetic structure, but certainly the heaviness just referred to and the continuing, unbroken downward progression are harmonious with the sensation that Dickinson describes. "Drum" suggests funeral drums; a tolling bell, also associated with funerals, prolongs the mood. "Wrecked," "broke," and "Crash" help suggest the destruction following the tolling of "Space." Careful examination reveals a remarkable harmony between what is being said and the connotations and sounds of the words that say it.

Within the unity of this brief poem, we find enough *variety* and *contrast* to hold our interest. A look at the funeral motif and the sound motif indicates that Dickinson used very subtle variety indeed. Too much variety within so brief a poem would seriously threaten unity, especially since contrast is so sharp. The poet's isolation is contrasted with the multiplicity of people in "Mourners" and "they all," until the isolation reaches its culmination in "I, and Silence . . . solitary." Their actions are contrasted with her immobility and numbing sensations. Space and the heavens are set off against weight and the tangible things of earth. Silence is set against a crescendo of sound. It is, in fact, because of these contrasts that the fulcrum operates so successfuly.

Balance and *proportion* offer no real problem here, since there are almost an equal number of lines and amount of emotional weight on either side of the fulcrum. The build-up to the fulcrum is steady. Immediately after the point of balance is reached, the action ceases momentarily; although the emotional and logical climaxes fall in the second portion of the poem, they do not overbalance the heaviness and familiarity of the funeral motif in the first section. Moreover, the emotional climax is controlled by abstractions: "the Heavens," "Being," and "strange Race." After the emotional climax, the speed picks up, and the repeated use of "and" tightens the progression to the conclusion.

Rhythm of content is strongest in the shifts from the poet to the mourners that we mentioned earlier and in the focus on their actions and then on her responses. Again, there is not enough room for an elaborate pattern of rhythm of content in twenty short lines. As we continue to look at the poem, however, we are aware that both the variety and the contrast make a rhythmic contribution, as do some of the elements in unity.

Innumerable small details also contribute to the intrinsic factors.

Line	Persons	Mental and Physical Motifs	Connectives	Verb Forms	Funeral Motifs	Sound and Silence
1	I my	I felt my brain		I felt	funeral	
2	mourners		and		mourners	
3	they (implied)	it seemed	till	kept treading treading it seemed		treading treading
4	my (implied)	sense		was breaking		
5	they (mourners)		and when	were seated		
6					service drum	drum
7	I	I thought	till	kept beating beating I thought		beating beating
8	my	my mind		was going		
9	I them (mourners)	I heard	and then	I heard lift	box	heard them
10	them (implied) my	my soul	and	creak		creak across
11	their (implied)				lead	boots of lead
12		space	then	began to toll	toll	toll FULCRUM
13		heavens		as [if] . . . were	bell	bell
14		being ear	and	as [if] . . . were (implied)		ear
15	I and silence	race	and . . . and	as [if] . . . were (implied)		silence
16				as [if] . . . were (implied)		solitary
17		reason	and then	broke		plank broke
18	I		and . . . and	dropped		
19	I (implied)		and	hit		crash
20	I (implied)	knowing	and then	got through		

We cannot resist calling attention to the remarkable spacing of "treading," "creak across," and "Plank," all of which suggest floor boards. They are placed with mathematical precision in lines 3, 10, and 17. The use of the already familiar "I" with "heard" controls the unity, and "heard" prepares us for "toll," "Bell," "Ear," "Silence," "Plank . . . broke," and finally "Crash."

Now what should you do with all this discovery? Use it fully and with complete confidence in the author. Whether the writer was conscious of using all the elements, or indeed of the intrinsic and extrinsic factors as such, is beside the point. It is your responsibility to find everything the writer has given you to work with.

Synthesis

The difficult task of synthesis comes next. Synthesis takes time — time to grow, correct, adjust, and grow again. In this process the interpreter begins to work as an artist. Slowly, step by step, all the parts are reassembled so that the selection is once more an ordered work of literary art and not a mere list of details. Don't expect to do it all at once. Putting a literary selection back together after analysis is as complex as reassembling a delicate watch, a complicated stereo system, or the engine of a car. Every piece must go where it belongs to function properly with every other piece. The process may seem like a juggling act the first few times you try it, but it will get easier and more interesting each time. You may not be entirely satisfied with your first few performances, but that is because now you know much more and no longer need to rely on good luck or slick tricks that you hope will work.

Rehearsing the Selection

It is impossible to set up a system that will work for every selection, because each piece of literature presents its own problems and opportunities. However, the following procedure may give you a general working outline.

Read the material aloud over and over and over, paying attention first to meaning, both what it means and how it means it.

Next, give some attention to the method of organization. Key words, phrases, and sentences come into play here, as do the denotations and connotations of words. Settle on the location of the climax or the fulcrum, and determine how the author brings the material to a close so that your audience will know where the selection is going and when it gets there.

Look at all the elements that contribute to unity and harmony. What holds the selection together and keeps it moving?

Spend some time examining the imagery in the selection for a full response with your mind and emotions. How does the imagery contribute to unity and harmony, and how and where does it provide variety and contrast? Don't forget the importance of connotation here.

Who is speaking in the selection? Is this persona thinking aloud for us to overhear, or addressing another person specifically? How would he or she respond to the connotation and imagery you have worked on? What is the locus — the physical, psychological, and temporal position — of the persona in relation to the experience being shared? Is it memory of the past, is it the present, or is it the future?

What help does the author give you in keeping the two parts on either side of the fulcrum in balance? Is there a strong rhythm of content either in the emotional build-ups and drops or in the alternation of attention to activity and passivity, past and present, or any other aspect?

Keep reading the selection aloud as you fit these pieces together. Start several days ahead so you have time to allow it to mellow. Be sure your vocal technique is serving all the things you have discovered. Reflect the imagery and connotations in your voice quality, pace, and volume. Give every word its full value of sound.

As you work aloud on a piece of literature, you gain new insights and hear new melodies. Thus, it is wise to begin oral preparation well in advance of performance. You need to let the writing work on you as you work on it. Always start your rehearsal session by reading the entire selection aloud.

As an interpreter, you should remember that your audience does not want to hear your analysis: it wants to share the experience of the literature. If the analysis has been thorough and the preparation sound, you may trust the author and yourself to give your full concentration to sharing the selection in its entirety. But unless you know exactly what the author has done, you cannot possibly perform the work to its full potential.

Excerpts and Introductions

Some selections in this text may be too long to be practical for a class assignment, but most of them offer units that may be used as excerpts. Feel free to use only a portion of a selection when time constrains you, but be careful not to damage the work in the process of selecting the words that will fill your requirements.

When you choose an excerpt from a play or a story, be sure to select a unit with at least a minor climax, so that your audience will get a clear sense that something is happening. You need to be aware of the key sentences or phrases in earlier sections that your audience must know about to understand and respond to the climax. One good way to use the author's words to introduce your performance is to select a sentence that features the key phrase or phrases, make a brief additional comment in your own words, and then proceed to the segment you will perform. Sometimes it will be clearer and smoother to explain the key phrases in your introduction. Although your introduction and necessary transitions do not tell the audience what they are going to hear (except, of course, for author and title), they do prepare your listeners with subtle clues about what is to come. It is wise to avoid cutting poetry until you have more experience, especially lyric poetry, because of its compactness.

Keep your introduction (and whatever additional material you need) as brief as possible; its style should be in harmony with the mood you want to create. Address your comments directly to the audience without using written notes. That way the audience can more easily believe that this is a special performance just for them. Introductions — and transitions, if they are necessary — should appear to be spontaneous. They are an important part of your performance, but they are not what your audience wants to hear. Before working on the porch, be sure the house is sturdy.

Analyzing the Performance

After you have finished your first performance, you must wait a few minutes before you have any realistic idea of how it went. In fact, it may not be until some hours later that you can get a clear evaluation of your success and your shortcomings. The line you "blew" or your break in concentration will stand blazing in your mind. Try not to lose your perspective. After you have settled back to normal and the adrenalin of performance has subsided, ask yourself some questions.

Did you keep your concentration steady from what the author had given you to your appropriate response and then out to communicate with the audience? If not, what caused the break? Where did it occur? Why there?

Did you control and preserve the unity so that there was an effective beginning, middle, and conclusion?

Did your introduction tell the audience what they needed for background, especially if you used an excerpt? Did it set the proper mood for the selection? Was it too long?

Were variety and contrast allowed to work effectively while remaining well within the essential unity and harmony? Did you allow for the rhythm of content while keeping the thread of unity firm and clear?

Did the audience respond as you expected? Did any of your performance mannerisms distract the audience from what they were hearing?

Part of your responsibility — and pleasure — in an interpretation class is to be a good audience. Put your own worries aside for a time and really *listen* and react to the readings of others. Often you learn as much or more from someone else's performance as from your own. Your instructor's comments may seem vague or theoretical until you see or hear someone else doing the same thing; suddenly you see how what someone else did helped communicate the selection or detracted from it.

You will probably be asked to comment about others' readings. In your comments about these performances, try to describe to the interpreter exactly what you saw and heard. Avoid such comments as "I liked it" or "It was nice." Of course, the reader will be pleased that you liked it, but without more specific comments on why you liked it, he or she will not know how to improve. Mention instead a specific moment in the performance. A comment like "The way you held your head made Mrs. Mallard seem very stern and cold at the end of the story" or "Your voice at the opening of 'I Felt a Funeral' was very high-pitched and sounded as if you were about to scream" will help the performer focus specifically on exactly what happened during the performance. Only in this way can the performer learn what he or she successfully communicated to you. Together you and the reader can examine the selection to see if it calls for the actions or mannerisms you describe. And you can compare your responses with those of other audience members to be sure that the performance was equally effective throughout the audience. Finally, we have found that performers are more likely to listen carefully if they think you enjoyed some aspect of the reading; why not begin your comment with something specific that succeeded in the performance and then move on to the elements that still need work?

Selections for Analysis and Oral Interpretation

Each of these selections must be analyzed thoroughly. Do not try to make each one follow the pattern of Chopin's story or Dickinson's poem, however, because every piece of writing is unique. Look for all the details that we have discussed. Then decide which ones contribute to unity and harmony and see where variety and contrast exist within the unity and harmony. Find the fulcrum and climaxes, and consider balance and proportion. Look carefully for rhythm of content. Remember that details may contribute to more than one of the intrinsic factors.

Begin with the whole selection and let it work on you until you feel comfortable with it. Then move into an objective analysis. After each step, go back to the complete selection and see how the pieces fit together. Remember that your audience wants the total effect, not the separate pieces. Each selection is followed by one or two bulleted questions to assist you in rehearsal or to begin class discussion.

Although these three poems all have stars as their main motif, they vary considerably in the ways this theme is treated. Each poem shows strong marks of individuality. In each case the persona is clearly the poet and the locus is here on earth. The poems make an interesting comparison. In the first poem, by Walt Whitman, repetition creates both frustration and relief. The exquisite delay that culminates in the last syllable of the last line must never become sluggish.

When I Heard the Learn'd Astronomer
WALT WHITMAN

When I heard the learn'd astronomer,
When the proofs, the figures, were ranged in columns before me,
When I was shown the charts and diagrams, to add, divide, and
        measure them,
When I sitting heard the astronomer where he lectured with much
        applause in the lecture-room,
How soon unaccountable I became tired and sick,
Till rising and gliding out I wander'd off by myself,
In the mystical moist night-air, and from time to time,
Look'd up in perfect silence at the stars.

❚ How can you demonstrate the persona's growing dismay?
❚ At what word did your persona first see the stars?

Sonnet
JOHN KEATS

Bright star! would I were as steadfast as thou art —
    Not in lone splendor hung aloft the night
And watching, with eternal lids apart,

Like nature's patient, sleepless Eremite,
The moving waters at their priest-like task
   Of pure ablution round earth's human shores,
Or gazing on the new soft fallen mask
   Of snow upon the mountains and the moors —
No — yet still steadfast, still unchangeable,
   Pillow'd upon my fair love's ripening breast,
To feel for ever its soft fall and swell,
   Awake for ever in a sweet unrest,
Still, still to hear her tender-taken breath,
   And so live ever — or else swoon to death.

> ▌ How did your performance of the *still*'s in the ninth line differ
> from the *still*'s in the thirteenth line? Why?

The Starlight Night

GERARD MANLEY HOPKINS

Look at the stars! look, look up at the skies!
   O look at all the fire-folk sitting in the air!
   The bright boroughs, the circle-citadels there!
Down in dim woods the diamond delves! the elves'-eyes!
The grey lawns cold where gold, where quickgold lies!
   Wind-beat whitebeam! airy abeles set on a flare!
   Flake doves sent floating forth at a farmyard scare!
Ah well! it is all a purchase, all is a prize.

Buy then! bid then! — What? — Prayer, patience, alms, vows.
Look, look: a May-mess, like on orchard boughs!
   Look! March-bloom, like on mealed-with-yellow sallows!
These are indeed the barn; withindoors house
The shocks. This piece-bright paling shuts the spouse
   Christ home, Christ and his mother and all his hallows.

> ▌ Did you see each manifestation of stars before moving on to the
> next?
> ▌ Did your audience see the auction that begins in the ninth line?

The narrator in this excerpt is clearly the grown man remembering a special time in his childhood. Although the characters vary considerably in age, their attitudes are perfectly attuned. All the speeches are given to the woman. Her short sentences have the excitement and vitality of immediacy, which gives nice contrast to the quieter but warm and happy memory of the narrator, thus providing an essential rhythm.

FROM *A Christmas Memory*
TRUMAN CAPOTE

Imagine a morning in late November. A coming of winter morning more than twenty years ago. Consider the kitchen of a spreading old house in a country town. A great black stove is its main feature; but there is also a big round table and a fireplace with two rocking chairs placed in front of it. Just today the fireplace commenced its seasonal roar.

A woman with shorn white hair is standing at the kitchen window. She is wearing tennis shoes and a shapeless gray sweater over a summery calico dress. She is small and sprightly, like a bantam hen; but, due to a long youthful illness, her shoulders are pitifully hunched. Her face is remarkable — not unlike Lincoln's, craggy like that, and tinted by sun and wind; but it is delicate too, finely boned, and her eyes are sherry-colored and timid. "Oh my," she exclaims, her breath smoking the windowpane, "it's fruitcake weather!"

The person to whom she is speaking is myself. I am seven; she is sixty-something. We are cousins, very distant ones, and we have lived together — well, as long as I can remember. Other people inhabit the house, relatives; and though they have power over us, and frequently make us cry, we are not, on the whole, too much aware of them. We are each other's best friend. She calls me Buddy, in memory of a boy who was formerly her best friend. The other Buddy died in the 1880's, when she was still a child. She is still a child.

"I knew it before I got out of bed," she says, turning away from the window with a purposeful excitement in her eyes. "The courthouse bell sounded so cold and clear. And there were no birds singing; they've gone to warmer country, yes indeed. Oh, Buddy, stop stuffing biscuit and fetch our buggy. Help me find my hat. We've thirty cakes to bake."

It's always the same: a morning arrives in November, and my friend, as though officially inaugurating the Christmas time of year that exhilarates her imagination and fuels the blaze of her heart, announces: "It's fruitcake weather! Fetch our buggy. Help me find my hat."

The hat is found, a straw cartwheel corsaged with velvet roses out-of-doors has faded: it once belonged to a more fashionable relative. Together, we guide our buggy, a dilapidated baby carriage, out to the garden and into a grove of pecan trees. The buggy is mine, that is, it was bought for me when I was born. It is made of wicker, rather unraveled, and the wheels wobble like a drunkard's legs. But it is a faithful object; springtimes, we take it to the woods and fill it with flowers, herbs, wild fern for our porch pots; in the summer, we pile it with picnic paraphernalia and sugar-cane fishing poles and roll it down to the edge of a creek; it has its winter uses, too: as a truck for hauling firewood from the yard to the kitchen, as a warm bed for Queenie, our tough little orange and white rat terrier, who has survived distemper and two rattlesnake bites. Queenie is trotting beside it now.

Three hours later we are back in the kitchen hulling a heaping buggyload of windfall pecans. Our backs hurt from gathering them: how hard they were to find (the main crop having been shaken off the trees and sold by the orchard's owners, who are not us) among the concealing leaves, the frosted deceiving grass. Caarackle! A cheery crunch, scraps of miniature thunder sound as the shells collapse and the golden mound of sweet oily ivory meat mounts in the milk-glass bowl. Queenie begs to taste, and now and again my friend sneaks her a mite, though insisting we deprive ourselves. "We musn't, Buddy: If we start, we won't stop. And there's scarcely enough as there is. For thirty cakes." The kitchen is growing dark. Dusk turns the window into a mirror: our reflections mingle with the rising moon as we work by the fireside in the firelight. At last, when the moon is quite high, we toss the final hull into the fire and with joined sighs, watch it catch flame. The buggy is empty, the bowl is brimful.

▮ Did your audience see, hear, touch, smell, and taste all of the elements described?

▮ Did you allow time for each image to sink in?

Anne Sexton is often spoken of as a poet of the "confessional" school. This poem is an outgrowth of her actual experience in an institution, but her skill takes it beyond fact. The long sentence with its nursery rhyme construction of clauses must be used as a connected unit. The last sentence is an important contrast. The speaker's mental disturbance must not be overplayed. She is perfectly, but detachedly, in control of her logic. Locus is obviously of great importance here.

Ringing the Bells
ANNE SEXTON

And this is the way they ring
the bells in Bedlam
and this is the bell-lady
who comes each Tuesday morning
to give us a music lesson
and because the attendants make you go
and because we mind by instinct,
like bees caught in the wrong hive,
we are the circle of crazy ladies
who sit in the lounge of the mental house
and smile at the smiling woman
who passes us each a bell,
who points at my hand
that holds my bell, E flat,
and this is the gray dress next to me
who grumbles as if it were special
to be old, to be old,
and this is the small hunched squirrel girl
on the other side of me
who picks at the hairs over her lip,
who picks at the hairs over her lip all day
and this is how the bells really sound,
as untroubled and clean
as a workable kitchen,
and this is always my bell responding
to my hand that responds to the lady
who points at me, E flat;
and although we are no better for it,
they tell you to go. And you do.

▮ How did you show your audience everyone else in "the circle of crazy ladies"?

"Wild Grapes" calls for considerable attention to locus. The narrative lines, of course, should be directed to the audience. The brother's first instructions are delivered as he stands beside the little girl; his "loud cries" are directed to her as she hangs suspended in the air.

Wild Grapes

ROBERT FROST

What tree may not the fig be gathered from?
The grape may not be gathered from the birch?
It's all you know the grape, or know the birch.
As a girl gathered from the birch myself
Equally with my weight in grapes, one autumn,
I ought to know what tree the grape is fruit of.
I was born, I suppose, like anyone,
And grew to be a little boyish girl
My brother could not always leave at home.
But that beginning was wiped out in fear
The day I swung suspended with the grapes,
And was come after like Eurydice
And brought down safely from the upper regions;
And the life I live now's an extra life
I can waste as I please on whom I please.
So if you see me celebrate two birthdays,
And give myself out as two different ages,
One of them five years younger than I look —
One day my brother led me to a glade
Where a white birch he knew of stood alone,
Wearing a thin head-dress of pointed leaves,
And heavy on her heavy hair behind,
Against her neck, an ornament of grapes.
Grapes, I knew grapes from having seen them last year.
One bunch of them, and there began to be
Bunches all round me growing in white birches,
The way they grew round Leif the Lucky's German;
Mostly as much beyond my lifted hands, though,
As the moon used to seem when I was younger,
And only freely to be had for climbing.

My brother did the climbing; and at first
Threw me down grapes to miss and scatter
And have to hunt for in sweet fern and hardhack;
Which gave him some time to himself to eat,
But not so much, perhaps, as a boy needed.

So then, to make me wholly self-supporting,
He climbed still higher and bent the tree to earth
And put it in my hands to pick my own grapes.
"Here, take a tree-top, I'll get down another.
Hold on with all your might when I let go."
I said I had the tree. It wasn't true.
The opposite was true. The tree had me.
The minute it was left with me alone
It caught me up as if I were the fish
And it the fishpole. So I was translated
To loud cries from my brother of "Let go!
Don't you know anything, you girl? Let go!"
But I, with something of the baby grip
Acquired ancestrally in just such trees
When wilder mothers than our wildest now
Hung babies out on branches by the hands
To dry or wash or tan, I don't know which,
(You'll have to ask an evolutionist) —
I held on uncomplainingly for life.
My brother tried to make me laugh to help me.
"What are you doing up there in those grapes?
Don't be afraid. A few of them won't hurt you.
I mean, they won't pick you if you don't them."
Much danger of my picking anything!
By that time I was pretty well reduced
To a philosophy of hang-and-let-hang.
"Now you know how it feels," my brother said,
"To be a bunch of fox-grapes, as they call them,
That when it thinks it has escaped the fox
By growing where it shouldn't — on a birch,
Where a fox wouldn't think to look for it —
And if he looked and found it, couldn't reach it —
Just then come you and I to gather it.
Only you have the advantage of the grapes
In one way: you have one more stem to cling by,
And promise more resistance to the picker."

One by one I lost off my hat and shoes,
And I still clung. I let my head fall back
And shut my eyes against the sun, my ears
Against my brother's nonsense; "Drop," he said,
"I'll catch you in my arms. It isn't far."
(Stated in lengths of him it might not be.)
"Drop or I'll shake the tree and shake you down."

Grim silence on my part as I sank lower,
My small wrists stretching till they showed the banjo strings.
"Why, if she isn't serious about it!
Hold tight awhile till I think what to do.
I'll bend the tree down and let you down by it."
I don't know much about the letting down;
But once I felt ground with my stocking feet
And the world came revolving back to me,
I know I looked long at my curled-up fingers,
Before I straightened them and brushed the bark off.
My brother said: "Don't you weigh anything?
Try to weigh something next time, so you won't
Be run off with by birch trees into space."

It wasn't my not weighing anything
So much as my not knowing anything —
My brother had been nearer right before.
I had not taken the first step in knowledge;
I had not learned to let go with the hands,
As still I have not learned to with the heart,
And have no wish to with the heart — nor need,
That I can see. The mind — is not the heart.
I may yet live, as I know others live,
To wish in vain to let go with the mind —
Of cares, at night, to sleep; but nothing tells me
That I need to learn to let go with the heart.

> ▌ Did you make the remembered scene vivid and present to your
> audience? How?

The choice of words in this poem provides an interesting contrast to that of
the Dickinson poem we have already analyzed within the chapter.

Because I Could Not Stop for Death
EMILY DICKINSON

Because I could not stop for Death —
He kindly stopped for me —
The Carriage held but just Ourselves —
And Immortality.

We slowly drove — He knew no haste
And I had put away

My labor and my leisure too,
For His Civility —

We passed the School, where Children strove
At Recess — in the Ring —
We passed the Fields of Gazing Grain —
We passed the Setting Sun —

Or rather — He passed Us —
The Dews drew quivering and chill —
For only Gossamer, my Gown —
My Tippet — only Tulle —

We paused before a House that seemed
A Swelling of the Ground —
The Roof was scarcely visible —
The Cornice — in the Ground —

Since then — 'tis Centuries — and yet
Feels shorter than the Day
I first surmised the Horses' Heads
Were toward Eternity —

▌ Did you perform the dashes in this poem? Do they all mean the
same thing?

You need to understand the grammatical structure of the sentences to make
the references clear when you read them aloud. This speaker seems thoroughly confident of his poetic ability. Why?

Sonnet 18

WILLIAM SHAKESPEARE

Shall I compare thee to a summer's day?
Thou art more lovely and more temperate:
Rough winds do shake the darling buds of May,
And summer's lease hath all too short a date:
Sometime too hot the eye of heaven shines,
And often is his gold complexion dimm'd;
And every fair from fair sometimes declines,
By chance, or nature's changing course untrimm'd;
But thy eternal summer shall not fade,
Nor lose possession of that fair thou ow'st,

Nor shall death brag thou wander'st in his shade,
When in eternal lines to time thou grow'st;
   So long as man can breathe, or eyes can see,
   So long lives this, and this gives life to thee.

▌ Who is being addressed here? Does the persona see the beloved
clearly?

This story about the death of a pet may remind you of Deborah Sherman's
"Dulce," but don't miss the distinctive differences. The present tense here
increases the immediacy of the tale as it moves Michael (the storyteller)
closer to us. Try to determine precisely what Keds's death means to him.

Homework

PETER CAMERON

My dog, Keds, was sitting outside of the A. & P. last Thursday when
he got smashed by some kid pushing a shopping cart. At first we
thought he just had a broken leg, but later we found out he was
bleeding inside. Every time he opened his mouth, blood would seep
out like dull red words in a bad silent dream.

Every night before my sister goes to her job she washes her hair
in the kitchen sink with beer and mayonnaise and eggs. Sometimes
I sit at the table and watch the mixture dribble down her white back.
She boils a pot of water on the stove at the same time; when she is
finished with her hair, she steams her face. She wants so badly to
be beautiful.

I am trying to solve complicated algebraic problems I have set
for myself. Since I started cutting school last Friday, the one thing I
miss is homework. Find the value for n. Will it be a whole number?
It is never a whole number. It is always a fraction.

"Will you get me a towel?" my sister asks. She turns her face
toward me and clutches her hair to the top of her head. The sprayer
hose slithers into its hole next to the faucet.

I hand her a dish towel. "No," she says. "A bath towel. Don't
be stupid."

In the bathroom, my mother is watering her plants. She has
arranged them in the tub and turned the shower on. She sits on the
toilet lid and watches. It smells like outdoors in the bathroom.

I hand my sister the towel and watch her wrap it round her head.
She takes the cover off the pot of boiling water and drops lemon
slices in. Then she lowers her face into the steam.

This is the problem I have set for myself:

$$\frac{245\,(n + 17)}{34} = 396\,(n - 45)$$

$n =$

Wednesday, I stand outside the high-school gym doors. Inside, students are lined up doing calisthenics. It's snowing, and prematurely dark, and I can watch without being seen.

"Well," my father says when I get home. He is standing in the garage testing the automatic door. Every time a plane flies overhead, the door opens or closes, so my father is trying to fix it. "Have you changed your mind about school?" he asks me.

I lock my bicycle to a pole. This infuriates my father, who doesn't believe in locking things up in his own house. He pretends not to notice. I wipe the thin stripe of snow off the fenders with my middle finger. It is hard to ride a bike in the snow. This afternoon on my way home from the high school I fell off, and I lay in the snowy road with my bike on top of me. It felt warm.

"We're going to get another dog," my father says.

"It's not that," I say. I wish everyone would stop talking about dogs. I can't tell how sad I really am about Keds versus how sad I am in general. If I don't keep these things separate, I feel as if I'm betraying Keds.

"Then what is it?" my father says.

"It's nothing," I say.

My father nods. He is very good about bringing things up and then letting them drop. A lot gets dropped. He presses the button on the automatic control. The door slides down its oiled tracks and falls shut. It's dark in the garage. My father presses the button again and the door opens, and we both look outside at the snow falling in the driveway, as if in those few seconds the world might have changed.

My mother has forgotten to call me for dinner, and when I confront her with this she tells me that she did, but that I was sleeping. She is loading the dishwasher. My sister is standing at the counter, listening, and separating eggs for her shampoo.

"What can I get you?" my mother asks. "Would you like a meat-loaf sandwich?"

"No," I say. I open the refrigerator and survey its illuminated contents. "Could I have some scambled eggs?"

"O.K.," says my mother. She comes and stands beside me and puts her hand on top of mine on the door handle. There are no eggs in the refrigerator. "Oh," my mother says; then, "Julie?"

"Did you take the last eggs?"

"I guess so," my sister says. "I don't know."

"Forget it," I say. "I won't have eggs."

"No," my mother says. "Julie doesn't need them in her shampoo. That's not what I bought them for."

"I do," my sister says. "It's a formula. It doesn't work without the eggs. I need the protein."

"I don't want eggs," I say. "I don't want anything." I go into my bedroom.

My mother comes in and stands looking out the window. The snow has turned to rain. "You're not the only one who is unhappy about this," she says.

"About what?" I say. I am sitting on my unmade bed. If I pick up my room, my mother will make my bed: that's the deal. I didn't pick up my room this morning.

"About Keds," she says. "I'm unhappy too. But it doesn't stop me from going to school."

"You don't go to school," I say.

"You know what I mean," my mother says. She turns around and looks at my room, and begins to pick things off the floor.

"Don't do that," I say. "Stop."

My mother drops the dirty clothes in an exaggerated gesture of defeat. She almost — almost — throws them on the floor. The way she holds her hands accentuates their emptiness. "If you're not going to go to school," she says, "the least you can do is clean your room."

In the algebra word problems, a boat sails down a river while a jeep drives along the bank. Which will reach the capital first? If a plane flies at a certain speed from Boulder to Oklahoma City and then at a different speed from Oklahoma City to Detroit, how many cups of coffee can the stewardess serve, assuming she is unable to serve during the first and last ten minutes of each flight? How many times can a man ride the elevator to the top of the Empire State Building while his wife climbs the stairs, given that the woman travels one stair slower each flight? And if the man jumps up while the elevator is going down, which is moving — the man, the woman, the elevator, or the snow falling outside?

The next Monday I get up and make preparations for going to school. I can tell at the breakfast table that my mother is afraid to acknowledge them for fear it won't be true. I haven't gotten up before ten o'clock in a week. My mother makes me French toast. I sit at the table and write the note excusing me for my absence. I am eighteen, an adult, and thus able to excuse myself from school. This is what my note says:

DEAR MR. KELLY [my homeroom teacher]:

Please excuse my absence February 17–24. I was unhappy and did not feel able to attend school.

Sincerely,
MICHAEL PECHETTI

This is the exact format my mother used when she wrote my notes, only she always said, "Michael was home with a sore throat," or "Michael was home with a bad cold." The colds that prevented me from going to school were always bad colds.

My mother watches me write the note but doesn't ask to see it. I leave it on the kitchen table when I go to the bathroom, and when I come back to get it I know she has read it. She is washing the bowl she dipped the French toast into. Before, she would let Keds lick it clean. He liked eggs.

In Spanish class we are seeing a film on flamenco dancers. The screen wouldn't pull down, so it is being projected on the blackboard, which is green and cloudy with erased chalk. It looks a little as if the women are sick, and dancing in Heaven. Suddenly the little phone on the wall buzzes.

Mrs. Smitts, the teacher, gets up to answer it, and then walks over to me. She puts her hand on my shoulder and leans her face close to mine. It is dark in the room. "Miguel," Mrs. Smitts whispers, *"Tienes que ir a la oficina de* guidance."

"What?" I say.

She leans closer, and her hair blocks the dancers. Despite the clicking castanets and the roomful of students, there is something intimate about this moment. *"Tienes que ir a la oficina de* guidance," she repeats slowly. Then, "You must go to the guidance office. Now. *Vaya."*

My guidance counsellor, Mrs. Dietrich, used to be a history teacher, but she couldn't take it anymore, so she was moved into guidance. On her immaculate desk is a calender blotter with "LUNCH" written across the middle of every box, including Saturday and Sunday. The only other things on the desk are an empty photo cube and my letter to Mr. Kelly. I sit down, and she shows me the letter as if I haven't yet read it. I reread it.

"Did you write this?" she asks.

I nod affirmatively. I can tell Mrs. Dietrich is especially nervous about this interview. Our meetings are always charged with tension. At the last one, when I was selecting my second-semester courses, she started to laugh hysterically when I said I wanted to take Boys' Home Ec. Now every time I see her in the halls she stops me and asks me how I'm doing in Boys' Home Ec. It's the only course of mine she remembers.

I hand the note back to her and say, "I wrote it this morning," as if this clarified things.

"This morning?"

"At breakfast," I say.

"Do you think this is an acceptable excuse?" Mrs. Dietrich asks. "For missing more than a week of school?"

"I'm sure it isn't," I say.

"Then why did you write it?"

Because it is the truth, I start to say. It is. But somehow I know that saying this will make me more unhappy. It might make me cry. "I've been doing algebra at home," I say.

"That's fine," Mrs. Dietrich says, "but it's not the point. The point is, to graduate you have to attend school for a hundred and eighty days, or have legitimate excuses for the days you've missed. That's the point. Do you want to graduate?"

"Yes," I say.

"Of course you do," Mrs. Dietrich says.

She crumples my note and tries to throw it into the wastepaper basket but misses. We both look for a second at the note lying on the floor, and then I get up and throw it away. The only other thing in her wastepaper basket is a banana peel. I can picture her eating a banana in her tiny office. This, too, makes me sad.

"Sit down," Mrs. Dietrich says.

I sit down.

"I understand your dog died. Do you want to talk about that?"

"No," I say.

"Is that what you're so unhappy about?" she says. "Or is there something else?"

I almost mention the banana peel in her wastebasket, but I don't. "No," I say. "It's just my dog."

Mrs. Dietrich thinks for a moment. I can tell she is embarrassed to be talking about a dead dog. She would be more comfortable if it were a parent or a sibling.

"I don't want to talk about it," I repeat.

She opens her desk drawer and takes out a pad of hall passes. She begins to write one out for me. She has beautiful handwriting. I think of her learning to write beautifully as a child and then growing up to be a guidance counsellor, and this makes me unhappy.

"Mr. Neuman is willing to overlook this matter," she says. Mr. Neuman is the principal. "Of course, you will have to make up all the work you've missed. Can you do that?"

"Yes," I say.

Mrs. Dietrich tears the pass from the pad and hands it to me. Our hands touch. "You'll get over this," she says. "Believe me, you will."

My sister works until midnight at the Photo-Matica. It's a tiny booth in the middle of the A. & P. parking lot. People drive up and leave their film and come back the next day for the pictures. My sister wears a uniform that makes her look like a counterperson in a fast-food restaurant. Sometimes at night when I'm sick of being at home I walk downtown and sit in the booth with her.

There's a machine in the booth that looks like a printing press, only snapshots ride down a conveyor belt and fall into a bin and then disappear. The machine gives the illusion that your photographs are being developed on the spot. It's a fake. The same fifty photographs roll through over and over, and my sister says nobody notices, because everyone in town is taking the same pictures. She opens up the envelopes and looks at them.

Before I go into the booth, I buy cigarettes in the A. & P. It is open twenty-four hours a day, and I love it late at night. It is big and bright and empty. The checkout girl sits on her counter swinging her legs. The Muzak plays "If Ever I Would Leave You." Before I buy the cigarettes, I walk up and down the aisles. Everything looks good to eat, and the things that aren't edible look good in their own way. The detergent aisle is colorful and clean-smelling.

My sister is listening to the radio and polishing her nails when I get to the booth. It is almost time to close.

"I hear you went to school today," she says.

"Yeah."

"How was it?" she asks. She looks at her nails, which are so long it's frightening.

"It was O.K.," I say. "We made chili dogs in Home Ec."

"So are you over it all?"

I look at the pictures riding down the conveyor belt. I know the order practically by heart: graduation, graduation, birthday, mountains, baby, baby, new car, bride, bride and groom, house . . . "I guess so," I say.

"Good," says my sister. "It was getting to be a little much." She puts her tiny brush back in the bottle, capping it. She shows me her nails. They're an odd brown shade. "Cinnamon," she says. "It's an earth color." She looks out at the parking lot. A boy is collecting the abandoned shopping carts, forming a long silver train, which he noses back toward the store. I can tell he is singing by the way his mouth moves.

"That's where we found Keds," my sister says, pointing to the Salvation Army bin.

When I went out to buy cigarettes, Keds would follow me. I hungout down here at night before he died. I was unhappy then, too. That's what no one understands. I named him Keds because he was all white with big black feet and it looked as if he had high-top sneakers on. My mother wanted to name him Bootie. Bootie is a cat's name. It's a dumb name for a dog.

"It's a good thing you weren't here when we found him," my sister says. "You would have gone crazy."

I'm not really listening. It's all nonsense. I'm working on a new problem: Find the value for n such that n plus everything else in your life makes you feel all right. What would n equal? Solve for n.

▌ How did you help your audience understand why Michael tells us this story?

This poem rewards performance in part because audiences respond so positively, and in part because we so fully understand the speaker's dilemma. Trust the line length completely; you will not be disappointed.

Upon Learning That a Junior High School Acquaintance Has Been Nominated for an Academy Award

JOANNE GILBERT

Ungainly in candy-striped pajamas as a Who
from whom the Grinch stole Christmas
temporarily —
she wasn't that memorable.
Tonight, same frizz of hair,
same awkward gait,
with much of the world watching,
she apparently is.

When I first started to see her in movies,
I wanted to
clench   the   screen,
tear
      great
         gobs
from her face, shouting,
"It's not fair!
It should be me!"
Cool rationality turned
my sour grapes to
sour wine and
I plotted her public embarrassment:
I would send our Junior High Yearbook to *The National Enquirer*
(anonymously, of course)
so the world could feast its eyes on her
chubby, orthodontic countenance.
Meanwhile, I worried I'd run into her at her films,
remaining invisible,
glowering
as she misremembered me.

Tonight she wears outrageous earrings and floats among the
    privileged,
eyes the golden statuette,

smiles benignly,
never once recalling
I live.
Chatting with heroes, this Amazon has no idea I know her battle
    scar;
a cyst on her egg sac — the whole untimely ripped at her
    ripening —
front cover material
most definitely.

The envelope please . . .
es me because it
does   not   grant
her wish.
An eye for an eye;
I am satisfied.
I was teased more than she, after all.
Justice as the camera — still trained on her — reveals nothing.
It is right; she was only a Who —
I was the narrator.

▌ How did you embody the speaker's wide range of physical and
vocal responses?

This powerful poem features a second-person narrator who comes to understand his brother and himself in ways he hadn't expected. The shape of
the lines trace the thoughts that race through his mind and describe the
change that occurs by the end. Lassell's poem is among the earliest — and
finest — of the works of art that speak to the holocaust of AIDS.

How to Watch Your Brother Die

MICHAEL LASSELL

When the call comes, be calm.
Say to your wife, "My brother is dying. I have to fly
to California."
Try not to be shocked that he already looks like
a cadaver.
Say to the young man sitting by your brother's side,
"I'm his brother."
Try not to be shocked when the young man says,
"I'm his lover. Thanks for coming."

Listen to the doctor with a steel face on.
Sign the necessary forms.
Tell the doctor you will take care of everything.
Wonder why doctors are so remote.

Watch the lover's eyes as they stare into
your brother's eyes as they stare into
space.
Wonder what they see there.
Remember the time he was jealous and
opened your eyebrow with a sharp stick.
Forgive him out loud
even if he can't understand you.
Realize the scar will be
all that's left of him.

Over coffee in the hospital cafeteria
say to the lover, "You're an extremely good-looking
young man."
Hear him say,
"I never thought I was good enough looking to
deserve your brother."
Watch the tears well up in his eyes. Say,
"I'm sorry. I don't know what it means to be
the lover of another man."
Hear him say,
"It's just like a wife, only the commitment is
deeper because the odds against you are so much
greater."
Say nothing, but
take his hand like a brother's.

Drive to Mexico for unproven drugs that might
help him live longer.
Explain what they are to the border guard.
Fill with rage when he informs you,
"You can't bring those across."
Begin to grow loud.
Feel the lover's hand on your arm,
restraining you. See in the guard's eye
how much a man can hate another man.
Say to the lover, "How can you stand it?"
Hear him say, "You get used to it."

Think of one of your children getting used to
another man's hatred.

Call your wife on the telephone. Tell her,
"He hasn't much time.
I'll be home soon." Before you hang up say,
"How could anyone's commitment be deeper than
a husband and wife?" Hear her say,
"Please, I don't want to know all the details."

When he slips into an irrevocable coma
hold his lover in your arms while he sobs,
no longer strong. Wonder how much longer
you will be able to be strong.
Feel how it feels to hold a man in your arms
whose arms are used to holding men.
Offer God anything to bring your brother back.
Know you have nothing God could possibly want.
Curse God, but do not
abandon Him.

Stare at the face of the funeral director
when he tells you he will not
embalm the body for fear of
contamination. Let him see in your eyes
how much a man can hate another man.
Stand beside a casket covered in flowers,
white flowers. Say,
"Thank you for coming" to each of several hundred men
who file past in tears, some of them
holding hands. Know that your brother's life
was not what you imagined. Overhear two mourners say,
"I wonder who'll be next."

Arrange to take an early flight home.
His lover will drive you to the airport.
When your flight is announced say,
awkwardly, "If I can do anything, please
let me know." Do not flinch when he says,
"Forgive yourself for not wanting to know him
after he told you. He did."
Stop and let it soak in. Say,
"He forgave me, or he knew himself?"
"Both," the lover will say, not knowing what else

to do. Hold him like a brother while he
kisses you on the cheek. Think that
you haven't been kissed by a man since
your father died. Think,
"This is no moment not to be strong." Fly
first class and drink scotch. Stroke
your split eyebrow with a finger
and think of your brother alive. Smile
at the memory and think
how your children will feel in your arms,
warm and friendly and without challenge.

▮ How did you demonstrate the wide range of physical responses
in the speaker?
▮ Where, specifically, in the speaker's world does his brother
exist?

Bibliography

These works discuss in different ways and with different goals some
of the chief philosophical foundations of literature, criticism, and the
interrelationship of performance and criticism. Many of their argu-
ments and conclusions complement positions taken in this chapter
and elsewhere in this book.

Adams, Hazard, ed. *Critical Theory Since Plato*. New York: Harcourt
Brace Jovanovich, 1971.
Anthology of major theoretical statements by literary critics from Plato
to the present with brief, helpful, introductions to each critic and sources
for further study.

Beardsley, Monroe, Robert Daniel, and Glenn Leggett. *Theme and
Form*. Englewood Cliffs, N.J.: Prentice-Hall, 1956.
Brief essays on the structure of the various modes of literature combined
with an anthology arranged according to themes.

Beckson, Karl and Arthur Ganz. *A Reader's Guide to Literary Terms*.
New York: Farrar, Straus & Giroux, 1960.
Similar to *A Dictionary of Literary Terms*, but somewhat more complex.

Butcher, Samuel Henry. *Aristotle's Theory of Poetry and Fine Art, with
a Critical Text and Translation of the Poetics*. 4th ed. New York:
Dover Publications, 1951.
A useful and readable translation of Aristotle's classic study, with an
essay on Aristotelian criticism by John Gassner.

Geiger, Don. *The Sound, Sense, and Performance of Literature.* Glenview, Ill.: Scott, Foresman and Company, 1963.
> The performer of literature is the focal point of this book, which is built on the premise that oral interpretation is in itself an act of criticism.

Langer, Susanne K. *Philosophy in a New Key.* Cambridge, Mass.: Harvard University Press, 1942.
> Discussion of art as cognitive discourse.

————. *Mind: An Essay on Human Feeling.* Vols. 1–3. Baltimore: Johns Hopkins University Press, 1967, 1972, 1982.
> Further development of the *act* as a basic unit of life forms.

Pepper, Stephen. *The Work of Art.* Bloomington: Indiana University Press, 1955.
> Propounds the author's theory of funding and fusion in response and contains a clarification of object and vehicle.

Richards, I. A. *Principles of Literary Criticism.* New York: Harcourt, Brace and Company, 1925.
> One of the classic works on modern literary criticism.

Rosenblatt, Louise M. *The Reader, the Text, the Poem: The Transactional Theory of a Literary Work.* Carbondale, Ill.: Southern Illinois University Press, 1978.
> An excellent and persuasive discussion of the reader's role as co-creator of a poem in the reading event. Explores implications for change in methods of evaluation that can easily be adapted to performance.

Scott, Wilbur. *Five Approaches to Literary Criticism.* New York: Collier Books, 1962.
> Brief discussions of moral, psychological, sociological, formalistic, and archetypal approaches to criticism followed by essays that illustrate each of these forms.

Vivas, Eliseo, and Murray Krieger. *The Problem of Aesthetics.* New York: Holt, Rinehart and Winston, 1935.
> Essays on the nature and problems of aesthetics as a discipline and on criteria for judgment.

Wellek, Rene, and Austin Warren. *Theory of Literature.* 3rd ed. New York: Harcourt, Brace and World, 1966.
> A discussion of the nature and function of literature, with helpful notes and a good bibliography.

Wheelwright, Philip. *Metaphor and Reality.* Bloomington: Indiana University Press, 1962.
> A cogent discussion of the relationship between being, presence, and reality.

The following collections are among the most popular anthologies available today.

Abcarian, Richard, and Marvin Klotz. *Literature: The Human Experience.* 5th ed. New York: St. Martin's Press, 1991.
This popular collection explores poetry, prose, and drama across historical and thematic categories.

Barnet, Sylvan, Morton Berman, and William Burto. *An Introduction to Literature.* 7th ed. Boston: Little, Brown and Company, 1981.
This impressive edition includes an excellent collection of poems, stories, and plays with useful, brief discussions of genres and modes.

Cassill, R. V. *The Norton Anthology of Short Fiction.* New York: W. W. Norton and Company, 1978.
These short stories, collected from classic and contemporary sources, offer rich and diverse challenges to the performer.

Hunt, Douglas. *The Riverside Anthology of Literature.* Boston: Houghton Mifflin Company, 1988.
This enormous collection traces the development of stories, poems, and plays from their earliest forms to the present day.

Main, C. F., and Peter J. Seng. *Poems.* 4th ed. Belmont, Calif.: Wadsworth Publishing Company, 1978.
A brief discussion of poetic techniques with a collection of poems from all periods.

Meyer, Michael. *The Bedford Introduction to Literature.* Boston: Bedford Books of St. Martin's Press, 1987.
A wide-ranging anthology that features an intensive study of one or two important writers.

. . . human voices vary even more. Each one possesses more notes than the richest instrument of music. And the combinations in which the voice groups these notes are as inexhaustible as the infinite variety of personalities.

Marcel Proust, Within a Budding Grove

VOICE DEVELOPMENT FOR ORAL INTERPRETATION

3

BODY AND VOICE TOGETHER BECOME a twofold instrument, and the modern interpreter must learn to control and coordinate them perfectly to communicate the full meaning of the literature. However, unless you can be heard and understood, your gestures and bodily responses, no matter how appropriate, will not be effective.

Most people speak adequately for general conversation and informal communication. But the oral interpretation of literature requires additional vocal flexibility and special control. The fact that you use a normal speaking voice every day and have done so since childhood is no guarantee that your voice is an adequate instrument for artistic re-creation. You need to know first of all just how your voice functions and how you can control and develop it to provide wider range in pitch, greater flexibility in volume and stress, richer variations in quality, and finer degrees of subtlety in duration and rate. Once you understand these factors, you should work to develop your voice as deliberately as a singer does. As your voice control improves, you will be increasingly able to meet, with intelligence and sensitivity, the demands of the various kinds of literary material.

Students who have had voice training may find the following discussion useful only as a review. We have made an effort, however, to apply some of the principles of voice training to specific problems facing interpreters. You will find that a few minutes spent on the exercises will be most valuable during rehearsal periods when you are working on a particularly demanding selection.

Breath Control

The first concern of anyone interested in voice improvement should be breath control because it is impossible to produce good vocal tone without it. Proper use of the normal breathing mechanism is simple. Any difficulties are probably due to bad habits, which may be the result of physical or psychological tensions. An understanding of the muscles involved in the breathing process and of the functions they perform may help you locate and release some of these tensions.

In *inhalation* — intake of air — the major concern is with the amount; in *exhalation* — letting out of air — the major concern is with control. The whole process of breathing rests on two aspects of a basic physiological and physical principle: the balance of tension and relaxation in opposing sets of muscles serves to control the creation of a vacuum.

When we inhale and pull a quantity of air into the body, the diaphragm — the large dome-shaped muscle at the floor of the chest — lowers and pushes downward against the *relaxed* abdominal muscles; thus, the lengthwise expansion of the chest is increased. As this action is taking place, the muscles between the outer surfaces of the ribs lift and extend the rib cage, and the side-to-side and front-to-back expansion of the chest is accomplished. This increase in size creates a vacuum inside the chest cavity. Atmospheric pressures force air into the vacuum, so that the pressure inside and outside of the body is equalized. The air is forced down through the windpipe (trachea) and through the bronchial tubes and finally comes to rest in the flexible air sacs in the lungs in which the bronchioli terminate. The air sacs in the lungs inflate as the air enters, and when the lungs are thus extended, the process of inhalation is complete. Obviously, breathing is an active muscular process.

When the mechanism is ready for the process of exhalation to take place (following the exchange of oxygen and carbon dioxide in the blood), the muscles in the diaphragm relax, and the diaphragm rises into the dome-shaped position again. The muscles on the outside of the rib cage relax as the ones between the ribs on the inside contract. This action pulls the extended rib cage inward. All of this pressure upward and inward acts on the elastic lung tissue containing the air that was forced in during inhalation. The elastic tissue begins to collapse, and the air is forced out of the lungs, up through the bronchial tubes and windpipe, and finally out of the nose or mouth. Thus, one cycle of respiration is completed.

In exhaling for speech, however, there is frequently another action besides the relaxing of the diaphragm in the lower chest area. This action is the firm contraction of the abdominal muscles that are relaxed for inhalation. As they contract for exhalation, they support the action accomplished by the relaxing of the diaphragm and in this way help control the outflow of air. This process is known as *forced exhalation*. The term is somewhat misleading, perhaps, because the contraction of the abdominal muscles should be an easy and natural process, particularly for a trained speaker who wishes support for a tone projected by sustained exhalation. Forced exhalation is simply the continuation of the action that takes place in the process of exhalation during silent breathing.

Where should you begin exercises to achieve greater breath capacity and better control over exhalation? You may want these muscular processes to function effectively to give smooth interpretation to long flowing lines of poetry. You may want to force a swift exhalation for command or expression of emotion in dramatic dialogue.

Proper breathing is possible only when your posture is good. If each muscle is to perform its assigned function, your body should be in a state of controlled relaxation — that is, in a state of nicely balanced relaxation and essential tension. Wrongly induced tension inhibits the flexibility of muscles that control the intake and the outward flow of air. One of the most frequent errors in breathing practice is forcing the muscles of the rib cage and the abdomen into a rigid position. These muscles must be firm, but they cannot function if they are locked.

In exercises for improved breathing habits, it is particularly important, when standing, to have your weight easily and comfortably supported by your feet and legs; to have your spinal column erect but not forced into position; and to have your shoulders level and the muscles that support your shoulders free from tension. Strong lifting of the shoulders, a common error in inhalation, serves only to put tension in the wrong area and has a negative effect on the vocal tone.

This simple four-step exercise to demonstrate the proper balance between tension and relaxation also tends to show *where* concentration of energy should be — at the beltline rather than in the throat. Lie on your back the first few times you do the first step so that you get used to the easy, relaxing, in-and-out movement of the muscles at the base of your ribs and below them.

1. Take a deep, comfortable breath and hold it. Contract your abdominal muscles *sharply* and force the air out of your chest on a single vocalization, such as "Ah — h — h," as if audibly sighing. Hold the contraction of these muscles an appreciable instant, and

then *suddenly* release the tension. Notice that the air rushes into the chest and fills the lower portion of the lungs (or perhaps more) when you release the tension. Exhale by forcing air out of your chest with the gradual contraction of your abdominal muscles as your diaphragm relaxes and returns to its dome-shaped position.

2. Stand easily erect and repeat the process described in step 1. As the air rushes in on the release of tension in the abdominal muscles, make a conscious effort to lift your upper rib cage slightly. (Be careful *not* to lift your shoulders!) More space will be created in your upper chest, and your whole chest will be well extended and able to accommodate a large intake of air. The upper portion of your lungs, as well as the lower, should be filled now. Exhale, pushing the air out with the relaxing of your diaphragm and the gradual contracting of your abdominal muscles and lowering of your rib cage. (Don't collapse and let your shoulders sag!)

3. Place your hands, palm in, on the lower portion of your rib cage so that your fingers are touching. Begin to inhale slowly. As you inhale, your ribs should push your hands apart. When the lower part of your breath cavity is full and you have allowed your chest to lift *slightly* until it, too, is full, you should have a full breath. Hold it for a second or two and let it out in a whoosh!

4. Repeat step 3, and when you have a full breath, tuck in your abdominal muscle slightly and hold your breath for a second until you feel in complete control. Now, as you start to exhale the full breath, begin to count aloud. As you begin to run out of breath for vocalizing, gradually contract your abdominal muscles (*not* the upper chest ones) as you continue counting. When you can no longer force air out of your chest by the strong but comfortable contraction of your abdominal muscles, stop the vocalized counting. Don't sacrifice a good quality of tone in the effort to "squeeze out" more sound. This will result only in undue tension in your upper chest and throat muscles — the very thing you want to avoid.

This exercise is basic to developing good breath control and should be used to begin any period of exercise. Many instructions say: "Breathe in," and *then* "breathe out." This exercise suggests breathing out first, to empty your chest of air at the beginning of the exercise. In this way, a "stuffing" of the chest is avoided. Then comes the breathing in, followed by the controlled breathing out. This is the inevitable order, whether or not you are "exercising," for you cannot hold your breath forever.

You should not continue to work steadily at this or any other exercise after you begin to feel tired. Until you grow used to a changed method of control or a marked effort to increase capacity, you should go back to your usual manner of breathing for a rest. As you follow this type of exercise, it should become increasingly clear that the sooner you can make this method automatic, the easier the whole breathing process will be.

As you become able to take in larger amounts of air with ease and to continue exhalation to support the tone, you should be able to count more numbers on one breath. With each exercise period try to say a few more, always being careful that there is no strain in your throat, no forcing of the tone, and no sacrifice of quality. You should count at what seems an easy volume and a pleasing level of pitch. When material is performed, some of the phrasal units need to be separated by pauses of varying lengths. During these pauses you have an opportunity to replenish your supply of breath. Take care not to let the pauses break the continuity of thought. The position and duration of the pauses should always grow out of the relationship of the phrases to each other and to the complete thought being expressed. Learn to breathe where you must pause, not pause in order to breathe. It is usually impossible to get a full breath except in the major pauses that complete the units of thought. Therefore, the final step in breath control is to learn to inhale quickly and unobtrusively, while still using the proper muscles.

Frequently a speaker inhales properly and uses the full capacity for breath but still cannot sustain a long flow of sound. The problem here is inadequate control of exhalation, not an insufficient supply of air. Inadequate control is one of the major causes of dropping final words or syllables so that they do not carry to the last row of the audience. A simple exercise will help determine whether the control muscles collapse instead of exerting steady pressure as they relax.

Inhale a full, comfortable breath. Be sure that your shoulders are relaxed. Hold a lighted match directly in front of your lips as close as your profile will allow. Start to count aloud in a full voice. You should be able to continue counting until the match burns down. If you blow out the flame, check the state of control of the muscles in and around your rib cage. Most of us exhale more than we need to on certain sounds, such as "two" or "three" or "four." Light another match, take another deep breath, and try the exercise again, speaking very softly with conscious control of the rate of relaxation of the muscles involved. You will feel as if you may explode, but you won't, and you will become aware of where the control must be exercised. As you gradually increase your volume to normal, you will find that the flame flickers but that you will not extinguish it by a sudden uncontrolled spurt of air.

Volume and Projection

Anyone who has been in an audience and strained to hear the speaker knows the tremendous importance of sufficient volume and good projection. After all, your purpose is to share your material with the audience. If you cannot be heard, you obviously have failed in your primary objective.

Actually, the words *volume* and *projection* are sometimes used interchangeably. Indeed, they are both part of your ability to be heard and understood. For greater clarity in this discussion, we consider *volume* to be the degree of loudness and *projection* to be the act of directing the voice to a specific target.

You should be able to make your voice fill the room in which the audience is gathered. You should learn to control the volume of your voice to fill a large space easily without distorting your voice and without blasting it down the back wall if space is limited. With practice, you will learn how much volume is required and how you can achieve the greatest possible flexibility within that requirement.

Control of Projection

Being understood also depends to a degree on the speaker's control of projection. The first requirement of adequate projection is to have enough volume and support so that the tone will carry as far as the material and situation demand. The second requirement is to have the proper mental attitude. Good communication is a product not only of breath control but also of your constant awareness of the listeners. This awareness is often spoken of in the theatre as *audience sense*. Although this sense is difficult to explain, it has its base in the speaker's attitude of reaching out toward an audience with every line. Regardless of the energy of the ideas or emotions being expressed, performers with a fine sense of audience participation have a psychological set that helps their voices reach out to the audience. As you perform, keep the back row of listeners in mind and be sure that your words reach them.

This mental attitude toward communication has a direct and observable effect on the physiological control of projection. By thinking *to* your listeners as well as *of* them, wanting to be sure that they hear and share the full effect of the literature, you will tend to keep your body erect and your head lifted slightly so that your throat is free from tension.

Focus of Projection

It is sometimes helpful to think of your voice as a tangible thing —
an object to be aimed and thrown at a target. This trick of *throwing
the voice* may smack of ventriloquism, yet it is a practice everyone
uses at times. A child calling to attract the attention of playmates
down the street sends his voice to where they are. Football fans
shouting advice to the players on the field direct their voices without
conscious thought to the exact spot where their attention is focused.
When carrying on a conversation in a room full of people, one person
may project across the room to answer a remark or add to a discussion. When people wish to be confidential, they let their voices drop,
and their circle of mental directness narrows to fill only the desired
area.

The following exercises for focus of projection can be practiced
most effectively in a large room. They have been conceived primarily
to apply to an imagined concrete situation. By thinking specifically
of what to do and by using any words that come to mind, the
interpreter can concentrate on the suggested volume and focus.

1. You are seated at a desk in the center front of the room. You see
    a friend at the door; you call an easy greeting. She waves and
    goes on. You think of something that you ought to tell her. You
    call her name quickly, but she apparently doesn't hear, for she
    keeps on going. Without leaving your place, call again; have a
    good full breath as you start to call and direct the sound at her
    quickly disappearing back. Do the same thing again with more
    volume and longer sounds supported by forced exhalation. Be
    sure that you catch her this time.

2. You are giving directions to a group of people about how to work
    out a diagram. The room is large, and everyone must hear. Direct
    your remarks to various places, thinking of certain people who
    might be there. After you have given instructions and the group
    starts to work, a person in the front of the group asks a question.
    You shift your focus of projection, reduce your volume, and
    answer the person who asked the question. Then you decide
    that others might need that special information, too. You raise
    your volume and expand your area of projection to attract every-
    one's attention, and then repeat to the group what you have said
    to the individual. As you do this, take care to direct your voice
    to the various parts of the room so that everyone will hear.

When you have made some progress in projection through these
exercises, move on to practice with literary material.

An interesting problem in projection is found in Shakespeare's

Julius Caesar. As Brutus goes up into the pulpit to make his famous speech to the crowd, he addresses a single remark to those near him. In the opening sentence, try to get the feeling of first speaking to those who stand around you, and then including the several hundred citizens who are milling around the Forum. It is necessary to quiet the crowd during the early part of the speech.

> BRUTUS: Be patient till the last. Romans, countrymen, and lovers! hear me for my cause, and be silent, that you may hear; believe me for mine honor, and have respect to mine honor, that you may believe; censure me in your wisdom, and awake your senses, that you may the better judge. If there be any in this assembly, any dear friend of Caesar's, to him I say, that Brutus' love to Caesar was no less than his. If then that friend demand why Brutus rose against Caesar, this is my answer: Not that I lov'd Caesar less, but that I lov'd Rome more.

In the following lines from the famous trial scene of Shakespeare's *The Merchant of Venice,* two characters are speaking. Our primary concern here is not with the difference in their voices or mental attitudes, but rather with the changes in focus and consequent projection in their speeches. (The parenthetical stage directions are inserted for this specific exercise and do not appear in the text of the play.) The Duke speaks to Portia at close range on his greeting and first question and on the opening line of his second speech. After "take your place," it is assumed that she moves away from him; thus, his question "Are you acquainted with the difference/That holds this present question in the court?" must carry over a greater distance than his first remarks but should still be addressed directly to Portia. His order to Antonio and Shylock to "stand forth" may be thought of as carrying even farther, since they are probably among a group of people outside the judge's area. Practice the Duke's speeches until you can place them where you want them, and then follow the same procedure in Portia's speeches.

> DUKE: Give me your hand. Came you from old Bellario?
> PORTIA: (To Duke as she gives him her hand) I did, my lord.
> DUKE: You are welcome; take your place.
>   Are you acquainted with the difference
>   That holds this present question in the court?
> PORTIA: (From her place a few feet away from the Duke) I am informed thoroughly of the cause.
>   (To the assemblage) Which is the merchant here, and which the Jew?

DUKE: Antonio and old Shylock, both stand forth.
PORTIA: (To Shylock after he has stepped forward from the crowd) Is your name Shylock?

In working to develop volume and projection, you are concentrating on one of the basic requirements of all speech: that it reach its audience. Volume depends largely on adequate breath supply and proper support in exhalation. Projection combines these physical aspects with the psychological aspect of mental directness. We discuss this concept of physical and mental focus more fully in later chapters. For the moment it is enough to recognize the relationship.

Pitch and Quality

Although pitch and quality are different attributes of sound, they are so closely related in origin and control in the human voice that they may be considered together. The way the vocal bands vibrate basically determines both the pitch and the quality of the vocal tone: the pitch is formed by the rate of vibration, the quality by the complexity of the vibration.

The *pitch* of a sound is its place on the musical scale. In terms of the scale range, pitch is high, medium, or low. It is important for interpreters to become skillful in using pitch to suggest shades of meaning and to build to climaxes. Changes in pitch give variety and contrast to the material being read and help hold the audience's attention. Because a change of pitch produces *inflection*, a speaker's *inflection range* is the entire pitch span between the highest and lowest tones that he or she is capable of making comfortably.

Any pattern in the variation of levels of pitch results in *melody*. When there are no discernible changes of pitch, the result is a *monotone*. Although melody is an asset to the interpreter, it can also become a problem. Most people have in their daily speech a characteristic pattern of inflections, which is part of their own personalities. This is highly commendable, and certainly it is to be expected that some of that pattern will be carried over into their work before an audience. Often, however, a reader's pattern is so marked that it calls attention to itself and thus gets in the way of re-creation of the material. For example, one of the most common and annoying vocal patterns in reading poetry permits each line or each new thought to start on a high pitch and drift to a low tone at the close. The following lines are an example of poetic structure in which this problem must be controlled.

The Wild Honeysuckle

PHILIP FRENEAU

Fair flower, that dost so comely grow,
Hid in this silent, dull retreat,
Untouched thy honied blossoms blow,
Unseen thy little branches greet:
    No roving foot shall crush thee here,
    No busy hand provoke a tear.

And again, in less conventional poetry:

FROM *I Hear America Singing*

WALT WHITMAN

I hear America singing, the varied carols I hear,
Those of mechanics, each one singing his as it should be blithe and
    strong,
The carpenter singing his as he measures his plank or beam,
The mason singing his as he makes ready for work, or leaves off
    work . . .

Quality, more difficult to define distinctively, can be described best as the characteristic of a tone that distinguishes it from all other tones of the same pitch and intensity. This is sometimes called *timbre*, or to use the German word, *Klang*, meaning the "ring" of the tone. In describing quality, one frequently uses words that suggest color — a *golden* tone, a *silver-voiced* orator, a *blue* note.

Quality of tone is perhaps most closely associated with mood and feeling. Connotation and emotional response have a strong effect on quality, and empathy (which we discuss more fully in the next chapter) plays its part in the degree of tension or relaxation it imposes on the vocal mechanism. Vocal quality is influenced by your empathic response to whatever elements of emotion, strength, and beauty are inherent in the material.

Pitch and quality working together, then, are invaluable in helping you bring out the universality and suggestion in a piece of literature. If you control these two aspects of vocal technique, they will contribute a great deal to the communication of emotional content.

Rate and Pause

The *rate* at which people speak is often habitual, a part of their personalities and their entire backgrounds. It probably serves them very well for ordinary conversation, but they may need to adjust their habitual rate to do justice to an author's style and purpose. Audiences cannot listen as rapidly as a performer can speak. Interpreters must learn to hear themselves in rehearsal and in conversation. There is no magic formula for slowing a too-rapid pace; to do this requires constant attention. It is helpful to select material that by its style and connotation encourages a slow pace of delivery. Frequently the mere physical process of forming a sequence of sounds affects the rate at which a sentence can be read intelligibly and effectively. Interpreters should control their rate of speaking so that they can form every sound accurately. Also, by changing the rate, interpreters can express subtle variety in a selection. Emotion, connotation, suggestion, and the combination of vowels and consonants all provide clues for knowing when to speed up one's speaking pace, and when to slow it down.

Rate is determined not only by the speed with which sounds are uttered in sequence but also by the length and frequency of pauses that separate the sequences of sounds. It is essential to recognize the *phrasal pause* that clarifies the relationships of words in phrases to convey units of thoughts. The pause also may become one of your most effective tools for building suspense and climaxes and for reinforcing emotional content.

Beginning interpreters are often afraid to hold the pause long enough for its dramatic effect to register with their listeners. If a pause is motivated by real understanding and by identification with the feeling suggested, it may be sustained for a much longer time and with greater effect than you might realize. You need only be sure that during the pause something relevant to the material is going on in your own mind and consequently in the minds of your listeners. Usually a pause provides a bridge between thoughts. It should always stay within the total concept of the selection and supply whatever transition or suspense is needed. You should work not only to use pauses in the most effective places but also to vary and sustain the lengths of the pauses as the material demands.

Punctuation is used on the printed page to signal the eyes. It guides the reader in establishing the relationship of words and phrases and their division into sentences. Interpreters can change pitch, quality, emphasis, or use a combination of these to signal the ears of their listeners. You do not always need to use a pause. Moreover, you should remember that rules and fashions change in punctuation. Your full understanding of and response to your material, together with a sense of responsibility to your audience, are the final determining factors in your use of pauses.

In the following scene from Edmond Rostand's *Cyrano de Bergerac,*

Cyrano is speaking of his monstrous nose and its effect on his entire being. You can make exquisite use of pause here. As you work on the interpretation, you will realize that the tempo of the scene changes with "Oh, not that ever!" You will see how this change to a faster, more smoothly flowing rate is effected. You also will realize that the change goes hand in hand with Cyrano's struggle to turn from his romantic, self-revelatory mood to his customary half-comic acceptance of his nose.

> CYRANO: My old friend — look at me,
>   And tell me how much hope remains for me
>   With this protuberance! Oh I have no more
>   Illusions! Now and then — bah! I may grow
>   Tender, walking alone in the blue cool
>   Of evening, through some garden fresh with flowers
>   After the benediction of the rain;
>   My poor big devil of a nose inhales
>   April . . . and so I follow with my eyes
>   Where some boy, with a girl upon his arm,
>   Passes a patch of silver . . . and I feel
>   Somehow, I wish I had a woman too,
>   Walking with little steps under the moon,
>   And holding my arm so, and smiling. Then
>   I dream — and I forget . . .
>   And then I see
>   The shadow of my profile on the wall!
> LEBRET: My friend! . . .
> CYRANO: My friend, I have my bitter days,
>   Knowing myself so ugly, so alone.
>   Sometimes —
> LEBRET: You weep?
> CYRANO: (Quickly) Oh, not that ever! No,
>   That would be too grotesque — the tears trickling down
>   All the long way along this nose of mine?
>   I will not so profane the dignity
>   Of sorrow. Never any tears for me!

To develop additional skill in your use of rate of speaking, try to work on selections that demand basically different rate patterns. As you read the material aloud with feeling, you will realize that you should effectively observe the *quantity*, or length, of the individual vowel and consonant sounds, as well as the length of pauses between sounds. In a prevailing rapid rate, the sounds as well as the pauses are often short; in a slower rate, they are long.

Many of the lyrics of the Gilbert and Sullivan operettas are wonderful examples of the way in which sound suggests rate. Note particularly the fast-moving "Nightmare Song" from *Iolanthe:*

> When you're lying awake with a dismal headache,
>   And repose is taboo'd by anxiety —
> I conceive you may use any language you choose
>   To indulge in, without impropriety . . .

Intelligibility of Speech

We mentioned earlier that to fulfill its basic function of communication, speech must be understandable and intelligible; hence, it must be heard. But to be fully intelligible, speech should be not only audible, but also distinct and accurate. Listeners cannot keep their attention on the material if they must constantly "translate" unclear speech sounds or mispronunciations. Therefore, all speech sounds should be correct as well as distinct and pleasing. Few things are more irritating to the listener than a speaker's self-conscious, overly careful mouthing of vowels and consonants. This conveys affectation and insincerity. Moreover, it violates the cardinal rule of interpretation because it draws attention to the reader's technique and away from the material. On the other hand, a reader who cannot be understood certainly cannot communicate. Consequently, you should learn to pronounce and articulate words with such clarity and accuracy that any audience is able to understand you.

A distinction between pronunciation and articulation may be helpful. *Pronunciation* refers to the *correctness* of sounds and accents in spoken words. *Articulation* refers to the *shaping* of the sounds by the speaker's lips, teeth, tongue, and hard and soft palates.

Pronunciation is considered to be acceptable when all the sounds of a word are uttered correctly in their proper order and with accent (stress) on the proper syllable. There is a big difference, for instance, between *refúse* and *réfuse*. Current good usage is the guide to correct pronunciation. A standard dictionary is the final authority. Unfamiliar polysyllabic words are not always the ones that trip up readers. Because you may distrust your pronunciation of such words, you probably will look them up in the dictionary. The real pitfalls are the common, everyday words that you may have fallen into the habit of pronouncing incorrectly. Mispronunciation can ruin a fine oral line, and may distract listeners so much that they momentarily lose the thought that you are trying to communicate.

Most of us have ingrained in our speech patterns certain regional or ethnic influences. These are usually slight deviations (from so-called standard speech) in some individual sounds, the melody pattern, or both. For instance, one need only consider the difference in pronunciation of |r| as one travels from New England through the Midwest and into the South to be aware that Standard American Speech is "standard" for very few of us. Further, audiences associate accents or dialects with certain stereotypes. Therefore, some effort should be made to develop Standard American Speech, if only to use it "on special occasions," when material and audiences are better served by the elimination of any regionalisms or obtrusive vocal mannerisms.

Dialect, or accent, is basically a matter of the way separate sounds are formed and, far more important, the use of a melodic or rhythmic flow as the sounds go together. An author who wants dialect to provide a part of the character may indicate this through spelling, syntax, word choice, or all three (look at Toni Cade Bambara's "The Lesson" at the end of this chapter). Because a writer is black or Chicano or British or from New England does not mean that the interpreter should strive for such regional speech. If the author wrote in dialect, you should read it as well as you can. If not, make your own speech sufficiently flexible to conform to the total demand of the selection you have chosen. When an interpreter's own dialect seems incongruous for the speaker in the selection, the contradiction can distract the listeners, particularly if the audience doesn't share the regional dialect. Test your progress by trying pieces of material that involve difficult combinations of sounds. Even experienced interpreters profit from an occasional session of careful listening for careless articulation. All this attention to vocal technique belongs in rehearsal periods; in performance you should concentrate on the literature you are sharing, not on your articulation.

Selections for Analysis and Oral Interpretation

In analyzing these selections, pay particular attention to the vocal problems each one presents. Almost all of the selections require more than a normal supply of breath because they either contain long, flowing sentences or demand an unusual amount of volume or force. Some pieces present interesting problems in projection. They all require that you work with a maximum flexibility of range to communicate the richness of sounds effectively. They also demand an awareness of your bodily responses.

The telling is almost more important than the tale itself in this segment from *Lake Wobegon Days*. Don't try to imitate Keillor's distinctive radio voice. Rather, focus on what interests this narrator most: the responsiveness of the people to the need they perceived. And be sure we see all of these characters as real people; no one is being mocked here.

FROM *Lake Wobegon Days*

GARRISON KEILLOR

People who visit Lake Wobegon come to see somebody, otherwise they missed the turn on the highway and are lost. *Ausländers*, the Germans call them. They don't come for Toast 'n Jelly Days, or the Germans' quadrennial Gesuffa Days, or Krazy Daze, or the Feast Day of St. Francis, or the three-day Mist County Fair with its exciting Death Leap from the top of the grandstand to the arms of the hay-stack for only ten cents. What's special about here isn't special enough to draw a major crowd, though Flag Day — you could drive a long way on June 14 to find another like it.

Flag Day, as we know it, was the idea of Herman Hochstetter, Rollie's dad, who ran the dry goods store and ran Armistice Day, the Fourth of July, and Flag Day. For the Fourth, he organized a double-loop parade around the block which allowed people to take turns marching and watching. On Armistice Day, everyone stepped outside at 11 A.M. and stood in silence for two minutes as Our Lady's bell tolled eleven times.

Flag Day was his favorite. For a modest price, he would install a bracket on your house to hold a pole to hang your flag on, or he would drill a hole in the sidewalk in front of your store with his drill gun powered by a .22 shell. *Bam!* And in went the flag. On patriotic days, flags flew all over; there were flags on the tall poles, flags on the short, flags in the brackets on the pillars and the porches, and if you were flagless you could expect to hear from Herman. His hairy arm around your shoulder, his poochlike face close to yours, he would say how proud he was that so many people were proud of their country, leaving you to see the obvious, that you were a gap in the ranks.

In June 1944, the day after D-Day, a salesman from Fisher Hat called on Herman and offered a good deal on red and blue baseball caps. "Do you have white also?" Herman asked. The salesman thought that white caps could be had for the same wonderful price. Herman ordered two hundred red, two hundred white, and one hundred blue. By the end of the year, he still had four hundred and eighty-six caps. The inspiration of the Living Flag was born from that overstock.

On June 14, 1945, a month after V-E Day, a good crowd assembled in front of the Central Building in response to Herman's ad in the paper:

Honor "AMERICA" June 14 AT 4 p.m. Be proud of "Our Land & People". Be part of the "LIVING FLAG". Don't let it be said that Lake Wobegon was "Too Busy". Be on time. 4 p.m. "Sharp".

His wife Louise handed out the caps, and Herman stood on a stepladder and told people were to stand. He lined up the reds and whites into stripes, then got the blues into their square. Mr. Hanson climbed up on the roof of the Central Building and took a photograph, they sang the national anthem, and then the Living Flag dispersed. The photograph appeared in the paper the next week. Herman kept the caps.

In the flush of victory, people were happy to do as told and stand in place, but in 1946 and 1947, dissension cropped up in the ranks: people complained about the heat and about Herman — what gave *him* the idea he could order *them* around? "People! Please! I need your attention! You blue people, keep your hats on! Please! Stripe No. 4, you're sagging! You reds, you're up here! We got too many white people, we need more red ones! Let's do this without talking, people! I can't get you straight if you keep moving around! Some of you are not paying attention! Everybody shut up! Please!"

One cause of resentment was the fact that none of them got to see the Flag they were in; the picture in the paper was black and white. Only Herman and Mr. Hanson got to see the real Flag, and some boys too short to be needed down below. People wanted a chance to go up to the roof and witness the spectacle for themselves.

"How can you go up there if you're supposed to be down here?" Herman said. "You go up there to look, you got nothing to look at. Isn't it enough to know that you're doing your part?"

On Flag Day, 1949, just as Herman said, "That's it! Hold it now!" one of the reds made a break for it — dashed up four flights of stairs to the roof and leaned over and had a long look. Even with the hole he left behind, it was a magnificent sight. The Living Flag filled the street below. A perfect Flag! The reds so brilliant! He couldn't take his eyes off it. "Get down here! We need a picture! Herman yelled up to him. "How does it look?" people yelled up to him. "Unbelievable! I can't describe it!" he said.

So then everyone had to have a look. "No!" Herman said, but they took a vote and it was unanimous. One by one, members of the Living Flag went up to the roof and admired it. It *was* marvelous! It brought tears to the eyes, it made one reflect on this great country and on Lake Wobegon's place in it. One wanted to stand up there all afternoon and just drink it in. So, as the first hour passed, and only forty of the five hundred had been to the top, the others got more and more restless. "Hurry up! Quit dawdling! *You've* seen it! Get down here and give someone else a chance!" Herman sent people up in groups of four, and then ten, but after two hours, the Living Flag became the Sitting Flag and then began to erode, as the members who had had a look thought about heading home to supper, which infuriated the ones who hadn't. "Ten more minutes!" Herman cried, but ten minutes became twenty and thirty, and people snuck off and the Flag that remained for the last viewer was a Flag shot through by cannon fire.

In 1950, the Sons of Knute took over Flag Day. Herman gave them the boxes of caps. Since then, the Knutes have achieved several good Flags, though most years the attendance was poor. You need at least four hundred to make a good one. Some years the Knutes made a "no-look" rule, other years they held a lottery. One year they experimented with a large mirror held by two men over the edge of the roof, but when people leaned back and looked up, the Flag disappeared, of course.

▌ How did your performance demonstrate the narrator's affection for the inhabitants of his town? Did they disappoint him?

You can find a classic example of the value of sound combinations in this familiar nonsense poem.

Jabberwocky
LEWIS CARROLL

'Twas brillig, and the slithy toves
    Did gyre and gimble in the wabe:
All mimsy were the borogoves,
    And the mome raths outgrabe.

"Beware the Jabberwock, my son!
    The jaws that bite, the claws that catch!
Beware the Jubjub bird, and shun
    The frumious Bandersnatch!"

He took his vorpal sword in hand;
    Long time the manxome foe he sought —

So rested he by the Tumtum tree,
  And stood awhile in thought.

And, as in uffish thought he stood,
  The Jabberwock, with eyes of flame,
Came whiffling through the tulgey wood,
  And burbled as it came!

One, two! One, two! And through and through
  The vorpal blade went snicker-snack!
He left it dead, and with its head
  He went galumphing back.

"And hast thou slain the Jabberwock?
  Come to my arms, my beamish boy!
O frabjous day! Callooh, Callay!"
  He chortled in his joy.

'Twas brillig, and the slithy toves
  Did gyre and gimble in the wabe:
All mimsy were the borogoves,
  And the mome raths outgrabe.

▌ There is nothing silly for the personae in this tale. How did
  your voice distinguish among the speakers?

There is great opportunity for vocal variety here. Let the young "interpreters"
in the story enjoy the elocutionary aspects of their selections. Note carefully
the narrator's descriptions of each of the girls' antics. Don't caricature these
young women — each is a character in herself.

FROM *The Little Girls*
ELIZABETH BOWEN

Thick cream glazed blinds were pulled most of the way down. Failing
to keep out the marine sunshine, they flopped lazily over the open
windows in the hot June breath rather than breeze haunting the
garden. St. Agatha's had been a house, IV-A Classroom probably
the morning-room. The blinds were lace-bordered. There was a gar-
landed wallpaper — called to order by having on it a bald, pontifical
clock, only a size or two smaller than a station one, a baize board
clustered with lists and warnings, and sepia reproductions of inspir-

ing pictures, among them "Hope," framed in oak. Of oak were the desks, to which were clamped high-backed seats. An aroma of Plasticine came from the models along the chimneypiece, and from jars of botanical specimens near a window whiffs of water slimy with rotting greenery were fanned in — the girl in charge of the specimens being absent with one of her summer colds. Chalk in the neighbourhood of the blackboard and ink thickening in china wells in the desks were the only other educational smells.

A dozen or so girls, most of them aged eleven, some ten, some twelve, sat at the desks. All wore their summer tunics of butcher-blue. By turning their heads, left, they could have seen strips of garden, parching away, between restless lace and stolid white window sills. Politely, however, most of them faced their teacher; this they could do for Miss Kinmate, if little else. This was the first lesson after mid-morning break with its milk and biscuits — even the slight feast had thrown IV-A into a gorged condition. But this also was the Tuesday poetry hour, to which Miss Kinmate attached hopes. Each girl (the idea was) chose for herself the short poem or portion of a longer one which, got by heart, she was to recite.

One more of them had just taken the stand.

"There *was* a time when meadow, grove and stream,
The earth and —"

"Stop!" cried Miss Kinmate. "Before we begin, not *too* much expression. Wordsworth was not as regretful as all that."

"I thought he was. Like some old, fat person saying, 'There *was* a time when I could jump over a ten-foot wall.'"

"That would be silly."

"Well, this is silly, in a way."

"Your old, fat man would not be speaking the truth. Have you any idea how high a ten-foot wall is?"

"Yes."

"I wonder whether you have. Because, even a Greek athlete could probably not jump over that." (From a back desk, a hand shot up.)

"*Yes*, Olive?"

"How high could a Greek athlete probably jump?"

"That would depend."

The child Clare, during this intermission, stood stonily contemplating her audience — hands behind her, back to the blackboard, feet planted apart, tongue exploring a cavity in a lower molar. At a moody sign from Miss Kinmate, she went on:

"— and every common sight,
To *me* did seem
Apparell'd in celestial *light,*
The glory and freshness of a dream.
It is *not* now as it has been of yore; —
Turn whereso'er I may,
By night *or* day,
The things which —"

"Stop! Oh dear, what are we to do?"

"I thought —"

"Well, don't — *try!* Otherwise, go and sit down. Ruining that beautiful poem!"

"Yes, Miss Kinmate."

"And don't make eyes at the others. Next time, choose a poem you understand."

"I do know another. Shall I try that?"

Miss Kinmate looked at the clock. The whole class (but for Sheila Beaker, who couldn't be bothered, and Muriel Borthwick, who having picked at a good big scab on her arm now dabbed blotting-paper at the resultant blood) did likewise, in an awed, considering way. "Very well," Miss Kinmate conceded. "Go on, Clare — though remember, there are others to come."

The child, having drawn a breath twice her size, launched with passion into her second choice:

"Last night among his fellow roughs
He jested, quaff'd and swore:
A drunken private of the Buffs,
Who never look'd before.
Today, beneath the foeman's frown,
He stands in Elgin's place,
Ambassador from Britain's crown,
And type of all her race.

Poor, reckless, rude, low-born, untaught,
Bewilder'd and alone,
A heart, with English instinct fraught,
He yet can call his own.
Ay! tear his body limb from limb,
Bring *cord,* or *axe,* or *flame!* —
He only knows, that not through him
Shall England come to shame.

Fair Kentish hopfields round him seemed
Like dreams to come and go;
Bright leagues of cherry blossom —"

"Stop! Time's up, I'm afraid. A pity, because you were doing better." Miss Kinmate's eye roved round. "Diana, try and not sit with your mouth open — wake up! What is the name of the poem Clare's just recited?"

"'The Drunken Private of the Buffs.'"

"Not exactly. — Well, who and whose poem next? Muriel: you!"

"I think I'm bleeding too much."

"What, cut yourself?"

"Not exactly."

"Better go and find Matron."

Gory Muriel left. Miss Kinmate had to cast round all over again. "*Sheila*, then. Sheila, we'll hear you now."

Southstone's wonder, the child exhibition dancer, rose, tossed back her silver-gold plaits, and habituatedly stepped forward into the limelight. An ornate volume, open at the required page and gildedly looking like a school prize (which it was, though not awarded to her), was bestowed by her upon Miss Kinmate, with what was less a bow than a flowerlike inclination of the head. She then half-turned, with a minor swirl of the tunic, and, facing the footlights, glided three steps sideways into the place of doom left vacant by Clare. Here reality struck the prodigy amidships. Bewitched, since she rose from her desk, by her own performance, she had lost sight for that minute or two of her entrance's true and hideous purpose. She was to be called upon not to spring about but to give tongue. A badgered hatred of literature filled her features. She did deliver her poem, though in the manner of one voicing, with wonderful moderation, a long-nursed and justifiable complaint:

"Up the airy mountain,
Down the rushing glen,
We daren't *go* a-hunting
For fear of little *men;*
Wee folk, good folk,
Trooping all together;
Green jacket, red cap,
And white owl's feather!

Down on the rocky *shore*
Some make their home;
They *live* on crispy pancakes
Of yellow tide-foam;
Some, in the reeds
Of the black mountain-lake,

With frogs for *their* watch-dogs,
All night awake.

High on the hill-top
The old *King* sits.
He is now so old and grey
He's nigh lost . . . ?
. . . his bridge of white wits?
. . . his mist of white wits?
. . . *his* bridge?
. . . *his* wits . . . ?"

She ran down, ticked over uncertainly, gave right out, and turned on Miss Kinmate a look as much as to say: "Well, there you are. What else would you expect?"

"Never mind," Miss Kinmate hastened to say. "It went nicely so far. Though a little mournful — fairies are gay things, aren't they?"

Sheila had no idea.

"And one word wrong in your second line. It should be 'rushy,' not 'rushing.' How could a glen rush?"

"I thought it meant they were all rushing about," said Sheila Beaker, still more deeply aggrieved.

"Sheila chose a delightful poem, at any rate," Miss Kinmate informed the class — who knew to a girl whose the choice had been: Mrs. Beaker's.

❚ How did you demonstrate Miss Kinmate's growing dismay?

Rhyme and speech cadences both strongly support this brief poem, but equally powerful are the images the speaker draws to our attention. Let the pauses fill the poem's development.

Home Is So Sad
PHILIP LARKIN

Home is so sad. It stays as it was left,
Shaped to the comfort of the last to go
As if to win them back. Instead, bereft
Of anyone to please, it withers so,
Having no heart to put aside the theft

And turn again to what it started as,
A joyous shot at how things ought to be,

Long fallen wide. You can see how it was:
Look at the pictures and the cutlery.
The music in the piano stool. That vase.

▌ How did you show us the speaker's location?
▌ What functions were served by the demonstrative pronoun?

Although this poem was written during the nineteenth century, it certainly
is relevant to the world today. The poem's strength lies in the quality of
mind and attitude that it reflects. The final sentence should be carefully
controlled vocally to keep the last part of the stanza from overbalancing the
important plea for fidelity.

Dover Beach

MATTHEW ARNOLD

The sea is calm tonight.
The tide is full, the moon lies fair
Upon the straits; — on the French coast the light
Gleams and is gone; the cliffs of England stand
Glimmering and vast, out in the tranquil bay.
Come to the window, sweet is the night-air!
Only, from the long line of spray
Where the sea meets the moon-blanched land,
Listen! you hear the grating roar
Of pebbles which the waves draw back, and fling,
At their return, up the high strand,
Begin, and cease, and then again begin,
With tremulous cadence slow, and bring
The eternal note of sadness in.

Sophocles long ago
Heard it on the Aegean, and it brought
Into his mind the turbid ebb and flow
Of human misery; we
Find also in the sound a thought,
Hearing it by this distant northern sea.

The Sea of Faith
Was once, too, at the full, and round earth's shore
Lay like the folds of a bright girdle furled.
But now I only hear
Its melancholy, long, withdrawing roar,

Retreating, to the breath
Of the night-wind, down the vast edges drear
And naked shingles of the world.

Ah, love, let us be true
To one another! for the world, which seems
To lie before us like a land of dreams,
So various, so beautiful, so new,
Hath really neither joy, nor love, nor light,
Nor certitude, nor peace, nor help for pain;
And we are here as on a darkling plain
Swept with confused alarms of struggle and flight,
Where ignorant armies clash by night.

▌ How did you vocally indicate the several shifts in locus?

Here is an essay about a very personal memory that, tellingly, describes a moment we have all encountered. Be sure that you portray the young Allison as clearly as you portray the man he has become.

Back at the Ranch
JAY ALLISON

A young boy molts. Tender skin falls off, or gets scraped off, and is replaced by a tougher, more permanent crust. The transition happens in moments, in events. All of a sudden, something is gone and something else is in its place. I made a change like that standing in the back of a pickup truck when I was 15.

It was 1967 and I had a summer job at a camp in Wyoming. It was beautiful there, high-pasture country with a postcard view of the Tetons. As an apprentice counselor I straddled the worlds of boys and men, breathing the high air, watching over kids, hanging out with cowboys. The cowboys wrangled the horses for the camp and were mostly an itinerant group, living in summer cabins below the barn, and they tolerated my loitering down there. I hitched up my jeans just like them, braided my lasso like them, smoked and cursed and slouched like them.

On the day it happened, I was standing with a group of cowboys by the ranch office. We heard the sound of a big engine coming in the long driveway, and after a while a red Corvette Sting Ray convertible, of all things, motored up in front of us. Conversation stopped. In the driver's seat was a hippie. His hair fell straight down his back and a bandanna was tied around his head. His style may have been standard for somewhere, but not for Jackson, Wyo.

The guy was decked out with beads and earrings and dressed in fantastic colors, and next to him his girlfriend, just as exotic, with perfect blond hair, looked up at us over little square glasses with a distracted, angelic expression. All in a red Corvette.

I was fascinated, mesmerized. I looked around me with a big grin and realized that I was alone in this feeling. The cowboys all had hard stares, cold eyes. I adjusted, a traitor to myself, and blanked out my expression in kind.

The hippie opened up a big smile, and said: "I went to camp here when I was a kid . . . came by to say hi. Is Weenie around?"

In that moment, Weenie, the owner of the place, having heard the throb of the engine, appeared in the ranch office door and walked toward us with a bowlegged stride, his big belt buckle coming first. He walked right up to the driver and looked down on him.

"Get out." Weenie didn't say hi. "Get out of here now."

"What? Wait a minute. I came to say hi. I went to camp here. I just came to say hi."

"Get the hell off this ranch. *Now.*" And staring at the hippie, Weenie kicked some dust up on the side of the Corvette.

"What's wrong with you, man?"

"You're what's wrong with me, son."

I noticed the cowboys were nodding. I nodded. Weenie's right. The guy should leave. He doesn't belong here.

"But you sent me a Christmas card!" By this time, the hippie had choked up a little. "I don't believe it. You sent me a goddamn Christmas card!"

The group of us closed in a little around the car. We-don't-like-that-kind-of-talk-from-a-hippie was the feeling I was getting. Thumbs came out of belt-loops. Jaws began to work.

"Looks like the little girlie's cryin'," said one of the cowboys, a tough one named Hondu. He spoke with his lips turned down on one side as if he was mouthing a cigarette. "Maybe the little girlie needs a haircut."

"Maybe so," said another, with mock consideration.

The notion rested in the air peacefully for a moment, then, in a sudden whipping motion, Hondu's jackknife was out, open and raised. With his other hand, he reached down and grabbed a fat bunch of the hippie's hair and pulled it toward him. Smiling grimly, he hacked it off and held it up for us to see.

During this, I looked down at the hippie's face, which was lifted up and sideways in such a way that he was looking right at me. Involuntarily, my head tilted just like his and we froze like that for a second.

"There now, that's better, ain't it?" asked Hondu.

The hippie, stunned, turned to his girlfriend, whose eyes and mouth had been wide open as long as he had been sitting there. Then he turned back to us, his face contorted, helpless. And then he went wild. He threw open his door and tried to jump up from the seat, but forgot that his seat belt was fastened and it held him in place. He struggled against it, screaming, swinging his arms like a bar fighter trying to shrug off his buddies restraining him. It was funny. Like a cartoon.

I looked around. We were all laughing. Our group closed up a little more, and came toward the car. The air bristled. He was the one who started the trouble. Well, he would get what he was looking for, all right.

The hippie stopped struggling, threw the Vette into gear, and fishtailed in the dust. We all jumped out of the way, but the open door of the car bumped into Weenie's favorite dog, a Rhodesian Ridgeback, an inside-out-looking animal that gave a wild yelp and ran straight into a willow thicket. We could hear his yips over the sound of the big engine as the hippie gunned it and took off.

That settled it. The hippie hit the dog.

Without hesitation, we jumped into one of the trucks. Rifles were drawn from the rack in the cab. Other weapons were thrown up into the bed of the pickup. I was standing there and caught one.

We took off, and because the rough road slowed down the Corvette, we were gaining. I was filled with a terrible, frightening righteousness. I was holding a rifle, chasing a man and a woman with a rifle in my hand. I looked around at my partners in the truck, and the air came out of me. We meant harm. We didn't care. I wondered who I was exactly. I needed to know. And in that moment, it happened: I switched sides and never said a word about it.

We hit the asphalt road and floored it, but we couldn't catch the Corvette. No way. The smoke from its exhaust settled around us like fog in the valley.

Still, 23 years later, I can see the two of us clearly, chosen by the same moment. Memory cuts back and forth between our faces. The wind pulls tears from the hippie's eyes; his long hair waves behind him in his fiery convertible rocketing down Route 191 under the Tetons. I with my short hair stand in the back of a pickup truck watching after him, chasing after him, following, facing the same wind.

▮ How did you demonstrate the fulcrum?
▮ What happened with your body and voice to suggest Allison's body?

This poem is devastating in the cold simplicity of its literary style. The attitude of the persona is underscored by the word choice, the stark syntax, and the stanza division counting off the three "places." Keep the quotations within the unity of this attitude.

Her Story
NAOMI LONG MADGETT

They gave me the wrong name, in the first place.
They named me Grace and waited for a light and agile dancer.
But some trick of the genes mixed me up
And instead I turned out big and black and burly.

In the second place, I fashioned the wrong dreams.
I wanted to dress like Juliet and act
Before applauding audiences on Broadway.
I learned more about Shakespeare than he knew about himself.
But of course, all that was impossible.
"Talent, yes," they would tell me,
"But an actress has to look the part."
So I ended up waiting on tables in Harlem
And hearing uncouth men yell at me:
"Hey momma, you can cancel that hamburger
And come on up to 102."

In the third place, I tried the wrong solution.
The stuff I drank made me deathly sick
And someone called a doctor.
Next time I'll try a gun.

▮ How did you demonstrate the internal state of the speaker prior to the first line?

The fierce resilience of this narrator is only partly a result of environment. The coarse language and rough behavior only disguise the crucial vulnerability of the speaker. The audience needs to see all the levels in performance, of course, but not all at once. Keep all the characters full, involved in the tale.

The Lesson
TONI CADE BAMBARA

Back in the days when everyone was old and stupid or young and foolish and me and Sugar were the only ones just right, this lady

moved on our block with nappy hair and proper speech and no
makeup. And quite naturally we laughed at her, laughed the way
we did at the junk man who went about his business like he was
some big-time president and his sorry-ass horse his secretary. And
we kinda hated her too, hated the way we did the winos who
cluttered up our parks and pissed on our handball walls and stank
up our hallways and stairs so you couldn't halfway play hide-and-
seek without a goddamn gas mask. Miss Moore was her name. The
only woman on the block with no first name. And she was black as
hell, cept for her feet, which were fish-white and spooky. And she
was always planning these boring-ass things for us to do, us being
my cousin, mostly, who lived on the block cause we all moved North
the same time and to the same apartment then spread out gradual
to breathe. And our parents would yank our heads into some kinda
shape and crisp up our clothes so we'd be presentable for travel with
Miss Moore, who always looked like she was going to church, though
she never did. Which is just one of the things the grownups talked
about when they talked behind her back like a dog. But when she
came calling with some sachet she'd sewed up or some gingerbread
she'd made or some book, why then they'd all be too embarrassed
to turn her down and we'd get handed over all spruced up. She'd
been to college and said it was only right that she should take
responsibility for the young ones' education, and she not even related
by marriage or blood. So they'd go for it. Specially Aunt Gretchen.
She was the main gofer in the family. You got some ole dumb shit
foolishness you want somebody to go for, you send for Aunt
Gretchen. She been screwed into the go-along for so long, it's a
blood-deep natural thing with her. Which is how she got saddled
with me and Sugar and Junior in the first place while our mothers
were in a la-de-da apartment up the block having a good ole time.

So this one day Miss Moore rounds us all up at the mailbox and
it's puredee hot and she's knockin herself out about arithmetic. And
school suppose to let up in summer I heard, but she don't never let
up. And the starch in my pinafore scratching the shit outta me and
I'm really hating this nappy-head bitch and her goddamn college
degree. I'd much rather go to the pool or to the show where it's cool.
So me and Sugar leaning on the mailbox being surly, which is a Miss
Moore word. And Flyboy checking out what everybody brought for
lunch. And Fat Butt already wasting his peanut-butter-and-jelly sandwich like the pig he is. And Junebug punchin on Q.T.'s arm for
potato chips. And Rosie Giraffe shifting from one hip to the other
waiting for somebody to step on her foot or ask her if she from
Georgia so she can kick ass, preferably Mercedes'. And Miss Moore

asking us do we know what money is, like we a bunch of retards. I mean real money, she say, like it's only poker chips or monopoly papers we lay on the grocer. So right away I'm tired of this and say so. And would much rather snatch Sugar and go to the Sunset and terrorize the West Indian kids and take their hair ribbons and their money too. And Miss Moore files that remark away for next week's lesson on brotherhood, I can tell. And finally I say we oughta get to the subway cause it's cooler and besides we might meet some cute boys. Sugar done swiped her mama's lipstick, so we ready.

So we heading down the street and she's boring us silly about what things cost and what our parents make and how much goes for rent and how money ain't divided up right in this country. And then she gets to the part about we all poor and live in the slums, which I don't feature. And I'm ready to speak on that, but she steps out in the street and hails two cabs just like that. Then she hustles half the crew in with her and hands me a five-dollar bill and tells me to calculate 10 percent tip for the driver. And we're off. Me and Sugar and Junebug and Flyboy hangin out the window and hollering to everybody, putting lipstick on each other cause Flyboy a faggot anyway, and making farts with our sweaty armpits. But I'm mostly trying to figure how to spend this money. But they all fascinated with the meter ticking and Junebug starts laying bets as to how much it'll read when Flyboy can't hold his breath no more. Then Sugar lays bets as to how much it'll be when we get there. So I'm stuck. Don't nobody want to go for my plan, which is to jump out at the next light and run off to the first bar-b-que we can find. Then the driver tells us to get the hell out cause we there already. And the meter reads eighty-five cents. And I'm stalling to figure out the tip and Sugar say give him a dime. And I decide he don't need it bad as I do, so later for him. But then he tries to take off with Junebug foot still in the door so we talk about his mama something ferocious. Then we check out that we on Fifth Avenue and everybody dressed up in stockings. One lady in a fur coat, hot as it is. White folks crazy.

"This is the place," Miss Moore say, presenting it to us in the voice she uses at the museum. "Let's look in the windows before we go in."

"Can we steal?" Sugar asks very serious like she's getting the ground rules squared away before she plays. "I beg your pardon," say Miss Moore, and we fall out. So she leads us around the windows of the toy store and me and Sugar screamin, "This is mine, that's mine, I gotta have that, that was made for me, I was born for that," till Big Butt drowns us out.

"Hey, I'm goin to buy that there."

"That there? You don't even know what it is, stupid."

"I do so," he say punchin on Rosie Giraffe. "It's a microscope."

"Whatcha gonna do with a microscope, fool?"

"Look at things."

"Like what, Ronald?" ask Miss Moore. And Big Butt ain't got the first notion. So here go Miss Moore gabbing about the thousands of bacteria in a drop of water and the somethinorother in a speck of blood and the million and one living things in the air around us is invisible to the naked eye. And what she say that for? Junebug go to town on that "naked" and we rolling. Then Miss Moore ask what it cost. So we all jam into the window smudgin it up and the price tag say $300. So then she ask how long'd take for Big Butt and Junebug to save up their allowances. "Too long," I say. "Yeh," adds Sugar, "outgrown it by that time." And Miss Moore say no, you never outgrow learning instruments. "Why, even medical students and interns and," blah, blah, blah. And we ready to choke Big Butt for bringing it up in the first damn place.

"This here costs four hundred eighty dollars," Say Rosie Giraffe. So we pile up all over her to see what she pointin out. My eyes tell me it's a chunk of glass cracked with something heavy, and different-color inks dripped into the splits, then the whole thing put into a oven or something. But for $480 it don't make sense.

"That's a paperweight made of semi-precious stones fused together under tremendous pressure," she explains slowly, with her hands doing the mining and all the factory work.

"So what's a paperweight?" asks Rosie Giraffe.

"To weigh paper with, dumbbell," say Flyboy, the wise man from the East.

"Not exactly," say Miss Moore, which is what she say when you warm or way off too. "It's to weigh paper down so it won't scatter and make your desk untidy." So right away me and Sugar curtsy to each other and then to Mercedes who is more the tidy type.

"We don't keep paper on top of the desk in my class," Say Junebug, figuring Miss Moore crazy or lyin one.

"At home, then," she say. "Don't you have a calendar and a pencil case and a blotter and a letter-opener on your desk at home where you do your homework?" And she know damn well what our homes look like cause she nosys around in them every chance she gets.

"I don't even have a desk," say Junebug. "Do we?"

"No. And I don't get no homework neither," says Big Butt.

"And I don't even have a home," say Flyboy like he do at school to keep the white folks off his back and sorry for him. Send this poor kid to camp posters, is his specialty.

"I do," says Mercedes. "I have a box of stationery on my desk and a picture of my cat. My godmother bought the stationery and the desk. There's a big rose on each sheet and the envelopes smell like roses."

"Who wants to know about your smelly-ass stationery," say Rosie Giraffe fore I can get my two cents in.

"It's important to have a work area all your own so that . . ."

"Will you look at this sailboat, please," say Flyboy, cuttin her off and pointin to the thing like it was his. So once again we tumble all over each other to gaze at this magnificent thing in the toy store which is just big enough to maybe sail two kittens across the pond if you strap them to the posts tight. We all start reciting the price tag like we in assembly. "Handcrafted sailboat of fiberglass at one thousand one hundred ninety-five dollars."

"Unbelievable," I hear myself say and am really stunned. I read it again for myself just in case the group recitation put me in a trance. Same thing. For some reason this pisses me off. We look at Miss Moore and she lookin at us, waiting for I dunno what.

"Who'd pay all that when you can buy a sailboat set for a quarter at Pop's, a tube of glue for a dime, and a ball of string for eight cents? It must have a motor and a whole lot else besides," I say. "My sailboat cost me about fifty cents."

"But will it take water?" say Mercedes with her smart ass.

"Took mine to Alley Pond Park once," say Flyboy. "String broke. Lost it. Pity."

"Sailed mine in Central Park and it keeled over and sank. Had to ask my father for another dollar."

"And you got the strap," laugh Big Butt. "The jerk didn't even have a string on it. My old man wailed on his behind."

Little Q.T. was staring hard at the sailboat and you could see he wanted it bad. But he too little and somebody'd just take it from him. So what the hell. "This boat for kids, Miss Moore?"

"Parents silly to buy something like that just to get all broke up," say Rosie Giraffe.

"That much money it should last forever," I figure.

"My father'd buy it for me if I wanted it."

"Your father, my ass," say Rosie Giraffe getting a chance to finally push Mercedes.

"Must be rich people shop here," say Q.T.

"You are a very bright boy," say Flyboy. "What was your first clue?" And he rap him on the head with the back of his knuckles, since Q.T. the only one he could get away with. Though Q.T. liable to come up behind you years later and get his licks in when you half expect it.

"What I want to know is," I says to Miss Moore though I never talk to her, I wouldn't give the bitch that satisfaction, "is how much a real boat costs? I figure a thousand'd get you a yacht any day."

"Why don't you check that out," she says, "and report back to the group?" Which really pains my ass. If you gonna mess up a perfectly good swim day least you could do is have some answers. "Let's go in," she say like she got something up her sleeve. Only she don't lead the way. So me and Sugar turn the corner to where the entrance is, but when we get there I kinda hang back. Not that I'm scared, what's there to be afraid of, just a toy store. But I feel funny, shame. But what I got to be shamed about? Got as much right to go in as anybody. But somehow I can't seem to get hold of the door, so I step away from Sugar to lead. But she hangs back too. And I look at her and she looks at me and this is ridiculous. I mean, damn, I have never ever been shy about doing nothing or going nowhere. But then Mercedes steps up and then Rosie Giraffe and Big Butt crowd in behind and shove, and next thing we all stuffed into the doorway with only Mercedes squeezing past us, smoothing out her jumper and walking right down the aisle. Then the rest of us tumble in like a glued-together jigsaw done all wrong. And people lookin at us. And it's like the time me and Sugar crashed into the Catholic church on a dare. But once we got in there and everything so hushed and holy and the candles and the bowin and the hand-kerchiefs on all the drooping heads, I just couldn't go through with the plan. Which was for me to run up to the altar and do a tap dance while Sugar played the nose flute and messed around in the holy water. And Sugar kept givin me the elbow. Then later teased me so bad I tied her up in the shower and turned it on and locked her in. And she'd be there till this day if Aunt Gretchen hadn't finally figured I was lyin about the boarder takin a shower.

Same thing in the store. We all walkin on tiptoe and hardly touchin the games and puzzles and things. And I watched Miss Moore who is steady watchin us like she waitin for a sign. Like Mama Drewery watches the sky and sniffs the air and takes note of just how much slant is in the bird formation. Then me and Sugar bump smack into each other, so busy gazing at the toys, 'specially the sailboat. But we don't laugh and go into our fat-lady bump-stomach routine. We just stare at that price tag. Then Sugar run a finger over the whole boat. And I'm jealous and want to hit her. Maybe not her, but I sure want to punch somebody in the mouth.

"Watcha bring us here for, Miss Moore?"

"You sound angry, Sylvia. Are you mad about something?" Givin me one of them grins like she tellin a grown-up joke that never turns out to be funny. And she's lookin very closely at me like maybe she plannin to do my portrait from memory. I'm mad, but I won't give her that satisfaction. So I slouch around the store being very bored and say, "Let's go."

Me and Sugar at the back of the train watchin the tracks whizzin by large then small then gettin gobbled up in the dark. I'm thinkin about this tricky toy I saw in the store. A clown that somersaults on a bar then does chin-ups just cause you yank lightly at his leg. Cost $35. I could see me askin my mother for a $35 birthday clown. "You wanna who that costs what?" she'd say, cocking her head to the side to get a better view of the hole in my head. Thirty-five dollars could buy new bunk beds for Junior and Gretchen's boy. Thirty-five dollars and the whole household could go visit Granddaddy Nelson in the country. Thirty-five dollars would pay for the rent and the piano bill too. Who are these people that spend that much for performing clowns and $1000 for toy sailboats? What kinda work they do and how they live and how come we ain't in on it? Where we are is who we are, Miss Moore always pointin out. But it don't necessarily have to be that way, she always adds then waits for somebody to say that poor people have to wake up and demand their share of the pie and don't none of us know what kind of pie she talking about in the first damn place. But she ain't so smart cause I still got her four dollars from the taxi and she sure ain't gettin it. Messin up my day with this shit. Sugar nudges me in my pocket and winks.

Miss Moore lines us up in front of the mailbox where we started from, seem like years ago, and I got a headache for thinkin so hard. And we lean all over each other so we can hold up under the draggy ass lecture she always finishes us off with at the end before we thank her for borin us to tears. But she just looks at us like she readin tea leaves. Finally she say, "Well, what did you think of F.A.O. Schwarz?"

Rosie Giraffe mumbles, "White folks crazy."

"I'd like to go there again when I get my birthday money," says Mercedes, and we shove her out the pack so she has to lean on the mailbox by herself.

"I'd like a shower. Tiring day," say Flyboy.

Then Sugar surprises me by sayin, "You know, Miss Moore, I don't think all of us here put together eat in a year what that sailboat costs." And Miss Moore lights up like somebody goosed her. "And?" she say, urging Sugar on. Only I'm standin on her foot so she don't continue.

"Imagine for a minute what kind of society it is in which some people can spend on a toy what it would cost to feed a family of six or seven. What do you think?"

"I think," say Sugar pushing me off her feet like she never done before, cause I whip her ass in a minute, "that this is not much of a democracy if you ask me. Equal chance to pursue happiness means an equal crack at the dough, don't it?" Miss Moore is besides herself and I am disgusted with Sugar's treachery. So I stand on her foot one more time to see if she'll shove me. She shuts up, and Miss Moore looks at me, sorrowfully I'm thinkin. And somethin weird is goin on, I can feel it in my chest.

"Anybody else learn anything today?"lookin dead at me. I walk away and Sugar has to run to catch up and don't even seem to notice when I shrug her arm off my shoulder.

"Well, we got four dollars anyway," she says.

"Uh hunh."

"We could go to Hascombs and get half a chocolate layer and then go to the Sunset and still have plenty money for potato chips and ice cream sodas."

"Uh hunh."

"Race you to Hascombs," she say.

We start down the block and she gets ahead which is O.K. by me cause I'm going to the West End and then over to the Drive to think this day through. She can run if she want to and even run faster. But ain't nobody gonna beat me at nuthin.

▌ How did you distinguish between the narrator's participation in scene and activity in telling?

▌ If you chose to perform only an excerpt from the story, how did you make the "lesson" of your segment clear to your audience?

This small fragment of a Navajo ceremonial chant presents a real challenge to the interpreter. The repetition and the end-stopped lines are important for the quality of ritual and chant, but they should not be allowed to become monotonous. There is no need to attempt a musical accompaniment or tone, because the writing itself is so rich. Pay particular attention to the variety found in the middle of the lines where there are subtle word shifts. It will help to think of the first lines as a cohesive unit; the "beauty" lines as a unit; and the last four lines as another phase of this prayer of purification. Remember the Indians' mystical kinship with the earth on which they walk.

FROM *The Night Chant*

NAVAJO CEREMONIAL CHANT, TRANSLATED BY WASHINGTON MATTHEWS

In beauty may I walk.
All day long may I walk.
Through the returning seasons may I walk.
On the trail marked with pollen may I walk.
With grasshoppers about my feet may I walk.
With dew about my feet may I walk.
With beauty may I walk.
With beauty before me, may I walk.
With beauty behind me, may I walk.
With beauty above me, may I walk.
With beauty below me, may I walk.
With beauty all around me, may I walk.
In old age wandering on a trail of beauty, lively, may I walk.
In old age wandering on a trail of beauty, living again, may I walk.
It is finished in beauty.
It is finished in beauty.

▌ Did your voice mark the differences in the repeated words?

▌ How did you avoid monotony?

William Least Heat Moon set out on the back roads and byways to discover something about himself and about America. His itinerary arose almost entirely by whim, but he often found unique people and learned subtle lessons, as in this segment from *Blue Highways*.

FROM *Blue Highways*
WILLIAM LEAST HEAT MOON

Had it not been raining hard that morning on the Livingston square, I never would have learned of Nameless, Tennessee. Waiting for the rain to ease, I lay on my bunk and read the atlas to pass time rather than to see where I might go. In Kentucky were towns with fine names like Boreing, Bear Wallow, Decoy, Subtle, Mud Lick, Mummie, Neon; Belcher was just down the road from Mouthcard, and Minnie only ten miles from Mousie.

I looked at Tennessee. Turtletown eight miles from Ducktown. And also: Peavine, Wheel, Milky Way, Love Joy, Dull, Weakly, Fly, Spot, Miser Station, Only, McBurg, Peeled Chestnut, Clouds, Topsy, Isoline. And the best of all, Nameless. The logic! I was heading east, and Nameless lay forty-five miles west. I decided to go anyway.

The rain stopped, but things looked saturated, even bricks. In Gainesboro, a hill town with a square of businesses around the Jackson County Courthouse, I stopped for directions and breakfast. There is one almost infallible way to find honest food at just prices in blue-highway America: count the wall calendars in a cafe.

No calendar: Same as an interstate pit stop.
One calendar: Preprocessed food assembled in New Jersey.
Two calendars: Only if fish trophies present.
Three calendars: Can't miss on the farm-boy breakfasts.
Four calendars: Try the ho-made pie too.
Five calendars: Keep it under your hat, or they'll franchise.

One time I found a six-calendar cafe in the Ozarks, which served fried chicken, peach pie, and chocolate malts, that left me searching for another ever since. I've never seen a seven-calendar place. But old-time travelers — road men in a day when cars had running boards and lunchroom windows said AIR COOLED in blue letters with icicles dripping from the tops — those travelers have told me the golden legends of seven-calendar cafes.

To the rider of back roads, nothing shows the tone, the voice of a small town more quickly than the breakfast grill or the five-thirty tavern. Much of what the people do and believe and share is evident then. The City Cafe in Gainesboro had three calendars that I could see from the walk. Inside were no interstate refugees with full bladders and empty tanks, no wild-eyed children just released from the glassy cell of a stationwagon backseat, no longhaul truckers talking in CB numbers. There were only townspeople wearing overalls, or catalog-order suits with five-and-dime ties, or uniforms. That is, here were farmers and mill hands, bank clerks, the dry goods merchant, a policeman, and chiropractor's receptionist. Because it was Saturday, there were also mothers and children.

I ordered my standard on-the-road breakfast: two eggs up, hashbrowns, tomato juice. The waitress, whose pale, almost translucent skin shifted hue in the gray light like a thin slice of mother of pearl, brought the food. Next to the eggs was a biscuit with a little yellow Smiley button stuck in it. She said, "You from the North?"

"I guess I am." A Missourian gets used to Southerners thinking him a Yankee, Northerner considering him a cracker, a Westerner sneering at his effete Easternness, and the Easterner taking him for a cowhand.

"So whata you doin' in the mountains?"

"Talking to people. Taking some pictures. Looking mostly."

"Lookin' for what?"

"A three-calendar cafe that serves Smiley buttons on the biscuits."

"You needed a smile. Tell me really."

"I don't know. Actually, I'm looking for some jam to put on this biscuit now that you've brought one."

She came back with grape jelly. In a land of quince jelly, apple butter, apricot jam, blueberry preserves, pear conserves, and lemon marmalade, you always get grape jelly.

"Whata you lookin' for?"

Like anyone else, I'm embarrassed to eat in front of a watcher, particularly if I'm getting interviewed. "Why don't you have a cup of coffee?"

"Cain't right now. You gonna tell me?"

"I don't know how to describe it to you. Call it harmony."

She waited for something more. "Is that it?" Someone called her to the kitchen. I had managed almost to finish by the time she came back. She sat on the edge of the booth. "I started out in life not likin' anything, but then it grew on me. Maybe that'll happen to you." She watched me spread the jelly. "Saw your van." She watched me eat the biscuit. "You sleep in there?" I told her I did. "I'd love to do that, but I'd be scared spitless."

"I don't mind being scared spitless. Sometimes."

"I'd love to take off cross country. I like to look at different license plates. But I'd take a dog. You carry a dog?"

"No dogs, no cats, no budgie birds. It's a one-man campaign to show Americans a person can travel alone without a pet."

"Cain't travel without a dog!"

"I like to do things the hard way."

"Shoot! I'd take me a dog to talk to. And for protection."

"It isn't traveling to cross the country and talk to your pug instead of people along the way. Besides, being alone on the road makes you ready to meet someone when you stop. You get sociable traveling alone."

She looked out toward the van again. "Time I get the nerve to take a trip, gas'll cost five dollars a gallon."

"Could be. My rig might go the way of the steamboat." I remembered why I'd come to Gainesboro. "You know the way to Nameless?"

"Nameless? I've heard of Nameless. Better ask the amlance driver in the corner booth." She pinned the Smiley on my jacket. "Maybe I'll see you on the road somewhere. His name's Bob, by the way."

"The ambulance driver?"

"The Smiley. I always name my Smileys — otherwise they all look alike. I'd talk to him before you go."

"The Smiley?"

"The amlance driver."

And so I went looking for Nameless, Tennessee, with a Smiley button named Bob.

❚ What did you do in your performance to suggest the sincerity of the narrator's interest in the people in the City Cafe?

Bibliography

The following books have specific exercises on voice and articulation. Consult them for help with minor problems that need attention.

Berry, Cicely. *Voice and the Actor.* New York: Macmillan, 1973.
    Practical exercises from the voice director of the Royal Shakespeare Company.

Crannell, Kenneth. *Voice and Articulation: Developing Career Speech.* 2nd ed. Belmont, Calif.: Wadsworth Publishing Company, 1991.
    Numerous useful exercises and an audio recording of important examples enrich this broad examination of the ways in which voice can suggest character.

Kenley, Joan. *Voice Power.* New York: Henry Holt, 1988.

> A well-written practical guide to vocal production, with useful exercises for control and sustenance.

Lessac, Arthur. *The Use and Training of the Human Voice.* 2nd ed. New York: Drama Book Specialists, 1967.

> This is a most effective book for students working with a knowledgeable instructor who has been trained in the Lessac method. Lessac divides what he calls "vocal life" into three basic parts: consonant action, structural action, and tonal action. The method depends not on imitation but upon the development of the potential of each individual student's given voice.

Linklater, Kristin. *Freeing the Natural Voice.* New York: Drama Book Specialists, 1976.

> Understanding the voice in human communication precedes a series of exercises to free, develop, and strengthen the instrument.

Machlin, Evangeline. *Speech for the Stage.* Rev. ed. New York: Theatre Arts Books, 1966.

> A serviceable book that makes use of the international phonetic alphabet and traditional approaches to training the voice for the stage. The approach is perhaps more imitative than innovative, but the book contains excellent breathing exercises, audition exercises, and warm-up exercises. It also includes a good section on speaking Shakespeare.

McCalleon, Michael. *The Voice Book.* London: Routledge, Chapman, Hall, 1989.

> A useful recent work with handy exercises for control and support.

O body swayed to music, O brightening glance.
How can we know the dancer from the dance?

W. B. Yeats, "Among School Children"

THE USE OF THE BODY IN ORAL INTERPRETATION

4

WHEN YOU HAVE DECIDED ON a piece of literature that interests you and is worth the time and effort you must spend in preparing for performance, your next responsibility is to work on understanding its elements — its logical meaning, its emotive overtones, and its qualities of literary craftsmanship. If you allow yourself to respond fully to all of the clues you find, the experience expressed in the writing will become an integral part of you. Finally, when you feel sure of where the material is going and how it gets there, you can turn your attention to the most effective way of communicating the literature to the audience. At this point control of the twofold instrument of body and voice becomes important. Just as a musician cannot give a satisfactory performance without having perfected the handling of his or her musical instrument, so an interpreter, who is both instrument and instrumentalist, must devote attention to technique.

The term *technique* does not imply artificiality in the use of body and voice. In fact, the finer the technique is, the less apparent it is to the audience. Technique may be defined as style of performance. The style of performance in the art of interpretation must be unobtrusive if the interpreter wants to focus the audience on the material.

Overt attention to technique belongs in the rehearsal period and has no place in performance. Display of vocal ability or physical virtuosity as an end in itself has been outmoded since the decline of the "mechanical" school of elocution in the nineteenth century. Such display is considered in poor taste today, and it is interesting only to the degree than an exhibition of calisthenics or a recital of scales and arpeggios would be interesting. The interpreter develops and uses technique as a means of communicating the material; the material is not used as a vehicle for displaying technique.

You develop vocal and bodily technique by practicing, so that your muscles will respond to the demands made on them without apparent prompting or effort. During a performance you should concentrate on the material and on the response of the audience to that material. If you are adequately prepared, the muscles of your vocal mechanism and of your entire body will respond according to the habits you set up in rehearsal. As your skill increases through experience, this habitual response will become more dependable.

Since oral interpretation obviously involves the use of the voice, it would seem that the vocal mechanism should be of first importance. It is a mistake, however, to overlook or underestimate the subtle but very significant role of the body in oral interpretation. As a matter of fact, the body begins the process of communication even before the voice is heard. From the moment the audience becomes aware of your physical presence, you are arousing a response, establishing in your listeners what psychologists call a "set," or condition of mental readiness, toward what they are about to hear. It is true that you may not begin to communicate the *specific* material until you speak, but by your bodily actions you give intimations of a particular mental attitude toward yourself, the audience, and the material.

Bodily action may be defined as any movement of the muscles of the body. This movement may be a full gesture or merely a relaxing or tensing of the small muscles around the eyes or mouth, across the shoulders and back, or in the legs. It may be a combination of any or all of these movements. Bodily action includes the approach to and departure from the platform or lectern. It also includes movements of the head, arms, shoulders, hands, torso, and legs, and changes in posture, facial expressions, and muscle tone of the entire body. Modern interpreters know that the test of bodily action is the ability to communicate the literature at hand. Bodily action is effective only when it suits the material and thus helps elicit the desired response.

Although we touch briefly on separate areas of bodily action, such as posture, gesture, muscle tone, and empathy, it is important to remember that no bodily movement exists in isolation. Moreover, for a movement to be significant, it must be considered within a specific context. Sometimes what the body is communicating is in deliberate contradiction to what the words and thus the voice are saying. This incongruity can be a very useful technique for certain kinds of comedy. But unless it is evident in the writer's style, it can also interfere with what an unwary interpreter is trying to accomplish. When what we see contradicts what we hear, we tend to give greater weight to visual clues than to auditory clues. But when what we see underscores what we hear, the impact of the material being communicated is sharpened considerably.

An audience is quick to resent an overbearing or cocky attitude. It is equally quick to question the authority of a speaker who seems unsure of his or her ability. You will strike a happy medium when you are confident that you are adequately prepared, that your material is well chosen, and that your audience is capable of understanding and responding to that material. When you have doubts about any of these points, your uncertainty will be reflected in your physical bearing. The audience will sense your insecurity and will unconsciously share your discomfort. It is important, then, for you to avoid any mannerisms that may give an unfavorable impression, whether of virtuosity, arrogance, or lack of self-confidence.

Just as bodily action in all its aspects gives the audience clues about the interpreter, it is essential in suggesting character and reflecting the attitude of the persona. We all have seen speakers whom we did not believe for a moment because what we saw contradicted what we heard. In drama, the way a character moves and the tone of his or her entire body often reveal as much as or more than the words he or she uses. The body and voice work together as you communicate your own thoughts in your introduction and transitions or convey those of the persona in the selection.

Posture

The basis of effective bodily action is good *posture,* which is primarily a matter of proper positional relations among the various parts of the body. Good posture is the arrangement of the bones and muscles that puts the body in its perfect natural alignment so that each unit does its job of supporting and controlling the bodily structure without undue tension or strain. When this arrangement is accomplished, the entire body is balanced, flexible, responsive, and coordinated. Good posture requires nothing more complicated than standing straight and easy from the ankle bone to the crown of the head, so that the various parts of the skeletal structure fall naturally into place.

Kinesics

The interaction between what the voice is saying and what the body is saying is explored in a fascinating area of research called *kinesics*. Some of the books in the bibliography at the end of this chapter give details on the extent of the research that continues to be of great value to the interpreter. Kinesics is sometimes popularly called body language or nonverbal or nonlinguistic communication.

Gesture

A *gesture* may be defined as any movement that helps express or emphasize an idea or emotional response. In its most modern sense, gesture embraces the entire field of kinesics and includes both clearly discernible bodily movement and subtle changes in posture and muscle tone. Many people still think of gesture in its narrowest sense — as overt actions of the hands and arms and occasionally the head and shoulders. These parts of the body do not function as separate entities, however. Rather, they involve a "follow-through" that both affects and is affected by the degree of muscular tension in every other part of the body. It is impossible to treat gesture separately from an awareness of the body as an organic whole.

Bear in mind that an effective gesture amplifies or enriches the meaning of the text; it does not simply repeat the denotative information of the words. If an action does not help communicate the material, it is not a gesture but only a distracting and extraneous movement violating the basic principle that no action by an interpreter should call attention to itself. This is not to say that hand and arm movements should not be used. It is to say that their use must be dictated by the demands of the material being presented.

Your use of hand and arm movements normally depends on two considerations. The first, as we have said, is your material. You should use whatever bodily action is necessary to make the meaning clear to your audience and to convey the emotional quality effectively. The second consideration is the personality of the interpreter. Some of us find it easier than others to respond physically. You should use whatever movement you wish in rehearsal until you can handle it effectively when you need it, but you should never let gestures as such become an issue when you are before an audience. In performance, when your concentration shifts from the material to the problem of what to do with your hands, the audience will be quick to sense your preoccupation.

Nevertheless, a responsive body is such an important factor in the total process of communication that you would do well to work on gestures conscientiously during rehearsal periods. In the early phases of rehearsal, it is often helpful to use large, exaggerated actions or to move freely about the room, responding consciously and overtly to all the empathic cues and muscle imagery in the selection. This overt response during preparation is the basis of *muscle memory*, in which the muscles "remember" the big action, and muscle tone reflects this remembering even after the specific overt gesture is discarded or modified.

If, on the other hand, you have a tendency to "talk with your hands," you should use whatever movements make you feel at ease and help communicate your material. It is important, however, to remember both facets of this advice: "make you feel at ease" and "help communicate." Be sure that what makes you feel at ease doesn't distract your audience and thus actually block communication.

Perhaps you have developed certain habitual physical actions that are not gestures at all in the sense that they do not help you express an idea. You may be using a repetitious movement, such as constantly raising and lowering one hand, tilting your head, or shrugging your shoulders. Such personal mannerisms, called *autistic gestures* because they grow out of your own personality, direct attention to you and prevent the audience from concentrating on your material. Moreover, they can seriously interfere with the creation of a character or the persona in the literature. An occasional checkup before a large mirror will help call this fault to your attention.

Muscle Tone

Muscle tone refers to the degree of tension or relaxation present in the entire body. It is extremely important to consider muscle tone when you are projecting material to an audience, because an audience responds to what it sees more strongly than to what it hears.

We have already referred to muscle tone in our discussion, because it is impossible to talk about any effective bodily action without considering it. Muscle tone happens as a result of muscle memory, complete response to the material, and the interpreter's concentration on sharing that material with the audience. It is vital to the fulcrum and climax of "Dulce" (Chapter 1), for example. Usually we are not aware of muscle tone as a separate aspect of bodily action and need only to be reminded occasionally that it must not distract from or negate the other aspects of performance.

When one's posture is good, the body is in a state of controlled relaxation, with no undue muscular strain or tension. The properly poised body is flexible and responsive, and it moves with coordination and fluidity. Controlled relaxation is not to be confused with apathy or lack of physical energy. The interpreter who looks too tired, depressed, or bored to stand up straight communicates an unfortunate impression to the audience and draws an undesirable response because the listeners reflect in their own muscle tone this sense of weariness, depression, or boredom. Relaxation is an easing of tension; it is not total disintegration. The degree of relaxation is controlled in the interest of dignity and poise, and it is dictated by the requirements of the material being presented.

Although muscle tone should be dictated by the literature, it is often affected by the performer's mental and emotional state. It varies from obvious tension to assured, controlled relaxation in direct proportion to your own self-confidence and your confidence in the material and the audience. Any performance will carry with it a degree of excitement, which is translated into physical tension. The secret is to channel that tension so that it becomes an asset instead of a hazard. "Butterflies" in your stomach are not a sign of fear but of excitement, which, properly understood and controlled, is communicated to the audience in terms of a vital, stimulating performance. Too frequently, however, the inexperienced performer attributes this tension to stage fright — and immediately sets up a fear pattern. If your material is acceptable and your preparation is adequate, then "butterflies" are a good sign. They are the result of your personal involvement, which your performance needs to succeed.

Sense Imagery

Literature rich in universality and suggestion depends for much of its effectiveness on the skillful use of sense imagery. Images that appeal predominantly to the sense of sight are called *visual*; to the sense of hearing, *auditory*; to the sense of taste, *gustatory*; and to the sense of smell, *olfactory*. The sense of touch is appealed to in *tactual* (or tactile) imagery, which involves a sensation of physical contact, pressure, or texture, and in *thermal* imagery, which refers to the feelings of heat and cold.

Two additional types of imagery appeal directly to the muscles or motor sense. The first is *kinetic imagery*, a large, overt action of the muscles: running, jumping, sitting down, walking away. The second type is *kinesthetic imagery*, which refers to muscle tension and relaxation. It is closely related to muscle memory and resultant muscle tone, and is likely to be present in any particularly rich sense appeal. Clearly, from what we know of muscle tone, and, indeed, the whole area of kinesics, these actions are invariably accompanied by tension or relaxation. Rarely in literature do you find a kinetic action or motor image that does not clearly indicate how and why one ran or jumped or sat or walked. There is a difference between "I was terrified and I ran" and "I ran for the sheer joy of being young in summer."

How an action is performed is kinesthetic — the degree of body tension or relaxation that goes along with the kinetic, overt action. The kinesthetic is governed by the emotional state of the person performing the action and helps communicate that emotional state to the audience. You should identify fully with the *how* and the *why* of the actions performed by the personae or characters in a selection. A kinesthetic response is also involved in our reactions to height and distance. It operates very strongly in Hopkins's "The Starlight Night" (Chapter 2), for instance. Let your whole body respond completely to these two contrasting phrases: "Right above my head there was a huge bumblebee"; "Far off on the horizon I could see a single gull flying high and then swooping low over the expanse of water." Your responses are kinesthetic as well as visual. There need be no overt action involving the persona. But the emotional states differ, just as they do between "She sat primly waiting" and "She sat dozing in the sun." A kinesthetic image, unlike a kinetic one, often can stand alone.

Sense imagery helps create distinct and individual personalities. Robert Browning is a master of this technique, especially in his monologues, and Theodore Roethke uses it brilliantly in "Old Lady's Winter Words" at the end of this chapter. A playwright also may use sense imagery to tell us about a character's background and set of values. Look, for example, at the visual imagery Sondheim gives George in "Finishing the Hat" (Chapter 8).

Rarely does an image appeal to only one sense. In most good literature, certainly in all literature that is rich in suggestion, the images carry a complex of appeals. Besides the primary sense appeal of a word, phrase, or thought unit, there are usually additional or secondary appeals. Look at the feast of images that fill Garret Hongo's "Who Among You Knows the Essence of Garlic?" (Chapter 10). When you examine a selection in detail, you become aware that imagery contributes strongly to the intrinsic factors — that it helps produce unity and harmony, variety and contrast, balance and proportion, and rhythm.

One of the most obvious methods of achieving unity through imagery is to use a single type of primary appeal throughout the unit, much as Singer so deftly does in "A Crown of Feathers" (at the end of this chapter) by focusing on the exotic, arcane, and mysterious in Akhsa's life.

Sometimes imagery displays very little unity of type but is held together by restrictions to a limited locale. This is true of the excerpt from Welty's "June Recital" (Chapter 5). Or the imagery may all be slanted toward one person or object, as in Faulkner's "Dry September" (Chapter 5); or it may focus on the parts of a series of details that relate to one object, place, or person. In the latter case, the effect is usually cumulative and must be handled to achieve the strongest ultimate impression. Charles Dickens uses this cumulative technique to describe a battle in *A Tale of Two Cities:*

> With a roar that sounded as if all the breath in France had been shaped into the detested word, the living sea rose, wave on wave, depth on depth, and overflowed the city to that point. Alarm-bells ringing, drums beating, the sea raging and thundering on its new beach, the attack began . . .
>
> Cannon, muskets, fire and smoke . . . Flashing weapons, blazing torches, smoking wagon-loads of wet straw, hard work at neighboring barricades in all directions, shrieks, volleys, execrations, bravery without stint, boom, smash and rattle, and the furious sounding of the living sea . . .

Dickens begins with the auditory appeal, to which he adds complexity that reaches its height in "cannon, muskets, fire and smoke." Then he shifts to the visual and kinetic imagery of "flashing weapons," returning almost at once to the auditory appeal in "shrieks, volleys," which comes to a climax in "boom, smash and rattle." Finally, he blends all this into "the furious sounding of the living sea."

Thomas Wolfe's "The Golden World" gives the interpreter a complex problem in unity through imagery. The following sentence illustrates his use of cumulative technique.

> He knew the good male smell of his father's sitting room; of the smooth worn leather sofa, with the gaping horse-hair rent; of the blistered varnished wood upon the hearth; of the heated calf-skin bindings; of the flat moist plug of apple tobacco, stuck with a red flag; of wood-smoke and burnt leaves in October; of the brown tired autumn earth; of honey-suckle at night; of warm nasturtiums; of a clean ruddy farmer who comes weekly with printed butter, eggs and milk; of fat limp underdone bacon and of coffee; of a bakery-oven in the wind; of large deep-hued string beans smoking-hot and seasoned well with salt and butter; of a room of old pine boards in which books and carpets have been stored, long closed; of Concord grapes in their long white baskets.[1]

---

1. Thomas Wolfe, *Look Homeward Angel.*

In this single sentence the imagery is predominantly olfactory, but within this unity of appeal there is a variety of place. The progression from interior to exterior and back to interior may prove troublesome unless the interpreter is careful to group the objects that appeal to the senses. The excerpt opens in the sitting room, where it remains through mention of the visual detail of "a red flag." Without warning or apparent motivation, the scene shifts to the outdoors, but the olfactory motif remains strong, and there is unity of appeal in the focus of attention on the earth and its produce. This speaker is following his nose. The "ruddy farmer" with his "butter, eggs and milk" sets up the train of thought that centers on the smell of food and calls up the rest of the images within the sentence. Included in these images is the "room of old pine boards in which books and carpets have been stored," an image that for the author belongs with these others, but to the interpreter may seem like an interpolation among the many references to food. The unifying factor here might be best classified as the author's presentation through a "stream of consciousness." To keep the transitions clear and acceptable, you should be careful to group the images by association of place or type of appeal, keeping in mind the importance of the primary olfactory appeal and the fact that the memories cluster around a single house. Do not forget, or allow your listeners to forget, that the sentence begins with "He knew the . . . smell of. . . ."

Obviously, the type and vividness of the imagery should be in harmony with the total intention of the piece of literature: harmonious with the character and setting in a narrative and with the tastes and experiences of the intended audience in didactic writing and essays. Even the adjectives used to give the objects added richness should be highly appropriate: "heated calf-skin bindings" and "burnt leaves," for example, in the excerpt from "The Golden World." Books bound in watered silk would certainly not be harmonious with the "good male smell."

A skillful author is acutely aware, consciously or subconsciously, of the speed with which the senses tire. Thus, as Thomas Wolfe does with his "red flag," an author suddenly will vary the appeal to allow readers to shift their response to another sense. When the writer returns to the original appeal, the readers' and listeners' responses are heightened because of this momentary relief. The same relieving function can be accomplished by contrast as well. Thus, imagery makes a particularly rich contribution to both variety and contrast and is itself intensified by variation and contrast. It is one of the interpreter's tasks not to allow the variety to overshadow or violate the essential unity, but rather to use this variety to fulfill its purpose of relief.

Usually an author provides help with this problem. On close observation, you will discover that the author has not really abandoned the primary appeal, but has only allowed it to shift momentarily to a secondary position. There may also be a fairly consistent relationship between two types of imagery.

In the matter of balance and proportion, imagery is often used to weight a unit so that with this added vividness the section is comparable to a more detailed unit. In this case, imagery is usually combined with other factors as well — especially to heighten a climax or to sharpen a contrast.

In some literary selections imagery provides an interesting rhythm of logical content and emotional quality. Kinesthetic response is so much a part of emotional response that it cannot be ignored or underestimated; it is also basic to the implementation of empathy.

Empathy

One of the interpreter's most powerful tools is the control and use of *empathy*. Although the roots of the word are Greek, "empathy" is a term borrowed from modern psychology. It means literally a "feeling into" and it results from one's ability and willingness to project oneself intellectually and emotionally into a piece of literature or any other type of art. This emotional association enables an interpreter to identify thoroughly with and embody the mental and the emotional states of the speaker and characters in the selection. Such identification results in a corresponding physical response. The *interaction* of these emotional and physical responses, as they intensify each other, is the basis of empathy as it concerns the interpreter.

Every writer who deals with emotions uses words and phrases in such a way as to cause some mental disturbance, which may take the form of pleasure or pain, activity or repose. As an interpreter, you respond fully to these words and phrases. If you have not experienced precisely what the author is describing or creating, recall some parallel or approximate situation that has evoked a comparable response in you. As you react emotionally to the written material, your muscles tighten or relax, usually without a conscious effort on your part. This tightening or relaxing of muscles affects the tone of your entire body.

Try the following simple experiment to experience how this interaction actually works:

1. Divorce your mind from your immediate surroundings and recall some occasion or experience that made you feel happy and ex-

hilarated. It does not matter in the least what the experience was, as long as it made you feel particularly pleased with yourself and with your world. Spend as long as you wish recapturing the circumstances and the accompanying response.

2. Next, turn your thoughts to a set of circumstances that once made you violently angry. Concentrate on every detail and allow yourself to become thoroughly resentful. This is your chance to say all the things you thought of after it was too late.

3. Now go back to the pleasant situation. Recapture the experience as completely as you can. As you allow your mood to change and the happy memory to take over, notice what is happening to your muscles.

4. Keeping your muscle tone exactly as it is, go back to the anger you felt before. Don't let a muscle tighten or change. It is clearly impossible to be as thoroughly angry as you were when your muscles were responding freely, although unconsciously.

Empathy works for the interpreter in three distinct steps: from the literature to the interpreter, from the interpreter to the audience, and from the audience back to the interpreter.

As we read a piece of literature, we relate to it actively. We all have had the experience of coming out of a concert, movie, or play or of finishing a book and being physically exhausted and, often, exhilarated. We are not worn out because we have been uncomfortable but because we have participated so thoroughly that our muscles are tired. This participation, which combines intellect, emotions, and body, is the first step in empathy. It is partly what makes us choose a selection to read in the first place. You may lose this empathic response in the middle phases of rehearsal while you are trying to determine climaxes, the fulcrum, the intrinsic factors, and all of the other elements involved in analysis. But when you get the material back together again and look forward to sharing it with an audience, the empathic response comes back, strengthened by your newly developed mastery over the parts that make up the whole. Thus, the first step in empathy is your own response to the stimulus provided by the literature. Without this response the second step is impossible.

The second step in empathy has to do with the audience's response to the interpreter's material. When you respond empathically to the selection, you give physical cues to the listeners. Thus, we return to the whole concept of kinesics or nonverbal communication. The audience imitates your muscle tone, usually unconsciously; this physical imitation intensifies or inhibits their emotional involvement, just as your muscle tone intensified or inhibited your own emotional response in the exercise just described. Have you ever noticed that simply because someone else is frowning, smiling, or yawning, you tend to frown and feel depressed or irritated, or to smile and feel happy, or to yawn and feel tired or bored?

Successful interpreters are aware of the value of empathy, even in the way they approach the platform. During your introduction you can use this element to help establish an emotional readiness in the audience. If the selection is brief and intense, like Dickinson's "Because I Could Not Stop for Death," you will find that the audience moves with you much more surely if you make full use of empathy. Their own mental and emotional states of readiness affect the tone of all their muscles. And the audience, by unconscious imitation of what it sees, will adopt the physical tone that you project. By imitating your physical tone, the audience puts itself into psychic readiness for the response you wish to get from your listeners.

The third step in empathy is the interpreter's ultimate reward: the audience sends back an empathic response through its concentration and its alternating tension and relaxation. Thus, the cycle is complete: from the printed page to the interpreter, out to the audience, and back to the interpreter.

Hints for Rehearsal

A study of mime is valuable to interpreters because it makes them acutely aware of how each separate muscle contributes to an overall impression. It demands subtle control and flexibility of the entire body working as a fluid unit. Similarly, any dance or physical exercise reminds us of how we move.

So-called sensitivity sessions or awareness exercises are as valuable to interpreters as they are to actors. They involve the conscious recall of sensuous experience. Because interpreters should consider all of the stimuli received from the senses, strong concentration and a responsive body are indispensable during your preparation and rehearsal periods. By making yourself more open to the experience of the literature you are reading, you will enrich both your own and your audience's pleasure. Therefore, such exercises are helpful in achieving the first step in empathy.

A word of warning: the muscular response is in itself a result of mental activity. The outward, physical signs are an indication of that inner activity, never a substitute for it. If the mental and emotional responses come first, the muscular response should follow. It doesn't work nearly so fully the other way around.

But richness of response is not enough for an interpreter. You must be able to channel and direct that response to your audience.

A good rehearsal technique to help achieve this second step in empathy is to work occasionally with other people and attempt to create a mood in them without words — a sort of silent game of charades. You will develop an awareness of the way in which a response can be turned out to include other people, and you will sharpen and refine both your muscle memory and posture control.

After you have developed your own capacity to respond and have learned the all-important method of directing that response out for an audience to share, you should return to the material as it is written. Carefully and objectively evaluate how relevant your response is to the experience the author has written about. Then eliminate the areas of your own subjectivity that conflict with the clues in the writing. Fidelity to the text must always be the controlling factor.

Analyzing the Performance

Before you begin to examine your degree of success in making your voice and body work together to give your audience the selection you chose in its *aesthetic entirety*, go back and recheck the questions in the "Analyzing the Performance" section in Chapter 2. During this performance you may have focused your attention on some of the problems that occurred in your earlier performances. Where was the improvement you were seeking? Don't be discouraged if you are still encountering the same problems. Slight progress is still progress; take some heart from what you have achieved rather than becoming discouraged with what you haven't yet achieved. However slight your improvement, remember that the fullest performance of a piece of good literature is the result of slow and continuing self-monitoring, careful attention to the responses of the audience, and hard work.

Don't try to solve every problem in every rehearsal. Instead, concentrate on the trickiest or most difficult problem. Work on it at every rehearsal until it begins to jell. For example, if you are reading a story, be sure that you are absolutely clear about what the narrator sounds like and looks like before you get too involved in the characters in the story. Have you chosen a lyric poem? Make sure your voice and your body accurately reflect the structure of the poem. Are you giving each line the weight it needs to carry the fullest possible meaning, or are you rushing through the piece just to be sure that you get all the words in? Solving the major problems will give you the luxury of working on the minor difficulties. As you seem to be making progress with the larger dilemmas, gradually add others — but don't forget that the foundation is getting better and better.

Each selection demands a fresh start and perhaps a different point of attack from the last one. Do not allow yourself to perform only one kind of literature because you are most comfortable with it. Instead, experiment with many different kinds of selections. If you respect the literature and yourself as a performer, your audience will find something of value to see and hear.

Although the following questions relate directly to the chapters on voice development and the use of the body, they also apply to any performance you give.

Could you be heard? Could you be understood? (These are not always the same thing; why?)

Was your breath control satisfactory and comfortable? Did you find yourself running out of breath at places you previously had under control? What happened in the lines just preceding these new problem areas?

Were you able to control and vary the pace to support the demands of your selection? Remember, audiences listen at a much slower rate than you can speak.

Were you careful to use pause effectively, being sure that you did not break the unity or destroy the harmony but made use of variety and contrast to achieve balance and proportion, to bring out the climaxes, and to suggest the fulcrum? Was your concentration steady during the pauses?

Was there a regional dialect or melody pattern that interfered with the audience's full enjoyment of the personae? Was monotone a problem?

Was your body communicating what your voice was communicating? Did your body and your voice complement each other? Did you remember that your performance begins the instant you leave your seat and continues until you return to it? The walk to the front of the room gives you a good opportunity to collect your thoughts for your introduction. Once on stage, take the time to get a good, satisfying (but inaudible) breath and to become comfortable behind the lectern. Get your body into easy alignment and focus your concentration on exactly what the persona is thinking immediately prior to the first words in your selection. When you are ready — and your audience is ready — begin.

Did your body respond to the imagery honestly without ignoring the intrinsic factors?

Did you notice any physical mannerisms that inhibited what you were trying to communicate?

Did you handle the physical text unobtrusively?

These questions are also helpful in analyzing the performances of other readers. Remember to be descriptive. Select one striking moment in another's performance and see if you can describe *precisely* what it was that the performer did to achieve such distinction. Take the time to sketch verbally exactly what the performer's body was doing and exactly how the performer's voice behaved at that moment. Compare your responses with those of your classmates. Now, together, compare all of these descriptions with the actual text of the selection. Did the performance coincide with the selection? How? Did it veer away from what the author intended? Where? How? Why?

Finally, ask yourself where in the performance (whether your own or another's) did literature and the reader correlate most closely? Why? Before you begin your next performance, try to remember what you did to achieve such a richly rewarding blend. But above all, begin to work on your next performance. There is no time to rest on easy victories, nothing to learn without valiant effort.

Selections for Analysis and Oral Interpretation

All of the following selections have a strong suggestion of physical action. In preparing them for oral interpretation, let your muscles respond completely, taking time in some cases to work out a specific action, which you may or may not use in performance, to help you achieve the proper empathy. Because your voice and body must work together, many of the selections at the end of Chapter 3 also provide opportunities for bodily action, although they were chosen primarily because of their vocal demands.

Remember that each selection must be analyzed for organization, attitude, the elements of literary art, and suggested bodily action.

Be sure you understand all the allusions in this first selection. The action described is not that of the speaker, but kinesthetic imagery is very strong.

The Second Coming
WILLIAM BUTLER YEATS

Turning and turning in the widening gyre
The falcon cannot hear the falconer;
Things fall apart; the centre cannot hold;

Mere anarchy is loosed upon the world,
The blood-dimmed tide is loosed, and everywhere
The ceremony of innocence is drowned;
The best lack all conviction, while the worst
Are full of passionate intensity.
Surely some revelation is at hand;
Surely the Second Coming is at hand.
The Second Coming! Hardly are those words out
When a vast image out of *Spiritus Mundi*
Troubles my sight: somewhere in sands of the desert
A shape with lion body and the head of a man,
A gaze blank and pitiless as the sun,
Is moving its slow thighs, while all about it
Reel shadows of the indignant desert birds.
The darkness drops again; but now I know
That twenty centuries of stony sleep
Were vexed to nightmare by a rocking cradle,
And what rough beast, its hour come round at last,
Slouches towards Bethlehem to be born?

▌ What physical behavior did you use to show the persona's rise in desperation and its troubled release?

Muscle tone and posture help suggest the power and strength of the Greek hero in the next selection. These qualities are more important than his age. His memories of past actions and his hope for future ones are strongly kinesthetic as he considers them, and they set up a clear rhythm of content.

Ulysses
ALFRED, LORD TENNYSON

It little profits that an idle king,
By this still hearth, among these barren crags,
Matched with an aged wife, I mete and dole
Unequal laws unto a savage race,
That hoard, and sleep, and feed, and know not me.
I cannot rest from travel; I will drink
Life to the lees. All times I have enjoyed
Greatly, have suffered greatly, both with those
That loved me, and alone; on shore, and when
Through scudding drifts the rainy Hyades
Vexed the dim sea. I am become a name;
For always roaming with a hungry heart
Much have I seen and known — cities of men,
And manners, climates, councils, governments,
Myself not least, but honored of them all, —
And drunk delight of battle with my peers,
Far on the ringing plains of windy Troy.
I am a part of all that I have met;
Yet all experience is an arch wherethrough
Gleams that untraveled world, whose margin fades
Forever and forever when I move.
How dull it is to pause, to make an end,
To rust unburnished, not to shine in use!
As though to breathe were life! Life piled on life
Were all too little, and of one to me
Little remains: but every hour is saved
From that eternal silence, something more,
A bringer of new things; and vile it were
For some three suns to store and hoard myself,
And this gray spirit yearning in desire
To follow knowledge, like a sinking star,
Beyond the utmost bound of human thought.

This is my son, my own Telemachus,
To whom I leave the sceptre and the isle, —
Well-loved of me, discerning to fulfil
This labor, by slow prudence to make mild
A rugged people, and through soft degrees
Subdue them to the useful and the good.
Most blameless is he, centred in the sphere
Of common duties, decent not to fail
In offices of tenderness, and pay
Meet adoration to my household gods,
When I am gone. He works his work, I mine.
    There lies the port; the vessel puffs her sail;
There gloom the dark broad seas. My mariners,
Souls that have toiled, and wrought, and thought with me, —
That ever with a frolic welcome took
The thunder and the sunshine, and opposed
Free hearts, free foreheads, — you and I are old;
Old age hath yet his honor and his toil.
Death closes all; but something ere the end,
Some work of noble note, may yet be done,
Not unbecoming men that strove with Gods.
The lights begin to twinkle from the rocks;
The long day wanes; the slow moon climbs; the deep
Moans round with many voices. Come, my friends,
'Tis not too late to seek a newer world,
Push off, and sitting well in order smite
The sounding furrows; for my purpose holds
To sail beyond the sunset, and the baths
Of all the western stars, until I die.
It may be that the gulfs will wash us down;
It may be we shall touch the Happy Isles,
And see the great Achilles, whom we knew.
Though much is taken, much abides; and though
We are not now that strength which in old days
Moved earth and heaven, that which we are, we are;
One equal temper of heroic hearts,
Made weak by time and fate, but strong in will
To strive, to seek, to find, and not to yield.

▋ Your audience should feel themselves a part of Ulysses' audience. What did you do physically to demonstrate locus and
character?

This is the beginning of a long and splendid story by the Nobel laureate Isaac Bashevis Singer. It is likely that the names and customs in the story will seem bizarre or mysterious to you, but they are the *life* of Akhsa and the other people who live in Krasnobród. And the narrator presides over it all with an alluring, enigmatic profundity. There are several sections that, with a careful introduction, will serve as good units for class assignments.

FROM *A Crown of Feathers*
ISAAC BASHEVIS SINGER

Reb Naftali Holishitzer, the community leader in Krasnobród, was left in his old age with no children. One daughter had died in childbirth and the other in a cholera epidemic. A son had drowned when he tried to cross the San River on horseback. Reb Naftali had only one grandchild — a girl, Akhsa, an orphan. It was not the custom for a female to study at a yeshiva, because "the King's daughter is all glorious within" and Jewish daughters are all the daughters of kings. But Akhsa studied at home. She dazzled everyone with her beauty, wisdom, and diligence. She had white skin and black hair; her eyes were blue.

Reb Naftali managed an estate that had belonged to the Prince Czartoryski. Since he owed Reb Naftali twenty thousand guldens, the prince's property was a permanent pawn, and Reb Naftali had built for himself a water mill and a brewery and had sown hundreds of acres with hops. His wife, Nesha, came from a wealthy family in Prague. They could afford to hire the finest tutors for Akhsa. One taught her the Bible, another French, still another the pianoforte, and a fourth dancing. She learned everything quickly. At eight, she was playing chess with her grandfather. Reb Naftali didn't need to offer a dowry for her marriage, since she was heir to his entire fortune.

Matches were sought for her early, but her grandmother was hard to please. She would look at a boy proposed by the marriage brokers and say, "He has the shoulders of a fool," or, "He has the narrow forehead of an ignoramus."

One day Nesha died unexpectedly. Reb Naftali was in his late seventies and it was unthinkable that he remarry. Half his day he devoted to religion, the other half to business. He rose at daybreak and pored over the Talmud and the Commentaries and wrote letters to community elders. When a man was sick, Reb Naftali went to comfort him. Twice a week he visited the poorhouse with Akhsa, who carried a contribution of soup and groats herself. More than once, Akhsa, the pampered and scholarly, rolled up her sleeves and made beds there.

In the summer, after midday sleep, Reb Naftali ordered his britska harnessed and he rode around the fields and village with Akhsa. While they rode, he discussed business, and it was known that he listened to her advice just as he had listened to her grandmother's.

But there was one thing that Akhsa didn't have — a friend. Her grandmother had tried to find friends for her; she had even lowered her standards and invited girls from Krasnobród. But Akhsa had no patience with their chatter about clothes and household matters. Since the tutors were all men, Akhsa was kept away from them, except for lessons. Now her grandfather became her only companion. Reb Naftali had met famous noblemen in his lifetime. He had been to fairs in Warsaw, Kraków, Danzig, and Koenigsberg. He would sit for hours with Akhsa and tell her about rabbis and miracle workers, about the disciples of the false messiah Sabbatai Zevi, quarrels in the Sejm, the caprices of the Zamojskis, the Radziwills, and the Czartoryskis — their wives, lovers, courtiers. Sometimes Akhsa would cry out, "I wish you were my fiancé, not my grandfather!" and kiss his eyes and his white beard.

Reb Naftali would answer, "I'm not the only man in Poland. There are plenty like me, and young to boot."

"Where, Grandfather? Where?"

After her grandmother's death, Akhsa refused to rely on anyone else's judgment in the choice of a husband — not even her grandfather's. Just as her grandmother saw only bad, Reb Naftali saw only good. Akhsa demanded that the matchmakers allow her to meet her suitor, and Reb Naftali finally consented. The young pair would be brought together in a room, the door would be left open, and a deaf old woman servant would stand at the threshold to watch that the meeting be brief and without frivolity. As a rule, Akhsa stayed with the young man not more than a few minutes. Most of the suitors seemed dull and silly. Others tried to be clever and made undignified jokes. Akhsa dismissed them abruptly. How strange, but her grandmother still expressed her opinion. Once, Akhsa heard her say clearly, "He has the snout of a pig." Another time, she said, "He talks like the standard letter book."

Akhsa knew quite well that it was not her grandmother speaking. The dead don't return from the other world to comment on prospective fiancés. Just the same, it was her grandmother's voice, her style. Akhsa wanted to talk to her grandfather about it, but she was afraid he would think her crazy. Besides, her grandfather longed for his wife, and Akhsa didn't want to stir up his grief.

When Reb Naftali Holishitzer realized that his granddaughter was driving away the matchmakers, he was troubled. Akhsa was now past her eighteenth year. The people in Krasnobród had begun to gossip — she was demanding a knight on a white horse or the moon in heaven; she would stay a spinster. Reb Naftali decided not to give in to her whims any more but to marry her off. He went to a yeshiva and brought back with him a young man named Zemach, an orphan and a devout scholar. He was dark as a gypsy, small, with broad shoulders. His sidelocks were thick. He was nearsighted and studied eighteen hours a day. The moment he reached Krasnobród, he went to the study house and began to sway in front of an open volume of the Talmud. His sidelocks swayed, too. Students came to talk with him, and he spoke without lifting his gaze from the book. He seemed to know the Talmud by heart, since he caught everyone misquoting.

Akhsa demanded a meeting, but Reb Naftali replied that this was conduct befitting tailors and shoemakers, not a girl of good breeding. He warned Akhsa that if she drove Zemach away he would disinherit her. Since men and women were in separate rooms during the engagement party, Akhsa had no chance of seeing Zemach until the marriage contract was to be signed. She looked at him and heard her grandmother say, "They've sold you shoddy goods."

Her words were so clear it seemed to Akhsa that everyone should have heard them, but no one had. The girls and women crowded around her, congratulating her and praising her beauty, her dress, her jewelry. Her grandfather passed her the contract and a quill, and her grandmother cried out, "Don't sign!" She grabbed Akhsa's elbow and a blot formed on the paper.

Reb Naftali shouted, "What have you done!"

Akhsa tried to sign, but the pen fell from her hand. She burst into tears. "Grandfather, I can't."

"Akhsa, you shame me."

"Grandfather, forgive me." Akhsa covered her face with her hands. There was an outcry. Men hissed and women laughed and wept. Akhsa cried silently. They half led, half carried her to her room and put her on her bed.

Zemach exclaimed, "I don't want to be married to this shrew!"

He pushed through the crowd and ran to get a wagon back to the yeshiva. Reb Naftali went after him, trying to pacify him with words and money, but Zemach threw Reb Naftali's banknotes to the ground. Someone brought his wicker trunk from the inn where he had stayed. Before the wagon pulled away, Zemach cried out, "I don't forgive her, and God won't, either."

For days after that, Akhsa was ill. Reb Naftali Holishitzer, who had been successful all his life, was not accustomed to failure. He became sick; his face took on a yellow pallor. Women and girls tried to comfort Akhsa. Rabbis and elders came to visit Reb Naftali, but he got weaker as the days passed. After a while, Akhsa gained back her strength and left her sickbed. She went to her grandfather's room, bolting the door behind her. The maid who listened and spied through the keyhole reported that she had heard him say, "You are mad!"

Akhsa nursed her grandfather, brought him his medicine and bathed him with a sponge, but the old man developed an inflammation of the lungs. Blood ran from his nose. His urine stopped. Soon he died. He had written his will years before and left one-third of his estate to charity and the rest to Akhsa.

According to the law, one does not sit shivah in mourning after the death of a grandfather, but Akhsa went through the ceremony anyway. She sat on a low stool and read the book of Job. She ordered that no one be let in. She had shamed an orphan — a scholar — and caused the death of her grandfather. She became melancholy. Since she had read the story of Job before, she began to search in her grandfather's library for another book to read. To her amazement, she found a Bible translated into Polish — the New Testament as well as the Old. Akhsa knew it was a forbidden book, but she turned the pages anyway. Had her grandfather read it, Akhsa wondered. No, it couldn't be. She remembered that on the Gentile feast days, when holy icons and pictures were carried in processions near the house, she was not allowed to look out of the window. Her grandfather told her it was idolatry. She wondered if her grandmother had read this Bible. Among the pages she found some pressed cornflowers — a flower her grandmother had often picked. Grandmother came from Bohemia; it was said that her father had belonged to the Sabbatai Zevi sect. Akhsa recalled that Prince Czartoryski used to spend time with her grandmother when he visited the estate, and praised the way she spoke Polish. If she hadn't been a Jewish girl, he said, he would have married her — a great compliment.

That night Akhsa read the New Testament to the last page. It was difficult for her to accept that Jesus was God's only begotten son and that He rose from the grave, but she found this book more comforting to her tortured spirit than the castigating words of the prophets, who never mentioned the Kingdom of Heaven or the resurrection of the dead. All they promised was a good harvest for good deeds and starvation and plague for bad ones.

On the seventh night of shivah, Akhsa went to bed. The light was out and she was dozing when she heard footsteps that she recognized as her grandfather's. In the darkness, her grandafther's figure emerged: the light face, the white beard, the mild features, even the skullcap on his high forehead. He said in a quiet voice, "Akhsa, you have committed an injustice."

Akhsa began to cry. "Grandfather, what should I do?"

"Everything can be corrected."

"How?"

"Apologize to Zemach. Become his wife."

"Grandfather, I hate him."

"He is your destined one."

He lingered for a moment, and Akhsa could smell his snuff, which he used to mix with cloves and smelling salts. Then he vanished and an empty space remained in the darkness. She was too amazed to be frightened. She leaned against the headboard, and after some time she slept.

She woke with a start. She heard her grandmother's voice. This was not a murmuring like Grandfather's but the strong voice of a living person. "Akhsa, my daughter."

Akhsa burst into tears. "Grandmother, where are you?"

"I'm here."

"What should I do?"

"Whatever your heart desires."

"What, Grandmother?"

"Go to the priest. He will advise you."

Akhsa became numb. Fear constricted her throat. She managed to say, "You're not my grandmother. You're a demon."

"I am your grandmother. Do you remember how we went wading in the pond that summer night near the flat hill and you found a gulden in the water?"

"Yes, Grandmother."

"I could give you other proof. Be it known that the Gentiles are right. Jesus of Nazareth is the Son of God. He was born of the Holy Spirit as prophesied. The rebellious Jews refused to accept the truth and therefore they are punished. The Messiah will not come to them because He is here already."

"Grandmother, I'm afraid."

"Akhsa, don't listen!" her grandfather suddenly shouted into her right ear. "This isn't your grandmother. It's an evil spirit disguised to trick you. Don't give in to his blasphemies. He will drag you into perdition."

"Akhsa, that is not your grandfather but a goblin from behind the bathhouse," Grandmother interrupted. "Zemach is a ne'er-do-well, and vengeful to boot. He will torment you, and the children he begets will be vermin like him. Save yourself while there is time. God is with the Gentiles."

"Lilith! She-demon! Daughter of Ketev M'riri!" Grandfather growled.

"Liar!"

Grandfather became silent, but Grandmother continued to talk, although her voice faded. She said, "Your real grandfather learned the truth in Heaven and converted. They baptized him with heavenly water and he rests in Paradise. The saints are all bishops and cardinals. Those who remain stubborn are roasted in the fires of Gehenna. If you don't believe me, ask for a sign."

"What sign?"

"Unbutton your pillowcase, rip open the seams of the pillow, and there you will find a crown of feathers. No human hand could make a crown like this."

Her grandmother disappeared, and Akhsa fell into a heavy sleep. At dawn, she awoke and lit a candle. She remembered her grandmother's words, unbuttoned the pillowcase, and ripped open the pillow. What she saw was so extraordinary she could scarcely believe her eyes: down and feathers entwined into a crown, with little ornaments and complex designs no worldly master could have duplicated. On the top of the crown was a tiny cross. It was all so airy that Akhsa's breath made it flutter. Akhsa gasped. Whoever had made this crown — an angel or a demon — had done his work in darkness, in the inside of a pillow. She was beholding a miracle. She extinguished the candle and stretched out on the bed. For a long time she lay without any thoughts. Then she went back to sleep.

In the morning when she awoke, Akhsa thought she had had a dream, but on the night table she saw the crown of feathers. The sun made it sparkle with the colors of the rainbow. It looked as if it were set with the smallest of gems. She sat and contemplated the wonder. Then she put on a black dress and a black shawl and asked that the carriage be brought round for her. She rode to the house were Koscik, the priest, resided. The housekeeper answered her knock. The priest was nearing seventy and he knew Akhsa. He had often come to the estate to bless the peasants' bread at Easter and to give rites to the dying and conduct weddings and funerals. One of Akhsa's teachers had borrowed a Latin-Polish dictionary from him. Whenever the priest visited, Akhsa's grandmother invited him to her parlor and they conversed over cake and vishniak.

The priest offered Akhsa a chair. She sat down and told him everything. He said, "Don't go back to the Jews. Come to us. We will see to it that your fortune remains intact."

"I forgot to take the crown. I want to have it with me."

"Yes, my daughter, go and bring it."

Akhsa went home, but a maid had cleaned her bedroom and

dusted the night table; the crown had vanished. Akhsa searched in the garbage ditch, in the slops, but not a trace could she find.

Soon after that, the terrible news was abroad in Krasnobród that Akhsa had converted.

■ How did your narrator physically demonstrate his easy control of the story?

Here are two works about that uniquely American obsession, high-school football. Let Wright's images appear clear and vivid; don't miss a syllable.

Autumn Begins in Martins Ferry, Ohio
JAMES WRIGHT

In the Shreve High football stadium,
I think of Polacks nursing long beers in Tiltonsville,
And gray faces of Negroes in the blast furnace at Benwood,
And the ruptured night watchman of Wheeling Steel,
Dreaming of heroes.

All the proud fathers are ashamed to go home.
Their women cluck like starved pullets,
Dying for love.

Therefore,
Their sons grow suicidally beautiful
At the beginning of October,
And gallop terribly against each other's bodies.

■ What happens to the speaker between "Dying for love" and "Therefore"?
■ How did you create the world that gives rise to the game?

H. G. Bissinger's controversial account of one season of the Odessa, Texas, Permian High School Panthers explores the impact of high-school football on a town, a school, and the people who play and watch it. In this excerpt he cannily captures the excitement, tension, and thrill of an opening game. Let your body show us the power of these descriptions and memories.

FROM Friday Night Lights
H. G. BISSINGER

"Some of you haven't played before, been in the spotlight," said assistant coach Tam Hollingshead in those waning hours before Permian would take the field against El Paso Austin. He knew what the jitters of the season opener could do, how the most talented kid could come unglued in the sea of all those lights and those thousands of fans. He offered some succinct advice.

"Have some fun, hustle your ass, and stick the hell out of 'em."

"It's not a party we're goin' to, it's a business trip," Mike Belew told the running backs. "If you get hurt, that's fine, you're hurt. But if you get a lick, and you're gonna lay there and whine about it, you don't belong on the field anyway."

The team left the field house and made its way to the stadium in a caravan of yellow school buses. They went through their pre-game warmups with methodical, meticulous determination. Then they went to the dressing room and sat in silence before Gaines called the team to huddle around him. He didn't say much. He didn't have to.

Everyone knew what was at stake, that if all went without a hitch, this game would be the beginning of a glorious stretch that would not end until the afternoon of December 17 with a state championship trophy. It would be a sixteen-game season, longer than that of any college team in America and as long as most of the pro teams' seasons. Three and a half months of pure devotion to football where nothing else mattered, nothing else made a difference.

"That 1988 season is four and a half minutes away," Gaines said quietly with a little smile still on his lips. "Let's have a great one."

At the very sight of the team at the edge of the stadium, hundreds of elementary school kids started squealing in delight. They wore imitation cheerleading costumes and sweatshirts that said PERMIAN PANTHERS #1. They began yelling the war cry of "MO-JO! MO-JO! MO-JO!" in frantic unison, rocking their arms back and forth. A little girl in glasses put her hand to her mouth, as if she had seen something incredible, and it made her momentarily speechless between screams. As the black wave of the Permian players moved out into the middle of the field, eight thousand other souls who had filled the home side rose to give a standing ovation. This moment, and not January first, was New Year's day.

Brian Johnson opened the season with a fifteen-yard run off the right side through a gaping hole to the Permian 47, lurching forward for every possible extra inch. Two quick passes from Winchell to split end Lloyd Hill gave Permian a first down at the El Paso Austin ten. Winchell looked good, setting up with poise in the pocket, throwing nicely, no rushed throws skittering off the hand.

Then Don Billingsley, the starting tailback for the Permian Panthers, got the ball on a pitch. He was a senior, and it was his debut as a starter.

The roars of the crowd got louder and louder as Don took the ball and headed for the goal line. A touchdown on the first drive of the season seemed destined, to the delight of the thousands who were there. And no one wanted it more, no one felt it more, than Charlie Billingsley.

It was his son Don down there on that field with the ball. But it was more than the natural swell of parental pride that stirred inside him.

Twenty years earlier, Charlie Billingsley himself had worn the black and white of Permian, not as some two-bit supporter but as a star, a legend. He still had powerful memories of those days, and as he sat in the stands on this balmy and beautiful night where the last wisps of clouds ran across the sky like a residue of ash from a once-brilliant fire, it seemed impossible not to look down on the field and see his own reflection.

❚ How did you suggest the attitudes of the many people who inhabit this excerpt?

❚ Did you carefully follow Bissinger's sentence length?

In recounting *One Writer's Beginnings*, Eudora Welty demonstrates how her enduring themes and her commanding skill came into being. This memoir allows the interpreter to enjoy both the immediacy of the scene and the acuity of reflection. Young Eudora listens with her whole body — be sure you tell the story the same way.

FROM *One Writer's Beginnings*

EUDORA WELTY

In that vanished time in small-town Jackson, most of the ladies I was familiar with, the mothers of my friends in the neighborhood, were busiest when they were sociable. In the afternoons there was regular visiting up and down the little grid of residential streets. Everybody had calling cards, even certain children; and newborn babies themselves were properly announced by sending out their tiny engraved calling cards attached with a pink or blue bow to those of their parents. Graduation presents to high-school pupils were often "card cases." On the hall table in every house the first thing you saw was a silver tray waiting to receive more calling cards on top of the stack already piled up like jackstraws; they were never thrown away.

My mother let none of this idling, as she saw it, pertain to her; she went her own way with or without her calling cards, and though she was fond of her friends and they were fond of her, she had little time for small talk. At first, I hadn't known what I'd missed.

When we at length bought our first automobile, one of our neighbors was often invited to go with us on the family Sunday afternoon ride. In Jackson it was counted an affront to the neighbors to start out for anywhere with an empty seat in the car. My mother sat in the back with her friend, and I'm told that as a small child I would ask to sit in the middle, and say as we started off, "Now *talk.*"

There was dialogue throughout the lady's accounts to my mother. "I said" . . . "He said" . . . "And I'm told she very plainly said" . . . "It was midnight before they finally heard, and what do you think it *was?*"

What I loved about her stories was that everything happened in *scenes.* I might not catch on to what the root of the trouble was in all that happened, but my ear told me it was dramatic. Often she said, "The crisis had come!"

This same lady was one of Mother's callers on the telephone who always talked a long time. I knew who it was when my mother would only reply, now and then, "Well, I declare," or "You don't say so," or "Surely not." She'd be standing at the wall telephone, listening against her will, and I'd sit on the stairs close by her. Our telephone had a little bar set into the handle which had to be pressed and held down to keep the connection open, and when her friend had said goodbye, my mother needed me to prize her fingers loose from the little bar; her grip had become paralyzed. "What did she say?" I asked.

"She wasn't *saying* a thing in this world," sighed my mother. "She was just ready to talk, that's all."

My mother was right. Years later, beginning with my story "Why I Live at the P.O.," I wrote reasonably often in the form of a monologue that takes possession of the speaker. How much more gets told besides!

This lady told everything in her sweet, marveling voice, and meant every word of it kindly. She enjoyed my company perhaps even more than my mother's. She invited me to catch her doodlebugs; under the trees in her backyard were dozens of their holes. When you stuck a broom straw down one and called, "Doodlebug, doodlebug, your house is on fire and all your children are burning up," she believed this is why the doodlebug came running out of the hole. This was why I loved to call up her doodlebugs instead of ours.

My mother could never have told me her stories, and I think I knew why even then: my mother didn't believe them. But I could listen to this murmuring lady all day. She believed everything she heard, like the doodlebug. And so did I.

This was a day when ladies' and children's clothes were very often made at home. My mother cut out all the dresses and her little boys' rompers, and a sewing woman would come and spend the day upstairs in the sewing room fitting and stitching them all. This was Fannie. This old black sewing woman, along with her speed and dexterity, brought along a great provision of up-to-the-minute news. She spent her life going from family to family in town and worked right in its bosom, and nothing could stop her. My mother would try, while I stood being pinned up. "Fannie, I'd rather Eudora didn't hear that." "That" would be just what I was longing to hear, whatever it was. "I don't want her exposed to gossip" — as if gossip were measles and I could catch it. I did catch some of it but not enough. "Mrs. O'Neil's oldest daughter she had her wedding dress *tried on*, and all her fine underclothes featherstitched and ribbon run in and then — " "I think that will do, Fannie," said my mother. It was tantalizing never to be exposed long enough to hear the end.

Fannie was the worldliest old woman to be imagined. She could do whatever her hands were doing without having to stop talking; and she could speak in a wonderfully derogatory way with any number of pins stuck in her mouth. Her hands steadied me like claws as she stumped on her knees around me, tacking me together. The gist of her tale would be lost on me, but Fannie didn't bother about the ear she was telling it to; she just liked telling. She was like an author. If fact, for a good deal of what she said, I daresay she *was* the author.

Long before I wrote stories, I listened for stories. Listening *for* them is something more acute than listening *to* them. I suppose it's an early form of participation in what goes on. Listening children know stories are *there*. When their elders sit and begin, children are just waiting and hoping for one to come out, like a mouse from its hole.

It was taken entirely for granted that there wasn't any lying in our family, and I was advanced in adolescence before I realized that in plenty of homes where I played with schoolmates and went to their parties, children lied to their parents and parents lied to their children and to each other. It took me a long time to realize that these very same everyday lies, and the stratagems and jokes and tricks and dares that went with them, were in fact the basis of the *scenes* I so well loved to hear about and hoped for and treasured in the conversation of adults.

My instinct — the dramatic instinct — was to lead me, eventually, on the right track for a storyteller: the *scene* was full of hints, pointers, suggestions, and promises of things to find out and know about human beings. I had to grow up and learn to listen for the unspoken as well as the spoken — and to know a truth, I also had to recognize a lie.

> ▌ How and where did your muscles show us the remembered pleasure the persona so obviously relishes?

This poem performs brilliantly, but be sure that you know *exactly* what the relationship is between the speaker and the events. And don't throttle the end — it will take care of itself.

The .38

TED JOANS

I hear the man downstairs slapping the hell out of his stupid wife
        again
I hear him push and shove her around the overcrowded room
I hear his wife scream and beg for mercy
I hear him tell her there is no mercy
I hear the blows as they land on her beautiful body
I hear glasses and pots and pans falling
I hear her fleeing from the room
I hear them running up the stairs
I hear her outside my door
I hear him coming toward her outside my door
I hear her banging on my door
I hear him bang her head on my door
I hear him trying to drag her away from my door
I hear her hands desperate on my doorknob
I hear the blows of her head against my door
I hear him drag her down the stairs
I hear her head bounce from step to step
I hear them again in their room
I hear a loud smack across her face (I guess)
I hear her groan — then
I hear the eerie silence
I hear him open the top drawer of his bureau (the .38 lives there)
I hear the fast beat of my heart
I hear the drops of perspiration fall from my brow
I hear him yell I warned you
I hear him say damn you I warned you and now it's too late
I hear the loud report of the thirty eight caliber revolver then

I hear it again and again the Smith and Wesson
I hear the bang bang bang of four death dealing bullets
I hear my heart beat faster and louder — then again
I hear the eerie silence
I hear him walk out of their overcrowded room
I hear him walk up the steps
I hear him come toward my door
I hear his hand on the doorknob
I hear the doorknob click
I hear the door slowly open
I hear him step into my room
I hear the click of the thirty eight before the firing pin hits the
      bullet

I hear the loud blast of the powder exploding in the chamber of
        the .38
I hear the heavy lead nose of the bullet swiftly cutting its way
        through the barrel of the .38
I hear it emerge into space from the .38
I hear the bullet of death flying toward my head the .38
I hear it coming faster than sound the .38
I hear it coming closer to my sweaty forehead the .38
I hear its weird whistle the .38
I hear it give off a steamlike noise when it cuts through my sweat
        the .38
I hear it singe my skin as it enters my head the .38 and
I hear death saying, *Hello, I'm here!*

▌ At what line did terror finally fill the speaker? What was your
body *doing*?

Here is a poem that may prove Wallace Stevens's opinion that poetry can
kill a man. Time operates here in a special way and permits the speaker to
check all the body's responses to invasions. Don't miss any of the opportunities for kinesthetic response.

Still Life
DIANE ACKERMAN

The bullet has almost entered the brain:
I can feel it sprint down the gunbarrel
rolling each bevel around like a hoop
on a pigslide of calibrated steel and oil.
Now it whistles free and aloft
in that ice-cold millimeter of air,
then boils as the first layer of skin
shales off like ragged leaves of soap.
The trigger's omnipresent click
makes triggers all over the body fire
to the sound of Japanese shutters closing
one by one a skein of threads.
Now it tunnels through palisades,
veins, arteries, white corpuscles
red and battered as swollen ghosts,
cuts the struts on a glacial bone
jutting out like the leg of a single flamingo,

feints and draws in close for the kill,
egged on by a mousegray parliament of cells.

▌ Where was your speaker's focus? Why?

As in the previous poems, there is no mistaking the strong kinetic and kinesthetic imagery throughout this selection. Although the style may seem closer to prose than to poetry, don't neglect the contribution of the lines as units of the thought progression. The insistent *I* is varied sufficiently by the insertions of indirect discourse to help control the pressure and rush of the bulk of the poem. The fulcrum is clear and comes just in time for the persona and for us. The last long sentence is gentle, and this contrast is helped considerably by the line lengths and punctuation.

The Race

SHARON OLDS

When I got to the airport I rushed up to the desk
and they told me the flight was cancelled. The doctors had
said my father would not live through the night
and the flight was cancelled. A young man with a
dark blond mustache told me
another airline had a non-stop
leaving in seven minutes — see that
elevator over there well go
down to the first floor, make a right you'll
see a yellow bus, get off at the
second Pan Am terminal — I
ran, I who have no sense of direction
raced exactly where he'd told me, like a fish
slipping upstream deftly against the
flow of the river. I jumped off that bus with my
heavy bags and ran, the bags
wagged me from side to side as if to
prove I was under the claims of the material, I
ran up to a man with a white flower on his breast,
I who always go to the end of the line, I said
Help me. He looked at my ticket, he said make a
left and then a right go up the moving stairs and then
run. I raced up the moving stairs
two at a time, at the top I saw the
long hollow corridor and
then I took a deep breath, I said
goodbye to my body, goodbye to comfort, I

used my legs and heart as if I would
gladly use them up for this, to
touch him again in this life. I ran and the
big heavy dark bags
banged me, wheeled and swam around me like
planets in wild orbits — I have seen
pictures of women running down roads with their
belongings tied in black scarves
grasped in their fists, running under serious
gray historical skies — I blessed my
long legs he gave me, my strong
heart I abandoned to its own purpose, I
ran to Gate 17 and they were
just lifting the thick white
lozenge of the door to fit it into the
socket of the plane. Like the man who is not
too rich, I turned to the side and
slipped through the needle's eye, and then I
walked down the aisle toward my father. The jet was
full and people's hair was shining, they were
smiling, the interior of the plane was filled with a
mist of gold endorphin light,
I wept as people weep when they enter heaven,
in massive relief. We lifted up
gently from one tip of the continent and
did not stop until we set down lightly on the
other edge, I walked into his room and
watched his chest rise slowly and
sink again, all night
I watched him breathe.

▌ How did you show that your muscles remembered the effort of
the race?

Langston Hughes was able to condense and make vivid the history of his race from its beginnings through the first quarter of the twentieth century in this brief poem. The repetitions are, of course, a strong unifying factor, as are the motifs. Be careful that they do not obscure the variety and progression. The pride and strength of the persona as he speaks in the first person but also as a voice for an entire race will influence empathy and muscle tone. Don't let the repetition at the beginning of lines become patterned. Allow the verbs to provide the clues for handling them.

The Negro Speaks of Rivers
LANGSTON HUGHES

I've known rivers:
I've known rivers ancient as the world and older than the flow of
    human blood in human veins.
My soul has grown deep like the rivers.
I bathed in the Euphrates when dawns were young.
I built my hut near the Congo and it lulled me to sleep.
I looked upon the Nile and raised the pyramids above it.
I heard the singing of the Mississippi when Abe Lincoln went
    down to New Orleans, and I've seen its muddy bosom turn all
    golden in the sunset.

I've known rivers:
Ancient, dusky rivers.

My soul has grown deep like the rivers.

▌ What physical differences occurred in your persona before the eighth line and before the tenth line? Why?

The old lady whose words we hear in this poem obviously once loved being alive and physically responsive. Be sure to emphasize her memory of the joy of her body. Note the inner strength and fire suggested in the two-line stanza. Rhythm of content reflects the rhythm of her life — as she remembers the past, is frozen in the present, and yearns for what is to come.

Old Lady's Winter Words
THEODORE ROETHKE

To seize, to seize, —
I know that dream.
Now my ardors sleep in a sleeve.
My eyes have forgotten.

Like the half-dead, I hug my last secrets.
O for some minstrel of what's to be,
A bird singing into the beyond,
The marrow of God, talking,
Full merry, a gleam
Gracious and bland,
On a bright stone.
Somewhere, among the ferns and birds,
The great swamps flash.
I would hold high converse
Where the winds gather,
And leap over my eye,
An old woman
Jumping in her shoes.
If only I could remember
The white grass bending away,
The doors swinging open,
The smells, the moment of hay, —
When I went to sea in a sigh,
In a boat of beautiful things.
The good day has gone:
The fair house, the high
Elm swinging around
With its deep shade, and birds.
I have listened close
For the thin sound in the windy chimney,
The fall of the last ash
From the dying ember.
I've become a sentry of small seeds,
Poking alone in my garden.
The stone walks, where are they?
Gone to bolster a road.
The shrunken soil
Has scampered away in a dry wind.
Once I was sweet with the light of myself,
A self-delighting creature,
Leaning over a rock,
My hair between me and the sun,
The waves rippling near me.
My feet remembered the earth,
The loam heaved me
That way and this.
My looks had a voice;
I was careless in growing.

If I were a young man,
I could roll in the dust of a fine rage.

The shadows are empty, the sliding externals.
The wind wanders around the house
On its way to the back pasture.
The cindery snow ticks over stubble.
My dust longs for the invisible.
I'm reminded to stay alive
By the dry rasp of the recurring inane,
The fine soot sifting through my south windows.
It is hard to care about corners,
And the sound of paper tearing.
I fall, more and more,
Into my own silences.
In the cold air,
The spirit
Hardens.

▌ Did your old lady have a clearly lived past *before* she began to
speak? How did you demonstrate this to your audience?

Let your muscles respond to this famous speech on the seven ages of man.
Remember the importance of muscle tone. Keep the progression firm and
unified, but allow time for the physical and emotional transitions. The person
himself does not age, but he visualizes and empathizes.

FROM *As You Like It*

WILLIAM SHAKESPEARE

ACT II, SCENE 7

JAQUES: All the world's a stage,
And all the men and women merely players.
They have their exits and their entrances,
And one man in his time plays many parts,
His acts being seven ages. At first the infant,
Mewling and puking in the nurse's arms.
Then the whining school-boy, with his satchel
And shining morning face, creeping like snail
Unwillingly to school. And then the lover,
Sighing like furnace, with a woeful ballad

Made to his mistress' eyebrow. Then a soldier,
Full of strange oaths, and bearded like the pard,
Jealous in honor, sudden, and quick in quarrel,
Seeking the bubble reputation
Even in the cannon's mouth. And then the justice,
In fair round belly with good capon lin'd,
With eyes severe and beard of formal cut,
Full of wise saws and modern instances;
And so he plays his part. The sixth age shifts
Into the lean and slipper'd pantaloon,
With spectacles on nose and pouch on side,
His youthful hose, well sav'd, a world too wide
For his shrunk shank, and his big manly voice,
Turning again toward childish treble, pipes
And whistles in his sound. Last scene of all,
That ends this strange eventful history,
Is second childishness and mere oblivion,
Sans teeth, sans eyes, sans taste, sans everything.

▌ How did your Jaques incorporate the kinesthetic imagery in
performance?

This memoir is probably as physical and spirited as Maya Angelou's early
life with her older brother, Bailey. Her fascination with everyone and everything in the Christian Methodist Episcopal Church in Stamps, Arkansas, has
not diminished with time. Keep those bodies alive!

FROM *I Know Why the Caged Bird Sings*
MAYA ANGELOU

In the Christian Methodist Episcopal Church the children's section
was on the right, cater-cornered from the pew that held those ominous women called the Mothers of the Church. In the young people's
section the benches were placed close together, and when a child's
legs no longer comfortably fitted in the narrow space, it was an
indication to the elders that that person could now move into the
intermediate area (center church). Bailey and I were allowed to sit
with the other children only when there were informal meetings,
church socials or the like. But on the Sundays when Reverend
Thomas preached, it was ordained that we occupy the first row,
called the mourners' bench. I thought we were placed in front because Momma was proud of us, but Bailey assured me that she just
wanted to keep her grandchildren under her thumb and eye.

Reverend Thomas took his text from Deuteronomy. And I was stretched between loathing his voice and wanting to listen to the sermon. Deuteronomy was my favorite book in the Bible. The laws were so absolute, so clearly set down, that I knew if a person truly wanted to avoid hell and brimstone, and being roasted forever in the devil's fire, all she had to do was memorize Deuteronomy and follow its teaching, word for word. I also liked the way the word rolled off the tongue.

Bailey and I sat alone on the front bench, the wooden slats pressing hard on our behinds and the backs of our thighs. I would have wriggled just a bit, but each time I looked over at Momma, she seemed to threaten, "Move and I'll tear you up," so, obedient to the unvoiced command, I sat still. The church ladies were warming up behind me with a few hallelujahs and Praise the Lords and Amens, and the preacher hadn't really moved into the meat of the sermon.

It was going to be a hot service.

On my way into church, I saw Sister Monroe, her open-faced gold crown glinting when she opened her mouth to return a neighborly greeting. She lived in the country and couldn't get to church every Sunday, so she made up for her absences by shouting so hard when she did make it that she shook the whole church. As soon as she took her seat, all the ushers would move to her side of the church because it took three women and sometimes a man or two to hold her.

Once when she hadn't been to church for a few months (she had taken off to have a child), she got the spirit and started shouting, throwing her arms around and jerking her body, so that the ushers went over to hold her down, but she tore herself away from them and ran up to the pulpit. She stood in front of the altar, shaking like a freshly caught trout. She screamed at Reverend Taylor. "Preach it. I say, preach it." Naturally he kept on preaching as if she wasn't standing there telling him what to do. Then she screamed an extremely fierce "I said, preach it" and stepped up on the altar. The Reverend kept on throwing out phrases like home-run balls and Sister Monroe made a quick break and grasped for him. For just a second, everything and everyone in the church except Reverend Taylor and Sister Monroe hung loose like stockings on a washline. Then she caught the minister by the sleeve of his jacket and his coattail, then she rocked him from side to side.

I have to say this for our minister, he never stopped giving us the lesson. The usher board made its way to the pulpit, going up both aisles with a little more haste than is customarily seen in church. Truth to tell, they fairly ran to the minister's aid. Then two of the deacons, in their shiny Sunday suits, joined the ladies in white on the pulpit, and each time they pried Sister Monroe loose from the preacher he took another deep breath and kept on preaching, and Sister Monroe grabbed him in another place, and more firmly. Reverend Taylor was helping his rescuers as much as possible by jumping around when he got a chance. His voice at one point got so low it sounded like a roll of thunder, then Sister Monroe's "Preach it" cut through the roar, and we all wondered (I did, in any case) if it would ever end. Would they go on forever, or get tired out at last like a game of blindman's bluff that lasted too long, with nobody caring who was "it"?

I'll never know what might have happened, because magically the pandemonium spread. The spirit infused Deacon Jackson and Sister Willson, the chairman of the usher board, at the same time. Deacon Jackson, a tall, thin, quiet man, who was also a part-time Sunday school teacher, gave a scream like a falling tree, leaned back on thin air and punched Reverend Taylor on the arm. It must have hurt as much as it caught the Reverend unawares. There was a moment's break in the rolling sounds and Reverend Taylor jerked around surprised, and hauled off and punched Deacon Jackson. In the same second Sister Willson caught his tie, looped it over her fist a few times, and pressed down on him. There wasn't time to laugh or cry before all three of them were down on the floor behind the altar. Their legs spiked out like kindling wood.

Sister Monroe, who had been the cause of all the excitement, walked off the dais, cool and spent, and raised her flinty voice in the hymn, "I came to Jesus, as I was, worried, wound, and sad, I found in Him a resting place and He has made me glad."

The minister took advantage of already being on the floor and asked in a choky little voice if the church would kneel with him to offer a prayer of thanksgiving. He said we had been visited with a mighty spirit, and let the whole church say Amen.

On the next Sunday, he took his text from the eighteenth chapter of the Gospel according to St. Luke, and talked quietly but seriously about the Pharisees, who prayed in the streets so that the public would be impressed with their religious devotion. I doubt that anyone got the message — certainly not those to whom it was directed. The deacon board, however, did appropriate funds for him to buy a new suit. The other was a total loss.

▌ How did you keep the turmoil from getting out of control?
▌ Did you fully embody Sister Monroe?
▌ Did you take enough time for your audience to see all of it happen?

This is the second poem in Thomas Hardy's *Satires of Circumstance in Fifteen Glimpses*. Be sure we see how thrilling the preacher's voice is to his pupil. Don't let the poem become more than a "glimpse."

In Church

THOMAS HARDY

"And now to God the Father," he ends,
And his voice thrills up to the topmost tiles:
Each listener chokes as he bows and bends,
And emotion pervades the crowded aisles.
Then the preacher glides to the vestry-door,
And shuts it, and thinks he is seen no more.

The door swings softly ajar meanwhile,
And a pupil of his in the Bible class,
Who adores him as one without gloss or guile,
Sees her idol stand with a satisfied smile
And re-enact at the vestry-glass
Each pulpit gesture in deft dumb-show
That had moved the congregation so.

▌ Did you show us the pupil's discovery? Where? How?

Bibliography

Most communication and interpretation textbooks discuss the role of the body in oral communication. These books address more technical and specialized needs. Consult them with specific problems to answer.

Berleant, Arnold. "The Verbal Presence: An Aesthetics of Literary Performance." *Journal of Aesthetics and Art Criticism*, 31 (Spring 1973), 339–346.
    Philosophical exploration of those components of performance that authenticate its aesthetic credentials.

Birdwhistle, Ray L. *Kinesics and Context: Essays on Body Motion and Communication*. Philadelphia: University of Pennsylvania Press, 1970.
    An expansion of one of the early basic studies in the relationship between kinesics and oral communication.

Blackmur, R. P. *Language as Gesture.* New York: Harcourt, Brace and
    Company, 1952.
    A detailed analysis of specific poems to illustrate the theory of poetry
    as language of gesture.

Burke, Kenneth. *The Philosophy of Literary Form: Studies in Symbolic
    Action.* Rev. ed. New York: Random House, Vintage Books, 1957.
    Essays on rhetoric and poetics, but basically a discussion of the theory
    of symbolic action.

Carlsöö, Sven. *How Man Moves.* London: Heinemann, 1975.
    Kinesiological methods and studies suggesting practical implications for
    performers in rehearsal.

Forrest, William Craig. "The Kinesthetic Feel of Literature." *Bucknell
    Review,* 16 (December 1968), 91–106.
    Useful discussion of the ways in which literature feels as it speaks.

Jordan, Richard Douglas. "Persona: The Dancer and the Dance."
    Quadrant, 20 (January 1976), 77–79.
    Brief discussion of the indivisibility of word and act in the speaking and
    the speaker of literature.

Katz, Robert L. *Empathy: Its Nature and Uses.* New York: Macmillan,
    1963.
    Emphasis on the dynamics of empathy and its social and aesthetic uses.

King, Nancy R. *A Movement Approach to Acting.* Englewood Cliffs,
    N.J.: Prentice-Hall, 1981.
    Program for movement training that begins with the performer's self-
    awareness and advances to difficult stage movement.

Klein, Maxine. *Time, Space, and Design for Actors.* Boston: Houghton
    Mifflin Company, 1975.
    Contains helpful theory and exercises for body relaxation, flexibility, and
    control.

Morris, Desmond, Peter Collett, Peter Marsh, and Marie O'Shaugh-
    nessy. *Gestures: Their Origins and Distributions.* New York: Stein
    and Day Publishers, 1979.
    An attempt to trace systematically the geographical range and antiquity
    of gesture.

Nelson, Cary. *The Incarnate Word: Literature as Verbal Space.* Urbana:
    University of Illinois Press, 1973.
    Broad and liberating explanation of the ways in which literature exists
    in the embodiment of language.

Pisk, Litz. *The Actor and His Body.* London: George C. Harrap &
    Company, 1975.
    Contains basic movement exercises that help the performer discover a
    state of "equilibrium" or "freedom" so that performance becomes a

reaction to a thought-feeling impulse rather than a matter of proscribed technique.

Vernon, John. *Poetry and the Body.* Urbana: University of Illinois Press, 1979.

Based largely on R. P. Blackmur's *Language as Gesture,* this study extends the idea that the poetic experience is essentially a kinetic experience activated through the reader's imaginative participation.

II

The Interpretation
of Prose

No difference between man and beast is more important than syntax.

Herbert Read, English Prose Style

SOME ASPECTS OF PROSE

5

In Part I we discussed aspects of analysis that are common to all types of writing. We also showed how we, as interpreters, use the knowledge gained through analysis and through observing the performance that surrounds us to communicate literature — with both our voices and our bodies. Part II concerns prose. Parts III and IV deal with drama and poetry, respectively.

Because all types of literature have certain elements in common, the basic principles of analysis and interpretation apply to all types. For example, an oral interpreter uses the same basic approach to poetry as to any other type of material. But poetry also demands special attention to condensation, sound patterns, and whatever strictures of stanzaic form, meter, and rhyme the poet has imposed. Drama requires special emphasis on character, time, place, and situation — and on the relationship among these elements that sets up an essential conflict. One also should be aware of the dramatic form, which may be either prose or poetry. Prose, on the other hand, may be primarily nondramatic yet may contain passages calling for attention to character and setting. Thus, it presents problems similar to those found in drama. Or prose may be highly suggestive and come very close to poetry in its use of imagery.

Classifying material as prose, drama, or poetry, with smaller subdivisions, should be regarded as only a convenience. Our concern is not with literary labels, except insofar as these labels help us analyze the material. Rather, we are interested in selecting suitable material and in completely understanding each piece of writing we wish to communicate to the listeners. Classification serves only as a starting point for detailed analysis.

An interpreter soon discovers the problems and advantages in each type of literature and then goes beyond this generalization to the specific, individual variations within a particular selection. Regardless of its form or type, each selection should be approached as an individual example. Before we consider various kinds of literature, we review some aspects of literary style found in all prose writing. Because subsequent chapters are devoted to drama and poetry, we focus here on nondramatic prose.

Style

The word *style* comes from the Latin *stilus,* which simply means a pointed instrument for writing. Even today, each writer has a different way of using a writing instrument and while it now may be a word processor rather than a quill, each author may be thought of as having a distinctive style. Indeed, by the end of the sixteenth century the word *style* came to mean a manner of writing or speaking.

George Bernard Shaw said, "He who has nothing to assert has no style." Style demonstrates character in the concrete, physical mode of written expression that appears on the page. Style embodies such technical considerations as overrall organization of ideas; the steps in development of a central idea, as they are evident in major thought units (stanzas in poetry, acts and scenes in drama, and paragraphs in prose); the syntactical characteristics of the sentences within these major thought units; and choice of words and the interrelationship of words within a sentence. Because interpreters are interested in communicating the written symbols orally, they are concerned with additional aspects of style: the way the sentences can be broken up into speech phrases; the relationship of the sounds of the words as they are combined; and the location of stresses, which are necessary for clarity.

As British novelist Arnold Bennett said, "When a writer conceives an idea he conceives it in a form of words. That form of words is his style. . . ." Thus, one's style is shaped by the kind of person one is, by one's general philosophy of life, and by the culture and age in which one lives. For example, what one person refers to as a "charming old inn" can be a "broken-down dump" to another. Style is dictated by the author's attitudes toward the subject matter and toward the intended audience — the readers. Style, the heart of the intrinsic factor of harmony, is basic in establishing the identity of the persona in a selection. Finally, style is also a mode of performance. The interpreter's goal is to match the style of performance with the style of the writing.

Paragraphs

The first step in examining the style of a selection is to become aware of its general organization. The next step is to discover how the organization and arrangement of the elements make up the whole. In prose this process involves a consideration of the major thought units, the *paragraphs.*

Each paragraph is a unit in the thought progression. The length and complexity of the unit and of the sentences that compose it reflect both the author's approach to the thought and the pace at which the idea is developed. In general, short, simple sentences and paragraphs indicate a direct approach and suggest immediacy of experience. Long, complicated sentences and paragraphs suggest a more sophisticated and evaluative approach, perhaps an intellectualization of experience or a reflection on past experiences.

Writers indicate degrees of relationship and importance by what they put together in the paragraphs. For instance, several relevant examples of a key idea may appear in one paragraph. Alternatively, each example may have a separate paragraph, thus adding to its individual importance by setting it off from the others. A paragraph is a distinct subdivision of the main thought; it deals with a particular point and terminates only when that point has been developed. It usually has a slight climax of its own, where a logical point or emotional level emerges and prepares the way for others to follow. Paragraphs are large stepping stones to the main climax and the conclusion.

Sentences

Sentences present practical concerns to the oral interpreter. Pay attention to length and grammatical construction as clues to attitude and tone and as guides to the use of the techniques of pause, rate, emphasis, and inflection in your performance.

Take note of elementary syntactical distinctions such as simple, complex, and compound sentences. Also, consider sentence length, position of subordinate elements, order of words, and use of such effects as parallelism and balanced construction. The syntax of a sentence is a way of grouping the words to show their relationship and to suggest degrees of importance. For example, contrast the syntax in these two sentences: "All the marigolds and pinks in the bungalow gardens were bowed to earth with wetness" and "Drenched were the cold fuchsias." In the first sentence, the order is normal and easily leads to the completed thought. We get an extended view of numerous flower beds. In the second sentence, however, "drenched" is given strong emphasis by its uncommon position at the beginning of the sentence, and our focus is on the degree of wetness, which is intensified by "cold." "Drenched" is much wetter than "wetness."

The writer of the following excerpt is describing how he felt when landing his plane after a dangerous and fantastic flight. He is unable to reflect on the experience he has been through and cannot translate it through his intellect into an ordered pattern. The succession of short sentences that combine statements, questions, and an exclamation gives an almost breathless sense of the writer's emotional exhaustion and his inability to put his experience into words:

> Had I been afraid? I couldn't say. I had witnessed a strange sight. What strange sight? I couldn't say. The sky was blue and the sea was white. I felt I ought to tell someone about it since I was back from so far away! But I had no grip on what I had been through.[1]

Longer sentences can be more formal and probably need to be broken down into speech phrases when they are read aloud. Long modifying phrases and clauses (italicized in the following examples) present the interpreter with a special challenge. Try to determine the core of the sentence. Modifiers at the beginning of a sentence prepare readers for the main idea and orient them toward it, and you must build up to the key words of the thought. A sentence whose elements occur out of the normal order so that the meaning is held up until near the very end of the sentence is said to be of *periodic* construction. Because the periodic sentence delays the completion of meaning, it creates suspense. Because it breaks the usual sentence pattern and alters the normal stresses, it can be especially emphatic:

> *Wandering through clear chambers where the general effect made preferences almost as impossible as if they had been shocks, pausing at open doors where vistas were long and bland,* she would, *even if she had not already known,* have discovered for herself that Poynton was the record of a life.[2]

1. Antoine de Saint Exupéry, *Wind, Sand and Stars.*
2. Henry James, *The Spoils of Poynton.* (Emphasis added.)

Modifiers in the middle of a sentence interrupt the main flow of the thought, even while explaining some elements within it. The meaning should be sustained, and the thread of the principal idea should be carried from one key word to another over the intervening material. At the same time, the contribution of those subordinate elements to the whole should not be nullified:

> The book in question, *which is at once a lasting contribution to English literature and a mere farrago of pretentious mediocrity,* was published about two months ago.[3]

Modifiers at the end of a sentence continue the main idea, expanding or qualifying it, although the skeletal frame of the thought is already complete without them:

> I was at incredible pains in cutting down some of the largest trees for oars and masts, *wherein I was, however, much assisted by his Majesty's shipcarpenters, who helped me in smoothing them after I had done the rough work.*[4]

Sentences that contain parallelism and balanced construction provide another challenge for the oral interpreter. Each of the two sentences that follow logically divides into modifiers and main ideas, and each develops the main idea in a characteristic way. Keep the parallel or coordinate elements equal in value at the same time you point out the connection or contrast between them. A compound sentence, which consists of two independent clauses connected by a conjunction, is an elementary example of syntactical parallelism. The clauses are related in grammatical construction because the ideas are closely connected and have equal value. The connective *and* (or sometimes a semicolon) is the signpost most often used for pointing out coordinations, as it does between parts of a compound subject or predicate. The parallelism may be a balanced construction, in which the parts are quite evenly set up against each other:

> No man is an island, entire of itself; every man is a piece of the continent, a part of the main.[5]

3. Virginia Woolf, *The Common Reader.* (Emphasis added.)

4. Jonathan Swift, *Gulliver's Travels.* (Emphasis added.)

5. John Donne, *Devotions, XVII.*

The parallelism here is easily demonstrated by lining up the parts:

| No man | is an island, | entire of itself; |
| every man | is a piece of the continent, | a part of the main. |

The parallelism also may be a series of elaborately wrought analogies and antitheses that are reflected in the form in which the sentence is cast, as in this example from Shakespeare's *Henry IV, Part I*:

> Harry, I do not only marvel where thou spendest thy time, but also how thou art accompanied; for though the camomile, the more it is trodden on the faster it grows, yet youth the more it is wasted the sooner it wears.

This sentence can be represented as follows:

Harry, I do	not only	marvel	where thou spendest thy time,
	but also		how thou art accompanied;
		for though	the camomile,
			the more it is trodden on
			the faster it grows,
	yet		youth
			the more it is wasted
			the sooner it wears.

The important thing to remember is that at the syntactical level, parallelisms indicate parts of a sentence that are equal in value, although they may not be equal in length or number of syllables. The ideas balance each other and contribute to each other.

Too many sentences of similar construction or similar length can result in a monotonous style that fails to hold the reader's attention. Some textbooks fall victim to this error. Skillful writers vary both the length and structure of sentences and hold their readers' sustained attention by subtle shifts of emphasis and pattern. For instance, an uphill climb through three or four rather lengthy and difficult sentences may be broken by a short sentence, which serves as a plateau on which one can catch one's breath and reorient oneself to the view. Although variety and rhythm in style are controlled by the writer, you should be aware of stylistic changes in pace and use them to emphasize shifts in tone and hold the audience's attention.

Speech Phrases

As we mentioned previously, you probably need to break long, grammatically complex sentences into speech phrases when you read the material aloud. In this way you can ensure that the relationship of the clauses and phrases will be clear.

Speech phrases are often more important to the interpreter than to the writer. The relative lengths of units within the sentence as well as the location of stresses become integral parts of the sound pattern as the interpreter uses them. The division of a sentence into speech phrases is dictated by its punctuation and grammatical structure and by the need to make mood and idea clear to an audience.

Punctuation is the first guide, even though it is meant for the eye rather than the ear. A comma, for example, prevents the eye from running ahead and mistaking the sense of the sentence, but in oral reading a comma does not always demand a pause. A change of the pitch, tempo, or volume of your voice can often serve the same purpose less obtrusively than a pause.

Important clues are also given by semicolons, colons, parentheses, and dashes. A semicolon marks a turn of the thought or a definite separation between two aspects of the same thought, and it usually requires a slight pause to make the relationship clear to the listeners. Parentheses and dashes, in pairs, also mark off distinct speech phrases, which are often interpolative ideas across which the main thought of the sentence should be carried. (Long interpolations, of course, need to be further subdivided for convenience and clarity when reading aloud.) A single dash, or a colon, often marks the pause that occurs just before a summing-up and implies a reference to some previous portion of the sentence.

Because punctuation is inserted as a visual aid in silent reading, unfortunately it does not serve as an infallible or complete guide to follow when establishing speech phrases. In fact, punctuation alone is often inadequate for aural comprehension, and you may need to insert slight pauses for clarity. It is often necessary to use pauses to emphasize similar or contrasting ideas, as in the following example:

> The same cartoon humor that shows goats munching tin cans depicts ostriches swallowing alarm clocks, monkey wrenches, and cylinder heads.[6]

Although the punctuation is correct in this sentence, a pause between "cans" and "depicts" helps balance the parallel ideas when the sentence is read aloud. The following single-sentence paragraph gives an even better example of the problem:

6. Bergen Evans, *The Natural History of Nonsense.*

> There is an amusing belief among many country boys, for instance, that an owl has to turn his head to watch you and must watch you if you are near him, so that if you will only walk completely around him he will wring his own neck.[7]

If this sentence were read aloud without a pause or any attention to the author's punctuation, it would quickly lose an audience in a maze of clauses, and it would convey little of the idea intended. When it is read aloud, with each mark of punctuation reflected in a change of pitch, pace, or volume, the sentence becomes somewhat clearer but still needs work: the punctuation does not take care of the parallel values in "that an owl has to turn his head to watch you and must watch you if you are near him," or of the suspension of thought from "so that" to "he will wring his own neck." Therefore, you need to break down these long units into shorter speech phrases. Be careful, of course, not to destroy the relationship between the parts and the whole.

Balancing Sentences

Some sentences may seem much too long to sustain your audience's attention. The following two sentences (a paragraph from the chapter in Lillian Hellman's *Pentimento* in which she describes the life of her cousin Bethe after her arrival in New Orleans) are good examples:

> Bethe for a short time lived in the modest house on Prytania Street, sleeping on a cot in the dining room, rising at five o'clock to carry it to the back porch, to be the first to heat the water, to make the coffee, to roll and bake the German breakfast rolls that nobody liked. Then, to save the carfare, she walked the long distance to the end of Canal Street, where she carried shoe box stacks back and forth all day, for the German merchant who ran a mean store for sailors off the wharves.

Such sentences understandably cause anxiety; after all, there are a lot of *words* there. Take courage! Every sentence has a fulcrum, or balancing point. Recall our discussion of fulcrums in Chapter 2 and our discussion of speech phrases earlier in this chapter. Paragraphs, stanzas, poems, stories, and sentences have fulcrums: that point where the action and language of the story, play, or poem pivot or balance. Sentences have their own point of balance, where the weight of the words in the first segment roughly equals the weight of the words in the second segment. Remember, there need not be exactly

7. Ibid.

the same number of words or syllables in both components. As you know, one large adult can balance five or six small children on a seesaw. But the weight of sense in the two parts of a sentence should be equal.

In the first of these sentences, then, where would you place the fulcrum? A case can be made for one or two other places, but perhaps the most even balance for this sentence occurs if the fulcrum is placed after "Prytania Street." Thus, the first half of the sentence concerns Bethe's first weeks in New Orleans: "Bethe for a short time lived in the modest house on Prytania Street." The second half of the sentence describes Bethe's life in the house as a succession of activities: "sleeping on a cot in the dining room, rising at five o'clock to carry it to the back porch, to be the first to heat the water, to make the coffee, to roll and bake the German breakfast rolls that nobody liked."

If you consider these parts equal in substance (although they are unequal in numbers of syllables or the time they take to say), you realize that your performance must demonstrate their relationship in a vocal and physical way. We have to see and hear that, to Bethe, living in the house means completing all these tasks — and that's even before leaving for work! If you make each of the tasks in the second part more difficult or onerous because it follows and precedes its neighbors, the audience can have a fuller idea of what Bethe's life was like. You and they will understand why Hellman (who could also write effective short sentences) chose to make this one so long.

Now consider the second sentence. This sentence, which describes a typical work day for the immigrant woman, has a much more typical structure than the first sentence. Where does the sentence logically and substantively divide? While some might place the fulcrum after "Then" (although as a critical and performance decision it seems eccentric), it is better to place the fulcrum after "Canal Street," nicely paralleling the fulcrum of the prior sentence. One part of the sentence then describes how Bethe got to work, and the other part tells what she did there. Thus, the fulcrum clarifies the arrangement of Bethe's day and helps us see clearly the progress and purpose of the sentence.

Taken together, these two long sentences suggest the multitude of activity and the continual pressure Bethe found in New Orleans. If you perform them carefully, the audience, too, can become awed by Bethe's endurance.

Choice of Words

Any discussion of words as an aspect of style to some extent overlaps our earlier discussion of words as an aspect of content, for style and content are obviously inseparable. Nevertheless, the writer's choice of words is a vital part of style and deserves special attention.

We have already made a distinction between the denotations and the connotations of words. Now we should remind ourselves of another important aspect of literary style — the writer's use of allusions, similes, and metaphors. These three types of figures of speech are all means of comparing one thing to another; thus, they are instruments of connotative meaning. They are used in all types of writing, of course, but they are basic to description. They contribute primarily to harmony by intensifying theme or underscoring attitude. This is certainly the function of the simile in Welty's "June Recital" (the studio "decorated like the inside of a candy box") that sets the tone for the excerpt (at the end of this chapter).

The length of words is a practical concern for one who is reading aloud, but from the point of view of style, what is important is whether words are formal, informal, or even colloquial and whether they are unusual or common in everyday speech. In any case, the words should be evaluated in terms of the prevailing tone of the selection. This sentence from Woolf's *The Common Reader*, which also appeared earlier in the chapter, is a delightful example of how word choice can shift within a single sentence to underscore attitude:

> The book in question, which is at once a lasting contribution to English literature and a mere farrago of pretentious mediocrity, was published about two months ago.[8]

Woolf begins with the straightforward, factual "The book in question." This is also the tone of the closing phrase. In the middle of the sentence, however, is the almost classic academic reference to "a lasting contribution to English literature" and the cutting, deliberately elaborate "mere farrago of pretentious mediocrity." It is amusing to know that *farrago* means a hodgepodge and comes from a Latin word meaning mixed fodder for cattle. The author has given a deadly criticism indeed! Although it will not always be necessary for you to delve into the origins and derivations of words, you should be prepared to do so if this would be helpful in bringing out the complete meaning of a sentence.

Tone Color

The sounds of the words an author has chosen are especially important for interpreters, since one of their tasks is to translate the written

8. Virginia Woolf, *The Common Reader*.

symbols into sound symbols for their listeners. Writers who are concerned with appealing to the senses and emotions of their readers carefully establish harmony between what they are describing and the sounds of the words with which they choose to describe it. Of course it is the words, not the separate sounds, that carry the meaning; and it is the connotations of the words that influence the interpreter's pace, vocal quality, and all the rest of the elements of his or her vocal technique. There are, for instance, more factors affecting the way one would say *sleep, slap, slip,* and *slop* than merely the difference in the vowels. Nevertheless, certain combinations of sounds produce articulation problems that slow the pace or give a sharpness to separate words, whereas other combinations lend themselves to smooth linking and help produce a flowing effect. The combination of sounds of vowels and consonants to achieve a particular effect is called *tone color.*

Read the following pair of examples aloud several times, fully realizing the imagery.

> The world was more wintry than he had expected. Hoarfrost lay white over the hard refrozen edges of things — the thatch that roofed the hovels, the ridges of mud, and the stones and rubbish in the lane.[9]

> The weather was airy and light; the stars came nightly into their appointed places; there were rills and cresses and kindling sticks, and fish for the catching in some of the streams.[10]

Now listen to how the sounds of the words in combination enhance and reinforce that imagery — and vice versa. There is a strong contrast in the syntactical structure of the two quotations that helps set up a harmonious rhythm in each. These things are important when a skilled interpreter handles these brief descriptions of weather. They were put there by the author for you to use. Enjoy them!

Prose Rhythm

Another important guide for the interpreter is the rhythm of a prose selection. All well-written prose has *rhythm* — not the formal, patterned rhythm of poetry, but a controlled flow of words that makes relationships clear and causes emphasis to fall on important words.

9. Gladys Schmitt, *The Godforgotten* (New York: Harcourt Brace Jovanovich, Inc., 1972), p. 250.
10. Ibid., p. 301.

We have already mentioned rhythm of content, which is established by the organization of the progression of thoughts and emotions. This type of rhythm depends on the placement of key words and phrases and of the major and minor climaxes, both logical and emotional, throughout the entire selection.

There is also a rhythm in *structure* that becomes evident when prose is read aloud. This prose rhythm is established by the length and grammatical construction of the sentences and speech phrases, and by the position of the stresses. As you group words into thought units and speech phrases, separating them with pauses of varying duration, you are creating cadences. A *cadence* is a flow of sound. Words that are grouped together form a flow of sound. A pause interrupts this flow, whether it is a terminal pause at the end of a sentence or a brief pause to set off a speech phrase. Thus, length and frequency of pauses also become part of prose rhythm.

The rate at which the flows of sound are uttered and the number of syllables within the flows affect the rhythm pattern. A mechanical measurement of the cadences in prose usually is not necessary, although it may prove interesting and helpful. The interpreter whose ear is trained is aware of the existence and contribution of cadences.

The element of *stress* in prose results from a number of factors: the demands of proper pronunciation, the need for clarity, the development of contrast, or the combining of particular sounds. The sentences from *Pentimento* quoted earlier illustrate this. The use of numerous one-syllable words in sequence, for instance, may produce a sharp staccato rhythm, especially if the content is forceful in meaning and if the cadences established by the length of sentences and speech phrases are short. The brief excerpt from *Wind, Sand and Stars* near the beginning of this chapter provides an interesting illustration of this type of cadence.

Description

The form that writing takes may be classified roughly as dialogue, narration, or description. These types are not mutually exclusive. Within the dialogue that makes up a play, characters often sketch in needed background about themselves or about past events. Sometimes they use description as well. Poetry may be purely narrative, purely descriptive, or a combination of the two forms. Most narratives, whether poetry or prose, contain dialogue and revealing sections of description. It is important to be aware of the purpose that is served by such blending of the three forms. We discuss narration and dialogue more thoroughly in chapters 6, 7, and 8 and concentrate here on description.

Descriptive writing appeals to the senses and explores the sensory qualities of people, places, things, and events and ensures vividness and clarity. It engages us physically as well as emotionally because it tells us how something looks, sounds, smells, or tastes. It may describe texture or pressure, heat or cold. It may show movement, energy, or light or may even convey a sense of bulkiness or weightlessness. In its rich appeals to the senses, descriptive writing is important in evoking empathic response.

When you examine a unit of descriptive writing, you may make associations from your own experience. This response should be followed by an objective analysis that enables you to communicate the experience that exists *within* the literature. Suppose, for example, that the subject is a storm at sea. You might never have known such an experience, and as you imagine it you know you would be terrified. The author, however, finds the storm exhilarating. Thus, you need to substitute the memory of another experience — one that had an exhilarating effect on you — to convey the emotion in the writing. An interpreter embodies the emotional experience within the framework of the writing.

When considering each descriptive image in detail, remember the sense of the entire thought unit. Consider, for instance, the thermal implications of the word *hot*. When the word is used in a phrase like "hot shower after a cold hike," one has a natural tendency to let the accompanying suggestion of relaxation show in one's muscles, in the slower tempo of the words, and in a more relaxed vocal tone. If, on the other hand, the word is used in the context of "Ouch! That water is hot!" your muscles become tense, the tempo of the words quickens, and the force and tension of your voice increase. In short, the image-bearing word or phrase should always be combined with the whole unit of thought.

Response to imagery affects your muscle tone and consequently the audience's empathic and emotional response. This is particularly true in the case of appeals to motor responses, but the attendant emotional associations the author has achieved through references to sights, sounds, tastes, and smells also make an empathic contribution.

After you have worked out the various images, consider next what aspects of the imagery contribute most to the total context of the selection. How can you perform particular images in such a way that they are a unifying force, and not a catalogue of separate items? In other words, which sense appeals contribute to unity and harmony, and which add variety and contrast within that unity? When the images are considered in relation to the whole, it is clear that some contribute more than others and should be stressed; those that provide variety within this unity may be played down.

Remember, seeing is believing. Your audience relies on you to see what they are unable to see. Your description is their only means of understanding what the author wants them to see. Until you see it clearly, no audience will be able to see it reflected in your voice and body. The elocutionists used to say, "Impression before expression." *See* what you are describing before telling your audience about it. Unless you do, the audience loses.

You may be tempted to overemphasize some especially vivid images, but you should remember that too much stress on descriptive detail may destroy the essential unity of the material. In your performance you should use the descriptive elements in the same way that you use every other aspect of content and form — subtly and unobtrusively. These elements are only part of the whole, and their importance is dictated by the author's larger purpose. The final step in preparation is to put the material back together so that all parts are coordinated. The final test of your performance is its honesty and the thoroughness of communication with your audience.

Types of Prose

Within the broad range of types of prose writing, there are numerous subdivisions that frequently overlap but differ according to the author's purpose. We look briefly at some of these types as they relate to interpretation.

Factual Prose

The interpreter is not likely to be working extensively with strictly factual prose. Obviously, you would seldom perform material from an encyclopedia or a chemistry textbook. Nevertheless, you may encounter passages or entire units in an essay that are technically factual and out of which the personal reflections of the author develop.

Factual prose, in the strictest definition of the term, is writing in which the author gives verifiable information. It states that something is so. The writer's personal comments are kept to a minimum. Unadulterated examples of this type of writing are probably found only in books on science and mathematics, where one is told, for instance, that "in an isosceles triangle the angles opposite the equal sides are themselves equal," or in an encyclopedia, which states on good authority that John Milton was born in England in 1608 and died in 1674. Objective journalistic reporting also may be considered factual when it limits itself to the simple formula of "who, where, when, what," and possibly "why." In short, factual prose informs, defines, and explains.

The interpreter is more likely to deal with prose in which the author is concerned with the implication or interpretation of the facts. Sometimes the facts provide a touch of humor or satire; in other cases, the implied comment of the author is the desired end, and the factual content is merely a means of achieving that end. The interpreter discovers how the author uses the information and ensures that this same purpose is achieved when the material is communicated to the audience.

The Personal Essay

Personal essays offer a wide variety of material to interest an audience. Their content includes broad humor, philosophy, politics, and religion. Because they have a highly personal point of view, persona and locus are very important. The writer's personality and values are reflected in the facts and concrete objects that have been selected to set up associations. This is especially true in accounts of travel and in autobiographical sketches. The associations and connotations lead readers and listeners beyond the facts and the denotations of words and phrases.

For example, Jacques Barzun describes a certain mathematics teacher by saying, "He would put the chalk to his lips, make a noise like a straining gear box, and write out the correct result." We have no idea what the man looks like, and we do not need to. The depiction of his characteristic gesture of putting chalk to his lips calls forth in us a mental picture of bemused, pedantic concentration. The "noise like a straining gear box" suggests that he is more of a machine than a man, and when the gears start to move, out comes the answer!

Often, especially in humorous essays, an author chooses to write in the first person, whether the selection is autobiographical or not. Certainly we are not expected to believe that James Thurber, for instance, actually experienced all the incidents he recorded in the first person! We are really not so concerned about the actual physical identity of the speaker as we are with the author's wit and sense of the ridiculous that has either exaggerated or played down the details of the incidents and ordered them for our enjoyment. We are often concerned with the age, sex, or social position of the speaker; but we care about these details as they relate to the speaker's situation and to the comments the author makes by implication or direct statement.

Sometimes essayists choose topics that seem impossible for a general audience. Not many people are vitally concerned about "the movement of water through aqueducts and siphons and pumps and forebays and afterbays and weirs and drains," but the novelist and essayist Joan Didion cares deeply about these topics. In "Holy Water" she describes a visit to the California State Water Projects Operations Control Center. For such a visit to mean something other than an odd place for an eccentric to visit, she must make her interest in water and drought have a broader appeal. The best personal essays make clear that what might seem like a peculiar individual concern is in fact remarkably close to a concern we all share — another aspect of the touchstones we mentioned in Chapter 1. Didion, in the first sentence of her essay, recognizes the problem her topic presents. "Some of us who live in arid parts of the world think about water with a reverence others might find excessive." Later, she states, "Not many people I know carry their end of the conversation when I want to talk about water deliveries . . ." But when, in the penultimate paragraph of the essay, she says, "Water is important to people who do not have it, and the same is true of control," we realize that she has, in fact, been talking about something that involves all of us. Needless to say it takes great skill on her part to keep us interested in the topic until we get to that conclusion, but such indirection is typical of one style of personal essay and permits the audience to become involved in a special way in the discovery of something personal about themselves.

A writer uses references for their universal appeal. References are also rooted in an author's background and experiences. They are selected very carefully. Scrutinize all expressions and references that seem to carry a comment, an evaluation, or a judgment. By understanding what all of the words mean and suggest, in themselves and in the total context, you can come to an understanding of who the author is and what the author is saying. Then you will be able to convey that attitude to an audience.

Journals, Diaries, Letters, Testimony, and Paraliterature

Journals and diaries often make excellent selections for performance, because they provide intimate glimpses into special moments in the lives of interesting people. Ostensibly, most diaries are written for the writer's private pleasure. They are likely to be less formal than essays, which are intended for public consumption. The organization of diaries often is dictated by highly subjective associations. A careful examination of the elements of style helps you learn about the writer's personality and reveals attitudes and degrees of emotional involvement. When working with so personal a revelation as a diary or journal, it is important to find out as much as possible about the writer's life and times, since the motivation for recording certain details probably grew directly out of his or her relationship to this environment and the people in it.

One may say that in their writing diarists are speaking to themselves in their own voices. But there is an element of danger in this idea. You must have sufficient projection, both psychological and vocal, to hold your audience's attention and interest. One of the ways to achieve this delicate balance between private thoughts and public expression of them is to allow the writer to "think aloud" while you put thoughts in order or reread them aloud. This procedure helps you remain actively engaged in organizing and expressing the entire entry.

In recent years a wealth of correspondence has been published. Much of the appeal of letters is undoubtedly the same as that of diaries and journals. Letters, however, present an added problem for the interpreter.

First, you need to distinguish whether they are public or private letters. Public letters may be handled very much as you would approach an oration or a public address. They are usually didactic, having been designed to persuade a large group of listeners or readers to a course of action or to the acceptance of an idea. The writer has selected details that have strong universal appeal and refer to matters with which the intended audience is easily familiar. The letter of St. Paul at the end of this chapter is an excellent example of a public letter; it is particularly interesting to examine for word choice and organization. Since the writer of a public letter is speaking to a specific audience, you may find it helpful to imagine that this particular audience and your own audience are identical. This approach helps achieve directness. You may address your listeners in the person of the writer or, more probably, in the person of someone selected to present the letter to the intended audience.

Private letters are likely to involve a complex relationship between writer and recipient, and you need to find out as much as possible about both parties. The letter you are reading may be the reply to a letter received earlier by the writer; consequently, a chain of references may have to be investigated. The method of organization and the style of writing reflect both the purpose of the letter and the relationship between the writer and the person to whom the letter is addressed. Henry James's letter to Grace Norton (at the end of this chapter) is an excellent example of this.

Sometimes you might be more interested in the reaction of the recipient than you are in the writer. In this case you might choose to read the letter as if you are the one to whom it is addressed. If this seems the more desirable approach, you must cope with a twofold problem: how to use the writer's style effectively and, at the same time, how to suggest the reaction of another person. Obviously, this approach is more useful when the relationship between the two people is clearly drawn or is so well known that the response is predictable. Letters are often used in this way within a play or narrative where the characters have been well established. The letter becomes virtually a part of the plot and motivation.

Increasingly, interpreters have found wonderful material for performance in collections of oral histories, testimony, depositions, and transcripts, which are sometimes grouped under the general heading *paraliterature*. This word suggests that in preparing such material an editor's skill is at least as important as the speaker's. But because the words began as speech, they carry with them an immediacy and a conviction that can be startling. In the past two decades, perhaps no one more than Studs Terkel has developed the art of oral history. In such works as *Hard Times, Division Street, Working,* and *The Good War,* Terkel, with his tape recorder, speaks with people from every level of society and in every possible occupation. He asks them to tell him what they have learned or discovered about their own lives, a special period, or an event. Then, with the skill of an artist, he splices together their words to make powerfully funny or poignant or telling testimony to the human condition. We see people whom we may easily know expressing something both unique and timeless. See "Terry Pickens" from *Working* at the end of this chapter.

Oral history projects frequently flourish where archives are housed and can often be the source of impressive and moving material for performance. At the end of this chapter, for example, are selections in which two soldiers in the Revolutionary War tell what they discovered about themselves from fighting. Compare their testimony to that in Al Santoli's *Everything We Had* (Chapter 11) and discover how little war's impact has changed. Sometimes court records provide exciting exchanges between litigants in important cases; the *Congressional Record* offers, on occasion, impressive speeches and exchanges between debating members of Congress. And do not neglect the various collections of memorabilia — letters, notes, journal entries, and reminiscences — that are assembled to mark historic events or to portray a locale or historic period. With careful editing, such prose works can give vivid and powerful glimpses of the personalities who shaped our lives, either in great office or in unrecognized occupations. Because such material records the immediate voices of people struggling to make themselves understood, their communicative effectiveness and power are greatly enhanced. These records are too rich a source for interpreters to overlook.

Folktales and Storytelling

Centuries-old folktales and their narrators — uniquely gifted men and women who tap the magic and mystery of ancient tales — represent the source of oral interpretation. Before an audience of hundreds, or with just a few lucky people around a fire, storytellers charm and enchant with tales whose meaning is larger (and often more touching) than can be easily explained.

Folktales, like folksongs, appeal to the ear and to human interest in organizing experience and learning from encounters with the world. Storytellers mine the vast resources of folktales, which live in all cultures and have thrived in all times; their similarity suggests something of the cohesiveness of human experience. The authoritative collection of these tales is Antti Aarne and Stith Thompson's *The Types of the Folktale*. In this work, the vast range of international folktales that have surmounted the barriers of language, geography, and culture has been catalogued.

Of course, merely consulting this monument of research doesn't make one a storyteller; for one reason, often several versions of a particular story will feature quite markedly different motifs. These differences are the work of the storyteller, the verbal fingerprints of the narrator who, at the moment of telling, shapes the events and dialogue and characters specifically to the attentive audience. For example, a storyteller who is particularly adept with dialects will, in all likelihood, include several speaking characters who will demonstrate that facility; a storyteller who sings well or makes realistic bird-calls will incorporate those skills into the story.

Remember that storytellers aren't verbal in the way writers of stories are verbal. Of course, both use words as the medium to convey the story, but the storyteller — working in the immediacy of any given telling — can't revise, edit, or erase. Storytellers constantly move the tale forward while engaging an audience eagerly listening at their feet. The story the audience sees and hears occurs not so much as carefully marshalled words (although, of course, tellers plan carefully the kinds of vivid language and compelling dialogue they intend to use). Rather, the audience experiences a series of pictures or images which the storyteller explains and explores, or they confront a succession of incidents that build to the point the teller wants to illustrate or celebrate. Each telling of the same tale by the same teller results in a new story that naturally resembles its predecessors in most ways and yet also differs significantly in other ways — ways chosen by the teller to tailor the story for each unique performance. You can begin to see how exhilarating — and challenging — such a task is!

Storytellers have been recorded — both electronically on audio and videotape and literarily in printed recensions or retellings — and students can consult these resources. But recordings are not, finally, the experiences, anymore than saying the words someone else said at another place and in another time will create again the magic for your audience. Consulting recordings will permit you to begin to test your own abilities as a teller of tales. In addition, your own experiences can be further developed by attending storytelling festivals and listening carefully to how others tell the tales that have been told for centuries. In this manner storytellers have always developed: first, awed by the wonder of the teller, they undertake to study (and, sometimes, convincingly imitate) storytellers who strike their interest, then they make their own stories and, finally, they develop their own personal storytelling style. The opportunities are endless, and in storytelling we can find the earliest, easiest, most accessible entry to understanding another culture's rich wisdom and profiting from their special sources of grace and wonder.

Selections for Analysis and Oral Interpretation

In addition to the following excerpts, you will find some interesting descriptive passages in the selections in earlier chapters and within the narratives in Chapter 6.

The style here is as packed as the recital room. Pay particular attention to the shift in imagery as you reach the last paragraph.

FROM *June Recital*
EUDORA WELTY

The night of the recital was always clear and hot; everyone came. The prospective audience turned out in full oppression.

In the studio decorated like the inside of a candy box, with "material" scalloping the mantel shelf and doilies placed under every movable object, now thus made immovable, with streamers of white ribbons and nosegays of pink and white Maman Cochet roses and the last MacLain sweetpeas dividing and re-dividing the room, it was as hot as fire. No matter that this was the first night of June; no electric fans were to whir around while music played. The metronome, ceremoniously closed, stood on the piano like a vase. There was no piece of music anywhere in sight.

When the first unreasoning hush — there was the usual series —

fell over the audience, the room seemed to shake with the agitation of palmetto and feather fans alone, plus the occasional involuntary tick of the metronome within its doors. There was the mixture together of agitation and decoration which could make every little forthcoming child turn pale with a kind of ultimate dizziness. Whoever might look up at the ceiling for surcease would be floundered within a paper design stemming out of the chandelier, as complicated and as unavailing as a cut-out paper snowflake.

Now Miss Eckhart came into the room all changed, with her dark hair pulled low on her brow, and gestured for silence. She was wearing her recital dress which made her look larger and closer-to than she looked at any other times. It was an old dress: Miss Eckhart disregarded her own rules. People would forget that dress between times and then she would come out in it again, the untidy folds not quite spotlessly clean, gathered about her bosom and falling heavy as a coat to the sides; it was tawny crepe-back satin. There was a bodice of browning lace. It was as rich and hot and deep-looking as a furskin. The unexpected creamy flesh on her upper arms gave her a look of emerging from it.

Miss Eckhart, achieving silence, stood in the shadowy spot directly under the chandelier. Her feet, white-shod, shod by Mr. Sissum for good, rested in the chalk circle previously marked on the floor and now, she believed, perfectly erased. One hand, with its countable little muscles so hard and ready, its stained, blue nails, went to the other hand and they folded quite still, holding nothing, until they lost their force by lying on her breast and made a funny little house with peaks and gables. Standing near the piano but not near enough to help, she presided but not with her whole heart on guard against disaster; while disaster was what remained on the minds of the little girls. Starting with the youngest, she called them out.

So they played, and except Virgie, all played their worst. They shocked themselves. Parnell Moody burst into tears on schedule. But Miss Eckhart never seemed to notice or to care. How forgetful she seemed at exactly the moments she should have been agonized! You expected the whip, almost, for forgetting to repeat before the second ending, or for failing to count ten before you came around the curtain at all; and instead you received a strange smile. It was as though Miss Eckhart, at the last, was grateful to you for *anything*.

▌ Did you take the time to allow your narrator to experience each image without being rushed?

▌ How hot was the room?

Joan Didion's skill as novelist, essayist, and screenwriter has been established in part by her flawless ability to select images that connote much wider implications. This speech describes something of her method as it demonstrates her sure shaping of sentences and paragraphs. Capture that distinctive sound.

FROM *"Why I Write"*
JOAN DIDION

Of course I stole the title for this talk, from George Orwell. One reason I stole it was that I like the sound of the words: Why I Write. There you have three short unambiguous words that share a sound, and the sound they share is this:

I

I

I

In many ways writing is the act of saying I, of imposing oneself upon other people, of saying Listen to me, see it my way, change your mind. It's an aggressive, even a hostile act. You can disguise its aggressiveness all you want with veils of subordinate clauses and qualifiers and tentative subjunctives, with ellipses and evasions — with the whole manner of intimating rather than claiming, of alluding rather than stating — but there's no getting around the fact that setting words on paper is the tactic of a secret bully, an invasion, an imposition of the writer's sensibility on the reader's most private space.

I stole the title not only because the words sounded right but because they seemed to sum up, in a no-nonsense way, all I have to tell you. Like many writers I have only this one "subject," this one "area": the act of writing. I can bring you no reports from any other front. I may have other interests: I am "interested," for example, in marine biology, but I don't flatter myself that you would come out to hear me talk about it. I am not a scholar. I am not in the least an intellectual, which is not to say that when I hear the word "intellectual" I reach for my gun, but only to say that I do not think in abstracts. During the years when I was an undergraduate at Berkeley I tried, with a kind of hopeless late-adolescent energy, to buy some temporary visa into the world of ideas, to forge for myself a mind that could deal with the abstract.

In short I tried to think. I failed. My attention veered inexorably back to the specific, to the tangible, to what was generally considered, by everyone I knew then and for that matter have known since, the peripheral. I would try to contemplate the Hegelian dialectic and would find myself concentrating instead on a flowering pear tree outside my window and the particular way the petals fell on my floor. I would try to read linguistic theory and would find myself wondering instead if the lights were on in the bevatron up the hill. When I say that I was wondering if the lights were on in the bevatron you might immediately suspect, if you deal in ideas at all, that I was registering the bevatron as a political symbol, thinking in shorthand about the military-industrial complex and its role in the university community, but you would be wrong. I was only wondering if the lights were on in the bevatron, and how they looked. A physical fact.

I had trouble graduating from Berkeley, not because of this inability to deal with ideas — I was majoring in English, and I could locate the house-and-garden imagery in "The Portrait of a Lady" as well as the next person, "imagery" being by definition the kind of specific that got my attention — but simply because I had neglected to take a course in Milton. For reasons which now sound baroque I needed a degree by the end of that summer, and the English department finally agreed, if I would come down from Sacramento every Friday and talk about the cosmology of *Paradise Lost*, to certify me proficient in Milton. I did this. Some Fridays I took the Greyhound bus, other Fridays I caught the Southern Pacific's City of San Francisco on the last leg of its transcontinental trip. I can no longer tell you whether Milton put the sun or the earth at the center of his universe in *Paradise Lost*, the central question of at least one century and a topic about which I wrote 10,000 words that summer, but I can still recall the exact rancidity of the butter in the City of San Francisco's dining car, and the way the tinted windows on the Greyhound bus cast the oil refineries around Carquinez Straits into a grayed and obscurely sinister light. In short my attention was always on the periphery, on what I could see and taste and touch, on the butter, and the Greyhound bus. During those years I was traveling on what I knew to be a very shaky passport, forged papers: I knew that I was no legitimate resident in any world of ideas. I knew I couldn't think. All I knew then was that I wasn't, and it took me some years to discover what I was.

Which was a writer.

By which I mean not a "good" writer or a "bad" writer but simply a writer, a person whose most absorbed and passionate hours are spent arranging words on pieces of paper. Had my credentials been in order I would never have become a writer. Had I been blessed with even limited access to my own mind there would have been no reason to write. I write entirely to find out what I'm thinking, what I'm looking at, what I see and what it means. What I want and what I fear. Why did the oil refineries around Carquinez Straits seem sinister to me in the summer of 1956? Why have the night lights in the bevatron burned in my mind for twenty years? What is going on in these pictures in my mind?

When I talk about pictures in my mind I am talking, quite specifically about images that shimmer around the edges. There used to be an illustration in every elementary psychology book showing a cat drawn by a patient in varying stages of schizophrenia. This cat had a shimmer around it. You could see the molecular structure breaking down at the very edges of the cat: the cat became the background and the background the cat, everything interacting, exchanging ions. People on hallucinogens describe the same perception of objects. I'm not a schizophrenic, nor do I take hallucinogens, but certain images do shimmer for me. Look hard enough, and you can't miss the shimmer. It's there. You can't think too much about these pictures that shimmer. You just lie low and let them develop. You stay quiet. You don't talk to many people and you keep your nervous system from shorting out and you try to locate the cat in the shimmer, the grammar in the picture.

Just as I meant "shimmer" literally I mean "grammar" literally. Grammar is a piano I play by ear, since I seem to have been out of school the year the rules were mentioned. All I know about grammar is its infinite power. To shift the structure of a sentence alters the meaning of that sentence, as definitely and inflexibly as the position of a camera alters the meaning of the object photographed. Many people know about camera angles now, but not so many know about sentences. The arrangement of the words matters, and the arrangement you want can be found in the picture in your mind. The picture dictates the arrangement. The picture dictates whether this will be a sentence with or without clauses, a sentence that ends hard or a dying-fall sentence, long or short, active or passive. The picture tells you how to arrange the words and the arrangement of the words tells you, or tells me, what's going on in the picture. Nota bene:

It tells you.

You don't tell it.

. . . I recall having a number of pictures in my mind when I began the novel I just finished, *A Book of Common Prayer.* As a matter of fact one of these pictures was of that bevatron I mentioned, although I would be hard put to tell you a story in which nuclear energy figured. Another was a newspaper photograph of a hijacked 707 burning on the desert in the Middle East. Another was the night view from a room in which I once spent a week with paratyphoid, a hotel room on the Colombian coast. My husband and I seemed to be on the Columbian coast representing the United States of America at a film festival (I recall invoking the name "Jack Valenti" a lot, as if its reiteration could make me well), and it was a bad place to have fever, not only because my indisposition offended our hosts but because every night in this hotel the generator failed. The lights went out. The elevator stopped. My husband would go to the event of the evening and make excuses for me and I would stay alone in this hotel room, in the dark. I remember standing at the window trying to call Bogotá (the telephone seemed to work on the same principle as the generator) and watching the night wind come up and wondering what I was doing eleven degrees off the equator with a fever of 103. The view from that window definitely figures in *A Book of Common Prayer,* as does the burning 707, and yet none of these pictures told me the story I needed.

The picture that did, the picture that shimmered and made these images coalesce, was the Panama airport at 6 A.M. I was in this airport only once, on a plane to Bogotá that stopped for an hour to refuel, but the way it looked that morning remained superimposed on everything I saw until the day I finished *A Book of Common Prayer*. I lived in that airport for several years. I can still feel the hot air when I step off the plane, can see the heat already rising off the tarmac at 6 A.M. I can feel my skirt damp and wrinkled on my legs. I can feel the asphalt stick to my sandals. I remember the big tail of a Pan American plane floating motionless down at the end of the tarmac. I remember the sound of a slot machine in the waiting room. I could tell you that I remember a particular woman in the airport, an American woman, a *norteamericana*, a thin *norteamericana* about 40 who wore a big square emerald in lieu of a wedding ring, but there was no such woman there.

I put this woman in the airport later. I made this woman up, just as I later made up a country to put the airport in, and a family to run the country. This woman in the airport is neither catching a plane nor meeting one. She is ordering tea in the airport coffee shop. In fact she is not simply "ordering" tea but insisting that the water be boiled, in front of her, for twenty minutes. Why is this woman in this airport? Why is she going nowhere, where has she been? Where did she get that big emerald? What derangement, or disassociation, makes her believe that her will to see the water boiled can possibly prevail?

> She had been going to one airport or another for four months, one could see it, looking at the visas or her passport. All those airports where Charlotte Douglas's passport had been stamped would have looked alike. Sometimes the sign on the tower would say 'Bienvenidos' and sometimes the sign on the tower would say 'Bienvenue,' some places were wet and hot and others dry and hot, but at each of these airports the pastel concrete walls would rust and stain and the swamp off the runway would be littered with the fuselages of cannibalized Fairchild F-227's and the water would need boiling.
> I knew why Charlotte went to the airport even if Victor did not.
> I knew about airports.

These lines appear about halfway through *A Book of Common Prayer*, but I wrote them during the second week I worked on the book, long before I had any idea where Charlotte Douglas had been or why she went to airports. Until I wrote these lines I had no character called "Victor" in mind: the necessity for mentioning a name, and the name "Victor," occurred to me as I wrote the sentence. I knew why Charlotte went to the airport sounded incomplete. I knew why Charlotte went to the airport even if Victor did not carried a little more narrative drive. Most important of all, until I wrote these lines I did not know who "I" was, who was telling the story. I had intended until that moment that the "I" be no more than the voice of the author, a 19th century omniscient narrator. But there it was:

> I knew why Charlotte went to the airport even if Victor did not.
> I knew about airports.

This "I" was the voice of no author in my house. This "I" was someone who not only knew why Charlotte went to the airport but also knew someone called "Victor." Who was Victor? Who was this narrator? Why was this narrator telling me this story? Let me tell you one thing about why writers write: had I known the answer to any of these questions I would never have needed to write a novel.

▮ How did you demonstrate her unique combination of confidence and vulnerability?
▮ Where is she bold? Where is she reticent?

Moses Hall and Garret Watts were foot soldiers in the Revolutionary War. In the following selections they recount their wartime experiences for a federal pension board many years after the events had occurred. Note carefully how vivid these recollections are; be sure to make your readers feel their impact.

Moses Hall served in a troop that had just defeated a detachment of British soldiers and mercenaries (Tories).

FROM *The Revolution Remembered*
JOHN C. DANN, EDITOR

Moses Hall

The evening after our battle with the Tories, we having a considerable number of prisoners, I recollect a scene which made a lasting impression upon my mind. I was invited by some of my comrades to go and see some of the prisoners. We went to where six were standing together. Some discussion taking place, I heard some of our men cry out, "Remember Buford," and the prisoners were immediately hewed to pieces with broadswords. At first I bore the scene without any emotion, but upon a moment's reflection, I felt such horror as I never did before nor have since, and, returning to my quarters and throwing myself upon my blanket, I contemplated the cruelties of war until overcome and unmanned by a distressing gloom from which I was not relieved until commencing our march next morning before day by moonlight. I came to Tarleton's camp, which he had just abandoned leaving lively rail fires. Being on the left of the road as we marched along, I discovered lying upon the ground something with appearance of a man. Upon approaching him, he proved to be a youth about sixteen who, having come out to view the British through curiosity, for fear he might give information to our troops, they had run him through with a bayonet and left him for dead. Though able to speak, he was mortally wounded. The sight of this unoffending boy, butchered rather than be encumbered in the [illegible] on the march, I assume, relieved me of my distressful feelings for the slaughter of the Tories, and I desired nothing so much as the opportunity of participating in their destruction.

▌ What difficulties did your Hall undergo in retelling his story? Why? How did your audience notice this in your performance?

Garret Watts served in the Continental army under the generals de Kalb and Dickson; he recalls a vivid moment from a battle with British forces under Lord Cornwallis.

Garret Watts

The two armies came near each other at Sutton's about twelve or one o'clock in the night (this was in the year 1780). The pickets fired several rounds before day. I well remember everything that occurred the next morning: I remember that I was among the nearest to the enemy; that a man named John Summers was my file leader; that we had orders to wait for the word to commence firing; that the militia were in front and in a feeble condition at that time. They were fatigued. The weather was warm excessively. They had been fed a short time previously on molasses entirely. I can state on oath that I believe my gun was the first gun fired, notwithstanding the orders, for we were close to the enemy, who appeared to maneuver in contempt of us, and I fired without thinking except that I might prevent the man opposite from killing me. The discharge and loud roar soon became general from one end of the lines to the other. Amongst other things, I confess I was amongst the first that fled. The cause of that I cannot tell, except that everyone I saw was about to do the same. It was instantaneous. There was no effort to rally, no encouragement to fight. Officers and men joined in the flight. I threw away my gun, and, reflecting I might be punished for being found without arms, I picked up a drum, which gave forth such sounds when touched by the twigs I cast it away. When we had gone, we heard the roar of guns still, but we knew not why. Had we known, we might have returned. It was that portion of the army commanded by de Kalb fighting still. De Kalb was killed. General Dickson was wounded in the neck and a great many killed and wounded even on the first firing. After this defeat, many of the dispersed troops proceeded to Hillsboro in North Carolina. I obtained a furlough from General Dickson and had permission to return home a short time. This last tour was for the space of three months and truly laborious.

▌ How did your body behave when Watts admitted he was a deserter?

There is remarkable unity of focus in this selection. Notice how the descriptive details and the progress of time work together. The sentence structure is characteristic of Faulkner's style. Close attention to imagery and the relationship of descriptive words to each other will help untangle it.

FROM *Dry September*
WILLIAM FAULKNER

She was thirty-eight or thirty-nine. She lived in a small frame house with her invalid mother and a thin, sallow, unflagging aunt, where each morning between ten and eleven she would appear on the porch in a lace-trimmed boudoir cap, to sit swinging in the porch swing until noon. After dinner she lay down for a while, until the afternoon began to cool. Then, in one of the three or four new voile dresses which she had each summer, she would go downtown to spend the afternoon in the stores with the other ladies, where they would handle the goods and haggle over the prices in cold, immediate voices, without any intention of buying.

She was of comfortable people — not the best in Jefferson, but good people enough — and she was still on the slender side of ordinary looking, with a bright, faintly haggard manner and dress. When she was young she had had a slender, nervous body and a sort of hard vivacity which enabled her for a time to ride upon the crest of the town's social life as exemplified by the high school party and church social period of her contemporaries while still children enough to be unclassconscious.

She was the last to realize that she was losing ground; that those among whom she had been a little brighter and louder flame than any other were beginning to learn the pleasure of snobbery — male — and retaliation — female. That was when her face began to wear that bright, haggard look. She still carried it to parties on shadowy porticoes and summer lawns, like a mask or a flag, with that bafflement of furious repudiation of truth in her eyes. One evening at a party she heard a boy and two girls, all schoolmates, talking. She never accepted another invitation.

She watched the girls with whom she had grown up as they married and got homes and children, but no man ever called on her steadily until the children of the other girls had been calling her "aunty" for several years, the while their mothers told them in bright voices about how popular Aunt Minnie had been as a girl. Then the town began to see her driving on Sunday afternoons with the cashier in the bank. He was a widower of about forty — a high-colored man, smelling always faintly of the barber shop or of whiskey. He owned the first automobile in town, a red runabout; Minnie had the first motoring bonnet and veil the town ever saw. Then the town began to say: "Poor Minnie." "But she is old enough to take care of herself," others said. That was when she began to ask her old schoolmates that their children call her "cousin" instead of "aunty."

It was twelve years now since she had been relegated into adultery by public opinion, and eight years since the cashier had gone to a Memphis bank, returning for one day each Christmas, which he spent at an annual bachelors' party at a hunting club on the river.

From behind their curtains the neighbors would see the party pass, and during the over-the-way Christmas day visiting they would tell her about him, about how well he looked, and how they heard that he was prospering in the city, watching with bright, secret eyes her haggard, bright face. Usually by that hour there would be the scent of whisky on her breath. It was supplied her by a youth, a clerk at the soda fountain: "Sure; I buy it for the old gal. I reckon she's entitled to a little fun."

Her mother kept to her room altogether now; the gaunt aunt ran the house. Against that background Minnie's bright dresses, her idle and empty days, had a quality of furious unreality. She went out in the evenings only with women now, neighbors, to the moving pictures. Each afternoon she dressed in one of the new dresses and went downtown alone, where her young "cousins" were already strolling in the late afternoons with their delicate, silken heads and thin, awkward arms and conscious hips, clinging to one another or shrieking and giggling with paired boys in the soda fountain when she passed and went on along the serried store fronts, in the doors of which the sitting and lounging men did not even follow her with their eyes any more.

▌ Why does this narrator describe Miss Minnie as "thirty-eight or thirty-nine"? Doesn't he know?

The letters of St. Paul are noted for their arresting figures of speech and their organization. Some are straightforward and businesslike; others are distinctly poetic. The following letter has a marked lyric quality, due in part to the choice of words and images and in part to the rhythmic sentence structure. The text is that of the King James Bible.

FROM *The New Testament*
ST. PAUL

First Corinthians, Chapter 13

Though I speak with the tongues of men and of angels, and have not charity, I am become as sounding brass, or a tinkling cymbal. And though I have the gift of prophecy, and understand all mysteries, and all knowledge; and though I have all faith, so that I could remove mountains, and have not charity, I am nothing. And though I bestow all my goods to feed the poor, and though I give my body to be burned, and have not charity, it profiteth me nothing. Charity suffereth long, and is kind; charity envieth not; charity vaunteth not itself, is not puffed up; Doth not behave itself unseemly, seeketh not her own, is not easily provoked, thinketh no evil; Rejoiceth not in iniquity, but rejoiceth in the truth; Beareth all things, believeth all things, hopeth all things, endureth all things. Charity never faileth: but whether there be prophecies, they shall fail; whether there be tongues, they shall cease; whether there be knowledge, it shall vanish away. For we know in part, and we prophesy in part. But when that which is perfect is come, then that which is in part shall be done away. When I was a child, I spake as a child, I understood as a child, I thought as a child: but when I became a man, I put away childish things. For now we see through a glass, darkly; but then face to face: now I know in part; but then shall I know even as also I am known. And now abideth faith, hope, charity, these three; but the greatest of these is charity.

▋ How did you convey the intensity of Paul's conviction in this letter?

This letter from the master novelist Henry James to Grace Norton is surely one of the most humanely considerate letters in the English language. The one long paragraph moves carefully through several concerns, but be sure that you are always aware of the persona's attitude toward Grace Norton. Imagine her sitting directly across from you; see her as you speak.

Letter to Grace Norton
HENRY JAMES

131 Mount Vernon St., Boston.
July 28th [1883].

My dear Grace,

Before the sufferings of others I am always utterly powerless, and your letter reveals such depths of suffering that I hardly know what to say to you. This indeed is not my last word — but it must be my first. You are not isolated, verily, in such states of feeling as this — that is, in the sense that you appear to make all the misery of all mankind your own; only I have a terrible sense that you give all and receive nothing — that there is no reciprocity in your sympathy — that you have all the affliction of it and none of the returns. However — I am determined not to speak to you except with the voice of stoicism. I don't know *why* we live — the gift of life comes to us from I don't know what source or for what purpose; but I believe we can go on living for the reason that (always of course up to a certain point) life is the most valuable thing we know anything about, and it is therefore presumptively a great mistake to surrender it while there is any yet left in the cup. In other words consciousness is an illimitable power, and though at times it may seem to be all consciousness of misery, yet in the way it propagates itself from wave to wave, so that we never cease to feel, and though at moments we appear to, try to, pray to, there is something that holds one in one's place, makes it a standpoint in the universe which it is probably good not to forsake. You are right in your consciousness that we are all echoes and reverberations of the *same,* and you are noble when your interest and pity as to everything that surrounds you, appears to have a sustaining and harmonizing power. Only don't, I beseech you, *generalize* too much in these sympathies and tendernesses — remember that every life is a special problem which is not yours but another's, and content yourself with the terrible algebra of your own. Don't melt too much into the universe, but be as solid and dense and fixed as you can. We all live together, and those of us who love and know, live so most. We help each other — even unconsciously, each in our own effort, we lighten the effort of others, we contribute to the sum of success, make it possible for others to live. Sorrow comes in great waves — no one can know that better than you — but it rolls over us, and though it may almost smother us it leaves us on the spot, and we know that if it is strong we are stronger, inasmuch as it passes and we remain. It wears us, uses us, but we wear it and use it in return; and it is blind, whereas we after a manner see. My dear Grace, you are passing through a darkness in which I myself in my ignorance see nothing but that you have been made wretchedly ill by it; but it is only a darkness, it is not an end, or *the* end. Don't think, don't feel, any more than you can help, don't conclude or decide — don't do anything but *wait.* Everything will pass, and serenity and *accepted* mysteries and disillusionments, and the tenderness of a few good people, and new opportunities and ever so much of life, in a word, will remain. You will do all sorts of things yet, and I will help you. The only thing is not to *melt* in the meanwhile. I insist upon the necessity of a sort of mechanical condensation — so that however fast the horse may run away there will, when he pulls up, be a somewhat agitated but perfectly identical G. N. left in the saddle. Try not to be ill — that is all; for in that there is a failure. You are marked out for success, and you must not fail. You have my tenderest affection and all my confidence. Ever your faithful friend —

Henry James

❚ Was your James clearly visualizing the grief-stricken Grace? How did your audience detect it?

This astonishing tale combines many prominent themes in black folklore, including flying Africans, disappearing slaves, and magic hoes. The story testifies powerfully to the enduring value of *telling,* since those who could not fly kept the dream alive.

The People Could Fly
Retold by VIRGINIA HAMILTON

They say the people could fly. Say that long ago in Africa, some of the people knew magic. And they would walk up on the air like climbin up on a gate. And they flew like blackbirds over the fields. Black, shiny wings flappin against the blue up there.

Then, many of the people were captured for Slavery. The ones that could fly shed their wings. They couldn't take their wings across the water on the slave ships. Too crowded, don't you know.

The folks were full of misery, then. Got sick with the up and down of the sea. So they forgot about flyin when they could no longer breathe the sweet scent of Africa.

Say the people who could fly kept their power, although they shed their wings. They kept their secret magic in the land of slavery. They looked the same as the other people from Africa who had been coming over, who had dark skin. Say you couldn't tell anymore one who could fly from one who couldn't.

One such who could was an old man, call him Toby. And standin tall, yet afraid, was a young woman who once had wings. Call her Sarah. Now Sarah carried a babe tied to her back. She trembled to be so hard worked and scorned.

The slaves labored in the fields from sunup to sundown. The owner of the slaves callin himself their Master. Say he was a hard lump of clay. A hard, glinty coal. A hard rock pile, wouldn't be moved. His Overseer on horseback pointed out the slaves who were slowin down. So the one called Driver cracked his whip over the slow ones to make them move faster. That whip was a slice-open cut of pain. So they did move faster. Had to.

Sarah hoed and chopped the row as the babe on her back slept.

Say the child grew hungry. That babe started up bawling too loud. Sarah couldn't stop to feed it. Couldn't stop to soothe and quiet it down. She let it cry. She didn't want to. She had no heart to croon to it.

"Keep that thing quiet," called the Overseer. He pointed his finger at the babe. The woman scrunched low. The Driver cracked his whip across the babe anyhow. The babe hollered like any hurt child, and the woman fell to the earth.

The old man that was there, Toby, came and helped her to her feet.

"I must go soon," she told him.

"Soon," he said.

Sarah couldn't stand up straight any longer. She was too weak. The sun burned her face. The babe cried and cried, "Pity me, oh, pity me," say it sounded like. Sarah was so sad and starvin, she sat down in the row.

"Get up, you black cow," called the Overseer. He pointed his hand, and the Driver's whip snarled around Sarah's legs. Her sack dress tore into rags. Her legs bled onto the earth. She couldn't get up.

Toby was there where there was no one to help her and the babe.

"Now, before it's too late," panted Sarah. "Now, Father!"

"Yes, Daughter, the time is come," Toby answered. "Go, as you know how to go!"

He raised his arms, holding them out to her. "*Kum . . . yali, kum buba tambe,"* and more magic words, said so quickly, they sounded like whispers and sighs.

The young woman lifted one foot on the air. Then the other. She flew clumsily at first, with the child now held tightly in her arms. Then she felt the magic, the African mystery. Say she rose just as free as a bird. As light as a feather.

The Overseer rode after her, hollerin. Sarah flew over the fences. She flew over the woods. Tall trees could not snag her. Nor could the Overseer. She flew like an eagle now, until she was gone from sight. No one dared speak about it. Couldn't believe it. But it was, because they that was there saw that it was.

Say the next day was dead hot in the fields. A young man slave fell from the heat. The Driver come and whipped him. Toby come over and spoke words to the fallen one. The words of ancient Africa once heard are never remembered completely. The young man forgot them as soon as he heard them. They went way inside him. He got up and rolled over on the air. He rode it awhile. And he flew away.

Another and another fell from the heat. Toby was there. He cried out to the fallen and reached his arms out to them. *"Kum kunka yali, kum . . . tambe!"* Whispers and sighs. And they too rose on the air. They rode the hot breezes. The ones flyin were black and shinin sticks, wheelin above the head of the Overseer. They crossed the rows, the fields, the fences, the streams, and were away.

"Seize the old man!" cried the Overseer. "I heard him say the magic *words.* Seize him!"

The one callin himself Master come runnin. The Driver got his whip ready to curl around old Toby and tie him up. The slaveowner took his hip gun from its place. He meant to kill old, black Toby.

But Toby just laughed. Say he threw back his head and said, "Hee, hee! Don't you know who I am? Don't you know some of us in this field?" He said it to their faces. "We are ones who fly!"

And he sighed the ancient words that were a dark promise. He said them all around to the others in the field under the whip, ". . . *buba yali . . . buba tambe. . . ."*

There was a great outcryin. The bent backs straighted up. Old and young who were called slaves and could fly joined hands. Say like they would ring-sing. But they didn't shuffle in a circle. They didn't sing. They rose on the air. They flew in a flock that was black against the heavenly blue. Black crows or black shadows. It didn't matter, they went so high. Way above the plantation, way over the slavery land. Say they flew away to *Free-dom.*

And the old man, old Toby, flew behind them, takin care of them. He wasn't cryin. He wasn't laughin. He was the seer. His gaze fell on the plantation where the slaves who could not fly waited.

"Take us with you!" Their looks spoke it but they were afraid to shout it. Toby couldn't take them with him. Hadn't the time to teach them to fly. They must wait for a chance to run.

"Goodie-bye!" The old man called Toby spoke to them, poor souls! And he was flyin gone.

So they say. The Overseer told it. The one called Master said it was a lie, a trick of the light. The Driver kept his mouth shut.

The slaves who could not fly told about the people who could fly to their children. When they were free. When they sat close before the fire in the free land, they told it. They did so love firelight and *Free-dom*, and tellin.

They say that the children of the ones who could not fly told their children. And now, me, I have told it to you.

❙ How did you keep alive the overpowering tension and fear when the Master, Overseer, and Driver were present?

Jane Tortillot kept a diary as she crossed the Great Plains from May to November 1862. On some days she was too busy to make any entries. When she did write, she gave a moving picture of the world of the wagon train; of her husband, Albert; of her life under extraordinarily difficult circumstances. To be sure, she suffered, but she didn't whine; keep her backbone strong!

FROM ***Women's Diaries of the Westward Journey***
LILLIAN SCHLISSEL, EDITOR

Jane Gould Tortillot

Friday, July 4   Today is the Fourth of July and here we are away off in the wilderness and can't even stay over a day to do any extra cooking. The men fired their guns. We wonder what the folks at home are doing and oh, how we wish we were there. Albert is not well today, so I drive. I have been in the habit of sleeping a while every forenoon, so naturally I was very sleepy driving. Went to sleep a multitude of times, to awaken with a start fancying we were running into gullies. After going a short distance we came in sight of a mail station, on the other side of the river there were several buildings. They are of adobe, I suppose. Nearly opposite on this side of the river we passed a little log hut which is used for a store. It was really a welcome sight after going four hundred miles without seeing a house of any kind. . . .

Saturday, July 5–Tuesday, July 8 . . .

Wednesday, July 9 . . .   We hear many stories of Indians depredations, but do not feel frightened yet. . . .

July 10 . . .

Friday, July 11 . . .   There was a little child run over by a wagon in Walker's train, who are just ahead of us. The child was injured quite seriously. . . . They sent for a German physician that belongs to our train, to see the child that was injured. He said he thought it would get better.

July 12–July 19 . . .

Sunday, July 20 . . .   The men had a ball-play towards night. Seemed to enjoy themselves very much, it seemed like old times.

Monday, July 21 . . .   Our men went to work this morning to building a raft. Worked hard all day. Half of the men in the water, too. . . .

Tuesday, July 22 . . .   Went to work this morning as early as possible to ferrying the wagons over. Had to take them apart and float the box and cover behind. The two boxes were fastened together by the rods, one before to tow in and the other to load. Worked till dark. We were the last but one to cross tonight. Got some of our groceries wet, some coffee, sugar dissolved.

July 24–July 25 . . .

Saturday, July 26 . . .   Annie McMillen had lagged behind, walking, when we stopped. The whole train had crossed the creek before they thought of her. The creek was so deep that it ran into the wagon boxes, so she could not wade. A man on horseback went over for her, and another man on a mule went to help her on. The mules refused to go clear across went where the water was very deep, threw the man off and almost trampled him, but he finally got out safe, only well wet and with the loss of a good hat, which is no trifling loss here.

Sunday, July 27 . . .

Monday, July 28 . . .   Came past a camp of thirty-six wagons who have been camped for some time here in the mountains. They have had their cattle stampeded four or five times. There was a woman died in this train yesterday. She left six children, one of them only two days old. Poor little thing, it had better have died with its mother. They made a good picket fence around the grave.

July 29–31, August 1–2 . . .

Sunday, August 3 . . .   We passed by the train I have just spoken of. They had just buried the babe of the woman who died days ago, and were just digging a grave for another woman that was run over by the cattle and wagons when they stampeded yesterday. She lived twenty-four hours, she gave birth to a child a short time before she died. The child was buried with her. She leaves a little two year old girl and a husband. They say he is nearly crazy with sorrow. . . .

August 4 . . .

Tuesday, August 5 . . .   Did not start very early. Waited for a train to pass. It seems today as if I *must* go home to fathers to see them all. I can't wait another minute. If I could only *hear* from them it would do some good, but I suppose I shall have to wait whether I am patient or not. . . .

August 6–9 . . .

Sunday, August 10   Traveled five or six miles when we came to Snake River. We stayed till two o'clock then traveled till about four or five, when *we* from the back end of the train saw those on ahead all get out their guns. In a short time the word came back that a train six miles on had been attacked by the Indians, and some killed and that was cause enough for the arming. In a short time were met by two men. They wanted us to go a short distance from the road and bring two dead men to their camp, five miles ahead.

Albert unloaded his little wagon and sent Gus back with them and about forty armed men from both trains, to get them. We learned that a train of eleven wagons had been plundered of all that was in them and the teams taken and the men killed. One was Mr. Bullwinkle who left us the 25th of last month, at the crossing of Green River. He went on with this Adams train. Was intending to wait for us but we had not overtaken him yet. He was shot eight times. His dog was shot four times before he would let them get to the wagon. They took all that he had in his wagon, except his trunks and books and papers. They broke open his trunks and took all that they contained. (He had six.) It is supposed that they took six thousand dollars from him, tore the cover from his wagon, it was oilcloth. He had four choice horses. They ran away when he was shot, the harnesses were found on the trail where it was cut from them when they went. It was a nice silver one. The Captain had a daughter shot and wounded severely. This happened yesterday. This morning a part of their train and a part of the Kennedy train went in pursuit of the stock. They were surrounded by Indians on ponies, two killed, several wounded and two supposed to be killed. They were never found. One of those killed was Capt. Adams' son, the other was a young man in the Kennedy train. Those that we carried to camp were those killed this morning. Mr. Bullwinkle and the two others were buried before we got to the camp. There were one hundred and fifty wagons there and thirty four of ours. Capt. Kennedy was severely wounded. Capt. Hunter of Iowa City train was killed likewise by an Indian. We camped near Snake River. We could not get George to ride after the news, he *would* walk and carry his loaded pistol to help.

Monday, August 11 . . .   The two men we brought up were buried early this morning with the other three, so they laid five men side by side in this vast wilderness, killed by guns and arrows of the red demons. The chief appeared yesterday in a suit of Mr. Bullwinkle's on the battlefield. . . .

Tuesday, August 12   Capt. Adams' daughter died this morning from the effects of her wound. Was buried in a box made of a wagon box. Poor father and mother lost one son and one daughter, all of his teams, clothing and four thousand dollars. Is left dependent on the bounty of strangers. . . . In the evening we took in Mrs. Ellen Ives, one of the ladies of the plundered train. Her husband goes in the wagon just ahead of us. She was married the morning she started for California. Not a very pleasant wedding tour. . . .

▌ How did you make your audience see the tensions building in
   Jane at the end of July and the beginning of August?

Terry Pickens, fourteen, is a newsboy. Together with his brother Cliff (who is twelve), he serves 111 customers, but Terry's route is more difficult. As he says, "Cliff hasn't got any hills. Mine's all hills." Be sure we see Terry think — he has become a very savvy young man. What question do you suppose Terkel asked to get him started?

FROM *Working*
STUDS TERKEL

Terry Pickens

I've been having trouble collecting. I had one woman hid from me once. I had another woman tell her kids to tell me she wasn't home. He says, "Mom, newsboy." She says (whispers), "Tell him I'm not home." I could hear it from the door. I came back in half an hour and she paid me. She's not a deadbeat. They'll pay you if you get 'em. Sometimes you have to wait . . .

If I don't catch 'em at home, I get pretty mad. That means I gotta come back and come back and come back and come back until I catch 'em. Go around about nine o'clock at night and seven o'clock in the morning. This one guy owed me four dollars. He got real mad at me for comin' around at ten o'clock. Why'd I come around so late? He probably was mad 'cause I caught him home. But he paid me. I don't care whether he gets mad at me, just so I get paid.

I like to have money. It's nice to have money once in a while instead of being flat broke all the time. Most of my friends are usually flat broke. I spent $150 this summer. On nothing — candy, cokes, games of pool, games of pinball. We went to McDonald's a couple of times. I just bought anything I wanted. I wonder where the money went. I have nothing to show for it. I'm like a gambler, the more I have, the more I want to spend. That's just the way I am.

It's supposed to be such a great deal. The guy, when he came over and asked me if I wanted a route, he made it sound so great. Seven dollars a week for hardly any work at all. And then you find out the guy told you a bunch of bull. You mistrust the people. You mistrust your customers because they don't pay you sometimes.

Then you get mad at the people at the printing corporation. You're supposed to get fifty-seven papers. They'll send me forty-seven or else they'll send me sixty-seven. Sunday mornings they get mixed up. Cliff'll have ten or eleven extras and I'll be ten or eleven short. That happens all the time. The printers, I don't think they care. They make all these stupid mistakes at least once a week. I think they're half-asleep or something. I do my job, I don't see why they can't do theirs. I don't like my job any more than they do.

Sunday morning at three — that's when I get up. I stay up later so I'm tired. But the dark doesn't bother me. I run into things sometimes, though. Somebody's dog'll come out and about give you a heart attack. There's this one woman, she had two big German shepherds, great big old things, like three or four feet tall. One of 'em won't bite you. He'll just run up, charging, bark at you, and then he'll go away. The other one, I didn't know she had another one — when it bit me. This dog came around the bush. (Imitates barking.) When I turned around, he was at me. He bit me right there (indicates scar on leg). It was bleeding a little. I gave him a real dirty look.

He ran over to the other neighbor's lawn and tried to keep me from gettin' in there. I walked up and delivered the paper. I was about ready to beat the thing's head in or kill it. Or something with it. I was so mad. I called up that woman and she said the dog had all its shots and "I don't believe he bit you." I said, "Lady, he bit me." Her daughter started giving me the third degree. "What color was the dog?" "How big was it?" "Are you sure it was our yard and our dog?" Then they saw the dogs weren't in the pen.

First they told me they didn't think I needed any shots. Then they said they'd pay for the doctor. I never went to the doctor. It wasn't bleeding a whole lot. But I told her if I ever see that dog again, she's gonna have to get her papers from somebody else. Now they keep the dog penned up and it barks at me and everything. And I give it a dirty look.

There's a lot of dogs around here. I got this other dog, a little black one, it tried to bite me too. It lunged at me, ripped my pants, and missed me. (With the glee of W. C. Fields) I kicked it *good*. It still chases me. There are two black dogs. The other one I've kicked so many times that it just doesn't bother me any more. I've kicked his face in once when he was biting my leg. Now he just stays under the bushes and growls at me. I don't bother to give him a dirty look.

There were these two other dogs. They'd always run out in the street and chase me. I kicked them. They'd come back and I'd kick 'em again. I don't have any problems with 'em any more, because they got hit chasin' cars. They're both dead.

I don't like many of my customers, 'cause they'll cuss me if they don't get their papers just exactly in the right place. This one guy cussed me up and down for about fifteen minutes. I don't want to repeat what he called me. All the words, just up and down. He told me he drives past all those blank drugstores on his blank way home and he could stop off at one of 'em and get a blank newspaper. And I'm just a blank convenience.

I was so mad at him. I hated his guts. I felt like taking a lead pipe to him or something. But I kept my mouth shut, 'cause I didn't know if the press guy'd get mad at me and I'd lose my route. You see, this guy could help me or he could hurt me. So I kept my mouth shut.

A lot of customers are considerate but a lot of 'em aren't. Lot of 'em act like they're doing you such a favor taking the paper from you. It costs the same dime at a drugstore. Every time they want you to do something they threaten you: (imitates nasty, nasal voice) "Or I'll quit."

What I really can't stand: you'll be collecting and somebody'll come out and start telling you all their problems. "I'm going to visit my daughter today, yes, I am. She's twenty-two, you know." "Look here, I got all my sons home, see the army uniforms?" They'll stand for like half an hour. I got two or three like that, and they always got something to say to me. I'll have like two hours wasted listening to these people blabbin' before they pay me. Mmm, I don't know.

Maybe they're lonely. But they've got a daughter and a son, why do they have to blab in my ear?

A lot of the younger customers have had routes and they know how hard it is, how mean people are. They'll be nicer to you. They tend to tip you more. And they don't blab all day long. They'll just pay you and smile at you. The younger people frequently offer me a coke or something.

Older people are afraid of me, a lot of them. The first three, four weeks — (muses) they seemed so afraid of me. They think I'm gonna rob 'em or something. It's funny. You wouldn't think it'd be like this in a small town, would you? They're afraid I'm gonna beat 'em up, take their money. They'd just reach through the door and give me the money. Now they know you so well, they invite you in and blab in your ear for half an hour. It's one or the other. I really don't know why they're afraid. I'm not old, so I wouldn't know how old people feel.

Once in a while I come home angry, most of the time just crabby. Sometimes kids steal the paper out of people's boxes. I lose my profits. It costs me a dime. The company isn't responsible, I am. The company wouldn't believe you probably that somebody stole the paper.

I don't see where being a newsboy and learning that people are pretty mean or that people don't have enough money to buy things with is gonna make you a better person or anything. If anything, it's gonna make a worse person out of you, 'cause you're not gonna like people that don't pay you. And you're not gonna like people who act like they're doing you a big favor paying you. Yeah, it sort of molds your character, but I don't think for the better. If anybody told me being a newsboy builds character, I'd know he was a liar.

I don't see where people get all this bull about the kid who's gonna be President and being a newsboy made a President out of him. It taught him how to handle his money and this bull. You know what it did? It taught him how to hate the people on his route. And the printers. And dogs.

▌ What did you do with your body and voice to let your audience see a fourteen-year-old boy eager to talk? What was his body doing?

Bibliography

Chatman, Seymour. ed. *Literary Style: A Symposium.* New York: Oxford University Press, 1971.

A collection of learned essays representing leading schools of thought in America, England, and continental Europe, integrating linguistics and literary theory, and suggesting a future for stylistic studies.

Connolly, Cyril. *The Evening Colonnade*. New York: Harcourt Brace Jovanovich, 1975.
A variety of essays on literary subjects and personalities.

Cowley, Malcolm. *And I Worked at the Writer's Trade: Chapters of Literary History, 1918–1978*. New York: Viking Press, 1978.
A consideration of the relationship of literary generations with interesting comments on changing themes and language.

Cowley, Malcom, ed. *Writers at Work: The "Paris Review" Interviews*. New York: Viking Press, 1961.
A collection of interviews on "How Writers Write." Sixteen interviews offer a range of styles and interests from E. M. Forster to Françoise Sagan.

Fiedler, Leslie, ed. *The Art of the Essay: Edited with Introduction, Notes and Exercise Questions*. New York: Thomas Y. Crowell Company, 1958.
An extensive collection of essays and travel accounts.

Gardner, John. *On Moral Fiction*. New York: Basic Books, 1978.
An examination of contemporary fiction measured against this outstanding novelist's premise that fiction is moral only when it attempts to share human values and efforts at human fulfillment.

Gibson, Walter. *Tough, Sweet & Stuffy: An Essay On Modern American Prose Style*. Bloomington, Indiana: Indiana University Press, 1966.
Countless intriguing examples illustrate a close analysis of words, modifiers, word groups, and sentences.

Graves, Robert, and Alan Hodge. *The Reader Over Your Shoulder*. 2nd ed. New York: Random House, 1971.
A practical discussion of the writer's responsibilities for clarity and the reader's need for precision.

Lanham, Richard A. *Style: An Anti-Textbook*. New Haven: Yale University Press, 1974.
A brief work with a decidedly unusual and interesting focus on the way in which words establish personality, suggest dimension, and interact to shape perception.

Mallon, Thomas. *A Book of One's Own*. New York: Ticknor & Fields, 1984.
A highly readable collection excerpting famous diaries and journals — and more that ought to be famous. Useful bibliography.

Read, Herbert. *English Prose Style*. Boston: Beacon Press, 1952.
Still the most complete discussion of prose style per se. The approach is first from the standpoint of composition and then from that of rhetoric.

Sawyer, Ruth. *Way of the Storyteller.* New York: The Viking Press, 1962.
An explanation of ways to learn a story and how to tell it: picture by picture — never word by word.

Thomas, Wright, and Stuart Gerry Brown. *Reading Prose: An Introduction to Critical Study.* New York: Oxford University Press, 1952.
An extensive collection of essays grouped thematically, with a brief section on experimental prose. The final section is a compact directive for developing a critical approach. The book has a helpful chronological index.

Zinsser, William. *On Writing Well.* New York: Harper, Row, 1976.
Enormously useful book for readers as well as writers. Practical advice about the shape and impact of sentences suggest a method of analysis.

**Well, you know or don't you kennet or haven't I
told you every telling has a taling and that's the
he and the she of it. Look, look, the dusk is
growing!**

James Joyce, Finnegans Wake

NARRATION

6

ALL OF US TELL STORIES even if they are only about what happened to us yesterday or just a moment ago. We tell stories because they authenticate our lives and experiences and help us make sense of who we are and what we are about. Good stories are good because the teller uses lively description to help listeners see what he or she has seen, because the teller is confident enough of the tale's interest to step aside to let other characters speak, and because the teller summarizes the important intervening events or time. But always, at the center, is the storyteller — *telling* a tale.

Narration, then, is more than plot. Whether in prose or in verse, narration includes the *telling* (remember that active form) by a *narrator* of something that has happened (to the narrator or to someone else) or that might happen.

When you prepare narration for performance, answer five important questions:

1. Who is telling this story? To whom?
2. Exactly what is going on here?
3. What sort of people live in this story?
4. What are they saying to each other?
5. Where is all of this taking place?

Frequently, answers to any of these five questions are really clusters of other questions, but if you are fully informed about each one of them, you will be well on your way to successful and engaging performances of narration.

Too often we read stories just to find out what happens, as if the words obstruct the facts or ideas or whatever might be conveyed by the story. The manner of telling the story, however, is just as important as the tale, for it reflects the unique personality of the narrator who shapes the tale, moves the event at the proper pace, and leads the reader to the planned conclusion. Along the way occur all the details that make this telling of the events unique. If you read rapidly, you may skip these vital clues, which are in fact the verbal fingerprints of the teller. So it's wisest to begin our analysis with strategies for answering the first question, "What sort of person is telling the story?"

Point of View

Every story has a storyteller, a person who selects what we see and hear, chooses the perspective from which we view the action, determines the details on which we linger, and decides how long it takes us to traverse time. Every story is shaped by its narrator, who establishes a *point of view,* a way to experience the world from a particular vantage point. Every narrator sets for us — by the position from which the action is viewed *and* by his or her unique personality — a characteristic way of showing and telling. This characteristic way of telling a story tells us about the narrator, too.

When we attend a film, everything we see has been selected by the eye of the camera. Although we might want desperately to see something else, we see only what the camera shows us. We watch the scene as long as the camera wants us to watch it, at the distance from which the camera wants us to see it, and lit in the manner the camera allows. Similarly, the narrator in a story selects and organizes what we see and hear, telling us what we must know or allowing us to overhear characters carrying on dialogue from which we draw our own conclusions. Storytellers have different attitudes and manners. Objective, clinical, cut-and-dried, black-and-white news stories look and feel different from stories that jump around in time and locale and are full of vivid happenings with improbable people doing impossible things. In all cases, though, the events are related according to the vision of the eye that both sees and speaks. At the center of a story, shaping, controlling, refining, and guiding us through the narrative, is what Henry James calls the "central intelligence." Your first task as an interpreter is to communicate the narrator.

First-Person Narrators

Two brief passages demonstrate how palpably present that central intelligence can be. The first is from *The Odyssey:*

> Tell me, Muse, of the man of many ways, who was driven far journeys, after he had sacked Troy's sacred citadel. Many were they whose cities he saw, whose minds he learned of, many the pains he suffered in his spirit on the wide sea, struggling for his own life and the homecoming of his companions.[1]

By the second syllable we know that the story is being told by a specific somebody. "Tell *me*, Muse," the narrator says. The invocation of the Muse and the simplicity and confidence of the words further suggest that the narrator is awed by the hero and his journey. Only if he is inspired by the gods can he convey the story of the "god-like Odysseus." Although the narrator seems to be at some distance from the events, they still impress him. These first few lines summarize the ordeal that is revealed in the story ahead, and the majesty in the words gives emotional impact to the beginning of this great tale.

Now look at the first paragraph of John Updike's "A & P" (the entire story can be found at the end of this chapter):

> In walks these three girls in nothing but bathing suits. I'm in the third checkout slot, with my back to the door, so I don't see them until they're over by the bread. The one that caught my eye first was the one in the plaid green two-piece. She was a chunky kid, with a good tan and a sweet broad soft-looking can with those two crescents of white just under it, where the sun never seems to hit, at the top of the back of her legs. I stood there with my hand on a box of HiHo crackers trying to remember if I rang it up or not. I ring it up again and the customer starts giving me hell. She's one of these cash-register-watchers, a witch about fifty with rouge on her cheekbones and no eyebrows, and I know it made her day to trip me up. She's been watching cash registers for fifty years and probably never seen a mistake before.

Here we meet Sammy, a boy with his eye on three girls. How else is he identified here? What — precisely — is he doing? Where is he doing it? How is it going to get him into trouble before the

---

1. Homer, *The Odyssey,* trans. Richmond Lattimore (New York: Harper and Row, 1967), p. 27.

paragraph is over? He is clearly interested in the girls and in their bathing suits, and he takes time from his tasks to describe the cut and color of one costume. But is his mind on his work? What is Sammy's attitude toward the people he meets during his job? He addresses us as if we were his friends. The vivid impression these girls make is marked for both Sammy and us by the use of the present tense in the first sentence. What happens to tense as the paragraph progresses?

We are located quickly in the familiar world of the A & P: we recognize the grocery store, and we know about lanes, checkers, cash-register-watchers, and HiHo crackers. We know the landscape; we're on Sammy's side, ready to hear about what happens to these three girls.

Sammy is obviously not the disembodied voice of Homer and he is surely not Updike, the author. The persona, Sammy, is simply the teller of a tale vivid and important enough to him to be worth telling to us; his language makes us his peers. When interpreting this story, you should create a Sammy to whom all of this story has happened and who, as he recalls it so vividly, needs to tell us about it.

Both *The Odyssey* and "A & P" are written in *first-person narration*. They are told by different kinds of narrators, and yet each narrator takes an active and lively part in telling something that happened to him.

In first-person narration, the person telling the story speaks directly to the reader as "I," and he or she is also the "eye" of the story. Sometimes the "I" is physically identified, as in Updike's story; in other cases, as with the narrator of Homer's epic, the "I" is not physically identified, although he or she definitely demonstrates a characteristic personality. The narrator may observe from either afar or quite near the events, may participate in the actions described or merely report what occurs, or may report and evaluate as well. But whatever the degree of physical presence in the story, the narrator remains very much at the center of things. The narrator's personality shapes and colors everything we see and hear.

The kind of first-person narration that is presented in "A & P" gives us all the vitality of a teller who lives through the tale. First-person narrators are peculiarly convinced of their own vision. They *know* it, because it happened to them. And like most people who live through experiences that they want to talk about later, first-person narrators are incapable of complete objectivity. They shape events to favor themselves and to prove their antagonists unreasonable, unattractive, and irresponsible. Such qualities do not make first-person narrators less interesting people; on the contrary, the foibles, idiosyncracies, and peculiar diction and vision of these narrators may present a special challenge to the interpreter. Only by assuming the personality of the narrator can the interpreter develop a believable response to the material. In this way the narrator, revealed in the way the story is told, becomes a full-blooded character, unquestionably the most important character you will present. An interpreter must move as the narrator moves, must sound as the *narrator* sounds. You must find within your body and your voice sufficient similarities to the body and voice of the storyteller to convince the audience that they are listening to a story told by someone to whom all of this actually happened.

First-person narrators, then, may be either central participants in the action of the story (like Sammy) or observers (like Homer's narrator). Each posture presents both benefits and liabilities to interpreters and their audiences. If you are telling a first-person story with an actively involved narrator, you obviously have immediate access to many of the events; you know precisely what is going on inside one of the major characters. But you are also restricted to that person's perception of the events, and you may find yourself the victim of some fancy elaboration of the truth. If you are telling a first-person story in which your narrator is chiefly observing the events, you get a much less subjective (although not entirely objective) picture of what is happening, but you do not get the inner concerns of any of the major characters. As an example, consider an automobile accident. Obviously, the driver of the car knew exactly what *he* was doing and thinking when the truck pulled out in front of him, but he could not see (and could not know) about the truck driver's fears about being late or the little puppy that jumped into the trucker's vision and caused the truck to swerve and collide with the car. Someone watching from the streetcorner may have seen many of these events happen, more or less clearly, but wouldn't know about any of the internal concerns of the participants. In either case, though, the narrator remains at the center of the story, and when we hear the words of the characters we hear them and see them *through* the voice of the narrator.

Second-Person Narrators

Among the most intriguing developments in contemporary fiction has been the explosion of interest in and experimentation with *second-person narrators*. Although such narratives do not appear as frequently as first- or third-person narratives, many strong second-person stories have been published in the last decade.[2]

---

2. Foremost among those whose recent scholarship explores the performance opportunities in second-person narratives is John Capecci; his research informs the next three paragraphs.

Two characteristics distinguish second-person narration: First, an explicit "you" is an actant (or partakes of the events) within the tale. Second, two "clocks" appear to be running simultaneously within the story: the clock that times the events of the story — and can be speeded up or slowed down according to the narrator's needs; and the clock that times the narrator's actual telling of the tale to the audience. These qualifications permit many variations, understandably, and authorial ingenuity encourages still other changes, so that any classification is bound to be an incomplete description. For our purposes, however, four kinds of second-person narrators exist, each characterized by a different way of responding to the questions, "Who is the speaker addressing? Just who is this *you* being mentioned?"

Briefly, the narrator may speak to someone *not* acting within the story who is within, or outside of, the situation being described. A narrator may specifically address someone who is clearly acting and involved in the story (as in Ann Beattie's "Snow," at the end of this chapter). A third choice is a narrator who is really addressing himself or herself disguised as a "you," giving a confessional or highly personal impression (Michael Lassell's poem, "How to Watch Your Brother Die," at the end of Chapter 2 is an example). Finally, there is the impersonal "you" with little or no specificity, the "you" of travel guides ("If you turn left at the next corner, Santa Cecilia will be the large building immediately in front of you") or cookbooks ("Now, you gradually fold in the beaten egg whites").

Discovering who "you" is and defining the essential characteristics of "you" begin a rehearsal process that involves all of the challenges of storytelling. Once you determine the type of second-person address, you can gauge the degree of ambiguity operating in the work. You'll probably want to define clearly some things about "you" — the physical and vocal effects "you" has on the narrator, for example. Other ambiguities may be more effective if left unresolved. Remember, suggestion enables us to explore literature rich in ambiguity. Still, the narrator needs clear definition, and because the story focuses on "you," clues about the speaking character's body and voice may *appear* elusive. Look carefully at the word choice of the narrator, at what the narrator chooses to include and to exclude, and you will begin to discover the distinctive flesh and blood who is telling the tale.

Experimentation with second-person narrators clarifies our experiences with first- and third-person narrators, broadens the field of material available for performance, and makes immediate and tangible other, new ways for tellers to tell stories. Moreover, because second-person narrators demand experimentation and creative solutions to performance problems, they encourage us to seek fresh answers to well-known problems.

Third-Person Narrators

Third-person narration is probably the most familiar to you. For most beginning interpreters, this form of narration may be the most difficult narrative posture of all, chiefly because the narrator seems to fade from existence or to resemble some sort of disembodied voice or uninflected reporter simply stating facts. Nothing could be further from the truth, for these narrators are lively and full-blooded, although discovering the ways in which they make their presence known requires careful scrutiny, a keenly deductive mind, and a spirited imagination.

There are many different forms of third-person narrators, and any extended study of narration will require you to become familiar with all of them. (The bibliography at the end of this chapter lists many books that can help you learn further.) For our purposes, we divide third-person narrators into two broadly inclusive groups: objective observers and omniscient observers. Generally, *objective observers* simply recount the events, incidents, dialogue, and activity that could be related by any reasonable individual present at the scene. *Omniscient observers* — and omniscience may be limited to only one character — have all of these powers as well as access to the internal life of a character or characters. Although these narrators *can* tell us about the inner fears and hopes, concerns, past, and future of a character who interests them, they do not *have* to tell us. Furthermore, they choose the time to tell us such internal details. In both kinds of third-person narration, though, careful examination of diction, grammar, and syntax help reveal the narrators' personalities. Note which kinds of events they dwell on and which they pass over. Inspect the relationship they establish with the characters in their tales. Some careful deductions will begin to flesh out the personality who is telling a particular tale and whom you must communicate to your audience.

Look at the opening of Eudora Welty's *Losing Battles:*

> When the rooster crowed, the moon had still not left the world but was going down on flushed cheek, one day short of the full. A long thin cloud crossed it slowly, drawing itself out like a name being called. The air changed, as if a mile or so away a wooden door had swung open, and a smell, more of warmth than wet, from a river at low stage, moved upward into the clay hills that stood in darkness.

Then a house appeared on its ridge, like an old man's silver watch pulled once more out of its pocket. A dog leaped up from where he'd lain like a stone and began barking for today as if he meant never to stop.

Then a baby bolted naked out of the house. She monkey-climbed down the steps and ran open-armed into the yard, knocking at the walls of flowers still colorless as faces, tagging in turn the four big trees that marked off the corners of the yard, tagging the gatepost, the well-piece, the birdhouse, the bell post, a log seat, a rope swing, and then, rounding the house, she used all her strength to push over a crate that let a stream of white Plymouth Rocks loose on the world. The chickens rushed ahead of the baby, running frantic, and behind the baby came a girl in a petticoat. A wide circle of curl-papers, paler than the streak of dawn, bounced around her head, but she ran on confident tiptoe as though she believed no eye could see her. She caught the baby and carried her back inside, the baby with her little legs still running like a windmill.

The distant point of the ridge, like the tongue of a calf, put its red lick on the sky. Mists, voids, patches of woods and naked clay, flickered like live ashes, pink and blue. A mirror that hung within the porch on the house wall began to flicker as at the striking of kitchen matches. Suddenly two chinaberry trees at the foot of the yard lit up, like roosters astrut with golden tails. Caterpillar nets shone in the pecan tree. A swollen shadow bulked underneath it, familiar in shape as Noah's Ark — a school bus.

Then as if something came sliding out of the sky, the whole tin roof of the house ran with new blue. The posts along the porch softly bloomed downward, as if chalk marks were being drawn, one more time, down a still misty slate. The house was revealed as if standing there from pure memory against a now moonless sky. For the length of a breath, everything stayed shadowless, as under a lifting hand, and then a passage showed, running through the house, right through the middle of it, and at the head of the passage, in the center of the front gallery, a figure was revealed, a very old lady seated in a rocking chair with head cocked, as though wild to be seen.

Then Sunday light raced over the farm as fast as the chickens were flying. Immediately the first straight shaft of heat, solid as a hickory stick, was laid on the ridge.

Miss Beulah Renfro came out of the passage at a trot and cried in the voice of alarm which was her voice of praise, "Granny! Up, dressed, and waiting for 'em! All by yourself! Why didn't you holler?"

There is no "I" in this account of dawn in the rural South, but there is a very strong "eye." Even though the speaker is an omniscient observer and even though this account is in the past tense, there is a sense of immediacy about it. A distinct personality emerges as each sentence reveals not only the illuminated details of the farm but also the character of the storyteller.

The passage is rich in imagery and metaphor. Faced with the task of preparing and performing this text, the interpreter should ask what sort of person is seeing this scene and describing it. What do the metaphors tell about the character of the narrator? The moon is going down "on flushed cheek." As the sun creeps nearer to the top of the ridge, the farmhouse appears "like an old man's silver watch pulled once more out of its pocket." The dog has been lying "like a stone." The naked baby "monkey-climbed" down the steps. The narrator knows that the chickens let loose in the new light are Plymouth Rocks. The curl-papers in the girl's hair are "paler than the streak of dawn." The baby's legs are "running like a windmill." The point of the ridge is "like the tongue of a calf." The mirror on the porch wall begins to flicker "as at the striking of kitchen matches." The shadows of the porch posts are like "chalk marks . . . being drawn." The heat that comes with Sunday's first light is "solid as a hickory stick."

The images used to detail the story belong to what kind of person? Does the speaker seem to be a stranger in these parts or a part of the world of the story? Do the images and metaphors reflect the world of the story, or do they seem literary or sophisticated when compared with the setting and the characters?

Of course, the narrator seems to know the locale; the images used as figures of comparison are homely, a part of the world of the story. The heat is not oppressive, not like a slab. It is solid like a hickory stick, an object that belongs to the people of the story as well as to the narrator, just like the bulky school bus and the shadows like chalk on slate. These metaphors all suggest the air of "country school" that hangs about the dawn in the rural South even on a Sunday. The narrator does not stand aloof from the characters and events in the story but seems rather to be a member of their community, one whose vision of this morning light is infused with affection for the land and its people.

Sometimes a film begins with shots that set the scene and give a sense of atmosphere before the main characters are introduced. Similarly, this narrator glides smoothly over the landmarks of the farm, as light glides, and then illuminates at last the character who is to be the central figure in the novel: the old lady seated in the rocker. Granny, whose birthday celebration is the occasion of the novel, has been up and dressed long before dawn. She was sitting there from the first word of the description but is not mentioned until the sun is fully up, and its light, as well as the narrator's eye, reveals her.

We see, then, that third-person narration (like first-person narration) has both advantages and disadvantages. Objective observers clearly are for some the most reliable of storytellers, because all they tell is what has verifiably occurred. This "just the facts, nothing but the facts" approach can allow an audience to deduce relationships and attitudes and temperament for themselves. At the same time, this form of narration tends to be less gripping and can be difficult to sustain over a long tale. Omniscient observers — in all of the many forms this narrative type takes — ideally provide us with access to the past, future, and internal life of characters who command central positions in the story. Like all the other narrators, however, omniscient observers can withhold information at crucial times, and their interest in a given character may inhibit or even preclude equal interest in another character. Nevertheless, both kinds of third-person narrators are real people. A narrator does not have to appear as a character in a story to breathe, sympathize, or grieve. Personality cannot help but emerge in all the little details that give away the concerns of the soul. Certainly, clear attitudes, reflected in the words the narrator selects, the images the narrator chooses, the angle of vision the narrator employs, and of course the incidents themselves selected for narration, are all integral parts of the sensibility telling the tale. Interpreters need to be keenly aware of all of the details that reveal personality and character, even if the narrator never speaks from the personal point of view. Remember, we can communicate narration only when we communicate the narrator.

Action and Plot

Once you understand who is telling a story, you need to understand precisely what is going on, how the narrative moves, and where it is going. You should ask of every story, "What is its action?" *Action* is the sequence of visible or discernible physical happenings, the movement that courses through events. How is the action of a story different from its plot? *Plot* is the term used to describe the scheme or plan or design of the action. Plot orders action and arranges it in a pattern. The plot may involve psychological or physical action, and it may turn when one of the characters undergoes a change that affects the outcome of the story.

The *crisis* of a narrative is the turning point of the action. Like the fulcrum in a poem, the crisis serves as the "point of no return"; it is that point after which there can be only one possible resolution.

Conflict is essential in narrative; it causes action and plot. As you know, most works of literature involve people facing problems. (We rarely find much interest in people who are happy, at peace, and have nothing to do.) In both comedy and tragedy characters face obstacles: comic characters tend to overcome their problems, and tragic characters succumb to them. But there are always some obstacles, some types of conflict. They may be internal and psychological, or external and social. Frequently, external and internal conflicts are combined, one accenting the other or causing the other. Characters may fight city hall, nature, their in-laws, society, massive machines, repressive traditions, or even an idea whose time has come.

Conflict need not be completely explained nor absolutely real; there need not even be an absolute logic in the design of the events. But each element must obey the rules the story sets up for itself. Meaning arises from the way in which the tale is true to itself. Just as the characters in Archibald Marshall's "The Detective" can speak without proper punctuation and still be very proper Englishmen, and just as Baucis and Philemon can become intertwined trees in Ovid's *Metamorphoses*, and just as the child responds only to the angular movements and jagged sounds of cranes in David Leavitt's *Lost Language of Cranes*, (all three selections appear at the end of this chapter), characters do what they must to live in the particular world of the work they inhabit. If narratives — indeed, if any works of art — can be said to obey rules at all, they obey the rules they set for themselves.

Character

At this point in our analysis, we have discovered who is telling the story and the general action (as ordered in the plot) of the tale itself. Now we must discover what sort of people the story is about, the third of the crucial questions we mentioned earlier. Without a narrator, of course, there would be no action; without action, the characters would have nothing to do — indeed, there would be no characters because we understand characters by examining what they do, what they say, and what others say about them. First and last, it is the people we encounter — the characters — who grasp us most when we read, who help us understand who *we* are.

Narrative discovers character through action. We learn about people from what others — including the narrator — say about them. And we learn about character from the manner in which the narrator supplies all this information (Setting, too, affects people and personality; we discuss setting later.) Most often, personality, habit, and response motivate a character's reaction to the forces that shape a story.

A third-person narrator may tell us all we need to know about a character's appearance, behavior, speech, or thoughts. To consolidate these clues we must add material from our own lives and experiences. Be sure to understand exactly why characters refer to each other in the manner they do. If Clara calls George a "bonehead," be sure you know what George calls her and why she considers George in such a light before you take her word as truth. And remember that unreliable narrators (first-person narrators) can sometimes change the truth of an event to suit their preferences.

Characters whom you confront may be simple (like those who populate Marshall's "The Detective"). Depth and development of character are not requirements for successful stories. Little Red Riding Hood just wants to get to her grandmother's house, and the tortoise beats the hare chiefly because he doesn't stop to munch a carrot. Not much more is needed, since the situation itself or the attitude of the storyteller to the events is what interests us.

Fuller characters — those that E. M. Forster calls "round characters"[3] — require an internal life that both corresponds to and illumines the external make-up of the character. Sometimes the physical lives of the characters predominate; sometimes the psychological components are primary. Most often, both aspects together sketch the outlines of the character — as happens with Tony/Tommy in Malamud's "The Prison" at the end of this chapter. Whatever component is emphasized, in performance the characters must be totalities. Only for purposes of analysis can we separate their components. As in life, so in narrative: the character is greater than the sum of his or her attributes.

Dialogue

The fourth question to answer is "What are they saying to each other?" Almost every narrator at some point allows the characters to speak for themselves, providing the audience immediate access to the scene of the story, affording variety through distinctive personalities and speech rhythms, and emphasizing vividness in characterization. Although it may be useful and convenient for the writer, dialogue can cause trouble for the interpreter.

Dialogue may be in the form of either direct or indirect discourse. *Direct discourse* is the verbatim recording of the words the character is speaking. It is usually marked by quotation marks, although you

3. E. M. Forster *Aspects of the Novel* (New York: Harcourt, Brace and Company, 1927).

cannot always depend on authors to use them; in "The Detective" Archibald Marshall doesn't. Dialogue tags like "she said" are not much help either, for they do not always precede or follow a speech. Direct discourse introduces in the place of narration the total presence of a character, as if the narrator has momentarily stepped aside to allow the character to assume fully the telling of the tale. The richness of the story is enhanced immeasurably by the immediacy of the character's voice and perspective. Direct discourse depends on the interchange of question, response, and opinion. Characters speak because they wish to be heard, if only by themselves. Audiences should always be aware of who is speaking and who is listening and the listener's effect on the speaker.

On the other hand, *indirect discourse* reports the words the characters spoke and depends on an articulated or assumed "that." For example, in "she admitted she would eat the turtle," only the first two words are unquestionably pure narration. The remainder blends both the narrator's reporting and the character's declaration. Thus, the interpreter must make clear who is speaking by suggesting the personality of the character through the skillful use of body, voice, and the appropriate mental and physical attitude while not neglecting the narrator.

Indirect discourse blends the presence of the narrator with the presence of the character, so that narrator and character seem to be seen and heard simultaneously. The degree to which the narrator adopts the language, diction, and sentiments of the character is the ratio of the blend of narrator and character that the audience sees and hears. A remembered remark, for example, would carry less of the character's attitude than a reiterated demand would, although in both cases both narrator and character appear. Narrators commonly use indirect discourse in either simple grammatical sentences like "He said that . . ." or in more complex forms such as "She remembered having heard him say that . . ."

Examine this sentence from Flannery O'Connor's "Greenleaf":

"I thank God for ever thang," said Mr. Greenleaf.

Now compare it with these two sentences:

Mr. Greenleaf said that he thanked God for ever thang.
Then Greenleaf acknowledged divine providence.

O'Connor's sentence clearly demonstrates direct discourse: from the opening quotation marks the character fully assumes the line, and the narrator does not reappear until the end of the sentence. The second sentence blends the character and the narrator; but because the narrator has clearly adopted the characteristic diction and figures of speech of the character ("ever thang"), this sentence may demonstrate the character's attitude more than the narrator's. Finally, the last sentence has a narrator who has retained only the character's idea and has transformed it into his or her own language — language that is much more sophisticated than the character. In performance this would be seen as a narrator who dominates, but does not obliterate, the character. Sometimes, when indirect discourse implies subsequent activity ("He finally decided that he'd leave the kitchen and see for himself"), there is a clear appeal to a character's muscle response. The narrator can both describe this appeal and suggest it by mentally projecting the decision and its result. In each of these cases, though, remember that your decisions on how to perform a line rest on stylistic as well as literal clues, since style reveals background, attitudes, and the degree of mental or emotional tension of the moment.

Understanding the differences between these two kinds of discourse can help you understand the various technical ways in which an interpreter can persuade an audience to believe that they are seeing before them not a student in a class but a character in a story. To achieve such belief, you must solve the technical problems that arise from performing dialogue. We discuss some of the techniques here. Also examine Chapter 8, particularly the section "Embodying Characters." Techniques for creating character are useful in narration as well as drama.

First, remember that characters are persons with bodies and voices. Read the story carefully to find all of the clues the narrator gives about the characters in the story. Note carefully the kinds of language the characters use, the kinds of things others say to and about the characters. Then begin to observe — very carefully — the world around you. Have you ever seen twelve-year-old boys coming home from school? How do they carry themselves? How does a thoughtful boy hold his head? What does a rambunctious boy do with his arms and legs? Your own age and gender are immaterial at this point. When you have some physical clues about these boys, you are beginning to prepare to perform Roth's "The Conversion of the Jews," which appears at the end of this chapter. But you have only *just* begun. Now start listening carefully. How do boys this age talk? Has the voice changed? Or is it in that horrible no man's land between soprano and baritone, where it hits most of the notes in the scale? Begin to play with your voice. See if you can make yourself sound that age. Your first efforts will probably make you want to consider changing stories, but keep your courage and stay with it. Now add your body to the voice. It ought to feel out of place because you are not twelve, and possibly not male. How can your body resemble the boys you observed? With a voice and body that begin to sound and look like something, it is often easier to undertake the biggest problem in creating characters.

You have established some external characteristics for the audience, but these will simply be externals until you provide the personality that sparks the voice and body to life. Are you thinking about these people in the worlds that they inhabit? Have you examined the part they play in the action of the tale?

Of course, no character exists apart from a story. That is why you should know as much as possible about the persons you are performing. Review the whole story and glean whatever clues you can from the information given, remembering that this overall view places the characters in proper perspective. Determine the character's gender, age, and maturity. Then define the personal characteristics that distinguish the character's attitude, degree of emotional intensity, and any peculiar or important personal traits. Be sure to notice explicit descriptions about how a speech is said or what state of mind has prompted it, for narrative writing is uniquely able to stop action and examine motivation. Don't miss the implicit clues contained in the style of the speech, in the narrator's understanding of and sympathy with the character, and in the way in which the character's position is presented to the audience. Finally, remember that however bizarre these characters may seem to you, they are real in their own worlds, and you should create them to live there on their terms, not within your world. In "Conversion of the Jews," for example, you should discover why the boys are concerned about Rabbi Binder. Be sure you understand why they act the way they do. Is your Ozzie making serious efforts to figure out what Rabbi Binder is arguing? Here concentration will become increasingly important: only if you commit yourself to the character's life can your audience fully perceive the character's goals. Once you have completed this process for one speaking character, repeat it for all the major characters in the passage you are reading.

When you speak the words of a character's dialogue, re-create in your mind the person who is being addressed; see that person vividly in front of you, established at a position slightly above and beyond the audience. This technique permits the audience to sit in the middle of the tension that ties the characters together and that prompts them to speak; it also protects any particular audience member from feeling directly addressed. Your mental and vocal projection should therefore be strong enough to carry slightly beyond the last row. When you resume the words of the narrator and describe or summarize, you will be able to speak directly to your audience and to establish rapport with them. If several characters speak in rapid succession, establish a place (a point of focus) for each of them, once again slightly above and beyond the audience. (You may wish to consult Chapter 8, particularly the section "Physical Focus," for a further discussion of the ways to solve this kind of problem.)

Remember that dialogue has different levels of intensity. Seek the degree of forcefulness that suggests the character's emotional and psychological state at the moment of speaking; casual comments can be delivered with less power than pleas for freedom are. Mind you, *mental* focus does not relax, but people ask for the butter more often than they scream for help. The key is spontaneity, since it acknowledges the other characters and motivates responses.

Although you may feel at this point that there isn't anything else you can learn about a story, much remains to be understood. We mentioned that characters live in their own worlds. Because we need to know not only what and why they act, but also *where* they act, we must examine the role setting plays in narration.

Setting

Setting is a matter not only of locale but also of style. Narrators can see the world through all kinds of spectacles, but where they allow their characters to interact and where they permit them to speak is as much a matter of the tale as it is a choice of the teller. If we learn that "Aunt Tillie Beta pours her tea each afternoon as the sun strikes four against the walnut bureau," we can see not only the aunt's habitual tea but also her residence; the narrator acknowledges her ritual by permitting the sun to toll its time as solemnly as a clock. Dylan Thomas weaves another kind of world in one of the stories from *Quite Early One Morning:*

I was born in a large Welsh town at the beginning of the Great War — an ugly, lovely town (or so it was and is to me), crawling by a long and splendid curving shore where truant boys and sandfield boys and old men from nowhere, beach-combed, idled and paddled, watched the dock-bound ships or the ships steaming away into wonder and India, magic and China, countries bright with oranges and loud with lions; threw stones into the sea for the barking outcast dogs; made castles and forts and harbours and race tracks in the sand; and on Saturday summer afternoons listened to the brass band, watched the Punch and Judy, or hung about on the fringes of the crowd to hear the fierce religious speakers who shouted at the sea, as though it were wicked and wrong to roll in and out like that, whitehorsed and full of fishes.[4]

What an abundance of things to see and hear and smell and touch and taste! And the rush of activity — presented in one massive, breathless sentence — surrounds the reader utterly. Notice how Thomas couples the items in the catalog: the town is ugly and lovely; boys and old men beach-comb, idle, and paddle; the sea that licks that splendid shore carries men to wonder and magic. Also, brass bands and summers; puppet plays and town prophets; charging and pulling seas finally full of nothing scarier than fishes: what a wonderful, breathless world!

To interpret the story, you need to capture that world. Develop a keen visual and physical sense, so that in performance the whirling scene is all around you and your audience. Don't begin until you do. Let your audience see the shore and the boys, and then (as in an aerial shot in a film) move to the ships, the stones, and continue on through the town. A gesture might locate those most important places as they pass before you; let that palpable, living world motivate your description. Put Thomas's world there, in front of you. Tell your listeners about it!

Although not every scene is as boisterous as this one, every scene affects the characters and at the same time locates the action. Travel and adventure stories, in particular, use place as a crucial element in the telling of the tale because landscape, climate, and time of day inevitably affect the characters. Biographies and autobiographies, histories and historical fiction all depend on an audience's acceptance of the vividness of the period, a sense that life was lived fully. Even the most fantastic story uses setting as an element to persuade an audience of the internal reality of the world of the tale, affecting the characters in obvious or subtle, superficial or profound ways.

Cutting and Excerpting

Only rarely do interpreters discover a poem, story, or play that fits exactly all of the many requirements that performers impose on texts: the right length, balance of characters, distribution of lines and action, and level of challenge. Consequently, interpreters have to take

4. Dylan Thomas, *Quite Early One Morning* (New York: New Directions, 1954).

on works that, in one way or another, do not measure up to the performance or time requirements imposed by the occasion or assignment. They must cut or excerpt the text.

As we have stressed, interpretation seeks to communicate a work of literary art in its intellectual, aesthetic, and emotional entirety. This does not necessarily mean that one must perform every syllable of a work; indeed, the *essence* of an entire piece of literature can successfully be conveyed through performance of only a selection from it. There is a crucial distinction between excerpting a segment from a longer work and cutting, or abridging, a work in an attempt to encompass the entire work in a short amount of time. You should be aware of problems and dangers in both methods.

In *excerpting* from a longer work, the interpreter chooses a scene or passage that, when taken on its own, displays a totality of action, theme, or character development. Claire Morrill's "Miss Lizzie" (Chapter 11) offers several episodes that can be successfully excerpted, as does Isaac Bashevis Singer's "A Crown of Feathers" (Chapter 4). In each of these selections various brief segments seem to be relatively complete. In excerpting a segment, you should supply — in a *brief* introduction or in transitional comments — all the information necessary for the audience to understand fully what happens in the story. The segment itself should remain uncut; that is, you do not need to make interlinear or internal cuts, since the range or length of the segment itself conforms to the various requirements imposed by the particular performance situation. A long chapter that boasts a particularly attractive opening scene and a vivid conclusion might tempt an interpreter to splice the two sections together. However, the splicing itself can dangerously impair the delicate rhythms established by the author. Why not admit frankly that you are presenting two scenes from the same chapter? Perform the whole compelling opening; then, in your own words, fill in the transition with whatever information is necessary for the audience to understand the conclusion, which then can be performed as written by the author. This method has at least three special benefits. First, you can more accurately suggest the intellectual, aesthetic, and emotional entirety of the complete work since you have not tampered with the internal tempo or development of the segments. Second, you can deal with the smaller segments more effectively in short periods of rehearsal time. Finally, because the segments themselves are more easily manageable, you have a better chance of capturing your audience's attention and appreciation. Best of all, of course, is the fact that excerpting allows you to select scenes from any work of literature that you want: the entirety of *Moby Dick* is impossible to perform, but numerous crucial scenes within the book can be presented rewardingly.

Cutting differs from excerpting in that it imposes on diverse or unrelated words, lines, or scenes a false consecutiveness or immediate relationship not intended by the author. Some interpreters refuse to eliminate anything from what they perform, because they do not wish to impose on the work a pattern or scheme that violates its integrity. For other interpreters, cutting presents no particular problem. A performance may be restricted by time, by financial or physical resources, or sometimes by the intent of the performance. In spite of these limitations, you should approach the task of cutting literature with respect and concern for its essence because the life of the work is what interests you; that life is what you seek to communicate in performance.

You should be fully aware of all of the problems that cutting can create. Of course, cutting a character who has one or two lines, such as a maid or an attendant lord whose chief responsibility is to announce an arrival or present a prop, usually does not impair the excitement of the scene; but be sure that the arriving character or the prop is not central to the scene itself.

Tempo and rhythm should be regarded with utmost caution when you are considering cutting. Look at the passage from Toni Morrison's *Sula* at the end of this chapter. Hannah repeats "Plum" and "Mamma" at crucial places. However tempting it may seem, avoid altering the delicate rhythm Morrison worked so hard to achieve. Let the story remain uncut.

A cutting that may be small or seem insignificant can strongly affect the sense of the story. Consider Malamud's "The Prison," where the performer — already undertaking the narrator, the central character Tony/Tommy, his wife Rosa, and the little girl — is confronted for only a moment by the little girl's mother, who appears briefly at the end of the tale. It would be easy to cut her line; it is tempting, too, because cutting it would eliminate another character to suggest. However, what she says ("You little thief, this time you'll get your hands burned good") tells us quickly and fully what drove the little girl to steal. Cutting the mother would drastically violate the achievement of the story.

So the interpreter alters a text with care and tact. We are not saying that you should never cut; we are saying that sensitive and experienced interpreters undertake cutting with great caution. If they can avoid cutting, they do. Think carefully and completely about what you are about to do, since cutting must not be some immediate response at an instant when it seems you'll never master the line.

Judge honestly what you will gain and what you will lose if you eliminate a line or a few sentences. If, however, there is no other, more discreet way to overcome the restrictions imposed by time or circumstance, cut only the minimum, and only what *must* be cut.

Analyzing the Performance

Before we concentrate on how successfully you performed narration and prose, recheck the questions in the "Analyzing the Performance" sections in chapters 2 and 4. Recall the problems that cropped up in your earlier readings. Have you improved your ability to concentrate? Have you paid clear and consistent attention to variety and contrast? Has your voice contributed to the unity and harmony of the selection? Has your body become more responsive to the imagery, particularly the kinesthetic images of your selection?

Such questions will never disappear from your performance analysis because whatever literature you select will challenge you in new and exciting ways. Don't allow yourself to become discouraged if some aspect of your performance seems to resist improvement. Sometimes skill requires considerably more effort than may be apparent. No one is instantly proficient at playing tennis or the violin. Constant, careful, and consistent concentration and commitment will produce the kinds of results you anticipate. One further thought about progress: be sure to listen carefully to and watch closely every other performer you can. You can always learn something instructive. At the same time, don't measure your own progress against others in your class. You are better off gauging your developing prowess against the fine difficulty of the works you choose to perform. The most significant development in performance comes from valiant efforts with literature that cause you to reach slightly beyond your grasp. Nothing is gained by repeating the easy.

If you have not yet begun to experiment, why not begin? If you have performed only verse thus far, now is the time to try prose. Have you been concentrating on contemporary literature? Try a passage from one of the classic authors. Have you attempted personae whose gender is opposite to yours? What about characters of different ages and background and dialects? The function of any class in oral interpretation is not to confirm you in your ability to perform melancholy young women disappointed in love or brash and joking dudes who always crack up audiences. Rather, oral interpretation asks that you experience the human condition in all its manifestations. Keep exploring yourself and your performance possibilities.

Now, together we can explore some common problems in performing prose. Again, try to respond to the questions as honestly as you can.

Did your analysis of the style of the writer suggest physical and vocal analogues to the literature? How did your compound and complex sentences look and sound?

Did your body and voice manifest the personality apparent in the speaker's word choice? Were you consistent?

Did you balance each sentence, locating the precise point for the most efficient placement of the fulcrum?

Did you control your physical and vocal resources to shape each sentence (and each paragraph) to the shape of the thought?

Were you attentive to parallel structure? Did you carefully attend to each speech phrase?

Did you allow your body and voice to reflect the fullest possible engagement with the tone color?

Did you carefully construct an internal and external life for your narrator? Was your audience always certain who was in charge? Did you permit the narrator to relinquish dominance during passages of scene and discourse?

Were your characters as full-blooded as those of the narrator? Did your narrator blend into the characters in the passage? Why?

Did you center the narrator's interest on the action and plot? Were your body and voice in control of the events?

Did the dialogue passages seem spontaneous and unforced? Was your audience certain who was speaking?

Did you excerpt without internal cutting?

These questions can also help you focus on the performance of others. In your classroom discussion, try to describe as precisely as possible at least two or three of the following concerns:

1. the nature of the narrator you *saw* and *heard:* his or her age and attitude toward events, characters, setting, and the audience to whom the tale is told

2. the relationships between the narrator and the characters, as demonstrated by the performer

3. the internal and external lives of the narrator and characters, as demonstrated by the performer

4. performance behavior that gave life to personalities in the story

5. facility in the management of dialogue, as demonstrated by the performer

6. the immediacy of the tale being told, as it is shown in the performance.

When differences of opinion arise, return to the literature being performed. Your job as critic is to describe what you saw and heard and then to compare that performance with the text you know. Possibly you have performed the same passage yourself and thus know some of the problems more thoroughly than your classmates. Still, keep your attention directed to what happened in the performance you *saw* and *heard*, not what might have happened or what didn't happen. It isn't very helpful to say to a performer, "I didn't see any anger in Rosa's response to Tommy." Rather, try to describe exactly what you did see and hear; for example, "I saw a Rosa who seemed very calm and relaxed; your rate and volume were very easygoing." When you combine your responses with those of other audience members — and with the performer — you are ready to re-examine the story to find those clues that suggest precisely how Rosa ought to sound and behave.

Performing takes courage. If you want to improve, it helps to feel secure enough with your fellow students to experiment. Such freedom is difficult to achieve if you expect to get "torn apart" each time you perform. Discussion of a performance permits everyone to learn *if* everyone listens carefully and everyone thinks for a moment before speaking. Any given performance is a step on the route to the best possible performance. If you genuinely want to be helped by your classmates, be genuinely helpful in what you say to them.

In Chapter 11, "The Group Performance of Literature," we describe the technique of Chamber Theatre, which is the staging of narrative. You may wish to examine this chapter for further ideas about performing narration. Although that chapter focuses on groups, many of the techniques it describes may spark your imagination with solutions that a solo performer can use. If you remember that your primary responsibility is to tell the audience a story — the tale that the author conceived and the narrator relates — your performance of narration will enlighten both you and your audience. You will discover the rare pleasure of having told it very well, very well indeed.

Selections for Analysis and Oral Interpretation

Because the narrator in this story understands Tommy's frustration much better than Tommy himself does, the audience receives a rich and complex picture of the young man's entrapment, his grim existence, and his future. Pay careful attention to the ways in which Malamud's language indicates shifts in the closeness of narrator and central character.

The Prison

BERNARD MALAMUD

Though he tried not to think of it, at twenty-nine Tommy Castelli's life was a screaming bore. It wasn't just Rosa or the store they tended for profits counted in pennies, or the unendurably slow hours and endless drivel that went with selling candy, cigarettes, and soda water; it was this sick-in-the-stomach feeling of being trapped in old mistakes, even some he had made before Rosa changed Tony into Tommy. He had been as Tony a kid of many dreams and schemes, especially getting out of this tenement-crowded, kid-squawking neighborhood, with its lousy poverty, but everything had fouled up against him before he could. When he was sixteen he quit the vocational school where they were making him into a shoemaker, and began to hang out with the gray-hatted, thick-soled-shoe boys, who had the spare time and the mazuma and showed it in fat wonderful rolls down in the cellar clubs to all who would look, and everybody did, popeyed. They were the ones who had bought the silver caffe espresso urn and later the television, and they arranged the pizza parties and had the girls down; but it was getting in with them and their cars, leading to the holdup of a liquor store, that had started all the present trouble. Lucky for him the coal-and-ice man who was their landlord knew the leader in the district, and they arranged something so nobody bothered him after that. Then before he knew what was going on — he had been frightened sick by the whole mess — there was his father cooking up a deal with Rosa Agnello's old man that Tony would marry her and the father-in-law would, out of his savings, open a candy store for him to make an honest living. He wouldn't spit on a candy store, and Rosa was too plain and lank a chick for his personal taste, so he beat it off to Texas and bummed around in too much space, and when he came back everybody said it was for Rosa and the candy store, and it was all arranged again and he, without saying no, was in it.

   That was how he had landed on Prince Street in the Village, working from eight in the morning to almost midnight every day, except for an hour off each afternoon when he went upstairs to sleep; and on Tuesdays, when the store was closed and he slept some more and went at night alone to the movies. He was too tired always for schemes now, but once he tried to make a little cash on the side by secretly taking in punchboards some syndicate was distributing in the neighborhood, on which he collected a nice cut and in this way saved fifty-five bucks that Rosa didn't know about; but then the syndicate was written up by a newspaper, and the punchboards all disappeared. Another time, when Rosa was at her mother's house, he took a chance and let them put in a slot machine that could guarantee a nice piece of change if he kept it long enough. He knew of course he couldn't hide it from her, so when she came and screamed when she saw it, he was ready and patient, for once not yelling back when she yelled, and he explained it was not the same as gambling because anybody who played it got a roll of mints every time he put in a nickel. Also the machine would supply them a few extra dollars cash they could use to buy television so he could see the fights without going to a bar; but Rosa wouldn't let up screaming, and later her father came in shouting that he was a criminal and chopped the machine apart with a plumber's hammer. The next day the cops raided for slot machines and gave out summonses wherever they found them, and though Tommy's place was practically the only candy store in the neighborhood that didn't have one, he felt bad about the machine for a long time.

Mornings had been his best time of day because Rosa stayed upstairs cleaning, and since few people came into the store till noon, he could sit around alone, a toothpick in his teeth, looking over the *News* and *Mirror* on the fountain counter, or maybe gab with one of the old cellar-club guys who had happened to come by for a pack of butts, about a horse that was running that day or how the numbers were paying lately; or just sit there, drinking coffee and thinking how far away he could get on the fifty-five he had stashed away in the cellar. Generally the mornings were this way, but after the slot machine, usually the whole day stank and he along with it. Time rotted in him, and all he could think of the whole morning, was going to sleep in the afternoon, and he would wake up with the sour remembrance of the long night in the store ahead of him, while everybody else was doing as he damn pleased. He cursed the candy store and Rosa, and cursed, from its beginning, his unhappy life.

It was on one of these bad mornings that a ten-year-old girl from around the block came in and asked for two rolls of colored tissue paper, one red and one yellow. He wanted to tell her to go to hell and stop bothering, but instead went with bad grace to the rear, where Rosa, whose bright idea it was to keep the stuff, had put it. He went from force of habit, for the girl had been coming in every Monday since the summer for the same thing, because her rock-faced mother, who looked as if she arranged her own widowhood, took care of some small kids after school and gave them the paper to cut out dolls and such things. The girl, whose name he didn't know, resembled her mother, except her features were not quite so sharp and she had very light skin with dark eyes; but she was a plain kid and would be more so at twenty. He had noticed, when he went to get the paper, that she always hung back as if afraid to go where it was dark, though he kept the comics there and most of the other kids had to be slapped away from them; and that when he brought her the tissue paper her skin seemed to grow whiter and her eyes shone. She always handed him two hot dimes and went out without glancing back.

It happened that Rosa, who trusted nobody, had just hung a mirror on the back wall, and as Tommy opened the drawer to get the girl her paper this Monday morning that he felt so bad, he looked up and saw in the glass something that made it seem as if he were dreaming. The girl had disappeared, but he saw a white hand reach into the candy case for a chocolate bar and for another, then she came forth from behind the counter and stood there, innocently waiting for him. He felt at first like grabbing her by the neck and socking till she threw up, but he had been caught, as he sometimes was, by this thought of how his Uncle Dom, years ago before he went away, used to take with him Tony alone of all the kids, when he went crabbing to Sheepshead Bay. Once they went at night and threw the baited wire traps into the water and after a while pulled them up and they had this green lobster in one, and just then this fat-faced cop came along and said they had to throw it back unless it was nine inches. Dom said it was nine inches, but the cop said not to be a wise guy so Dom measured it and it was ten, and they laughed about that lobster all night. Then he remembered how he had felt after Dom was gone, and tears filled his eyes. He found himself thinking about the way his life had turned out, and then about this girl, moved that she was so young and a thief. He felt he ought to do something for her, warn her to cut it out before she got trapped and fouled up her life before it got started. His urge to do this was strong, but when he went forward she looked up frightened because he had taken so long. The fear in her eyes bothered him and he didn't say anything. She thrust out the dimes, grabbed at the tissue rolls and ran out of the store.

He had to sit down. He kept trying to make the desire to speak to her go away, but it came back stronger than ever. He asked himself what difference does it make it she swipes candy — so she swipes it; and the role of reformer was strange and distasteful to him, yet he could not convince himself that what he felt he must do was unimportant. But he worried he would not know what to say to her. Always he had trouble speaking right, stumbled over words, especially in new situations. He was afraid he would sound like a jerk and she would not take him seriously. He had to tell her in a sure way so that even if it scared her, she would understand he had done it to set her straight. He mentioned her to no one but often thought about her, always looking around whenever he went outside to raise the awning or wash the window, to see if any of the girls playing in the street was her, but they never were. The following Monday, an hour after opening the store he had smoked a full pack of butts. He thought he had found what he wanted to say but was afraid for some reason she wouldn't come in, or if she did, this time she would be afraid to take the candy. He wasn't sure he wanted that to happen until he had said what he had to say. But at about eleven, while he was reading the *News,* she appeared, asking for the tissue paper, her eyes shining so he had to look away. He knew she meant to steal. Going to the rear he slowly opened the drawer, keeping his head lowered as he sneaked a look into the glass and saw her slide behind the counter. His heart beat hard and his feet felt nailed to the floor. He tried to remember what he had intended to do, but his mind was like a dark, empty room so he let her, in the end, slip away and stood tongue-tied, the dimes burning his palm.

Afterwards, he told himself that he hadn't spoken to her because it was while she still had the candy on her, and she would have been scared worse than he wanted. When he went upstairs, instead of sleeping, he sat at the kitchen window, looking out into the back yard. He blamed himself for being too soft, too chicken, but then he thought, no there was a better way to do it. He would do it indirectly, slip her a hint he knew, and he was pretty sure that would stop her. Sometime after, he would explain to her why it was good she had stopped. So next time he cleaned out this candy platter she helped herself from, thinking she might get wise he was on to her, but she seemed not to, only hesitated with her hand before she took two candy bars from the next plate and dropped them into the black patent leather purse she always had with her. The time after that he cleaned out the whole top shelf, and still she was not suspicious, and reached down to the next and took something different. One Monday he put some loose change, nickels and dimes, on the candy plate, but she left them there, only taking the candy, which bothered him a little. Rosa asked him what he was mooning about so much and why was he eating chocolate lately. He didn't answer her, and she began to look suspiciously at the women who came in, not excluding the little girls; and he would have been glad to rap her in the teeth, but it didn't matter as long as she didn't know what he had on his mind. At the same time he figured he would have to do something sure soon, or it would get harder for the girl to stop her stealing. He had to be strong about it. Then he thought of a plan that satisfied him. He would leave two bars on the plate and put in the wrapper of one a note she could read when she was alone. He tried out on paper many messages to her, and the one that seemed best he cleanly printed on a strip of cardboard and slipped it under the wrapper of one chocolate bar. It said, "Don't do this any more or you will suffer your whole life." He puzzled whether to sign it A Friend or Your Friend and finally chose Your Friend.

This was Friday, and he could not hold his impatience for Monday. But on Monday she did not appear. He waited for a long time, until Rosa came down, then he had to go up and the girl still hadn't come. He was greatly disappointed because she had never failed to come before. He lay on the bed, his shoes on, staring at the ceiling. He felt hurt, the sucker she had played him for and was now finished with because she probably had another on her hook. The more he thought about it the worse he felt. He worked up a splitting headache that kept him from sleeping, then he suddenly slept and woke without it. But he had awaked depressed, saddened. He thought about Dom getting out of jail and going away God knows where. He wondered whether he would ever meet up with him somewhere, if he took the fifty-five bucks and left. Then he remembered Dom was a pretty old guy now, and he might not know him if they did meet. He thought about life. You never really got what you wanted. No matter how hard you tried you made mistakes and couldn't get past them. You could never see the sky outside or the ocean because you were in a prison, except nobody called it a prison, and if you did they didn't know what you were talking about, or they said they didn't. A pall settled on him. He lay motionless, without thought or sympathy for himself or anybody.

But when he finally went downstairs, ironically amused that Rosa had allowed him so long a time off without bitching, there were people in the store and he could hear her screeching. Shoving his way through the crowd he saw in one sickening look that she had caught the girl with the candy bars and was shaking her so hard the kid's head bounced back and forth like a balloon on a stick. With a curse he tore her away from the girl, whose sickly face showed the depth of her fright.

"Whatsamatter," he shouted at Rosa, "you want her blood?"

"She's a thief," cried Rosa.

"Shut your face."

To stop her yowling he slapped her across her mouth, but it was a harder crack than he had intended. Rosa fell back with a gasp. She did not cry but looked around dazedly at everybody, and tried to smile, and everybody there could see her teeth were flecked with blood.

"Go home," Tommy ordered the girl, but then there was a movement near the door and her mother came into the store.

"What happened?" she said.

"She stole my candy," Rosa cried.

"I let her take it," said Tommy.

Rosa stared at him as if she had been hit again, then with mouth distorted began to sob.

"One was for you, Mother," said the girl.

Her mother socked her hard across the ear. "You little thief, this time you'll get your hands burned good."

She pawed at the girl, grabbed her arm and yanked it. The girl, like a grotesque dancer, half-ran, half-fell forward, but at the door she managed to turn her white face and thrust out at him her red tongue.

▌ How did you embody the relationship between the narrator and Tommy?

▌ How much of Tommy did we see during indirect discourse?

The narrator of this story by John Updike treats us as his friends, and the events he tells us about have affected him deeply, but he is not lugubrious. Don't let him become overbearing or dimwitted, either. Why does he quit his job?

A & P

JOHN UPDIKE

In walks these three girls in nothing but bathing suits. I'm in the third checkout slot, with my back to the door, so I don't see them until they're over by the bread. The one that caught my eye first was the one in the plaid green two-piece. She was a chunky kid, with a good tan and a sweet broad soft-looking can with those two crescents of white just under it, where the sun never seems to hit, at the top of the backs of her legs. I stood there with my hand on a box of HiHo crackers trying to remember if I rang it up or not. I ring it up again and the customer starts giving me hell. She's one of these cash-register-watchers, a witch about fifty with rouge on her cheekbones and no eyebrows, and I know it made her day to trip me up. She'd been watching cash registers for fifty years and probably never seen a mistake before.

By the time I got her feathers smoothed and her goodies into a bag — she gives me a little snort in passing, if she'd been born at the right time they would have burned her over in Salem — by the time I get her on her way the girls had circled around the bread and were coming back, without a pushcart, back my way along the counters, in the aisle between the checkouts and the Special bins. They didn't even have shoes on. There was this chunky one, with the two-piece — it was bright green and the seams on the bra were still sharp and her belly was still pretty pale so I guessed she just got it (the suit) — there was this one, with one of those chubby berry-faces, the lips all bunched together under her nose, this one, and a tall one, with black hair that hadn't quite frizzed right, and one of these sunburns right across under the eyes, and a chin that was too long — you know, the kind of girl other girls think is very "striking" and "attractive" but never quite makes it, as they very well know, which is why they like her so much — and then the third one, that wasn't quite so tall. She was the queen. She kind of led them, the other two peeking around and making their shoulders round. She didn't look around, not this queen, she just walked straight on slowly, on these long white prima-donna legs. She came down a little hard on her heels, as if she didn't walk in her bare feet that much, putting down her heels and then letting the weight move along to her toes as if she was testing the floor with every step, putting a little deliberate extra action into it. You never know for sure how girls' minds work (do you really think it's a mind in there or just a little buzz like a bee in a glass jar?) but you got the idea she had talked the other two into coming in here with her, and now she was showing them how to do it, walk slow and hold yourself straight.

She had on a kind of dirty-pink — beige maybe, I don't know — bathing suit with a little nubble all over it and, what got me, the straps were down. They were off her shoulders looped loose around the cool tops of her arms, and I guess as a result the suit had slipped a little on her, so all around the top of the cloth there was this shining rim. If it hadn't been there you wouldn't have known there could have been anything whiter than those shoulders. With the straps pushed off, there was nothing between the top of the suit and the top of her head except just *her*, this clean bare plane of the top of her chest down from the shoulder bones like a dented sheet of metal tilted in the light. I mean, it was more than pretty.

She had sort of oaky hair that the sun and salt had bleached, done up in a bun that was unraveling, and a kind of prim face. Walking into the A & P with your straps down, I suppose it's the only kind of face you *can* have. She held her head so high her neck, coming up out of those white shoulders, looked kind of stretched, but I didn't mind. The longer her neck was, the more of her there was.

She must have felt in the corner of her eye me and over my shoulder Stokesie in the second slot watching, but she didn't tip. Not this queen. She kept her eyes moving across the racks, and stopped, and turned so slow it made my stomach rub the inside of my apron, and buzzed to the other two, who kind of huddled against her for relief, and then they all three of them went up the cat-and-dog-food-breakfast-cereal-macaroni-rice-raisins-seasonings-spreads-spaghetti-soft-drinks-crackers-and-cookies aisle. From the third slot I look straight up this aisle to the meat counter, and I watched them all the way. The fat one with the tan sort of fumbled with the cookies, but on second thought she put the package back. The sheep pushing their carts down the aisle — the girls were walking against the usual traffic (not that we have one-way signs or anything) — were pretty hilarious. You could see them, when Queenie's white shoulders dawned on them, kind of jerk, or hop, or hiccup, but their eyes snapped back to their own baskets and on they pushed. I bet you could set off dynamite in an A & P and the people would by and large keep reaching and checking oatmeal off their lists and muttering "Let me see, there was a third thing, began with A, asparagus, no, ah, yes, applesauce!" or whatever it is they do mutter. But there was no doubt, this jiggled them. A few houseslaves in pin curlers even looked around after pushing their carts past to make sure what they had seen was correct.

You know, it's one thing to have a girl in a bathing suit down on the beach, where what with the glare nobody can look at each other much anyway, and another thing in the cool of the A & P, under the fluorescent lights, against all those stacked packages, with her feet paddling along naked over our checkerboard green-and-cream rubber-tile floor.

"Oh Daddy," Stokesie said beside me. "I feel so faint."

"Darling," I said. "Hold me tight." Stokesie's married, with two babies chalked up on his fuselage already, but as far as I can tell that's the only difference. He's twenty-two, and I was nineteen this April.

"Is it done?" he asks, the responsible married man finding his voice. I forgot to say he thinks he's going to be manager some sunny day, maybe in 1990 when it's called the Great Alexandrov and Petrooshki Tea Company or something.

What he meant was, our town is five miles from a beach, with a big summer colony out on the Point, but we're right in the middle of town, and the women generally put on a shirt or shorts or something before they get out of the car into the street. And anyway these are usually women with six children and varicose veins mapping their legs and nobody, including them, could care less. As I say, we're right in the middle of town, and if you stand at our front doors you can see two banks and the Congregational church and the newspaper store and three real-estate offices and about twenty-seven old freeloaders tearing up Central Street because the sewer broke again. It's not as if we're on the Cape; we're north of Boston and there's people in this town haven't seen the ocean for twenty years.

The girls had reached the meat counter and were asking McMahon something. He pointed, they pointed, and they shuffled out of sight behind a pyramid of Diet Delight peaches. All that was left for us to see was old McMahon patting his mouth and looking after them sizing up their joints. Poor kids, I began to feel sorry for them, they couldn't help it.

Now here comes the sad part of the story, at least my family says it's sad, but I don't think it's so sad myself. The store's pretty empty, it being Thursday afternoon, so there was nothing much to do except lean on the register and wait for the girls to show up again. The whole store was like a pinball machine and I didn't know which tunnel they'd come out of. After a while they come around out of the far aisle, around the light bulbs, records at discount of the Caribbean Six or Tony Martin Sings or some such gunk you wonder they waste the wax on, sixpacks of candy bars, and plastic toys done up in cellophane that fall apart when a kid looks at them anyway. Around they come, Queenie still leading the way, and holding a little gray jar in her hand. Slots Three through Seven are unmanned and I could see her wondering between Stokes and me, but Stokesie with his usual luck draws an old party in baggy gray pants who stumbles up with four giant cans of pineapple juice (what do these bums *do* with all that pineapple juice? I've often asked myself) so the girls come to me. Queenie puts down the jar and I take it into my fingers icy cold. Kingfish Fancy Herring Snacks in Pure Sour Cream: 49¢. Now her hands are empty, not a ring or a bracelet, bare as God made them, and I wonder where the money's coming from. Still with that prim look she lifts a folded dollar bill out of the hollow at the center of her nubbled pink top. The jar went heavy in my hand. Really, I thought that was so cute.

Then everybody's luck begins to run out. Lengel comes in from haggling with a truck full of cabbages on the lot and is about to scuttle into that door marked MANAGER behind which he hides all day when the girls touch his eye. Lengel's pretty dreary, teaches Sunday school and the rest, but he doesn't miss that much. He comes over and says, "Girls, this isn't the beach."

Queenie blushes, though maybe it's just a brush of sunburn I was noticing for the first time, now that she was so close. "My mother asked me to pick up a jar of herring snacks." Her voice kind of startled me, the way voices do when you see the people first, coming out so flat and dumb yet kind of tony, too, the way it ticked over "pick up" and "snacks." All of a sudden I slid right down her voice into her living room. Her father and the other men were standing around in ice-cream coats and bow ties and the women were in sandals picking up herring snacks on toothpicks off a big glass plate and they were all holding drinks the color of water with olives and sprigs of mint in them. When my parents have somebody over they get lemonade and if it's a real racy affair Schlitz in tall glasses with "They'll Do It Every Time" cartoons stenciled on.

"That's all right," Lengel said. "But this isn't the beach." His repeating this struck me as funny, as if it had just occurred to him, and he had been thinking all these years the A & P was a great big dune and he was the head lifeguard. He didn't like my smiling — as I say he doesn't miss much — but he concentrates on giving the girls that sad Sunday-school-superintendent stare.

Queenie's blush is no sunburn now, and the plump one in plaid, that I like better from the back — a really sweet can — pipes up, "We weren't doing any shopping. We just came in for the one thing."

"That makes no difference," Lengel tells her, and I could see from the way his eyes went that he hadn't noticed she was wearing a two-piece before. "We want you decently dressed when you come in here."

"We *are* decent," Queenie says suddenly, her lower lip pushing, getting sore now that she remembers her place, a place from which the crowd that runs the A & P must look pretty crummy. Fancy Herring Snacks flashed in her very blue eyes.

"Girls, I don't want to argue with you. After this come in here with your shoulders covered. It's our policy." He turns his back. That's policy for you. Policy is what the kingpins want. What the others want is juvenile delinquency.

All this while, the customers had been showing up with their carts but, you know, sheep, seeing a scene, they had all bunched up on Stokesie, who shook open a paper bag as gently as peeling a peach, not wanting to miss a word. I could feel in the silence everybody getting nervous, most of all Lengel, who asks me, "Sammy, have you rung up their purchase?"

I thought and said "No" but it wasn't about that I was thinking. I go through the punches, 4, 9, GROC, TOT — it's more complicated than you think, and after you do it often enough, it begins to make a little song, that you hear words to, in my case "Hello (*bing*) there, you (*gung*) hap-py *pee*-pul (*splat*)! — the *splat* being the drawer flying out. I uncrease the bill, tenderly as you may imagine, it just having come from between the two smoothest scoops of vanilla I had ever known were there, and pass a half and a penny into her narrow pink palm, and nestle the herrings in a bag and twist its neck and hand it over, all the time thinking.

The girls, and who'd blame them, are in a hurry to get out, so I say "I quit" to Lengel quick enough for them to hear, hoping they'll stop and watch me, their unsuspected hero. They keep right on going, into the electric eye; the door flies open and they flicker across the lot to their car, Queenie and Plaid and Big Tall Goony-Goony (not that as raw material she was so bad), leaving me with Lengel and a kink in his eyebrow.

"Did you say something, Sammy?"

"I said I quit."

"I thought you did."

"You didn't have to embarrass them."

"It was they who were embarrassing us."

I started to say something that came out "Fiddle-de-doo." It's a saying of my grandmother's, and I know she would have been pleased.

"I don't think you know what you're saying," Lengel said.

"I know you don't," I said. "But I do." I pull the bow at the back of my apron and start shrugging it off my shoulders. A couple customers that had been heading for my slot begin to knock against each other, like scared pigs in a chute.

Lengel sighs and begins to look very patient and old and gray. He's been a friend of my parents for years. "Sammy, you don't want to do this to your Mom and Dad," he tells me. It's true, I don't. But it seems to me that once you begin a gesture it's fatal not to go through with it. I fold the apron, "Sammy" stitched in red on the pocket, and put it on the counter, and drop the bow tie on top of it. The bow tie is theirs, if you've ever wondered. "You'll feel this for the rest of your life," Lengel says, and I know that's true, too, but remembering how he made that pretty girl blush makes me so scrunchy inside I punch the No Sale tab and the machine whirs "pee-pul" and the drawer splats out. One advantage to this scene taking place in summer, I can follow this up with a clean exit, there's no fumbling around getting your coat and galoshes, I just saunter into the electric eye in my white shirt that my mother ironed the night before, and the door heaves itself open, and outside the sunshine is skating around on the asphalt.

I look around for my girls, but they're gone, of course. There wasn't anybody but some young married screaming with her children about some candy they didn't get by the door of a powder-blue Falcon station wagon. Looking back in the big windows, over the bags of peat moss and aluminum lawn furniture stacked on the pavement, I could see Lengel in my place in the slot, checking the sheep through. His face was dark gray and his back stiff, as if he'd just had an injection of iron, and my stomach kind of fell as I felt how hard the world was going to be to me hereafter.

❚ We must see Sammy clearly — how did you show your audience the audience he is telling his story to?

In this second-person narration, Beattie quietly, chillingly, and achingly details a memory that will not leave the speaker. We must see the description completely if we are to understand its powerful impact. And take your time: this memory haunts.

Snow

ANN BEATTIE

I remember the cold night you brought in a pile of logs and a chipmunk jumped off as you lowered your arms. "What do you think *you're* doing in here?" you said, as it ran through the living room. It went through the library and stopped at the front door as though it knew the house well. This would be difficult for anyone to believe, except perhaps as the subject of a poem. Our first week in the house was spent scraping, finding some of the house's secrets, like wallpaper underneath wallpaper. In the kitchen, a pattern of white-gold trellises supported purple grapes as big and round as Ping-Pong balls. When we painted the walls yellow, I thought of the bits of grape that remained underneath and imagined the vine popping through, the way some plants can tenaciously push through anything. The day of the big snow, when you had to shovel the walk and couldn't find your cap and asked me how to wind a towel so that it would stay on your head — you, in the white towel turban, like a crazy king of the snow. People liked the idea of our being together, leaving the city for the country. So many people visited, and the fireplace made all of them want to tell amazing stories: the child who happened to be standing on the right corner when the door of the ice-cream truck came open and hundreds of Popsicles cascaded out; the man standing on the beach, sand sparkling in the sun, one bit glinting more than the rest, stooping to find a diamond ring. Did they talk about amazing things because they thought we'd turn into one of them? Now I think they probably guessed it wouldn't work. It was as hopeless as giving a child a matched cup and saucer. Remember the night, out on the lawn, knee-deep in snow, chins pointed at the sky as the wind whirled down all that whiteness? It seemed that the world had been turned upside down, and we were looking into an enormous field of Queen Anne's lace. Later, headlights off, our car was the first to ride through the newly fallen snow. The world outside the car looked solarized.

You remember it differently. You remember that the cold settled in stages, that a small curve of light was shaved from the moon night after night, until you were no longer surprised the sky was black, that the chipmunk ran to hide in the dark, not simply to a door that led to its escape. Our visitors told the same stories people always tell. One night, giving me a lesson in storytelling, you said, "Any life will seem dramatic if you omit mention of most of it."

This, then, for drama: I drove back to that house not long ago. It was April, and Allen had died. In spite of all the visitors, Allen, next door, had been the good friend in bad times. I sat with his wife in their living room, looking out the glass doors to the backyard, and there was Allen's pool, still covered with black plastic that had been stretched across it for winter. It had rained, and as the rain fell, the cover collected more and more water until it finally spilled onto the concrete. When I left that day, I drove past what had been our house. Three or four crocus were blooming in the front — just a few dots of white, no field of snow. I felt embarrassed for them. They couldn't compete.

This is a story, told the way you say stories should be told: Somebody grew up, fell in love, and spent a winter with her lover in the country. This, of course, is the barest outline, and futile to discuss. It's as pointless as throwing birdseed on the ground while snow still falls fast. Who expects small things to survive when even the largest get lost? People forget years and remember moments. Seconds and symbols are left to sum things up: the black shroud over the pool. Love, in its shortest form, becomes a word. What I remember about all that time is one winter. The snow. Even now, saying "snow," my lips move so that they kiss the air.

No mention has been made of the snowplow that seemed always to be there, scraping snow off our narrow road — an artery cleared, though neither of us could have said where the heart was.

> ▌ In the next-to-last paragraph, how did you demonstrate what
> the narrator is thinking? Doing? Feeling?

From the Eighth Book of Ovid's *The Metamorphoses* (as translated by the American poet Rolfe Humphries) comes this tale of an old couple able to stay together even after death. Be sure you understand why Lelex (the narrator) tells this tale. Trust the line length to help you balance these long sentences.

FROM **The Metamorphoses**
OVID

The Story of Baucis and Philemon

                    An oak-tree stands
Beside a linden, in the Phrygian hills.
There's a low wall around them. I have seen

The place myself; a prince once sent me there
To land ruled by his father. Not far off
A great marsh lies, once habitable land,
But now a playground full of coots and divers.
Jupiter came here, once upon a time,
Disguised as mortal man, and Mercury,
His son, came with him, having laid aside
Both wand and wings. They tried a thousand houses,
Looking for rest; they found a thousand houses
Shut in their face. But one at last received them,
A humble cottage, thatched with straw and reeds.
A good old woman, Baucis, and her husband,
A good old man, Philemon, used to live there.
They had married young, they had grown old together
In the same cottage; they were very poor,
But faced their poverty with cheerful spirit
And made its burden light by not complaining.
It would do you little good to ask for servants
Or masters in that household, for the couple
Were all the house; both gave and followed orders.
So, when the gods came to this little cottage,
Ducking their heads to enter, the old man
Pulled out a rustic bench for them to rest on,
As Baucis spread a homespun cover for it.
And then she poked the ashes around a little,
Still warm from last night's fire, and got them going
With leaves and bark, and blew at them a little,
Without much breath to spare, and added kindling,
The wood split fine, and the dry twigs, made smaller
By breaking them over the knee, and put them under
A copper kettle, and then she took the cabbage
Her man had brought from the well-watered garden,
And stripped the outer leaves off. And Philemon
Reached up, with a forked stick, for the side of bacon,
That hung below the smoky beam, and cut it,
Save up so long, a fair-sized chunk, and dumped it
In the boiling water. They made conversation
To keep the time from being too long, and brought
A couch with willow frame and feet, and on it
They put a sedge-grass mattress, and above it
Such drapery as they had, and did not use
Except on great occasions. Even so,
It was pretty worn, it had only cost a little
When purchased new, but it went well enough

With a willow couch. And so the gods reclined.
Baucis, her skirts tucked up, was setting the table
With trembling hands. One table-leg was wobbly;
A piece of shell fixed that. She scoured the table,
Made level now, with a handful of green mint,
Put on the olives, black or green, and cherries
Preserved in dregs of wine, endive and radish,
And cottage cheese, and eggs, turned over lightly
In the warm ash, with shells unbroken. The dishes,
Of course, were earthenware, and the mixing-bowl
For wine was the same silver, and the goblets
Were beech, the inside coated with yellow wax.
No time at all, and the warm food was ready,
And wine brought out, of no particular vintage,
And pretty soon they had to clear the table
For the second course: here there were nuts and figs
And dates and plums and apples in wide baskets —
Remember how apples smell? — and purple grapes
Fresh from the vines, and a white honeycomb
As centerpiece, and all around the table
Shone kindly faces, nothing mean or poor
Or skimpy in good will.
                  The mixing-bowl,
As often as it was drained, kept filling up
All by itself, and the wine was never lower.
And this was strange, and scared them when they saw it.
They raised their hands and prayed, a little shaky —
"Forgive us, please, our lack of preparation,
Our meagre fare!" They had one goose, a guardian,
Watchdog, he might be called, of their estate,
And now decided they had better kill him
To make their offering better. But the goose
Was swift of wing, too swift for slow old people
To catch, and they were weary from the effort,
And could not catch the bird, who fled for refuge,
Or so it seemed, to the presence of the strangers.
"Don't kill him," said the gods, and then continued:
"We are gods, you know: this wicked neighborhood
Will pay as it deserves to; do not worry,
You will not be hurt, but leave the house, come with us,
Both of you, to the mountain-top!" Obeying,
With staff and cane, they made the long climb, slowly
And painfully, and rested, where a bowman

Could reach the top with a long shot, looked down,
Saw water everywhere, only their cottage
Standing above the flood. And while they wondered
And wept a little for their neighbors' trouble,
The house they used to live in, the poor quarters
Small for the two of them, became a temple:
Forked wooden props turned into marble columns;
The thatch grew brighter yellow; the roof was golden;
The doors were gates, most wonderfully carved;
The floor that used to be of earth was marble.
Jupiter, calm and grave, was speaking to them:
"You are good people, worthy of each other,
Good man, good wife — ask us for any favor,
And you shall have it." And they hesitated,
Asked, "Could we talk it over, just a little?"
And talked together, apart, and then Philemon
Spoke for them both: "What we would like to be
Is to be priests of yours, and guard the temple,
And since we have spent our happy years together,
May one hour take us both away; let neither
Outlive the other, that I may never see
The burial of my wife, nor she perform
That office for me." And the prayer was granted.
As long as life was given, they watched the temple,
And one day, as they stood before the portals,
Both very old, talking the old days over,
Each saw the other put forth leaves, Philemon
Watched Baucis changing, Baucis watched Philemon,
And as the foliage spread, they still had time
To say "Farewell, my dear!" and the bark closed over
Sealing their mouths. And even to this day
The peasants in that district show the stranger
The two trees close together, and the union
Of oak and linden in one. The ones who told me
The story, sober ancients, were no liars,
Why should they be? And my own eyes have seen
The garlands people bring there; I brought new ones,
Myself, and said a verse: *The gods look after*
Good people still, and cherishers are cherished.

▌ What happened to *your* body and voice when the narrator described the transformation?

This passage from the novel *Sula* is powerfully moving. Pay close attention to its moment-by-moment build-ups. The language hints at Plum's addiction and his behavior bears out Eva's decision. The final paragraphs will require a total commitment from the interpreter.

FROM *Sula*

TONI MORRISON

So late one night in 1921, Eva got up from her bed and put on her clothes. Hoisting herself up on her crutches, she was amazed to find that she could still manage them, although the pain in her armpits was severe. She practiced a few steps around the room, and then opened the door. Slowly, she manipulated herself down the long flights of stairs, two crutches under her left arm, the right hand grasping the banister. The sound of her foot booming in comparison to the delicate pat of the crutch tip. On each landing she stopped for breath. Annoyed at her physical condition, she closed her eyes and removed the crutches from under her arms to relieve the unaccustomed pressure. At the foot of the stairs she redistributed her weight between the crutches and swooped on through the front room, to the dining room, to the kitchen, swinging and swooping like a giant heron, so graceful sailing about in its own habitat but awkward and comical when it folded its wings and tried to walk. With a swing and a swoop she arrived at Plum's door and pushed it open with the tip of one crutch. He was lying in bed barely visible in the light coming from a single bulb. Eva swung over to the bed and propped her crutches at its foot. She sat down and gathered Plum into her arms. He woke, but only slightly.

"Hey, man. Hey. You holdin' me, Mamma?" His voice was drowsy and amused. He chuckled as though he had heard some private joke. Eva held him closer and began to rock. Back and forth she rocked him, her eyes wandering around his room. There in the corner was a half-eaten store-bought cherry pie. Balled-up candy wrappers and empty pop bottles peeped from under the dresser. On the floor by her foot was a glass of strawberry crush and a *Liberty* magazine. Rocking, rocking, listening to Plum's occasional chuckles, Eva let her memory spin, loop and fall. Plum in the tub that time as she leaned over him. He reached up and dripped water into her bosom and laughed. She was angry, but not too, and laughed with him.

"Mamma, you so purty. You so purty, Mamma."

Eva lifted her tongue to the edge of her lip to stop the tears from running into her mouth. Rocking, rocking. Later she laid him down and looked at him a long time. Suddenly she was thirsty and reached for the glass of strawberry crush. She put it to her lips and discovered it was blood-tainted water and threw it to the floor. Plum woke up and said, "Hey, Mamma, whyn't you go on back to bed? I'm all right. Didn't I tell you? I'm all right. Go on, now."

"I'm going, Plum," she said. She shifted her weight and pulled her crutches toward her. Swinging and swooping, she left his room. She dragged herself to the kitchen and made grating noises.

Plum on the rim of a warm light sleep was still chuckling. Mamma. She sure was somethin'. He felt twilight. Now there seemed to be some kind of wet light traveling over his legs and stomach with a deeply attractive smell. It wound itself — this wet light — all about him, splashing and running into his skin. He opened his eyes and saw what he imagined was the great wing of an eagle pouring a wet lightness over him. Some kind of baptism, some kind of blessing, he thought. Everything is going to be all right, it said. Knowing that it was so he closed his eyes and sank back into the bright hole of sleep.

Eva stepped back from the bed and let the crutches rest under her arms. She rolled a bit of newspaper into a tight stick about six inches long, lit it and threw it onto the bed where the kerosene-soaked Plum lay in snug delight. Quickly, as the *whoosh* of flames engulfed him, she shut the door and made her slow and painful journey back to the top of the house.

Just as she got to the third landing she could hear Hannah and some child's voice. She swung along, not even listening to the voices of alarm and the cries of the Deweys. By the time she got to her bed someone was bounding up the stairs after her. Hannah opened the door. "Plum! Plum! He's burning, Mamma! We can't even open the door! Mamma!"

Eva looked into Hannah's eyes. "Is? My baby? Burning?" The two women did not speak, for the eyes of each were enough for the other. Then Hannah closed hers and ran toward the voices of neighbors calling for water.

❚ Did your audience see what it cost Eva to make her move? How?

This is a complete chapter from David Leavitt's novel. Jerene is one of the characters who interacts with the novel's protagonist, but here we learn about her internal life. Let her increasing fascination with the account she reads be apparent to the audience, and then let us see where she makes the material she read her own.

FROM *The Lost Language of Cranes*
DAVID LEAVITT

The Crane Child

Jerene found it by accident. She was working in the library one afternoon — wasting time, really — skimming through indexes of psychoanalytic journals and papers in search of something, anything that would give her a clue, a new grounding, that would illuminate the way out of the mammoth, unruly dissertation in which she was lost. Over a period of seven years its subject had changed a dozen times — from child abandonment to the phenomenology of adoption, and onto lost languages, children babbling in their bedrooms. Still her fellowship had been renewed, and would be renewed indefinitely, it seemed, for many of the professors on the philosophy faculty thought her a genius in the raw, a great philosophical mind, while the rest feared she might go off the deep end if they turned her down for money, feared she might come in with a sawed-off shotgun and blow their brains out, like that deranged mathematics graduate student at Stanford. Scanning the index, a little bored, beginning to think about lunch, she read the abstract of a case history that intrigued her. It was in a collection of psychoanalytic papers, shelved in a distant stack. She followed the trail of the call number; took the book from a shelf; read the article quickly the first time, a little anxious, skipping sentences to find the thesis as she had trained herself long ago to do. She read it again, slowly. By the time she was finished she was breathing unevenly, loudly, her foot drumming the dark metal floor of the stacks, her heart pounding.

A baby, a boy, called Michel in the article, was born to a disoriented, possibly retarded teenager, the child of a rape. Until he was about two years old, he lived with his mother in a tenement next to a construction site. Every day she stumbled in and around and out of the apartment, lost in her own madness. She was hardly aware of the child, barely knew how to feed or care for him. The neighbors were alarmed at how Michel screamed, but when they went to knock at the door to ask her to quiet him, often she wasn't there. She would go out all hours, leaving the child alone, unguarded. Then one day, quite suddenly, the crying stopped. The child did not scream, and he did not scream the next night either. For days there was hardly a sound. Police and social workers were called. They found the child lying on his cot by the window. He was alive and remarkably well, considering how severely he appeared to have been neglected. Quietly he played on his squalid cot, stopping every few seconds to look out the window. His play was unlike any they had ever seen. Looking out the window, he would raise his arms, then jerk them to a halt; stand up on his scrawny legs, then fall; bend and rise. He made strange noises, a kind of screeching in his throat. What was he doing? the social workers wondered. What kind of play could this be?

Then they looked out the window, where some cranes were in operation, lifting girders and beams, stretching out wrecker balls on their single arms. The child was watching the crane nearest the window. As it lifted, he lifted; as it bent, he bent; as its gears screeched, its motor whirred, the child screeched between his teeth, whirred with his tongue.

They took him away. He screamed hysterically and could not be quieted so desolate was he to be divided from his beloved crane. Years later, Michel was an adolescent, living in a special institution for the mentally handicapped. He moved like a crane, made the noises of a crane, and although the doctors showed him many pictures of toys, he only responded to the pictures of cranes, only played with the toy cranes. Only cranes made him happy. He came to be known as the "crane-child." And the question Jerene kept coming up against, reading the article, was this: What did it sound like? What did it feel like? The language belonged to Michel alone; it was forever lost to her. How wondrous, how grand those cranes must have seemed to Michel, compared to the small and clumsy creatures who surrounded him. For each, in his own way, she believed, finds what it is he must love, and loves it; the window becomes a mirror; whatever it is that we love, that is who we are.

After Jerene xeroxed the article, she left the library. There was a brisk wind outdoors; she turned her collar up. Some construction was going on nearby — cranes working, lifting beams to the hard-hatted men who swarmed the precarious frame of a rising condominium. The cranes looked like a species of gigantic, long-limbed insect. Transfixed, Jerene approached the makeshift wooden fence that surrounded the construction site. There was a crudely cut peephole in the fence, and through it she stared at the vast pit from which the building would rise, watched the cranes lunge and strain. She stood in the deafening roar of the cranes. In the grinding, the churring, the screeching, in the universe of the cranes, the womb of the cranes, she stood there, eyes open, and listened.

▮ How did you demonstrate the narrator's comfortable relationship with Jerene?
▮ Does Jerene become a crane child? Why?

This simple story is sheer nonsense and wonderful fun if you succumb to the spirit of its irrepressible narrator. What seems like eccentric punctuation in fact is a splendid performance clue.

The Detective
ARCHIBALD MARSHALL

Once there was a detective who was good at finding out crimes, and one day a gentleman came to him and said somebody has just tried to murder my rich aunt, do you think you could find out for me who it was?

And the detective said well I might, but why not let sleeping dogs lie?

And he said well when she comes to she may think that I did it because of her money, and it will be rather awkward for me.

So the detective said yes I can quite see that, and I will find out for you who it was and you can go back to your wife and your three little girls and tell them not to worry, and you needn't be late for breakfast any more.

And he said how do you know I have a wife and three little girls and that I was late for breakfast?

And the detective said oh that is quite easy, you have three spots of marmalade on your face where they kissed you good morning, and if your wife had been dead you would be wearing a black tie instead of a blue one with red anchors on it, and you must have been late for breakfast because your little girls had finished theirs or they would have left egg or porridge or bacon on your face but not marmalade.

So he said well it is very wonderful, and the detective said oh that is nothing to what I can find out if I like, did the man who tried to murder your rich aunt leave any finger-prints or things like that behind him?

And he said well he did leave a photograph of himself with his name and address on it, I suppose it fell out of his pocket.

The detective said well that might be of some help if everything else fails, now I had better see your rich aunt and then I shall have something more to go on.

And he said oh you can't do that, she hasn't come to yet.

But the detective said oh that doesn't matter, and he took him to see his rich aunt, and she was lying in a bed with a pink eider-down on it.

So when the detective had looked all round the room, especially on the toilet-table, he said I am glad I came here, it is quite easy now and by the time your rich aunt comes to I shall be able to tell you who tried to murder her.

So the next morning the gentleman went to him again, and he said my rich aunt has come to now, and she wants to know who tried to murder her, if you have found out I shall be glad if you will tell me because she thinks I tried to do it because of her money.

And the detective said oh yes, I have found out who it was, I told you it would be quite easy, you know that shop Bigg and Bolt in the High Street?

And he said he did.

And the detective said well if you go there you will find a man serving in the shop with black hair rather rough, and if a policeman goes with you he can take him to prison because he is the one.

And he said it is very wonderful, how did you find out?

And the detective said oh it was quite easy, that pink eider-down was a new one and it had the name of that shop on it, and I knew the man who had sold it to your rich aunt would want to see what it looked like on her bed, and his hair was rough because he brushed it with your rich aunt's hairbrush before he went away, I found a black hair on it and hers is more mouse-coloured.

Well the gentleman asked a policeman to go with him, but they were all ladies serving in that shop and their hair was more lemon-coloured, and they said they hadn't stocked pink eider-downs for a long time and if his rich aunt's eider-down looked new perhaps she had laid it by. And Mr Bigg who was quite bald said he was sorry somebody had tried to murder the gentleman's rich aunt because she had been a good customer, and if it had been anybody in his shop he would have spoken about it but it must have been somebody else. And Mr Bolt said so too, and his hair was red so it couldn't have been him either.

So the policeman didn't take up anybody there and the gentleman went back to the detective and he said look here you must have made a mistake about this.

And the detective said well I did, I have been looking at that hair through a microscope and it belongs to a black spaniel, and if your rich aunt keeps one I expect she brushes it with her own hairbrush sometimes.

And he said well she does keep a black spaniel called Fido, and perhaps she does brush it sometimes with her own hairbrush, her habits were always rather dirty.

And the detective said why didn't you tell me that, it would have made all the difference, if you keep things back I'm afraid I can't go on any more for you.

So the gentleman said don't you think it would be worth while to try that man who left the photograph of himself behind, with his name and address on it?

And the detective said well you can do that if you like, it isn't the sort of clue I care about myself, it is too easy, but if anybody ever tries to murder your rich aunt again you can come to me and perhaps I shall have better luck next time.

So the gentleman gave the photograph to the police and they had the man sent to prison, and the gentleman's rich aunt was pleased with him for finding out who had tried to murder her, and she said she would leave him all her money because he hadn't tried to do it himself.

❙ How did you distinguish among the speakers?
❙ What posture did your narrator adopt? Why?

Since so much of Philip Roth's story below begins during a scene, the narrator emerges only gradually as the tale unfolds. Don't be tempted to skimp on preparation, for the narrator's complex understanding of Ozzie's dilemma is central to the total effect of the story. Ozzie and Itzie are two full-blooded twelve-year-old boys who are radically different yet remarkably similar.

FROM *The Conversion of the Jews*
PHILIP ROTH

"You're a real one for opening your mouth in the first place," Itzie said. "What do you open your mouth all the time for?"

"I didn't bring it up, Itz, I didn't," Ozzie said.

"What do you care about Jesus Christ for anyway?"

"I didn't bring up Jesus Christ. He did. I didn't even know what he was talking about. Jesus is historical, he kept saying. Jesus is historical." Ozzie mimicked the monumental voice of Rabbi Binder.

"Jesus was a person that lived like you and me," Ozzie continued. "That's what Binder said —"

"Yeah? . . . So what! What do I give two cents whether he lived or not. And what do you gotta open your mouth!" Itzie Lieberman favored closed-mouthedness, especially when it came to Ozzie Freedman's questions. Mrs. Freedman had to see Rabbi Binder twice before about Ozzie's questions and this Wednesday at four-thirty would be the third time. Itzie preferred to keep *his* mother in the kitchen; he settled for behind-the-back subtleties such as gestures, faces, snarls and other less delicate barnyard noises.

"He was a real person, Jesus, but he wasn't like God, and we don't believe he is God." Slowly, Ozzie was explaining Rabbi Binder's position to Itzie, who had been absent from Hebrew School the previous afternoon.

"The Catholics," Itzie said helpfully, "they believe in Jesus Christ, that he's God." Itzie Lieberman used "the Catholics" in its broadest sense — to include the Protestants.

Ozzie received Itzie's remark with a tiny head bob, as though it were a footnote, and went on. "His mother was Mary, and his father probably was Joseph," Ozzie said. "But the New Testament says his real father was God."

"His *real* father?"

"Yeah," Ozzie said, "that's the big thing, his father's supposed to be God."

"Bull."

"That's what Rabbi Binder says, that it's impossible —"

"Sure it's impossible. That stuff's all bull. To have a baby you gotta get laid," Itzie theologized. "Mary hadda get laid."

"That's what Binder says: 'The only way a woman can have a baby is to have intercourse with a man.' "

"He said *that*, Ozz?" For a moment it appeared that Itzie had put the theological question aside. "He said that, intercourse?" A little curled smile shaped itself in the lower half of Itzie's face like a pink mustache. "What you guys do, Ozz, you laugh or something?"

"I raised my hand."

"Yeah? Whatja say?"

"That's when I asked the question."

Itzie's face lit up. "Whatja ask about — intercourse?"

"No, I asked the question about God, how if He could create the heaven and earth in six days, and make all the animals and the fish and the light in six days — the light especially, that's what always gets me, that He could make the light. Making fish and animals, that's pretty good —"

"That's damn good." Itzie's appreciation was honest but unimaginative: it was as though God had just pitched a one-hitter.

"But making light . . . I mean when you think about it, it's really something," Ozzie said. "Anyway, I asked Binder if He could make all that in six days, and He could *pick* the six days he wanted right out of nowhere, why couldn't He let a woman have a baby without having intercourse."

"You said intercourse, Ozz, to Binder?"

"Yeah."

"Right in class?"

"Yeah."

Itzie smacked the side of his head.

"I mean, no kidding around," Ozzie said, "that'd really be nothing. After all that other stuff, that'd practically be nothing."

Itzie considered a moment. "What'd Binder say?"

"He started all over again explaining how Jesus was historical and how he lived like you and me but he wasn't God. So I said I under*stood* that. What I wanted to know was different."

What Ozzie wanted to know was always different. The first time he had wanted to know how Rabbi Binder could call the Jews "The Chosen People" if the Declaration of Independence claimed all men to be created equal. Rabbi Binder tried to distinguish for him between political equality and spiritual legitimacy, but what Ozzie wanted to know, he insisted vehemently, was different. That was the first time his mother had to come.

Then there was the plane crash. Fifty-eight people had been killed in a plane crash at La Guardia. In studying a casualty list in the newspaper his mother had discovered among the list of those dead eight Jewish names (his grandmother had nine but she counted Miller as a Jewish name); because of the eight she said the plane crash was "a tragedy." During free-discussion time on Wednesday Ozzie had brought to Rabbi Binder's attention this matter of "some of his relations" always picking out the Jewish names. Rabbi Binder had begun to explain cultural unity and some other things when Ozzie stood up at his seat and said that what he wanted to know was different. Rabbi Binder insisted that he sit down and it was then that Ozzie shouted that he wished all fifty-eight were Jews. That was the second time his mother came.

"And he kept explaining about Jesus being historical, and so I kept asking him. No kidding, Itz, he was trying to make me look stupid."

"So what he finally do?"

"Finally he starts screaming that I was deliberately simpleminded and a wise guy, and that my mother had to come, and this was the last time. And that I'd never get bar-mitzvahed if he could help it. Then, Itz, then he starts talking in that voice like a statue, real slow and deep, and he says that I better think over what I said about the Lord. He told me to go to his office and think it over." Ozzie leaned his body towards Itzie. "Itz, I thought it over for a solid hour, and now I'm convinced God could do it."

Ozzie had planned to confess his latest transgression to his mother as soon as she came home from work. But it was a Friday night in November and already dark, and when Mrs. Freedman came through the door she tossed off her coat, kissed Ozzie quickly on the face, and went to the kitchen table to light the three yellow candles, two for the Sabbath and one for Ozzie's father.

When his mother lit the candles she would move her two arms slowly towards her, dragging them through the air, as though persuading people whose minds were half made up. And her eyes would get glassy with tears. Even when his father was alive Ozzie remembered that her eyes had gotten glassy, so it didn't have anything to do with his dying. It had something to do with lighting the candles.

As she touched the flaming match to the unlit wick of a Sabbath candle, the phone rang, and Ozzie, standing only a foot from it, plucked it off the receiver and held it muffled to his chest. When his mother lit candles Ozzie felt there should be no noise; even breathing, if you could manage it, should be softened. Ozzie pressed the phone to his breast and watched his mother dragging whatever she was dragging, and he felt his own eyes get glassy. His mother was a round, tired, gray-haired penguin of a woman whose gray skin had begun to feel the tug of gravity and the weight of her own history. Even when she was dressed up she didn't look like a chosen person. But when she lit candles she looked like something better; like a woman who knew momentarily that God could do anything.

After a few mysterious minutes she was finished. Ozzie hung up the phone and walked to the kitchen table where she was beginning to lay the two places for the four-course Sabbath meal. He told her that she would have to see Rabbi Binder next Wednesday at four-thirty, and then he told her why. For the first time in their life together she hit Ozzie across the face with her hand.

All through the chopped liver and chicken soup part of the dinner Ozzie cried; he didn't have any appetite for the rest.

On Wednesday, in the largest of the three basement classrooms of the synagogue, Rabbi Marvin Binder, a tall, handsome, broad-shouldered man of thirty with thick strong-fibered black hair, removed his watch from his pocket and saw that it was four o'clock. At the rear of the room Yakov Blotnik, the seventy-one-year-old custodian, slowly polished the large window, mumbling to himself, unaware that it was four o'clock or six o'clock, Monday or Wednesday. To most of the students Yakov Blotnik's mumbling, along with his brown curly beard, scythe nose, and two heel-trailing black cats, made of him an object of wonder, a foreigner, a relic, towards whom they were alternately fearful and disrespectful. To Ozzie the mumbling had always seemed a monotonous, curious prayer; what made it curious was that old Blotnik had been mumbling so steadily for so many years. Ozzie suspected he had memorized the prayers and forgotten all about God.

"It is now free-discussion time," Rabbi Binder said. "Feel free to talk about any Jewish matter at all — religion, family, politics, sports —"

There was silence. It was a gusty, clouded November afternoon and it did not seem as though there ever was or could be a thing called baseball. So nobody this week said a word about that hero from the past, Hank Greenberg — which limited free discussion considerably.

And the soul-battering Ozzie Freedman had just received from Rabbi Binder had imposed its limitation. When it was Ozzie's turn to read aloud from the Hebrew book the rabbi had asked him petulantly why he didn't read more rapidly. He was showing no progress. Ozzie said he could read faster but that if he did he was sure not to understand what he was reading. Nevertheless, at the rabbi's repeated suggestion Ozzie tried, and showed a great talent, but in the

midst of a long passage he stopped short and said he didn't understand a word he was reading, and started in again at a drag-footed
pace. Then came the soul-battering.

Consequently when free-discussion time rolled around none of
the students felt too free. The rabbi's invitation was answered only
by the mumbling of feeble old Blotnik.

"Isn't there anything at all you would like to discuss?" Rabbi
Binder asked again, looking at his watch. "No questions or
comments?"

There was a small grumble from the third row. The rabbi re-
quested that Ozzie rise and give the rest of the class the advantage
of his thought.

Ozzie rose. "I forget it now," he said, and sat down in his place.

Rabbi Binder advanced a seat towards Ozzie and poised himself
on the edge of the desk. It was Itzie's desk and the rabbi's frame
only a dagger's-length away from his face snapped him to sitting
attention.

"Stand up again, Oscar," Rabbi Binder said calmly, "and try to
assemble your thoughts."

Ozzie stood up. All his classmates turned in their seats and
watched as he gave an unconvincing scratch to his forehead.

"I can't assemble any," he announced, and plunked himself
down.

"Stand up!" Rabbi Binder advanced from Itzie's desk to the one
directly in front of Ozzie; when the rabbinical back was turned Itzie
gave it five-fingers off the tip of his nose, causing a small titter in
the room. Rabbi Binder was too absorbed in squelching Ozzie's nonsense once and for all to bother with titters. "Stand up, Oscar. What's
your question about?"

Ozzie pulled a word out of the air. It was the handiest word.
"Religion."

"Oh, now you remember?"

"Yes."

"What is it?"

Trapped, Ozzie blurted the first thing that came to him. "Why
can't He make anything He wants to make!"

As Rabbi Binder prepared an answer, a final answer, Itzie, ten
feet behind him, raised one finger on his left hand, gestured it
meaningfully towards the rabbi's back, and brought the house down.

Binder twisted quickly to see what had happened and in the
midst of the commotion Ozzie shouted into the rabbi's back what he
couldn't have shouted to his face. It was a loud, toneless sound that
had the timbre of something stored inside for about six days.

"You don't know! You don't know anything about God!"

The rabbi spun back towards Ozzie. "What?"

"You don't know — you don't — "

"Apologize, Oscar, apologize!" It was a threat.

"You don't — "

Rabbi Binder's hand flicked out at Ozzie's cheek. Perhaps it had only been meant to clamp the boy's mouth shut, but Ozzie ducked and the palm caught him squarely on the nose.

The blood came in a short, red spurt on to Ozzie's shirt front.

The next moment was all confusion. Ozzie screamed, "You bastard, you bastard!" and broke for the classroom door. Rabbi Binder lurched a step backwards, as though his own blood had started flowing violently in the opposite direction, then gave a clumsy lurch forward and bolted out the door after Ozzie. The class followed after the rabbi's huge blue-suited back, and before old Blotnik could turn from his window, the room was empty and everyone was headed full speed up the three flights leading to the roof.

▌ Ozzie is serious and intelligent, but he isn't solemn. How did you demonstrate to your audience his continued efforts to understand?

Bibliography

Bakhtin, M. M. *The Dialogic Imagination: Four Essays.* Ed. Michael Holquist. Trans. Caryl Emerson and Michael Holquist. Austin: University of Texas Press, 1981.

    An important study that provides new insights into the peculiar use of language in the novel as well as the various ways in which time and space intersect in various forms of the novel.

Bentley, Phyllis. *Some Observation on the Art of Narrative.* New York: Macmillan Company, 1947.

    Extensive treatment of summary, description, and scene. A standard reference work for analysis of narratives.

Booth, Wayne C. *The Rhetoric of Fiction.* 2nd ed. Chicago: University of Chicago Press, 1983.

    The expanded second edition of this classic in criticism of prose fiction extends and clarifies concepts explored in the first edition.

Capecci, John. "Performing the Second-Person." *Text and Performance Quarterly* January 1989, pp. 42–52.

    The best discussion of the performance problems and opportunities in second-person narration. Very useful bibliography.

Cohn, Dorritt. *Transparent Minds: Narrative Modes for Presenting Consciousness.* Princeton, N.J.: Princeton University Press, 1978.
Thoughtful examination of three fundamental options a narrator has for presenting a character's consciousness in first- and third-person narrative.

Forster, E. M. *Aspects of the Novel.* New York: Harcourt, Brace and Company, 1927.
A splendidly readable, enormously practical book that clearly explains the implications of theoretical problems facing novelists.

Genette, Gerard. *Narrative Discourse.* Trans. Jane E. Lewin. Ithaca, N.Y.: Cornell University Press, 1980.
An impressive categorization of the functions and effects of narrative techniques that deserves close scrutiny.

James, Henry. *The Art of Fiction.* New York: Oxford University Press, 1948.
A classic work by an author who was himself a master in the field of fiction.

Kawin, Bruce F. *The Mind of the Novel: Reflexive Fiction and the Ineffable.* Princeton, N.J.: Princeton University Press, 1982.
An exploration of the underlying voice in first-person fiction as it is revealed apart from the conscious projection of an image of self by the narrator.

Lanser, Susan Snaider. *The Narrative Act: Point of View in Prose Fiction.* Princeton, N.J.: Princeton University Press, 1981.
An analysis of point of view grounded in speech act theory that examines the narrator's *status* in relation to the speech act, *contact* with the audience, and *stance* with regard to the narrated word.

Pratt, Mary Louise. *Toward a Speech Act Theory of Literary Discourse.* Bloomington: Indiana University Press, 1981.
This study refutes the distinction between literary and nonliterary uses of language, arguing that literature is a speech act that is best analyzed in terms of the speaker's attempt to control the focus of the reader.

Stevick, Phillip, ed. *The Theory of the Novel.* New York: Free Press, 1967.
A collection of excerpts by noted authors and critics from books, essays, and the introductions to novels on topics ranging from "Point of View" to "Narrative Technique."

Thompson, David W., and Virginia Fredricks. *Oral Interpretation of Fiction: A Dramatic Approach.* Minneapolis: Burgess Publishing Company, 1964.
A solid brief text stressing a "dramatistic" approach to oral interpretation, based on the theory that "the total symbolic action in literature and in the reader's oral interpretation of it can be discovered only from exploring all the interacting relationships of Scene-Role-Gesture."

III

The Interpretation
of Drama

Imitations produce pain or pleasure, not because they are mistaken for realities, but because they bring realities to mind.

Samuel Johnson, Preface to The Plays of William Shakespeare

THE SOLO PERFORMANCE OF DRAMA

7

AUDIENCES WATCH PLAYS BECAUSE DRAMA is more interesting than life. Like real life, dramatic life has a beginning, a middle, and an end (or, in terms of the play, a point to which the audience must be brought); but unlike real life, dramatic life consists of selected events, each of which takes place for a discernible reason. In even the most convoluted play, everything that happens on stage is subordinate to the central action. That action involves a conflict among two or more forces, and the excitement of the conflict arises from the equality of the matched contestants. Thus, to understand drama one studies people, conflict, life, and choices, because people in conflict making choices about their lives is the essence of drama.

But drama is also *play* in the sense of make-believe, game, and ritual. The actress playing Juliet pretends to die, speaking iambic pentameter, while the audience willingly suspends disbelief. To help create the illusion that the events the audience observes are happening for the first time, the characters must seem to live in the world each play creates. This means that the actors must speak and move as they do not because of their rehearsals or the audience but because this is the way real people lead their lives. As you interpret drama, you too must create a completely convincing illusion.

Western drama, which began in the religious celebrations of ancient Greece, still includes rituals, and sometimes the rituals are

so widely accepted that they become rules or conventions. For example, performers in a play speak, performers in a musical or opera
sing, and performers in a ballet dance. Each form has its own rules,
and each performance and production must be true to the form as
well as to its story. Every play follows its own set of rules; even the
most experimental play by the most determined iconoclast follows
rules. When the eighteenth-century critic Samuel Johnson said that
"the drama's laws the drama's patrons give," he meant that, for the
drama to exist, the audience must be sufficiently pleased not to leave
the theatre before the play is over.

Whether you perform drama in a classroom, on a podium, or in
an auditorium; whether or not you use a lectern; or whether or not
you decide to carry a manuscript, you create about yourself and
inhabit the world of the play. Today we can see drama performed at
almost any place or time. Like other kinds of plays, however, drama
is always performed in a place that both performer and audience
acknowledge as the playing space. Actors appearing on stage are
expected to fill that space with their energy, concentration, and commitment and to sketch the boundary within which they exist. Around
them the audience constructs the frame of seeing. The audience
attends to that space diligently, not wanting to miss a thing, and so
long as they are not misled, they accept the world the performer
suggests.

A great deal of concentration and commitment is also required
for the solo performance of drama. No audience will ever accept the
reality of the world of the play unless the interpreter believes in the
characters and setting and, through concentration, communicates
that belief to the audience. Concentration allows you to supplant
temporarily all the details of personal life with the intricate truth of
the characters' lives; commitment enables you to accept the world of
the play (and the rules of that world) as your own.

Of course, concentration and commitment alone are not enough:
the interpreter should communicate the drama through body and
voice. Unlike the actor, the interpreter works alone in a playing space
that is reduced to the boundaries sketched by one body and one
voice. You will succeed only by training your body and voice to bring
the world of the play to life. In chapters 3 and 4 we discussed the
use of voice and body in interpretation; review these chapters as
preparation for the performance of drama.

Finally, the performance of literature requires that you make
choices on such matters as how to say a word and where to stress a
point. Drama is no exception. Each choice you make measures your
sensitivity, acuity, and accuracy as an interpreter. Each choice testifies
to the work done — or ignored. No performer is ever more important

than the play, and no play is ever more important than the performer. With proper preparation, the right choice will appear; if you're constantly wondering when you should gesture, perhaps you haven't really finished your homework. Keep these responsibilities in mind as you read the next few sections and also remember as you proceed that you have something unique to offer an audience in your performance.

The Purpose of Solo Performance

Because the process of performing drama may seem formidable, beginning interpreters frequently have a question that they are reluctant to ask in class: "What is to be gained by one person's doing something that was clearly written to be done by a group?" If you are harboring such a doubt, the next few paragraphs are for you.

Performing drama requires considerable coordination of all the skills that are used in performing other genres, and as in any art based on skills, mastering the basic skills requires considerable practice. The skills of the solo performer of drama are also skills used to perform poetry and prose.

In part, the solo performance gives you a unique way of knowing the play. Actors "know" their lines, dancers "know" the steps, typists "know" the keyboard; they have acquired a special understanding of what they study. Like an actor, the interpreter communicates the play with body and mind and emotional make-up. Unlike an actor, however, the interpreter takes on *all* the characters. An interpreter's knowledge will encompass more than an actor's knowledge because the interpreter's task is to communicate the *entirety* of the play.

An audience benefits from a solo performance because it sees the play from a unique perspective: the shifting focus of the speaking character. A person watching a staged production may be distracted from the point that the actors and the director want to emphasize. But in your solo performance no one can upstage you; no one moves on your line; no one covers you. The audience sees how individual forces acting on each other make the play what it is. Your audience also takes part in the play's creation, since they must imaginatively provide the spectacle that you suggest.

Even the play benefits from a solo performance because it has a unique embodiment — you. You take on the entire play: your vision informs the audience without the difficulties that can accompany a staged performance. Only the play and the interpreter and the audience exist. If taken seriously by serious students, solo performance is one exciting way of experiencing the world of drama.

Acting and Interpretation

Another important question that students ask is "What is the difference between acting and interpretation?" In recent years, few issues
for performance theorists have raised more passions. Some people
argued that any sort of movement automatically makes interpreters
into actors (although, of course, eyes blink and mouths move). Others have said that interpreters use books when they perform, and
actors don't. Still others have said that actors perform plays, and
interpreters perform stories and poems. Each of these qualifications
has met reasonable questions, such as "If actors use a book in rehearsal, are they interpreters?" and "What happens when an actor
reads a story?" Many theorists have felt the need to define the limits
of what an interpreter does, although distinguishing between these
two forms of performance became more difficult when students taking courses in both acting and interpretation used techniques learned
in one course when performing in the other. What is clear is that
one method is not better than the other; both offer distinct rewards,
and each can be powerfully moving.

Interpretation is marked by emphasizing the text and minimizing
physical activity, some theorists argue, although they agree that interpretation and acting are more similar than different. Because similarities between the two forms abound, differences may be less
important — but they are no less keenly felt. Both acting and interpretation begin with a script that is carefully studied and thoroughly
understood. Actors tend to limit themselves to plays, and usually to
one character; interpreters perform all types of literature. Both kinds
of performers must have supple, responsive bodies that can communicate fine degrees of emotion and activity to audiences; both
must have voices distinguished by clear diction, adequate volume,
and sufficient flexibility. Both rehearse their materials by basing their
performance choices on their own experiences as well as close study
of the text. Little wonder confusion arises, especially since actors
often become interpreters and interpreters become actors.

Nevertheless, there are distinct differences between acting and
interpretation. The interpreter of drama is charged with becoming *all*
of the characters in a scene, and, more importantly, of communicating the *whole* of the scene. The interpreter must communicate not
just one character, but the sum of all the characters. This whole adds
up to more than the sum of its parts if the drama is to be conveyed
in its intellectual, emotional, and aesthetic entirety.

Standing alone in performance, your body creates the frame from
within which half of the scene is played. The other half exists at the

end of a character's line of tension with an opponent, just out beyond the far edge of the audience. The character speaks. The audience sees him demand the knife from the deranged woman, who clearly refuses to give it up. The tension arising from their conflict crackles along a line that *parallels* the sight lines of the audience, who find themselves in the middle of the excitement without analyzing how it is happening.

Actors, on the other hand, completely memorize their lines and ask the audience to believe that they are actually the people to whom the events happen. Each actor portrays only one character at a time; this portrayal is aided by other members of the cast, scenery, costume, make-up, and properties. The scene is *onstage* and exists around the players; while the audience watches, its sight lines *perpendicular* to the lines of tension that excite the staged production. Each actor is one element in the total work, one part of the whole. Each is surrounded by the reality of the play, though that reality may penetrate or include the audience as well as the stage. Every actor is, of course, conscious of the audience — sensing their responses, waiting for their laughs, and taking care to project to be heard in the last row of the balcony.

Briefly, then, an interpreter shares the actor's commitment to a faithful creation of the play, but from a different perspective. You are all of the characters in the scene and each individual character, one at a time. As you speak, you create an illusion of the simultaneous presence of all of the characters in the scene by letting them really and honestly respond and listen to one another. You share with actors the ability to *react* as well as to *act*. Your body and voice create the performance frame. Though this frame is smaller than the stage, everything you do and say takes on greater significance, and the power of every gesture is magnified. Each lifted eyebrow fills more of the total picture than an actor or actress can manage. Together, the interpreter and the audience create the world of the drama; together they are living in it, jointly committed to its conclusion.

Structural Elements of a Play

Plays are organized on the principles of unity and probability, and their basic ingredient is conflict. The ways in which conflict is presented, developed, and resolved vary widely. In general, however, the opening scenes of a play are devoted to exposition through action and dialogue. Then comes the challenge that introduces the inciting or exciting force. There may be several such units as the play develops. The primary challenge that is touched on in the exposition may be reintroduced and intensified by developing action or relationships so that it becomes more acute. This is usually followed by moves and countermoves among the characters who are most involved, thus producing a tightening of conflict and what is often termed the *rising action*. The rising action comes to a point of decision in the crisis. The *crisis* is that moment of limitation that directs the action to its final outcome. The crisis makes inevitable and brings about the *climax*, the culmination of all the elements of the conflict. This is followed by the *denouement* or *resolution*, or, in tragedy, the inevitable catastrophe.

The events of most dramas follow some variation of this general form; in the changes and alterations each drama achieves its unique pattern of emotional build-ups, intensity, and pace. These bare events or occurrences should not be confused with plot. As we discuss in Chapter 6, plot cannot be separated from the characters. We call *plot* all that which the characters say and do, and we know about characters from what they say and do and from what others say about and do to them. Chekhov's *The Three Sisters*, some people say, is about three women who don't go to Moscow, and it is true that the sisters never reach that goal. Still, this description shows very little understanding of what the sisters *do* reach, or how they get it, or what it costs, or what happens along the way.

When you are studying a play during your rehearsal period, proceed carefully with each speech, being sure that everything that is happening onstage is clear to you and that you understand everything that is being said. Sometimes a small stage map helps clarify where everyone is; sometimes you might want to develop a close, literal paraphrase of a difficult speech. Remember that the paraphrase is not an end but one means of understanding the speech itself. Don't proceed to the next speech until you are sure that you understand what the speaker is saying and doing and what everyone else onstage (or about to come onstage) is doing. Are all the others listening to the speaking character? What is on their minds? What are they *not* saying? What is the speaker thinking? What is the speaker doing? What is the speaker trying to hide? Where is everyone looking? What should an audience know about the movement onstage?

Since explicit clues about what is happening, and particularly what the characters are thinking, are not always provided in the drama, be on the lookout for implicit or even concealed clues in a given scene, speech, line, or word. Interpreters must discover how the scheme of events figures in the total work, for each scene may have a crisis and a climax just as the entire play does.

Analyzing a Scene

Let us examine a scene together to find some of these explicit and hidden clues about character. Perhaps our discussion of a scene from *The Three Sisters*, a play about time filled with the minutiae of life, will resolve some questions. Much of the action doesn't seem to get anybody anywhere. But Chekhov recognized what we all know: only rarely do lives change because of drastic or melodramatic events. More often changes "just happen" without our direction — as we drink coffee, turn the page of a newspaper, or stroll along a walkway overlooking the water.

In the following scene, almost at the end of the play, Irina, the youngest sister, converses with her new fiancé, the Baron Tuzenbach. For three and one-half acts the Baron has carefully courted Irina, who has quietly rejected all his tenuous but persistent offers and has been pained by his declarations because she has dreamed of marrying a Prince Charming, who would come to rescue her on a white horse. Time has pulled that dream apart; Irina has grown up and settled for the Baron, perhaps as the last hope to get her out of the small town where her culture and achievements are "like a sixth finger." Settling for the Baron has cost quite a high price, too, for he is painfully ugly. But his devotion to her never flags, and he even challenges a rival to a duel. As the scene begins, the Baron is about to leave for the duel; he may die because of it (and thereby destroy even this fragment of Irina's dream), but he will not tell her of that future.

[*Enter* IRINA *and* TUZENBACH, TUZENBACH *wearing a straw hat;* KULYGIN *crosses the stage, calling "Aa-oo, Masha! Aa-oo!"*]

TUZENBACH: That seems to be the only man in town who's glad the officers are leaving.
IRINA: It's understandable. [*Pause*] Our town is going to be empty now.
TUZENBACH: Dear, I'll be back shortly.
IRINA: Where are you going?
TUZENBACH: I must go into town . . . to see my comrades off.
IRINA: That's not true . . . Nikolai, why are you so distracted today? [*Pause*] What happened yesterday near the theater?
TUZENBACH [*with a gesture of impatience*]: I'll come back in an hour and be with you again. [*Kisses her hands.*] My beloved. . . . [*Looks into

her face.] It's five years now that I have loved you, and I still can't get used to it, and you seem always more beautiful to me. What lovely, wonderful hair! What eyes! Tomorrow I shall carry you off, we'll work, and be rich, and my dreams will come true. You shall be happy. There is only one thing, only one: you do not love me!

IRINA: That is not within my power! I'll be your wife, faithful and obedient, but it's not love, I can't help it! [*Weeps.*] I have never in my life been in love. Oh, how I have dreamed of love, dreamed of it for a long time now, day and night, but my soul is like a fine piano that is locked, and the key lost. [*Pause*] You look troubled.

TUZENBACH: I haven't slept all night. There is nothing in my life so terrible as to frighten me, only that lost key racks my soul and will not let me sleep. . . . Tell me something. . . . [*Pause*] Tell me something. . . .

IRINA: What? What shall I say? What?

TUZENBACH: Something.

IRINA: Don't! Don't! [*Pause*]

TUZENBACH: What trifles, what silly little things in life will suddenly, for no reason at all, take on meaning. You laugh at them just as you've always done, consider them trivial, and yet you go on, and you feel that you haven't the power to stop. Oh, let's not talk about that! I feel elated, I see these fir trees, these maples and birches, as if for the first time, and they all gaze at me with curiosity and expectation. What beautiful trees, and, in fact, how beautiful life ought to be with them! [*A shout of: "Aa-oo! Yoo-hoo!"*] I must go, it's time. . . . There's a tree that's dead, but it goes on swaying in the wind with the others. So it seems to me that if I die, I'll still have a part in life, one way or another. Good-bye, my darling. . . . [*Kisses her hands.*] The papers you gave me are on my table, under the calendar.

IRINA: I am coming with you.

TUZENBACH [*alarmed*]: No, no! [*Quickly goes, then stops in the avenue.*] Irina!

IRINA: What?

TUZENBACH [*not knowing what to say*]: I didn't have any coffee this morning. Ask them to make me some. [*Quickly goes out.*]

[IRINA *stands lost in thought, then goes to the back of the stage and sits down in the swing.*]

On a first reading, there does not seem to be much happening here: man and woman enter, talk about love, happiness, a piano, some trees, and the man runs off. All that is true. Lest we miss something complex or subtle, it would be wise to reread the scene carefully, speech by speech, to see what else, indeed, is happening.

The Baron enters with Irina. He had renounced his aristocracy to join the army, and now he has even renounced the army — he wants to join Irina and work for their future together. Although Irina has accepted this comically ugly man whom her sister recommended to her, can you imagine her mixed feelings when she gave up her dream of a dashing hero gloriously whisking her off? Irina and the Baron stand onstage together, silent. Each contemplates marriage. Do they touch? The text does not tell us.

Irina breaks the pause with "Our town is going to be empty now." Tuzenbach looks at his watch (he must not be late for the duel in which he is to be killed) and reassures Irina that he will return shortly. Anxious and distracted, he stumbles through his half-lie about saying good-bye to friends. Irina senses his fear, knows that he isn't telling her the truth, and gently encourages him to confide in her.

Time presses. This silent Tuzenbach — agonized because he displeases and worries the woman he never dreamed would say yes — resembles the earlier, silent Tuzenbach, who is awed by Irina's beauty. Impatiently he ignores the repeated question with a repeated assurance. He kisses her hand and looks directly into her eyes to repeat the love he has declared so often in the past. (Remember what he looks like, how his looks are a silent reminder to her of what her dreams have come to.) Exclaiming over her beautiful eyes and hair, he begins to sketch their future; but notice carefully what he says and how he says it: "Tomorrow I shall carry you off, we'll work, and be rich, and my dreams will come true. You shall be happy."

Consider those personal pronouns carefully: Baron Tuzenbach wants to be sure that *he* fulfills Irina's dreams by taking her away, as a knight on a charger rescues a damsel in distress. The kingdom he offers her is the simple life of working together and being rich together, as if one inevitably followed the other, as if work were as simple as saying it. When all of this occurs, Tuzenbach assures, then "*my*" dreams of five years will all be true. But will they? Will Irina love him? Will she love this ugly man as he loves her? Tuzenbach knows she doesn't love him, and fears that more than his imminent death. And he admits that fear: she doesn't love him, but he assures her that *she'll* be happy.

Irina's honest answer does not intend cruelty, although it must have ravaged the Baron, particularly when he is about to duel with a rival for her love. She agrees to be a wife, but it must be with open eyes and without pretenses, for dreams have evaporated. And with those dreams so changed in front of her, she begins to cry about what has become of her ambitions. At last she is passionate about something she *isn't*; her "soul is like a fine piano that is locked, and the key lost."

More time passes. Tuzenbach admits that he does not shirk the future, even death; only death without her love tortures him, terrifies him. He is willing not to be the pianist on the expensive piano of her soul; he will settle with being the key, if only she will let him. In some concealed, bravely disguised misery, they stand silent. Time passes. Now he begs her to speak to him.

The conflict that both joins them and sets them apart emerges more obviously. Begging some assurance that he is valued or even respected, Tuzenbach is at his most vulnerable. The only cover is Irina's insipid "What? What shall I say? What?" She isn't being coy or heartless. She doesn't know his future, knows only of their future together that she doesn't love him, can't love him, and mustn't pretend to love him. On the verge of tears and almost numb, he offers one word in isolation; but he gets the response a mother might give a distraught child. Surely the hero going off to battle needs something else from his beloved, but he asks for that which Irina does not have and cannot give. They stand together, silent again. Time presses.

Tuzenbach's only complaining lines appear here when he speaks of how "trifles" (like duels) and "silly little things" (like phrases uttered without thinking — even by a woman who has told him that it does not lie in her power to love him) come to matter in his life. It takes a moment for Tuzenbach's admirable optimism to assert itself. But on reflection he admits that he is curiously happy. He has waited for Irina, and she has agreed; looking around him he sees the trees that enchanted him in the first and second acts (and that will be cut down as soon as the curtain falls): "What beautiful trees, and, in fact, how beautiful life ought to be with them!" With the special clarity of the condemned, he values any world that can make them both so miserable as it rewards them. The subjunctive mood used in the second half of the line qualifies his future, just as he suddenly stiffens when he hears the call from the duel, a hello that means good-bye. Death waits for them all — it is only a matter of time. But he still will not succumb; even the dead, dried-up tree partakes somehow of life with the others, is moved as they move, and so Tuzenbach knows that he will live some kind of life after the duel. At last he takes her hand and kisses it.

Irina knows that this emotional farewell is not typical and moves to protect the man. She will go with him. Tuzenbach, alarmed, refuses to consider it and moves, now, to join those trees both living and dead with whom he has linked himself. He cannot let her know what will happen; she mustn't be hurt. Abruptly he stops, turning once more to glimpse her eyes and her hair (that charm against confusion) and calls out for her. He wants to say "Good-bye," and "I love you," and "I'm doing this for you," and "Please just tell me that you love me." And Irina, alone, unsure, afraid, confused, echoes what she said before: "What?" — as much an answer as a question about his needs and her ability to fill them. What more can either say? He requests some coffee, and in the last moment onstage finds himself caught between saying everything and nothing. Refusing to collapse, he gets one more glimpse. Just as he is about to break, he dashes off. She stands alone. Time passes.

These apparently patternless events actually disguise careful plotting of speech, incident, and silence. Each of these components furthers the action of the play. Tuzenbach must repeat his love to Irina and then somehow prepare her for the future that might not include him. Irina must make clear to Tuzenbach just what her agreement to marry him does and does not include. Neither can leave the stage until these objectives are fulfilled, and the conflict arises from the unresolvable tasks both characters undertake. Through their language, the characters convey their limitations and the degree to which they are willing to expose themselves: Tuzenbach speaks almost constantly. In dismay Irina responds briefly until her one long speech during which Tuzenbach learns the futility of his hopes. He moves toward her, away from her, and then finally runs off; she tolerates, accepts, endures.

Then they are silent. Admittedly, characters must speak for an audience to achieve the fullest possible understanding of their lives. But in drama some of the most moving moments are silent ones. Do not presume that nothing happens during a pause. A great deal happens, which even words cannot convey. Chekhov places five pauses in this brief scene, all at moments when nothing that the characters can say demonstrates their agony as effectively as their momentary speechlessness. "What shall I say?" Irina asks, as if to admit that even together she and Tuzenbach are more than ever apart and alone.

In patterning this scene, Chekhov creates a telling rhythm with long speeches that allow for prolonged self-disclosure (Tuzenbach on Irina's beauty, Irina on her inability to love Tuzenbach, Tuzenbach on the trees) set against brief questions and answers. Midscene the impasse between the two characters is clearest, and the language breaks down almost completely. It is possible, therefore, to detect rich and poignant resources for performance when you understand clearly when and how to look for them.

This brief excerpt is not Chekhov's entire play, of course. It is only a fragment through which the characters progress as they attempt to achieve their goals. These particular moments are possible only because the stage frees the characters to be alone; offstage all the other characters pursue their own goals.

Working a Scene

Knowing how and where to look for clues to understand a character is only the beginning of the interpreter's preparation. Using these techniques you need to answer countless questions about a scene to be sure that you fully understand the shape of the action onstage and can therefore draft a performance that will communicate the scene to your audience.

Let us look briefly at a scene from a different kind of play to see if by charting the action we can determine the nature of the characters and their unique relationship. Try to answer the questions that are asked as the discussion proceeds, and be sure to take the time to incorporate all of your discoveries into the performance preparation.

These scenes occur in the beginning of Edward Albee's *Who's Afraid of Virginia Woolf?* George is a forty-six-year-old associate professor of history; his fifty-two-year-old wife, Martha, is the daughter of the president of the college. It is after two in the morning, and husband and wife have just returned from a party given by Martha's father to welcome new faculty. At the party Martha has met a new biology professor and his wife and has invited them home for a nightcap. George, exhausted and more harassed than usual by his boisterous wife, has complained about their guests' tardiness. Martha retorts:

MARTHA [*after a moment's consideration*]:   You make me puke!

GEORGE: What?

MARTHA: Uh . . . you make me puke!

GEORGE [*thinks about it . . . then . . .*]:   That wasn't a very nice thing to say, Martha.

MARTHA: That wasn't *what*?

GEORGE: . . . a very nice thing to say.

MARTHA: I like your anger. I think that's what I like about you most . . . your anger. You're such a . . . such a simp! You don't even have the . . . the what? . . .

GEORGE: . . . guts? . . .

MARTHA: PHRASEMAKER! [*Pause . . . then they both laugh.*] Hey, put some more ice in my drink, will you? You never put any ice in my drink. Why is that, hunh?

GEORGE [*takes her drink*]:   I always put ice in your drink. You eat it, that's all. It's that habit you have . . . chewing your ice cubes . . . like a cocker spaniel. You'll crack your big teeth.

MARTHA: THEY'RE MY BIG TEETH!

GEORGE: Some of them . . . some of them.

MARTHA: I've got more teeth than you've got.

GEORGE: Two more.

MARTHA: Well, two more's a lot more.

GEORGE: I suppose it is. I suppose it's pretty remarkable . . . considering how old you are.

MARTHA: YOU CUT THAT OUT! [*Pause.*] You're not so young yourself.

GEORGE [*with boyish pleasure . . . a chant*]: I'm six years younger than you are . . . I always have been and I always will be.

MARTHA [*glumly*]: Well . . . you're going bald.

GEORGE: So are you. [*Pause . . . they both laugh.*] Hello, honey.

MARTHA: Hello. C'mon over here and give your Mommy a big sloppy kiss.

GEORGE: . . . oh, now. . . .

MARTHA: I WANT A BIG SLOPPY KISS!

GEORGE [*preoccupied*]: I don't *want* to kiss you, Martha. Where *are* these people? Where are these *people* you invited over?

MARTHA: They stayed on to talk to Daddy. . . . They'll be here. . . . *Why* don't you want to kiss me?

GEORGE [*too matter-of-fact*]: Well, dear, if I kissed you I'd get all excited . . . I'd get beside myself, and I'd take you, by force, right here on the living room rug, and then our little guests would walk in, and . . . well, just think what your father would say about *that*.

MARTHA: You pig!

GEORGE [*haughtily*]: Oink! Oink!

MARTHA: Ha, ha, ha, HA! Make me another drink . . . lover.

GEORGE [*taking her glass*]: My God, you can swill it down, can't you?

MARTHA [*imitating a tiny child*]: I'm firsty.

GEORGE: Jesus!

MARTHA [*swinging around*]: Look, sweetheart, I can drink you under any goddamn table you want . . . so don't worry about me!

GEORGE: Martha, I gave you the prize years ago. . . . There isn't an abomination award going that you. . . .

MARTHA: I swear . . . if you existed I'd divorce you. . . .

GEORGE: Well, just stay on your feet, that's all. . . . These people are your guests, you know, and. . . .

MARTHA: I can't even see you . . . I haven't been able to see you for years. . . .

GEORGE: . . . if you pass out, or throw up, or something . . .

MARTHA: . . . I mean, you're a blank, a cipher . . .

GEORGE: . . . and try to keep your clothes on, too. There aren't many more sickening sights than you with a couple of drinks in you and your skirt up over your head, you know. . . .

MARTHA: . . . a zero . . .

GEORGE: . . . your *heads*, I should say. . . .

[*The front doorbell chimes.*]

MARTHA: Party! Party!

GEORGE [*murderously*]: I'm really looking forward to this, Martha. . . .

MARTHA [*same*]: Go answer the door.

GEORGE [*not moving*]: You answer it.

MARTHA: Get to that door, you. [*He does not move.*] I'll fix you, you. . . .
GEORGE [*fake-spits*]:   . . . to you. . . .

[*Door chime again.*]

MARTHA [*shouting . . . to the door*]:   C'MON IN! [*To* GEORGE, *between her
teeth.*] I said, get over there!
GEORGE [*moves a little toward the door, smiling slightly*]:   All right, love . . .
whatever love wants. [*Stops.*] Just don't start on the bit, that's all.
MARTHA: The bit? The bit? What kind of language is that? What are you
talking about?
GEORGE: The bit. Just don't start in on the bit.
MARTHA: You imitating one of your students, for God's sake? What are
you trying to do? WHAT BIT?
GEORGE: Just don't start in on the bit about the kid, that's all.
MARTHA: What do you take me for?
GEORGE: Much too much.
MARTHA [*really angered*]:   Yeah? Well, I'll start in on the kid if I want to.
GEORGE: Just leave the kid out of this.
MARTHA [*threatening*]:   He's mine as much as he is yours. I'll talk about
him if I want to.
GEORGE: I'd advise against it, Martha.
MARTHA: Well, good for you. [*Knock.*] C'mon in. Get over there and
open the door!
GEORGE: You've been advised.
MARTHA: Yeah . . . sure. Get over there!
GEORGE [*moving toward the door*]:   All right, love . . . whatever love wants.
Isn't it nice the way some people have manners, though, even in
this day and age? Isn't it nice that some people won't just come
breaking into other people's houses even if they *do* hear some
subhuman monster yowling at 'em from inside . . . ?
MARTHA: SCREW YOU!

[*Simultaneously with* MARTHA's *last remark,* GEORGE *flings open the front door.*
HONEY *and* NICK *are framed in the entrance.*]

First, let's be clear: this scene does not depict a typical academic
couple at home. To understand the play completely, you must determine exactly what happens in the scene, and then determine how
this action arises from the characters' needs and goals. Albee's stage
directions greatly aid analysis, as does his curious use of ellipsis to
indicate both pause and thought at the same time.

We can begin by analyzing this scene together. You will develop
your own method by a process of trial and error as you gain experience with different kinds of plays. The first steps in analyzing
character should always be taken in terms of the entire play. Carefully
follow the patterns of action and inaction, silence and speech. What

do George and Martha say? In what circumstances do they say it? How does what they say further the development of their goals?

Understanding the physical activity that occurs during the scene enables us to understand the changes in persona that constantly occur in George and Martha. Where does Martha drop one role and assume another? There are several such points before the front door-bell chimes. Where does George shift his role? How frequently do these shifts occur? Who changes personality more often? How are George and Martha different by the last line of this scene? Keeping in mind this rough sketch of the ground to be covered, go back to the beginning and determine how to approach these moments most efficiently.

Once you know the content of the scene, you should consider the relationship of the characters to the setting in which they live. Albee has set this scene "in the living room of a house on campus of a small New England college." It is not difficult to believe that George and Martha are sloppy housekeepers; moreover, they have lived here for more than twenty years, and the accumulations of their lives fill this home. Books probably abound; are they all neatly shelved? Now ask the further questions that your answers imply. You can probably imagine fairly accurately the rest of their world. Might the ashtrays be full? Are the glasses empty and sweating on the table? Is it likely that George has suddenly taken out the vacuum and begun to tidy up? What are they wearing? Does what you know about Martha suggest a smart, chic woman, svelte and haughtily fashionable? Might her clothes be tighter, smaller, younger looking than she is? Why? Does George look like an illustration from *Gentlemen's Quarterly*? Why?

Consider the differences between them. How do they compare, contrast, and balance in terms of temperament, maturity, and cultural background? The variety and contrast of the play as a whole are achieved by pitting remarkable differences against each other and by comparing the tiny differences that loom larger when so many other things are similar. George appears willing to submit to Martha's abuse, but doesn't he taunt her, too? Both delight in word play; each is able to learn new rules as quickly as the other changes the game. Such interdependence arises out of years of practice, as well as out of some fundamental unity, something that they share. Look at George and Martha again from this perspective. It has been said that married couples tend to resemble each other after many years; is this true for George and Martha? Do their similarities outnumber or outweigh their differences? Why have they been together for so long? They fight viciously, so conflict obviously exists. In this scene, apart from the couple's obvious physical differences, what are the chief points of opposition between them? How do these different temperaments appear in the lines? Is either partner obliterated by the other? Why?

Answer these preliminary questions before you proceed with any detailed analysis of this scene. Every scene requires such close examination because the lives of the characters are both internal and external, as your life is. Your room may look immaculate or messy, you may have a favorite item of apparel, a manner of talking or habit of smoking, but you are surely not just the woman with the southern accent who wears scarves or the man in the bomber jacket who reads *Sports Illustrated.* Characters are much more than their appearance.

Focusing attention on one character at a time (starting with the person who has the most lines), apply the now-familiar process of understanding logical content, giving careful attention to climaxes and focal points, style and rhythm, and the denotative and connotative richness of all the words. Once you are sure of the content, you are ready to study the fusion of external and internal activity that makes a character appear to be alive.

Look closely at Martha. Albee describes her as "a large, boisterous woman, 52, looking somewhat younger. Ample but not fleshy." All external clues should be taken into consideration here, so Martha must also be capable of rapid changes in personality: she is a braying woman, a mommy, a tiny child, a vituperative wife, a shouting harridan. How do these changes occur in Martha? Where do these shifts take place? What do they arise from? Why does shared laughter accelerate the change? Does Martha need to move out of her chair? Why? Is there any difference among the kinds of anger Martha shows? All of these are *outward* characteristics. When you know what must be seen by the audience, you can clarify better both what internal life gives rise to these elements and how these responses affect other characters.

Now apply the same kinds of questions to George, whom Albee tellingly describes as "her husband, 46. Thin; hair going gray." Not much to build on there, one might think. But there is a great deal here, for George is six years younger than Martha, and he taunts her with this fact. He is described as "her husband," an adjunct to her, rather than a man or a history professor or a "failure," though he is all of these things, too. His physical spareness — borne out in his lines and perhaps even in his volume — contrasts with her abundance. His mildness is not passivity, since he is capable both of succumbing to her commands and annoying her, of submitting as well as dominating. Can you point to moments when he does each? Is there any way in which "giving in" can be considered a victory? Does "submission" mean a loss of dignity? Is it ever easier to do something than to fight about it? Martha calls George "a blank, a cipher" and moments later "a zero": is he? Are they unequally matched? George opens the door at the end of the scene, as Martha has ordered — why? He is clearly the more physically active of the two in this scene; does this movement parallel another kind of flexibility, his submissiveness, or both?

The interpreter of drama should follow much the same method of characterization as a conscientious actor does. You need to know how a character looks, lives, thinks, and behaves long before the play or the scene takes place. The playwright does not always give this complete information, and you may need to depend on your knowledge of human nature and your skills at observing others to supply the omitted details. Go behind the exterior manifestations to discover the motivations. You are dealing with human actions and reactions, and the more you know of your fellow creatures, the more easily you can understand and communicate to the audience the complexities of the characters in the play.

With the physical, psychological, and emotional background filled in, the interpreter can begin to study the sources of the incidents in the play. From examining this segment can you project what George and Martha were doing immediately before their entrance? Did George enjoy his father-in-law's party? Did he remember the young biology professor? Why did George and Martha go to the party? Why did Martha remember the biology professor? Why did they leave the party? Why do you suppose Martha put off telling her husband about the late guests? Did George expect any of this? Are they both prepared for what happens in the scene?

All characters in drama, as do people in life, represent at least the sum of their past experiences. All people behave in response to pressures and needs of a given situation on the basis of the events of their past. Psychologists have taught us how much of adult human behavior and personality is really a response, a *reaction*, both to the world as it was learned in childhood and also to the primal relationship of parent and child. Such substance renders much of the excitement of this scene, and many of its difficulties as well. How do George and Martha live with each other? Why have they put up with all this abuse for so long? They are not a couple who would refuse to consider divorce from any religious scruple. Martha mentions divorce, surely not for the first time. Can you fight over something you don't care about? The first act is called "Fun and Games," and both characters change considerably, even during this scene; how do they know when a new game is being played? George appears to submit to Martha; does Martha ever give in to George? How do they "weigh out" in the match between them? They certainly laugh a great deal — together and separately; does one person's laughter ridicule or scorn the other? What is so funny about "PHRASEMAKER," which elicits their first laugh together? When George cautions Martha not to "start in on the bit about the kid," is it a threat, a taunt, or a caution? Does he expect Martha to obey him? Does the reaction of either partner surprise the other? Why?

When you answer all of these questions — and many others that will occur to you — incorporate the answers into your performance. Some words of caution are due here, now that so much information has been gathered and so much work has been done. Beginning interpreters often become so enamored of a favorite character in a play or a scene that the rest of the characters never appear. Continue careful analysis of each character, studying each as an individual and evaluating his or her relationship to every other individual. Remember that your responsibility is to the scene as a whole, to the play as Albee wrote it. Balance your own observations with the play's truth, keeping in mind that while the audience wants to see and hear you (which will happen in any case), they also want to see and hear Albee's play.

Rhythm

As your characters begin to jell, some of the most exciting moments in rehearsal occur. As the rhythms of the individuals' speeches become more and more obvious, the ways in which speeches work off each other become more apparent and important. The rhythm of a play is extremely interesting and somewhat complex. First, at the stylistic level there is the individual speech rhythm of each character. Second, in terms of both content and form, there are important fluctuations in emotional tension. Third, there is the inevitable alternation between activity and passivity. We demonstrated this alternation in the scene from *The Three Sisters*. Of course, because a play depends on action for development, no part of a good play is ever really passive. Some scenes or portions of scenes may consist primarily of exposition and may serve the same purpose as transitional units in narrative. They may clarify cause and effect, present necessary relationships, allow the playwright to plead a case through one of the characters, or provide the needed suspense in preparation for a climax. This alternation between active and passive elements affects the tempo at which the various scenes and speeches move. It also determines the speed with which they build toward minor climaxes and finally toward the main climax, whether in terms of action or character development or both. In a well-written play, these transitional, static scenes are used sparingly and present nothing that does not bear on the ultimate outcome of the action. The playwright's arrangement of these scenes probably is governed by the same principles that influence the writer of narrative prose: how much the audience must know about background and where added background material can be most effectively inserted. The playwright also takes into account the need for relaxation from tension and intense activity and channels the audience's concentration into another area, which is different in kind if not in degree.

As is apparent in *Who's Afraid of Virginia Woolf?* and *The Three Sisters*, changes in rhythm are caused by changes of content as well as by stylistic, linguistic, grammatical, or syntactical changes. The words Chekhov uses range from spare to elaborate, but each word exists because at that particular moment with those people, at that point in their lives, only that combination of words expresses the complexity of their characters. Albee allows George and Martha to complete each other's lines, but he achieves their characteristic attitudes through techniques that include careful management of punctuation and pause. The patterning of silences to achieve a specific tempo appears often in contemporary drama. Harold Pinter, in particular, has elevated the pause to a dramatic force that can be both menacing and pitiful, ominous and poetic.

Style

Dialogue style includes what a character omits as well as what he or she says; playwrights don't leave characters speechless because they can't think of anything for them to say. In discovering the elements of dialogue style, interpreters learn about another part of a character's life. The language a character uses indicates a great deal about background and attitude. The arrangement of ideas gives a clue to the person's clarity of thinking and is likely to reflect intensity of emotion. The length of the thought units also may reveal much about a character's personality, forcefulness, and authority as well as the degree of psychological tension. Read Pinter's *Betrayal* (Chapter 8) with this aspect of character development in mind.

Style is an interesting consideration in contemporary drama. At the heart of absurdist drama is the human inability to communicate with one's fellows and even to put into words the frustrations and fears of one's own mind. Thus, you should examine motivation and character interaction differently from the way you approach those elements in a traditional play. The motivation for both speech and action is often confined to the character's own mind and formed by a sense of isolation from the world or by acceptance of the belief that people, the world, life, love, and death are equally absurd. The dialogue often takes the form of extremely long near-monologues or soliloquies. These are difficult for an interpreter to sustain, not only because they are subjectively motivated but also because they are highly repetitious. This aspect of repetition is used as a device for anticlimax in the structure of many contemporary plays. Likewise, the action is often either violent and almost stylized or statically impotent. When you are interpreting, the shifts in your muscle tone should be swift and sharp. Thorough analysis and considerable patience are necessary to make such scenes credible and dramatic, but they provide extraordinary rewards to the solo performer.

Scenography

When you go to the theatre, you are likely to see costumed performers on a carefully lighted stage that probably has properties and set pieces to suggest the period and social status of the world of the play. When done most elaborately, these technical achievements can astonish an audience: watch a three-masted ship in full sail explode into flames under a starry sky while seventy-eight choristers and six principals in seventeenth-century Venetian costume sing lustily. The spectacle will amaze you. Setting tends to be easily achieved by dramatists because they can put whatever information is necessary into stage directions and descriptions that precede or come between the scenes. Renaissance dramatists evoke setting within the speeches of the characters; contemporary dramatists specify lighting, setting, and costume. George Bernard Shaw provides voluminous and minute description for almost every second. In whatever period, drama always has been partly spectacle.

A solo performer appears in street clothes, possibly behind a lectern, probably carrying a book or a script. How can this interpreter hope to compete with the visually pleasing sets and costumes that surround actors? Carefully consider what you are doing. The technical resources that create visual statements in realistic dramas do not exist for the solo interpreter. But such resources aren't any more necessary to the interpreter than they were to Shakespeare or Sophocles. And although spectacle is part of drama, the spectacle need not be the fact of a staged production. Some realistic dramas of the late nineteenth and early twentieth centuries attempted to convince the audience of the reality of stage activity by featuring objects and details of real life (real bacon frying in a real cast-iron skillet over a real fire built on real sod). Proponents of these outlandish experiments (the real sod, after all, rested on a stage floor and was lit by stage lights) forget that belief is not as much a matter of what goes on in front of the audience's eyes as it is a matter of what goes on inside the audience's minds, for there illusion is made real. Absolutely crucial stage directions and descriptions can always be given by the performer (not the characters) before the performance begins. Audiences do not expect one performer to be eighty-four performers, nor do they expect the lavish spectacle of the stage. Your listeners assist in creating the scenographic elements in the performance with their imaginations, and they can do this quite well when their imaginations are carefully guided. For the scene to exist within the space filled by the audience, the space that surrounds the performer should resemble the space that surrounds the audience; all of it is set, lit, and costumed in the combined imaginations of audience and performer.

Sometimes, of course, the interpreter is called on to describe some intensely interpersonal activity that one person simply cannot duplicate — a pie fight, swordplay resulting in death, a wrestling match, a kiss. Or the interpreter is presented with some vast or intricate set piece or design requirement. Under such circumstances it is far wiser for the performer (*not* one of the characters) to describe the action as the playwright describes it in the stage directions.

In Shaw's *Candida*, for example, nearly a thousand words of stage directions precede the rise of the curtain on Act I. Some of this information is of immediate interest to the audience, but a great deal of it is aimed primarily at establishing the background out of which the characters have come and against which they develop. Consequently, in giving the stage directions, the interpreter could omit from performance the detailed information (using it, of course, in preparation as a guide to plot motivation and character development). Since the scene is not going to be presented scenographically to the audience, the interpreter, by selecting the important details, can enable the listeners to focus on essential background information. On the other hand, the audience needs the description of the sphinx from Shaw's *Caesar and Cleopatra* (at the end of this chapter), although most of the specific description of the characters might well be omitted.

Scenography is responsible for more than lavish sets, costumes, and lights. Period manners, social customs, and economic conditions all are communicated to an audience and all affect the characters. Writers of narratives can and do often remind their readers of the physical and psychological impact of surroundings on character; interpreters of drama constantly should scrutinize the world they are attempting to suggest to be sure that the telltale parts clearly appear in their performance. Tuzenbach keenly feels the impact of the birches as he and Irina stand in front of the house; George surely feels once again the messiness of his house as it is to be seen for the first time by the guests.

Place can establish a motive, motivate an action, describe a world, limit alternatives, or impede the achievement of a goal. Properties and various details of the sets may also play an important part in the action; the river separating Simon and Grusha in Brecht's *Caucasian Chalk Circle* (Chapter 11) intensifies the poignancy of their scene. In *Antony and Cleopatra* (at the end of this chapter), Cleopatra needs an asp to die. Shakespeare stresses the snake's presence, and the visual image of a woman with an asp at her breast was a standard Elizabethan icon. But no interpreter ought to reject this scene simply because of the inability to recruit a snake. If, as Cleopatra, you believe you are holding the asp and show your audience that you are, they will believe. (We discuss the management of properties more fully in Chapter 8.)

Putting It Together

If the list of responsibilities and problems you are likely to encounter in performing drama seems daunting, some words of encouragement may help. First, the solo performance *can* be done; richly rewarding performances occur when serious students work conscientiously. In drama, perhaps more than in any other genre, the key is not to take anything for granted: take the time for a *thorough* rehearsal of a three-minute segment rather than ask the same amount of rehearsal to prepare a five-minute scene. Next, don't expect it all to happen instantly. You know how long you took on your earlier performances; allot yourself at least half again as much time to work up this performance. Last, remember our opening comments about drama as "play." If you have rehearsed carefully, you have every reason to enjoy what you are doing. If you have studied the scene carefully, you have no reason to be surprised.

Perhaps the most difficult thing about interpreting drama, aside from the purely mechanical or technical problems of suggesting character and action, is keeping the numerous threads of character development and reaction separated and yet related. This demands careful preparation and a high degree of concentration during performance. The interpreter must check carefully, especially during preparation, to avoid presenting a mere series of character sketches, each complete in itself but unrelated to the others. Besides having a thorough knowledge of each character, you should have a constant awareness of relationships and of progressions in these relationships. As the actor must learn to *hear* the speeches of other characters, the interpreter must learn to *have heard*, to be sure each character is responding to what has gone before. All the characters must stay "in scene" and be ready to pick up the progression as they speak.

Thus, the interpreter needs to select for each character enough significant physical and vocal details so that the listeners can themselves fill in the outline to make a three-dimensional, believable person. It is impractical and even dangerous to offer specific directions for achieving this final communication of character because each personality in each play presents its own slightly different problems. Some suggestions for handling mechanical details — and they are suggestions only — are given in the next chapter. For the moment, however, it is enough to be aware that the interpreter needs to spend considerable time and effort perfecting control of voice and body, and should exert extreme care in performance to remain unobtrusive.

Selections for Analysis and Oral Interpretation

This scene opens the second act of *5th of July*. Shirley, fourteen, is the somewhat precocious and self-dramatizing niece of Jed's lover, Ken. All have assembled at the Talley farm near Lebanon, Missouri, for a celebration presided over by Sally, the aunt of Ken and the great-aunt of Shirley. Jed — an almost silent listener — is essential for Shirley to achieve her effect. Don't let either character become outlandish.

FROM *5th of July*
LANFORD WILSON

The porch. JED *is sitting in the sunshine, referring back and forth between two books, trying to compose a letter on a legal-size yellow pad. A bell tolls in the distance, fifteen seconds between each deep, heavy stroke.*

SHIRLEY *enters. She enjoys being alone with* JED *for a moment. She looks out over the garden, quite forgetting that* JED *does not see her there. She notices the bell.*

SHIRLEY: Oh! Listen!
JED: (*Jumps a foot*) Oh, God.
SHIRLEY: "Ask not for whom the bell tolls . . . "
JED: It tolls for Harley Campbell.
SHIRLEY: Who?
JED: Your Aunt Sally went to the funeral. They ring the bell before the service and after the service.

SHIRLEY: Oh. Oh, God, now it sounds horrible. Oh, God, that's mournful.

JED: If the man made more than a hundred thousand a year and left a widow, they ring it all during the service as well.

SHIRLEY: We, of course, are the first. (*He looks at her, not understanding*) To arise this morning.

JED: You're the last.

SHIRLEY: Last?

JED: You're up in time for brunch. . . .

SHIRLEY: Gwen is up?

JED: Yeah. And on the phone.

SHIRLEY: Uncle Kenny's up?

JED: Yeah, Sally and I had breakfast at seven, I drove her to church, woke up Ken, and we made an herbal anti-fungus concoction guaranteed to fail, and sprayed thirty-five phlox plants. With Wes's, uh . . . supervision.

SHIRLEY: (*Adjusts*) Oh. Yes . . . I slept . . . fitfully. I tossed, I . . .

JED: Turned?

SHIRLEY: I had this really weird dream. I was being chased by a deer. All through the woods, over bridges, this huge deer. What does a dream like that mean?

JED: Did he have antlers?

SHIRLEY: I don't remember. Why? (JED goes back to his books)

JED: If you happen to dream about seven fat cows and seven lean cows, I know what that one means.

SHIRLEY: I would never dream of a cow.

JED: Not a feisty young heifer? Jumping fences, trying to get into the corn?

SHIRLEY: Oh, please. I certainly hope you don't think of me like that! I am not a common cow! I am a . . . flower, Jed. Slowly and frighteningly opening her petals onto the spring morning. A trimu-a-timulus, a timu —

JED: What? A mimulus? You're probably a mimulus.

SHIRLEY: What's a mimulus?

JED: Mimulus is a wild flower. Pinkish-yellow, the monkey flower, they call —

SHIRLEY: No, not that one. Not a monkey flower! I am a . . .

JED: What?

SHIRLEY: Well, not — I don't know. And it's important, too. But . . . I can *see* it. A nearly white, small, single . . .

JED: What about an apple blossom? The first tree of spring to —

SHIRLEY: No, oh, God, no. And grow into an apple? A fat, hard, red, bloated, tasteless apple? For some crone to bake in a pie for her ditchdigger husband to eat without even knowing it? Oh,

God. Never. I'm more than likely the daughter of an Indian chief. My mother was very broad-minded and very promiscuous.

JED: So I've heard.

SHIRLEY: (*Thinks*) I am a blossom that opens for one day only . . . and I fall. I am not pollinated. It's too early for the bees. They don't find me. And I fade. Dropping my petals one by — what kind of flower is that? (*She thinks a moment*) A wild rose?

JED: No, you wouldn't flower till May at the earliest. There'd be bees lined up around the block.

SHIRLEY: Well, *what*? God. Daisies are when? (*He shakes his head*) Peony?

JED: There are some anemones . . . that bloom very early.

SHIRLEY: An anemone . . .

JED: The original ones are from Greece, so they're all claimed by heroes who fell in battle and their blood seeped into the ground and anemones sprang up, but I think they've found one or two somewhere else that haven't been claimed yet. I have a picture of them somewhere.

SHIRLEY: Could you find it?

JED: It's around; I'll look it up.

SHIRLEY: (*Hand on sleeve*) Jed. Thank you. This is, you know, very important to me.

JED: (*Mock seriousness*) Shirley. It's important to us all.

SHIRLEY: I know.

JED: We don't dwell on it because we try to spare you the pressure of all our expectations. We multitudes.

SHIRLEY: I know. But don't. Don't spare me. It makes me strong.

▌ How did you show the audience the seriousness underlying
Shirley's humor and the humor underlying Jed's seriousness?

Following are excerpts from three plays about Cleopatra. Each picture of this
notorious queen reflects the changing world as she ages, as well as the
attitudes and concerns about the age in which the play was written. The
most recent of the plays — Shaw's *Caesar and Cleopatra* — also portrays the
queen at her youngest. This Cleopatra is a frightened and superstitious little
girl. Julius Caesar is an old campaigner at the twilight of his career. Wandering away from his army, he comes on and addresses a sphinx, who
responds in the voice of a girl. Caesar can only believe he is dreaming.

FROM *Caesar and Cleopatra, Act I*

GEORGE BERNARD SHAW

CAESAR [*to himself*]   What a dream! What a magnificent dream! Only
let me not wake, and I will conquer ten continents to pay for
dreaming it out to the end. [*He climbs to the Sphinx's flank, and
presently reappears to her on the pedestal, stepping round its right
shoulder.*]

CLEOPATRA.   Take care. That's right. Now sit down: you may have
its other paw. [*She seats herself comfortably on its left paw*]. It is
very powerful and will protect us; but [*shivering, and with plaintive
loneliness*] it would not take any notice of me or keep me company. I am glad you have come: I was very lonely. Did you
happen to see a white cat anywhere?

CAESAR [*sitting slowly down on the right paw in extreme wonderment*]   Have you lost one?

CLEOPATRA.   Yes: the sacred white cat: is it not dreadful? I brought
him here to sacrifice him to the Sphinx; but when we got a little
way from the city a black cat called him, and he jumped out of
my arms and ran away to it. Do you think that the black cat can
have been my great-great-great-grandmother?

CAESAR [*staring at her*]   Your great-great-great-grandmother! Well,
why not? Nothing would surprise me on this night of nights.

CLEOPATRA.   I think it must have been. My great-grandmother's
great-grandmother was a black kitten of the sacred white cat;
and the river Nile made her his seventh wife. That is why my
hair is so wavy. And I always want to be let do as I like, no
matter whether it is the will of the gods or not: that is because
my blood is made with Nile water.

CAESAR.   What are you doing here at this time of night? Do you live
here?

CLEOPATRA.   Of course not: I am the Queen; and I shall live in the palace at Alexandria when I have killed my brother, who drove me out of it. When I am old enough I shall do just what I like. I shall be able to poison the slaves and see them wriggle, and pretend to Ftatateeta[1] that she is going to be put into the fiery furnace.

CAESAR.   Hm! Meanwhile why are you not at home and in bed?

CLEOPATRA.   Because the Romans are coming to eat us all. You are not at home and in bed either.

CAESAR [*with conviction*]   Yes I am. I live in a tent; and I am now in that tent, fast asleep and dreaming. Do you suppose that I believe you are real, you impossible little dream witch?

CLEOPATRA [*giggling and leaning trustfully towards him*]   You are a funny old gentleman. I like you.

CAESAR.   Ah, that spoils the dream. Why don't you dream that I am young?

CLEOPATRA.   I wish you were; only I think I should be more afraid of you. I like men, especially young men with round strong arms; but I am afraid of them. You are old and rather thin and stringy; but you have a nice voice; and I like to have somebody to talk to, though I think you are a little mad. It is the moon that makes you talk to yourself in that silly way.

CAESAR.   What! you heard that, did you? I was saying my prayers to the great Sphinx.

CLEOPATRA.   But this isn't the great Sphinx.

CAESAR [*much disappointed, looking up at the statue*]   What!

CLEOPATRA.   This is only a dear little kitten of a Sphinx. Why, the great Sphinx is so big that it has a temple between its paws. This is my pet Sphinx. Tell me: do you think the Romans have any sorcerers who could take us away from the Sphinx by magic?

CAESAR.   Why? Are you afraid of the Romans?

CLEOPATRA [*very seriously*]   Oh, they would eat us if they caught us. They are barbarians. Their chief is called Julius Caesar. His father was a tiger and his mother a burning mountain; and his nose is like an elephant's trunk. [*Caesar involuntarily rubs his nose*]. They all have long noses, and ivory tusks, and little tails, and seven arms with a hundred arrows in each; and they live on human flesh.

CAESAR.   Would you like me to shew you a real Roman?

CLEOPATRA [*terrified*]   No. You are frightening me.

CAESAR.   No matter: this is only a dream —

CLEOPATRA [*excitedly*]   It is not a dream: it is not a dream. See, see. [*She plucks a pin from her hair and jabs it repeatedly into his arm*].

1. Cleopatra's imperious maid.

CAESAR.   Ffff — Stop. [*Wrathfully*] How dare you?

CLEOPATRA [*abashed*]   You said you were dreaming. [*Whimpering*] I only wanted to shew you —

CAESAR [*gently*]   Come, come: don't cry. A queen mustn't cry. [*He rubs his arm, wondering at the reality of the smart*]. Am I awake? [*He strikes his hand against the Sphinx to test its solidity. It feels so real that he begins to be alarmed, and says perplexedly*] Yes, I — [*quite panicstricken*] no: impossible: madness, madness! [*Desperately*] Back to camp — to camp. [*He rises to spring down from the pedestal*].

CLEOPATRA [*flinging her arms in terror round him*]   No: you shan't leave me. No, no, no: don't go. I'm afraid — afraid of the Romans.

CAESAR [*as the conviction that he is really awake forces itself on him*]   Cleopatra: can you see my face well?

CLEOPATRA.   Yes. It is so white in the moonlight.

CAESAR.   Are you sure it is the moonlight that makes me look whiter than an Egyptian? [*Grimly*] Do you notice that I have a rather long nose?

CLEOPATRA [*recoiling, paralysed by a terrible suspicion*]   Oh!

CAESAR.   It is a Roman nose, Cleopatra.

CLEOPATRA.   Ah! [*With a piercing scream she springs up; darts round the left shoulder of the Sphinx; scrambles down to the sand; and falls on her knees in frantic supplication, shrieking*] Bite him in two, Sphinx: bite him in two. I meant to sacrifice the white cat — I did indeed — I [*Caesar, who has slipped down from the pedestal, touches her on the shoulder*] — Ah! [*She buries her head in her arms*].

CAESAR.   Cleopatra: shall I teach you a way to prevent Caesar from eating you?

CLEOPATRA [*clinging to him piteously*]   Oh do, do, do. I will steal Fta-tateeta's jewels and give them to you. I will make the river Nile water your lands twice a year.

CAESAR.   Peace, peace, my child. Your gods are afraid of the Romans: you see the Sphinx dare not bite me, nor prevent me carrying off to Julius Caesar.

CLEOPATRA [*in pleading murmurings*]   You won't, you won't. You said you wouldn't.

CAESAR.   Caesar never eats women.

CLEOPATRA [*springing up full of hope*]   What!

CAESAR [*impressively*]   But he eats girls [*she relapses*] and cats. Now you are a silly little girl; and you are descended from the black kitten. You are both a girl and a cat.

CLEOPATRA [*trembling*]   And will he eat me?

CAESAR.   Yes; unless you make him believe that you are a woman.

CLEOPATRA.   Oh, you must get a sorcerer to make a woman of me. Are you a sorcerer?

CAESAR.   Perhaps. But it will take a long time; and this very night you must stand face to face with Caesar in the palace of your fathers.

CLEOPATRA.   No, no. I daren't.

CAESAR.   Whatever dread may be in your soul — however terrible Caesar may be to you — you must confront him as a brave woman and a great queen; and you must feel no fear. If your hand shakes: if your voice quavers; then — night and death! [*She moans*]. But if he thinks you worthy to rule, he will set you on the throne by his side and make you the real ruler of Egypt.

▌ How did you demonstrate Caesar's growing interest in Cleopatra?

▌ How did your Cleopatra exhibit the potential for greatness Caesar detects?

Caesar now is dead. Cleopatra is many years older and loves Antony. For political reasons, however, Antony has married a distinguished Roman matron. In the following brief segment from *All for Love*, John Dryden presents Octavia, the recent bride of Antony, confronting Cleopatra, the one woman her husband will love beyond his destruction. Notice how differently these two characters speak of the same man — and how different this Cleopatra is from Shaw's portrayal of her at an earlier age. Be sure your performance demonstrates the differences between Octavia and Cleopatra. (Cleopatra's servant Alexas speaks first.)

FROM *All for Love*, Act III

JOHN DRYDEN

Alexas manet.

Enter CLEOPATRA, [*and Cleopatra's attendants*] CHARMION, IRAS, [*and*] *train.*

ALEX.   O madam, I have seen what blasts my eyes!
Octavia's here!

CLEO.   Peace with that raven's note.
I know it too; and now am in
the pangs of death.

ALEX.   You are no more a queen;
Egypt is lost.

CLEO.   What tell'st thou me of Egypt?
My life, my soul is lost! Octavia has him! —
O fatal name to Cleopatra's love!
My kisses, my embraces now are hers;

While I — But thou hast seen my rival; speak,
Does she deserve this blessing? Is she fair?
Bright as a goddess? And is all perfection
Confined to her? It is. Poor I was made
Of that coarse matter, which, when he was finished,
The gods threw by, for rubbish.
ALEX.   She's indeed a very miracle.
CLEO.   Death to my hopes, a miracle!
ALEX. (*bowing*)   A miracle;
I mean of goodness; for in beauty, madam,
You make all wonders cease.
CLEO.   I was too rash:
Take this in part of recompense. But, oh!

(Giving a ring.)

I fear thou flatter'st me.
CHAR.   She comes! she's here!
IRAS.   Fly, madam, Caesar's sister!
CLEO.   Were she the sister of the thund'rer Jove,
And bore her brother's lightning in her eyes,
Thus would I face my rival.

Meets **OCTAVIA** *with* **VENTIDIUS.** **OCTAVIA** *bears up to her. Their trains come
up on either side.*

OCTAV.   I need not ask if you are Cleopatra;
Your haughty carriage —
CLEO.   Shows I am a queen:
Nor need I ask you who you are.
OCTAV.   A Roman:
A name that makes and can unmake a queen.
CLEO.   Your lord, the man who serves me, is a Roman.
OCTAV.   He was a Roman, till he lost that name,
To be a slave in Egypt; but I come
To free him thence.
CLEO.   Peace, peace, my lover's Juno.
When he grew weary of that household clog,
He chose my easier bonds.
OCTAV.   I wonder not
Your bonds are easy; you have long been practised
In that lascivious art: he's not the first
For whom you spread your snares: let Caesar witness.
CLEO.   I loved not Caesar; 'twas but gratitude
I paid his love. The worst your malice can,

Is but to say the greatest of mankind
Has been my slave. The next, but far above him
In my esteem, is he whom law calls yours,
But whom his love made mine.
OCTAV. (*coming up close to her*)   I would view nearer
That face which has so long usurped my right,
To find th' inevitable charms that catch
Mankind so sure, that ruined my dear lord.
CLEO.   Oh, you do well to search; for had you known
But half these charms, you had not lost his heart.
OCTAV.   Far be their knowledge from a Roman lady,
Far from a modest wife! Shame of our sex,
Dost though not blush to own those black endearments
That make sin pleasing?
CLEO.   You may blush, who want 'em.
If bounteous nature, if indulgent heav'n
Have giv'n me charms to please the bravest man,
Should I not thank 'em? Should I be ashamed,
And not be proud? I am, that he has loved me;
And, when I love not him, heav'n change this face
For one like that.
OCTAV.   Thou lov'st him not so well.
CLEO.   I love him better, and deserve him more.
OCTAV.   You do not — cannot: you have been his ruin.
Who made him cheap at Rome, but Cleopatra?
Who made him scorned abroad, but Cleopatra?
At Actium, who betrayed him? Cleopatra.
Who made his children orphans, and poor me
A wretched widow? only Cleopatra.
CLEO.   Yet she who loves him best is Cleopatra.
If you have suffered, I have suffered more.
You bear the specious title of a wife,
To gild your cause, and draw the pitying world
To favor it: the world contemns poor me,
For I have lost my honor, lost my fame,
And stained the glory of my royal house,
And all to bear the branded name of mistress.
There wants but life, and that too I would lose
For him I love.
OCTAV.   Be't so, then; take thy wish.

Exit cum suis.

CLEO.   And 'tis my wish,
Now he is lost for whom alone I lived.

My sight grows dim, and every object dances,
And swims before me, in the maze of death.
My spirits, while they were opposed, kept up;
They could not sink beneath a rival's scorn:
But now she's gone, they faint.

ALEX.   Mine have had leisure
To recollect their strength, and furnish counsel,
To ruin her, who else must ruin you.

CLEO.   Vain promiser!
Lead me, my Charmion; nay, your hand too, Iras:
My grief has weight enough to sink you both.
Conduct me to some solitary chamber,
And draw the curtains round;
Then leave me to myself, to take alone
My fill of grief

> There I till death will his unkindness weep;
> As harmless infants moan themselves asleep.

Exeunt.

▌ Both women genuinely love the same man. How did you demonstrate their equal degree of affection but distinctively different methods of showing it?

Shakespeare, the earliest of the three playwrights, gives the final picture of Cleopatra. Antony has committed an ignominious suicide, and Cleopatra has been captured by Roman forces but bargains for time — enough time to conclude her own life. The women who have served her remain faithful until their deaths. Through the magic of some of Shakespeare's most shimmering poetry, Cleopatra embodies fidelity even beyond the grave. For her, at least, this death is the richest victory.

FROM *Antony and Cleopatra,* Act V, Scene II
WILLIAM SHAKESPEARE

[*Enter* IRAS *with a robe, crown, etc.*]

CLEO.   Give me my robe, put on my crown, I have
281   Immortal longings in me. Now no more
The juice of Egypt's grape shall moist this lip.
Yare, yare, good Iras; quick. Methinks I hear
Antony call; I see him rouse himself
285   To praise my noble act. I hear him mock
The luck of Caesar, which the gods give men

To excuse their after wrath. Husband, I come!
Now to that name my courage prove my title!
I am fire and air; my other elements
290   I give to baser life. So, have you done?
Come then, and take the last warmth of my lips.
Farewell, kind Charmian, Iras, long farewell.

[*Kisses them. Iras falls and dies.*]

Have I the aspic in my lips? Dost fall?
If thou and nature can so gently part,
295   The stroke of death is as a lover's pinch,
Which hurts, and is desir'd. Dost thou lie still?
If thus thou vanishest, thou tell'st the world
It is not worth leave-taking.
CHAR.   Dissolve, thick cloud, and rain, that I may say
The gods themselves do weep!
CLEO.   This proves me base.
301   If she first meet the curled Antony,
He'll make demand of her, and spend that kiss
Which is my heaven to have. Come, thou mortal wretch,

[*To an asp, which she applies to her breast.*]

With thy sharp teeth this knot intrinsicate
305   Of life at once untie. Poor venomous fool,
Be angry, and dispatch. O, could'st thou speak,
That I might hear thee call great Caesar ass
Unpolicied!
CHAR.   O eastern star!
CLEO.   Peace, peace!
309   Dost thou not see my baby at my breast,
That sucks the nurse asleep?
CHAR.   O, break! O, break!
CLEO.   As sweet as balm, as soft as air, as gentle —
O Antony! — Nay, I will take thee too:

[*Applying another asp to her arm.*]

What should I stay —   *Dies.*
CHAR.   In this [vile] world? So fare thee well!

287. **their**: i.e. the gods   288. **title**: right.   289. **other elements**: i.e. earth and water.
290. **baser**: i.e. mortal.   293. **aspic**: asp.   298. **leave-taking**: taking leave of
302. **make . . . her**: i.e. ask her for news of me.   **spend**: i.e. reward her with.
303. **mortal wretch**: deadly creature.   304. **intrinsicate**: intricate.
308. **Unpolicied**: outdone in craftiness (in the contest with Cleopatra).
313. **What**: why.

315   Now boast thee, death, in thy possession lies
       A lass unparallel'd. Downy windows, close,
       And golden Phoebus never be beheld
       Of eyes again so royal! Your crown's [awry],
319   I'll mend it, and then play —

▌ With so much going on in this scene, it is easy to get flustered
  or rushed. Did you give your audience time to see Cleopatra's
  transformation?
▌ How did you create the voice and body of "a lass unparallel'd"?

Bibliography

Corrigan, Robert W. *The Context and Craft of Drama: An Anthology of
    Critical Essays on the Nature of Drama and Theatre*. San Francisco:
    Chandler Publishing Company, 1964.
    A collection of contemporary dramatic criticism presented in two divi-
    sions. Context includes discussions of the nature, language, structure,

and criticism of drama; craft discusses the role of the playright, actors, director, designer, and critic.

Gassner, John. *Form and Idea in Modern Theatre*. New York: Holt, Rinehart and Winston, 1956.
Considerations of dramatic structure and style within a historical development.

Joseph, B. L. *Acting Shakespeare*. New York: Theatre Arts Books, 1960.
Problems in creating characters in verse dramas, with particular attention to Shakespeare.

Magarshack, David. *Stanislavsky on the Art of the Stage*. New York: Hill and Wang, 1961.
A translation of this famous classic with an introductory essay on the Stanislavsky system.

Technique is a test of a man's sincerity.

Ezra Pound

TECHNIQUE IN DRAMA

8

PERFORMING DRAMA OBVIOUSLY DEMANDS GREAT SKILL. Actors or interpreters need to understand and respond emotionally, mentally, and physically to the aesthetic entirety of a play. Unlike actors, who embody characters with lives independent of the audience, an interpreter, employing selectivity and suggestion, creates a life that emanates from the performer and includes the audience. Interpreter and audience together create the scene. The interpreter's skillful use of body and voice persuades the audience to believe that the characters they jointly created move about the world they jointly designed, costumed, and lighted.

To achieve this goal, interpreters must solve the technical problem of solo performance. This chapter suggests several ways to address some of these problems, but suggestions are not rules. You should develop your own individual method of handling the problems posed by each new scene. Remember that interpreters communicate the total achievement of the playwright, however, whether they are performing the entire play or only a single scene. All the technical expertise of the interpreter should be directed to that end.

Technique in Interpretation

An interpreter spends a great deal of time and effort in disciplining voice and body to respond without hesitation to the dictates of a scene. As we discuss in Chapter 7, you often may have to go over and over a difficult speech or exchange or scene, working it out the way a dancer perfects a complicated step. Only such in-depth rehearsal can bring your resources to the point where you communicate the scene rather than embellish or exhibit it or yourself. Of course, none of these rehearsal devices is apparent to an audience; you have worked them out so thoroughly before performance that your audience's attention is focused strictly on the material you are presenting.

Technique is the *most economical management of a performer's resources*. Every work of art demands some technique that has been refined in a unique way by each artist. Although one artist's technique differs from another's, there are always some fundamental similarities. What is achieved must be more than just a lecture or demonstration of technique. Technical mastery of body and voice allows the interpreter to communicate to the audience all the discoveries made during the rehearsal process.

Beginning actors often have some common misunderstandings about technique that have led to countless misconceptions about performance, interpretation, and acting. Some actors believe that a technically proficient actor is a hollow performer who substitutes a supple body and resonant voice for the character's life. On the other hand, performers committed to technical proficiency retort that the internal-reality performer merely grunts and stumbles in a display of personal anguish that also has nothing to do with the character's life. Both extremes typify selfish performers, whether they are actors or interpreters. Without the ability to project and refine gesture, internal commitment to the reality of the play is worthless. Without internal commitment, technical mastery simply shows — with striking clarity — how empty the interpreter really is. As you become more familiar with the performance of drama, it will become increasingly apparent to you that certain kinds of gestures or vocal habits impress the audience. You will be developing a bag of tricks. Tricks are not technique. Tricks deceive in order to puzzle or amuse. Technique refines and clarifies. Skill in execution and economy in performance present the selection instead of the performer.

Control

Some beginning performers erroneously believe that an interpreter should not respond emotionally to a scene during performance or

rehearsal. Make no mistake — the intensity of the interpreter's response is as great as the actor's. Controlling the outward manifestations of an emotion is not suppressing it. You well know that when
you must "hold your tongue" that you do not eliminate emotional
involvement. Both audience and interpreter have as their goal the
fullest possible life for the scene or the play; but interpreters always
remember that the characters, the action, the author's intentions, and
their own personal preferences should all be directed to the life of
the play. None is an end in itself.

Misunderstanding the interpreter's role has led to other problems. Some people have even claimed that interpreters are so concerned with control that the scenes they present are pale and lifeless.
You manage your emotional commitment as you do the other components of your performing instrument, remembering, of course,
that *you* manage *them*, they do not manage you. The principle of
aesthetic distance does not require lessened intensity in commitment
or in execution; it requires greater control over the intensity.

This concept may be the single most difficult principle for performers to understand. Yet it is the one principle that, if ignored,
leads to the most trouble in performance. Control in a scene is like
paying taxes: if you give less than required, you get into trouble; if
you give more, you are either foolish or careless. Interpreters in
control of a scene spend just enough resources to be sure that the
audience fully experiences the life of the drama. As performers, they
may not be experiencing precisely the same emotions as is the audience; but as characters, they are suggesting the emotional fullness
of the role. Interpreters should not confuse their personal response
to a character's plight (from the examples in Chapter 7, sorrow at
Irina's loss or anger at Martha) with the intention of the character;
and they should channel the character's intention into the scene's
intention. By controlling their personal response to the scene, interpreters give the audience room to fulfill its part in the experience.
An audience wants to focus on the life of the scene, not on the
personal travails and traumas of the interpreter as a performer. Excessive displays only display excess.

Memorizing Lines

Happily, we are now past the days when interpreters were told that
memorizing means acting. Constant repetition of a scene or a passage
allows the performer to become so familiar with the emotional and
intellectual progress of the speech that the words become inevitable
parts of the character, as they should be. It is not necessary to
memorize a scene — and surely it would be extraordinarily difficult

to memorize an entire play. Still, there are times when memorizing may be useful.

When a scene features two or three characters whose rapid, short dialogue prevents graceful consultation with the text (Dryden's *All for Love* at the end of Chapter 7), memorizing allows the pace of the scene to continue unabated. Sometimes transitions between characters are intricate and one character may interrupt the speaker with one or two words; in this case it is far easier to memorize the lines surrounding the interruptions to ensure that the audience has the benefit of your full-front placement and projection in clarifying the change in character. A particularly involved gesture demanded by the scene may prohibit consulting a text. In this case, you should be fully aware of the lines as you move from the lectern; if you move tentatively away from the text, you can make your audience nervous. Generally, it is more graceful to pick up the lines that you don't know by glancing at the text while you are speaking lines that you *do* know. Your rehearsal will have been extensive enough so that a key word or phrase triggers the rest of the line in your mind. Memorizing can help you enormously because it allows you to spend your resources directly with the audience. If you are tied to the text, with your face forever buried in paper, no audience will ever see the life of the characters. Even exemplary vocal projection suffers when it is directed to the floor.

However, memorizing carries with it some problems of its own that should be avoided. The most dangerous pitfall is a *set-speech* attitude: the type of delivery made by children who have had their "piece" drummed into them for the grade-school pageant and say all the words as rapidly as they can — and with very little sense of what they are saying. This lifelessness shows that the performer has memorized the text — but little more. Words mean things, ideas, hopes, and actions; words communicate to audiences and disclose the world that lives within the playwright. When a performer simply rattles off words, all the audience perceives is the rattling off of words.

Perhaps the best method to understand the needs of a scene is to ask whether the scene can be presented most fully if it is completely memorized, memorized in small or large part, or presented entirely from the text. Think carefully and keep this question as your guide: *During this scene what does the audience need to see?*

Setting the Scene

When people attend a play they receive programs with the characters' names, actor's names, setting and time, act divisions, and program notes. The interpreter, on the other hand, is responsible for presenting all of these elements. But the burden isn't so grim as it may sound.

The audience probably knows your name already, so your concern should be with the characters who appear in your scene. Be sure that whatever information you give is restricted to what is needed in the scene you are performing. The *Dramatis Personae* usually lists whatever additional information an audience should know, although if you begin the play after the opening curtain, it is helpful to tell your audience what has happened prior to the first line of your scene. You might also take the time at the beginning to indicate the arrival of any characters who will appear during the scene.

As you are standing at the lectern, remember that the picture you present to the audience is the general *frame* of your performance; the audience focuses its attention within this frame. Moreover, you are flexible, and the lectern is defined, rigid, and strict. If you plan to move about the lectern, you might extend the frame by delivering the necessary opening comments from the side of the lectern. As the scene begins, you will not need to repeat each character's name because the characterizations you present, coupled with your placement of characters out front, should clarify that matter sufficiently for the audience.

When stage directions appear important, they can be incorporated into the performance by the interpreter (*not* by the characters), who presents whatever necessary material should be communicated directly to the audience — as a narrator does with summary in a story. You may want to give some indication of time and locale, if they are not made clear by the lines of the play and are crucial to understanding the scene. If there is a rapid passage of time between two or three scenes you have selected to perform, relay this fact to the audience at the least obtrusive moment during your performance, usually at the end of one scene or just prior to an important segment. Once again the question that must be answered is this: *Is the performance fuller with this information supplied explicitly rather than understood implicitly?*

Sometimes it is necessary to provide scenographic information that is crucial to an understanding of the scene. In George Bernard Shaw's *Caesar and Cleopatra* (Chapter 7), for instance, the audience should know that the set of the first act requires a sphinx. In some scenes, the lines of the play can themselves set the scene much more effectively than any explanation by the performer. It is not necessary for an audience to know minor details when the broadest outline can allow them to both follow the playwright's requirements and complete the details in their imaginations.

Entrances and exits during the course of a scene may occasionally cause some difficulty. If a character's exit occurs at the close of a speech and indicates the completion of a key scene, the interpreter may simply turn away from the scene established. If there are elaborate activities accompanying the departure, the performer (*not* the character) may describe the action: "She pauses a moment, slipping on the long white gloves, gently grasping the parasol in her left hand, and turning ever so delicately toward the French doors, where she finds herself moments later as the curtain falls." If the audience's attention should remain with the character or characters onstage, you can adjust the description to reflect the departing character's activity while allowing the remaining characters to resume the scene. If a character enters mid-scene — or later — you may have to give that identification with a two- or three-word description. You will want to place such an entrance according to the world you and your audience have created ("She enters from the porch"), rather than from some stage-setting location ("She enters up left"); the world of the play is not on the stage but includes your audience.

When a character enters or departs during another character's speech, careful handling of placement of character and offstage focus can indicate to the audience that someone has either entered or left the room. You can welcome an arriving character or bid farewell to a departing character with a slight rise in mental and vocal projection, reaching over the greater distance. (Try these techniques with Lady Capulet's departure in *Romeo and Juliet* at the end of this chapter.) The best guide to keep in mind remains the answer to this question: *How can I lead my audience to understand the activity of this scene without diverting their attention from the scene itself?*

Moreover, audiences come to your performance prepared to believe what they see; they want to believe, and they want to participate in the creation of the world of the scene, provided you let them in on the scene and do not give them false clues or misdirect their attention. Present your suggestions with economy; your physical presence restricts the frame within which the audience follows the speaking character, and your opportunity to create the scene arises chiefly through the shifting focus of the speaking character. If you remember these guidelines, your responsibilities are clear, and you can make difficult judgments with greater confidence and skill.

Properties

Properties can cause many types of problems for performers. If you use real properties, be sure that all the characters who appear in the scene use the *same* prop, or you will be asking your audience to permit and dismiss reality without regard for the play's requirements.

Sometimes, however, it is necessary to present a mimed prop. If anything, mimed props should be treated more carefully than real properties because the performer carefully establishes, nurtures, and concludes their existence. The danger is that the scene might become a scene about a prop rather than a scene in which the prop helps the characters in their attempts to reach their goals. It is important to use the imaginary prop insofar as it touches the characters' lives and the purpose of the scene.

In the potion scene in *Romeo and Juliet*, Juliet has a vial. Stage tradition suggests that she lift it high for the audience to see, just as she shows a dagger later in the same speech. An interpreter with a text at a sloping lectern faces some problems in trying to juggle book, bottle, and knife. The energy used in finding and mastering the props would be better spent in rehearsing the scene and attempting to convey Juliet's dilemma. By barely sketching the gesture of holding a vial in hand, you can convey the mixture of fear and anticipation with which Juliet regards the liquid. If you project the muscle response that accompanies that tension, you will further create the power that piece of glass has over Juliet; this, after all, is the point of the scene. When, a few lines later, Juliet picks up the dagger, you can establish the presence of the knife by a similar gesture, slightly to the right or left of whatever you have placed the vial. As your body remembers what your muscles did in picking up the dagger, you can persuade the audience that Juliet is considering hefting the dagger. If you have suggested the action economically, the only performance action the audience may in fact see is the opening of a hand. They will imagine that Juliet has considered and rejected the dagger and has returned to the vial to complete the scene. Perhaps at the end you will have Juliet raise her hand and touch her lips with her fingers, almost in a farewell kiss.

The interpreter should be careful not to fall into the trap of too-explicit gestures, shuttling imaginary properties from hand to hand, plucking others from mid-air and laying them down on nothingness. Even though a scene may need a lot of tension, and the fullest response requires some physical activity, the interpreter should guard against overt representations or mimetic gestures. They often cause more trouble than they are worth and require effort that should be used more effectively elsewhere. Remember that your goal is to enable the audience to see the scene in their minds and feel it in their muscles: Juliet's agony of decision is the point of the scene; the properties are secondary. *Suggestion* keeps you from plucking at the air; *empathy* allows the audience to feel what the characters feel;

controlled intensity pinpoints the conflict, increasing the density of the scene's power.

Embodying Characters

As an interpreter, you must feel in your muscles the physical lives of the characters in the scene if the audience is to respond. It is sometimes helpful to go through the entire selection and develop a physical technique for one character at a time, concentrating wholly on those speeches and actions as if you were going to act that part — and only that part — on the stage. In making this type of study, you will use the other characters merely as line feeders until you feel that the main character is clearly and lastingly instilled in your mind, muscles, and voice. Then, one by one, allow the other characters to emerge with their individualities, progressions, and interrelationships. You may find it helpful to "walk" the main character, and the others in their turn, to rehearse relevant business exactly as if you were going to do it with properties and scenery. All this is an invaluable aid to timing, pace, and muscle tension, as well as to the motivation of changes in thought, the means for suggesting the character to your audience. Since this suggested procedure is time-consuming, you should select for your classroom assignment a brief scene with relatively few characters, so that you may prepare thoroughly. After the habits of preparation are set, the process becomes less puzzling, because you know what you are looking for and where to find it.

After the characters are "set," the next step is vocal and physical selectivity. It is here that the paths of actor and interpreter of drama separate. The interpreter, like the actor, has created an explicit character with individual mental, emotional, physical, and vocal traits. The interpreter now decides which vocal elements — such as tempo, rhythm, inflection, range, and quality — will most accurately and swiftly suggest each character to the audience. The interpreter now depends primarily on posture, muscle tone, and kinesthetic response to suggest physical characteristics whenever they aid communication.

The time spent in rehearsing the actual business is by no means lost, however, because the *memory* of it will add to the vitality, pace, and general effectiveness of the performance. This principle of muscle memory is sometimes referred to as the *theory of remembered action*. Muscle memory affects the reader's empathy and aids in suggesting hurry or leisure, activity or passivity, tension or relaxation as the scenes progress. In this way climaxes are built more effectively.

To test the effectiveness of this theory of muscle memory, read the following scene from Ibsen's *Hedda Gabler* aloud, ignoring the stage directions for the moment. Of course, it is necessary to consider this scene in the context of the entire play before complete character development can emerge. Nevertheless this excerpt as it stands will serve our purpose as an illustration.

> BRACK: No. But you will have to answer the question: Why did you give Eilert Lövborg the pistol? And what conclusions will people draw from the fact that you did give it to him?
>
> HEDDA (*Lets her head sink*):   That is true, I did not think of that.
>
> BRACK: Well, fortunately, there is no danger, so long as I say nothing.
>
> HEDDA (*Looks up at him*):   So I am in your power, Judge Brack. You have me at your beck and call, from this time forward.
>
> BRACK (*Whispers softly*):   Dearest Hedda — believe me — I shall not abuse my advantage.
>
> HEDDA: I am in your power none the less. Subject to your will and your demands. A slave, a slave then! (*Rises impetuously.*) No, I cannot endure the thought of that! Never!
>
> BRACK (*Looks half-mockingly at her*): People generally get used to the inevitable.
>
> HEDDA (*Returns his look*):   Yes, perhaps. (*She crosses to the writing table.*)

After analyzing the elements of content and style and the relationship of the characters so that you are certain of their interplay, go through the excerpt again, and follow the directions for action that Ibsen has given. Start perhaps with Brack, since he does not change his position. Assume that he is standing, leaning against a chair. Get the feeling in your muscles of one who leans on a chair, perfectly in control of the situation. Let Brack look down at Hedda, who is seated. He will probably straighten slightly and shift his focus as she rises. Act out the excerpt exactly as you would if you were rehearsing his lines for the stage. Next, take Hedda from a sitting position, through the drooping of her head and the upward look that follows, her sudden rising, and her cross to the table. Repeat as often as necessary to perfect the timing. You will note that it is easier to vary pace and inflection, as well as muscle tone and emotional tension, when the action accompanies the words. Now, applying the theory of muscle memory, reread the scene without making the overt physical movements for either character. You will be able to retain the vocal variety as well as the physical variety for a strong degree of suggested activity.

Answer this question: *Which significant physical and vocal details will permit the listeners to fill in a three-dimensional, believable person?*

Building Bodies and Voices of Characters

As an interpreter you do not represent the characters; rather, you suggest them to an audience so that, together, you and the audience create the life of the character. Suggestion does not diminish your responsibility to give a full performance; nor does it alter the need for real people — not shadows — to speak the lines.

All characters have bodies. Sometimes they are buried to their necks, sometimes they are chained to garbage cans, sometimes they appear odd or marvelously strange or fiendishly elusive; but in performance, they all have bodies. The performer's body should be sufficiently flexible to suggest a number of characters without worrying about false wigs, noses, or humps.

The first worry for most interpreters is the matter of gender: can a male performer ever persuade an audience that he is really Irina or Martha? How can a female ever convince an audience that she is Caesar? An interpreter can suggest either gender quite satisfactorily because audiences want to believe. You are not asking them to believe you are physically a particular character; you are asking them to imagine a character who behaves and thinks in the fashion you are suggesting and who happens to be a male or a female. Like age and infirmity, gender is finally a matter of characterization; neither age, infirmity, nor gender alone is sufficient to create a character.

Faced with the problem of performing a character of the opposite sex, the interpreter first should determine precisely the size and shape of the character. Not all women look like Cleopatra; not all men look like Mark Antony. Try to find real people who seem to you to look like the character. See how they carry themselves; watch them walk. Be on the lookout for people who may provide you with the perfect telltale gesture to clarify a goal or finish a scene. Note in particular what happens to a person's hips, thighs, shoulders, and hands as the person moves, walks, and sits. As movement takes place, what happens to the center of gravity? Actors sometimes find animals that resemble their characters and watch them carefully. Use any technique you need, but be sure that you are fully aware of how the body moves.

Now look at what you have to work with — yourself. Where do you carry your weight? Are there any similarities between the ways you and your characters move that you can use? Some men may find that the way they sit is similar to the way that Martha sits; some women may find that they make certain motions that resemble the way in which Tuzenbach looks back at Irina. You probably will develop many of the character's gestures and motions from observation and from trying different things with your own body. Use a full-length mirror. And practice alone, because you can concentrate better on the way you know you want to look.

Women who want to perform male characters have found that, generally, straightening their shoulders, increasing the feel of weight in their forearms and hands, and broadening their stance gets them moving in the right direction. Not all male characters will require all of these elements; some will require none. These simply are ways to start the trial-and-error process. Men who want to perform female characters have found that, generally, narrowing their base of support; lightening the weight in their hands, forearms, and upper legs; and drawing in their shoulders will help them begin to suggest some female characters. Once again, this is simply one way to begin the process.

Once you have developed a character's body, you must put some clothes on it. Your own clothes may restrict movement in ways that period costume does not, and vice versa. If you intend, for example, to perform a scene from *All for Love* (Chapter 7) in jeans, you need to know how Octavia's body can be suggested by yours, how her movement can be suggested by yours. Costumes restrict physical activity and enforce specific kinds of postures: because of his girth and sloppy demeanor, Falstaff would not be able to stand at attention successfully. Corsets, skirts, and swords all hamper agility and restrict freedom of gesture.

When you are costumed in what you will wear in the performance — in what you see the character wearing — move, stand, sit, and jump in the body of the character. Note how your body moves through the passages in the scene, trying any particularly active movements several times. Does the restricted frame of the lectern inhibit any activity? How does your costumed body feel in that frame?

Finally, see what voice emerges from the body you have made and dressed. Try not to force wide variations in pitch, range, or volume. Does this newly costumed body create a voice by itself? Without imposing any preconceptions on the voices, try the central lines for each body you have created. Run the scene entirely as the character you have created, moving as the character might in a staged version. How does it feel and sound? Don't expect instant success; you will need to practice. Work through the scene again, this time without saying a word. Do you remember what differences the voice made? What the body felt like? How the voice and the body together arose from the situation? Listen to people whose voices sound like your characters, and try those voices out on the new bodies. You have begun to build characters, and that is the beginning of building a scene.

Sometimes characters with physical infirmities pose special problems. The best way to deal with these characters is to examine how the infirmity affects their living in the scene. Although some octogenarians are lively and spry, others are feeble. How do their bodies differ *specifically:* is it simply that they gesture more slowly and deliberately? Or is the character arthritic, showing pain with each movement? Remember that habit creates character: Tiresias in Sophocles' *Oedipus the King* (at the end of this chapter) is well accustomed to his blindness, and his infirmity doesn't hinder him from recognizing how little he has to fear from his tragically deluded king.

Interpreters should be careful not to impose stock physical attributes on the characters they are depicting. It is true that some old people have voices that crack piteously, but not all old voices crack; it is true that age bends some men and women, but you know old people who are erect and vigorous. Be sure that the character's infirmity arises from the text, that you do not impose it in an excess of zeal for characterization.

Your attention to specific detail is the key to effective depiction of characters. Each moment and each movement should clarify a new bit of information for the audience. Each must contribute something different to the picture the audience is assembling and to which they are adding their own discoveries as well. Each movement arises out of the prior movement, leads into the following movement, and suggests the complexity that makes a character a vital human being. Bodies and characters are never divorced, they never cease their intricate dance of information.

Physical Contact

Physical contact is difficult for the solo performer to achieve, but audiences can believe it is happening. Audiences want to believe the scene, and they will fill in generously, as everyone does at movies that ask us to believe that flickering shadows are real people. Interpersonal activity is almost impossible to convey, because anything that requires repeated, flesh-on-flesh contact cannot be duplicated successfully by one person. If there is a swordfight, or a boxing match, or a pistol whipping, or even several punches that motivate the plot or initiate crucial character development, it is wisest to narrate the conflict, allowing the imagination of the audience to stage the scene more fully than any solo performer can manage.

Sometimes, though, scenes that appear to be intensely physical on first or second reading are in fact marvelous opportunities for the solo performer to stretch the possibilities of the craft and challenge technical facility. The key to detecting these scenes is to remember that what the audience always sees is the speaking character: as the line shifts, so does the speaking character. Ask yourself how the activity immediately *touches* the speaking character. Using the speaking character as the recipient or initiator of the action, reconsider the scene. What can the speaking character do that will suggest activity on the part of the silent characters? Such behavior is called *reflexive physical activity* because it suggests activity on the part of someone other than the speaker. For example, suppose a silent character picks up a vase to throw at the speaking character; if the speaking character keeps focus on the silent character and on the vase, increasing the tension, excitement, and volume, the audience will believe that something they can't see is causing the character's increased concern. When the silent character finally lets the object fly, the speaker can dodge the vase as it narrowly misses him, or, if it finds its mark, can quickly grasp his forehead to cover the blood, and then complete the speech, still suffering from the blow.

It is impossible to formulate general rules that can be applied to all types of physical contact scenes; each presents its own problems, and each interpreter is at a different level of technical proficiency. Remember that technique is the economical management of your *resources,* and audience belief is one of them. Again we can provide some questions to help you determine some workable solutions to try in rehearsal: *How explicit must I be for the audience to believe the action? Will the technique I have chosen call the audience's attention to a trick or to me and away from the scene?*

If you move, bend, and sway as the text permits, you will determine that what the audience sees is the movement of the scene and the character — not the clever or not-so-clever jumping around of the performer. Go to both extremes during your rehearsal. Stage the scene fully, and find out what the lives of the characters feel like. Then eliminate all activity so that your muscles remember, and you can clear away all the unnecessarily distracting movements. Somewhere between these two extremes you will discover the form that most fully communicates the total scene — all its elements in proper proportion — to an audience eager to fulfill its part in the creation.

Interplay of Characters

After you have discovered a body and a voice for each character in your scene and decided how to cope with their physical contact, something else remains. You want them to appear to listen to each other. Obviously, you cannot listen as one character while you speak as another. Interpreters of drama develop the ability to pick up a speech midway into a train of thought, to "have heard," which requires split-second response and complete control of the characters. You are not going to become split personalities but rather compound ones, each with a sharp focus on what is happening, where it is happening, and how what is happening affects everyone else. All of this effort is necessary because drama arises from the interplay of the characters whose goals engage each other, either because they share these goals or oppose them. You do not want your audience to feel that they are watching a number of people speaking from a series of disconnected islands.

It is now time to repeat some of the questions that you asked at the beginning of your preparation. When the bodies of the characters have been assembled, ask yourself again: "Why are these people continuing to talk to each other?" "What keeps them onstage dealing with each other?" "What does this character hope to gain by continuing his attention to that character?" Relationships are built through the sequences of speeches; as each character speaks, the other listens carefully and joins the dialogue without a pause when the first stops speaking.

Characters interacting in this way seem to be together on the same stage, carrying on their conversations, creating the tension that is the heartbeat of the *scene*, the interpreter's real goal. When characters at last begin to live in the scene, they *lean into* the action. This does not mean that they incline their bodies forward over the reading stand, although they may do that. Leaning into the scene is the way to demonstrate their need to get at the object of their discussion, there, in front of them; it embodies their intention to connect with another character, to whom they speak with earnest conviction. If the character who is being addressed moves, the speaking character follows, always keeping the person in focus and clearly as the object of the speech. And then, instantly, without any gap in which one character is dropped and another assumed, the audience sees the next speaking character.

Picking Up Cues

In picking up cues, the solo performance of drama is at its most artificial, the problems for the performer are the greatest, and the potential liabilities the most dangerous. Poor planning is frequently responsible for most problems here, and lack of foresight or insufficient rehearsal can destroy all the effort that has been made. With transitions, remember to focus the audience's attention on what *is* there (the speaking character) and not to distract them with what isn't there. There are no empty spaces in life — and there should be no empty spaces in the scene either. You are laboring to achieve the totality of the scene, and lapses break or kill the continuity.

When the audience is constantly seeing character, they do not have the time to see the machinery of the interpreter's efforts; they do not have the time to see you groping for lines or pausing to think about what comes next. Maintaining the forcefulness of the scene requires some attention to what the body is doing during the transitions. Try to ensure that whatever posture the character may be in at the conclusion of a line is not so extreme as to require the next character to make any extravagant movement. This does not mean that characters cannot move. It means that eccentric postures should be adjusted and resolved by the time the line is concluded, so that the performer is in a posture that is neutral enough to conclude one character and begin the next fluently. Without the need for any excessive or radical alteration in posture, the interpreter can shift the focus to the new character and begin the line effortlessly, and the audience will not be jolted.

Thorough rehearsal will make these transitions come more readily to the performer. Vocal and physical changes will occur so rapidly that an audience will not have time for a lapse in belief. Begin your rehearsal well in advance of the performance, so that there is time to evolve the habits of each character and to develop ease in assuming characters. Many brief practice sessions are far superior to one long session, for the interpreter must live with the characters to get to know them. One general question subsumes many other allied concerns: *How can a performer focus the audience's attention on what is there and divert attention from what isn't there?*

Physical Focus

The action of the scene should move along a line that stretches from the performer through the audience to the opposing character or characters, who exist just above and beyond the listeners' heads. This arrangement places the audience at the center of the interaction, with the interpreter providing the constant source of information and activity within the scene. Characters who are being addressed live at some distance from the speaker who addresses them; this distance should be bridged by the performer's intensity and commitment. The audience will support and enhance the tension among the characters, but only if they have something to go on, some life to sustain the excitement and direction of the scene. The source of this life should be the performer facing them. The physical focus of the scene should exist out front. Resist any temptation to place other characters on stage, to your right or left, leaving you in profile. Not only would the audience be denied the cues that your face and body can give them, but their attention also would be drawn away from what is in front of them. Keep the characters talking to other characters, and be sure that all the characters exist out front.

Methods of Focus

When the interpreter needs to distinguish between different heights or eye levels for the characters, the difference should not be even slightly exaggerated because the audience can grossly distort the intended angle of placement. You usually can make sufficient distinction with your eyes, and you need never substantially alter the horizontal angle of your head.

Consider this analogy: in the movie *Gone with the Wind*, you see Rhett Butler and Scarlett O'Hara in their final scene together confront each other for the last time in front of the staircase. You know that they are talking to each other, but there in front of you at one moment is a tight closeup of Clark Gable speaking directly to *you*; then, in turn, there is a similar closeup of Vivien Leigh's face as she talks directly to *you*. Of course both performers are speaking directly to the camera, but if you had seen the segment on the stage, you would have seen only the two actors speaking to each other directly. In the film, the camera is interposed between the characters; because the camera is there, so are you. You can see in their eyes and their mouths all of the tension of that moment.

Much the same phenomenon occurs in the solo performance of drama, except that instead of interposing the camera between the characters, the performer allows the audience the fullest view. We accept this convention because our experience with watching films and television renders it perfectly natural for two people who in fact are talking to each other to appear to be addressing the audience. If you keep in mind the analogy between the placement of the camera and that point where the audience enters the excitement of the scene, your initial fears about audience belief may be calmed. But remember that the performers in the film were so skillful that they made you believe that their characters were talking to each other. What the camera does is help us see more — and differently — than we could ever see on a stage.

If the action of a scene is elaborate, you can use an explanatory narrative technique to describe it. If the action is important primarily for its revelation of an attitude or an emotional state, then the audience should be made aware of the cause rather than the action itself.

The action, after all, is the outward manifestation of the interior response, and this gives the interpreter an important clue to the way action should be handled. It is not so much *what* the characters do as *how* they do it that reveals what they are thinking and feeling. If, for example, a character sinks dejectedly into a chair, it is not the process of sitting down that is important; it is the dejection that is emphasized by the action. Dejection shows itself in the muscle tone of the interpreter's entire body, in the pace of speech, in vocal quality, and in other ways. In rehearsal, the staged scene should certainly be practiced in detail, and the act of sitting should be synchronized with the speech so that voice and body are saying the same thing. In performance, however, your sinking into a set-piece chair would pull the scene up on stage instead of keeping it out front. It would be thoroughly impractical and cause needless complications, because you would need a chair to sink into and you need to get up in time to deliver the other characters' lines. Such activity draws attention to what isn't there at the expense of what is. Continue standing throughout the scene, and suggest a particular attitude not by an overt bodily activity but by empathy, muscle tone, and whatever aspects of focal technique are appropriate.

Angle of Placement

Onstage, actors move from place to place, and we watch them and follow them as they move. Part of the spectacle of a play is formed by the interesting and artful management of moving bodies. Understandably, solo interpreters cannot show such compositions in their performances. Through careful character placement, however, they can imply the movement of characters and suggest to the audience something of the essential movement of the play. After all, spatial relationships among characters contribute to their motivations and their lives.

Furthermore, interpreters can clarify the speaker's position by directing comments to specific locales. Too often, however, the angle of character placement is substituted for characterization; it is merely a tool to assist characterization. Placement of characters comes among the last of the responsibilities the interpreter need face.

There are at least two popular methods used to place characters out front. The easiest one is to locate a point for each character that is slightly above and slightly beyond the audience, and to address all of the character's lines to that point. When these points are placed reasonably close together — not so far apart that they require a large turn of the head — an interpreter can locate five or six characters very neatly. This method ensures that a specific character always looks in the same direction, no matter who the listener is. The interpreter's eyes are not glued to one spot since several people can be addressed in succession by a slight eye movement within the area that has been indicated for a particular character. An audience always knows that a particular character's comments are addressed to a particular area; by retaining for each character's speeches the same relative position, the beginning interpreter can become accustomed to a nearly automatic pickup of focus and muscle tone that is set for each character.

Another method, which is much more difficult and should not be attempted unless you are willing to spend hours in practicing its execution, uses the stage picture for its foundation. Picture a scene in which Arnold addresses Betty: he directs his comments to the imagined Betty. Then he has a line to Conrad, and he turns slightly to address these words to the imagined Conrad. When you become Betty in performance, you, too, address your comments to Conrad to the same place that Arnold looked when he spoke to Conrad, the difference between Arnold and Betty being distinguished by different characterization and different physical and vocal quality. Your goal is to make the audience believe that Arnold and Betty and Conrad are behind them, all in a kind of proximity to each other that permits movement on the characters' part and allows the speaking character to address the other characters as individuals.

Whatever method you choose, be sure that the important characters are in the center of the audience and that less important characters are grouped accordingly, only slightly to either side of that center line. If you place characters too far apart, you will constantly be moving your head back and forth. The extra time spent on transitions will allow the audience to pick up on the artificialities of the performing method, and they will focus their attention on what is *not* there, rather than what *is*.

The method you adopt must be the one that you feel gives the audience the clearest, least ambiguous information. The audience should always know who is speaking. Whatever the method, any reasonable activity can occur within a given speech, provided that the activity is begun and concluded by the interpreter's focusing at the agreed-upon character point and that the speech remains addressed to characters within the play.

The interpreter generally does not have any direct audience contact during the passages in which characters talk to characters. But when you present any narrative material or explanation, you can establish audience contact since you are delivering that material as yourself (consider the Singer in *The Caucasian Chalk Circle* in Chapter 11). Characters themselves occasionally speak directly to the audience in a soliloquy or an aside. In any case, avoid addressing your words to a single member of the audience, because that person might become uneasy under the constant gaze of the performer. Also, as an interpreter, you do not need to be thrown off your performance by connecting with individual expressions in the audience.

This does not mean that the audience will be ignored in your performance. You are engaged in this performance for them, and they are actively involved in creating characters and places and ideas with your guidance. If you are constantly in character, giving your listeners new information, alive and fully aware of the excitement of your scene, they will be with you, enthralled, absorbed, and perhaps as exhausted as you are by the conclusion.

The Reading Stand

For many people, the reading stand or lectern[1] is one of the hallmarks of the interpreter. It can be used or ignored. There are a number of reasons for using a lectern. It holds the script nicely and liberates the performer's hands and arms for gesture. If the lectern is used, however, it should not be ignored, and the text not consulted. Its use allows for greater freedom and flexibility in suggestion, since it allows the performer to make easy transitions from character to character and can serve as a table, a bar, a counter, a ledge, a tray, or any other necessary stage piece to support the performer's body.

There is an aesthetic element to the lectern: it provides a frame for the performance. An interpreter appears before the audience as a person with a book. Around this person the audience unconsciously creates a frame, since any performer is a presentational object. The performer is then responsible for filling the frame with the life of the play — with becoming the impulse that triggers the audience to share the experience of the play. Thus framed, the performer is given, in the audience's mind, an immediate restriction of movement; of course, movement to and from the lectern is allowed. But like many restrictions, this one carries with it a certain kind of freedom: the freedom that allows suggestion to assist the audience in creating the world of the play. In a staged production, an actor must compete for the audience's attention with set and costume and all the other actors; dramatic gestures must be sufficiently grand to fill a large space. Because they are restricted, interpreters can use

1. A *lectern* is a reading stand; it should not be confused with a *podium*, which is an elevated platform on which one stands.

substantially more refined, more economical activity than actors. Thus, they become capable of more variety, subtlety, and nuance in their physical world because they can achieve the same effect with less and because the audience itself is cooperating.

There is one other practical matter about lecterns that should be mentioned: unfortunately, they can obliterate carefully planned gestures and obscure delicate muscle memory. Rehearse with one, if at all possible.

Cutting and Excerpting

In Chapter 6 we discussed some of the most responsible techniques of excerpting, and every interpreter is sooner or later confronted by this delicate task. The safest, most conservative rule regarding cutting and excerpting remains: the less, the better. Since each text is unique and every performer and performance situation varies from every other, we cannot establish any set rules for excerpting. But we are quick to recognize that drama frequently requires some kind of condensation, particularly for a solo interpreter.

Because time limitations can cause problems, it is wisest to excerpt a segment from a longer work that adequately fills the time limit without any internal cutting. You are able to benefit from the carefully constructed rhythmic patterns of the play; the intricate, involved structure that sometimes hides itself at first glance emerges during your rehearsal process. Moreover, as you build the scene, you will have all the benefits of the author's craft on your side. If your segment should occur midway in the play, you can describe to the audience what has happened just prior to the scene; if subsequent events are important for an understanding of your passage, you can relate them after you have finished. If you start at the beginning of a play, your audience can join the performance as if they are watching a staged production because your performance will present all the required information. All the dramatic selections reprinted here are such excerpts, although not all occur at the beginning of the play.

Sometimes, though, it is necessary to cut the material, and you must be extremely careful how you do this. Often a performer's reflexive physical activity can suggest an action that has been performed: a speaking character is allowed to continue speaking, while the performer nods to an imaginary butler and mimes the action of picking up a letter from a proferred tray. If this is the butler's only appearance and his only line, the audience will scarcely miss him; if, however, your play is one in which "the butler did it," cutting his appearance here would deprive your audience of crucial information.

Before cutting anything, try conscientiously to include everything; most often you will be surprised at how unnecessary any cutting is. Only extraordinary circumstances should require you to cut more than a few words. If these circumstances do arise, at all costs avoid interlinear cutting because it defeats your purpose, misrepresents the play, and confuses the audience. Keep the speech whole.

Analyzing the Performance

Begin your analysis with an update and a review. By now you should be familiar with the performance problems that habitually plague you. Have you spent sufficient time on rehearsal? Have you been maintaining concentration? Have you made substantial and serious efforts to transform the literary analysis into performance behavior? Is your body responding more flexibly? Has your voice continued to demonstrate the tone color and vocal variety that marks successful interpretation? As we have said, these questions will never disappear. They will shift focus and degree, of course, with each selection you prepare and each performance you deliver, but the fundamental concerns of interpretation remain the same for beginning students as for veterans.

Performing drama affords another opportunity to broaden your experiences. Drama presents special problems in creating character, managing dialogue, and demonstrating action. These problems, of course, also appear when performing narration, and some types of poetry — particularly confessional poems — require similar effort for the construction of character. Thus, the skills you develop in these performances rest on the skills you have already established, and they will also be useful when you confront the special problems of performing poetry.

Try to respond, then, to the following questions about your performance of drama not simply in terms of this genre's unique concerns, but in terms of the *process* you undertake in performing any literary selection. Although these questions may seem specifically related to drama, they intimately involve your development as an interpreter of all kinds of literature.

Was your commitment to the scene total? Did your audience see only character during the time of the performance? When did the interpreter emerge? Why? Was it planned?

Did you carefully analyze the structure of your scene, taking time to establish clearly all the principal components of the action?

Did your close analytical reading disclose hidden clues about characters?

How did you find appropriate bodies and voices for the people in your scene? Gestures?

How was silence used in your scene? Did your characters fill the silences with their personalities? Did the speaker watch carefully for responses from the silent characters?

Did you stage the scene for yourself during rehearsal? Did you carefully imagine and define the settings and properties filling the world of the scene? Did you dress these characters appropriately?

Did your movement through the scene clarify the reason each character speaks and why the character chooses the language used? Did you need a paraphrase to understand the intellectual component of the scene?

Were properties necessary? Were they kept alive? Did you *economically* suggest stage movement? Did your audience always know where the characters were, in addition to who was speaking? How did you solve the scenographic requirements of the play?

Were you sensitive to the rhythm of the speeches? Did you allow each character a distinctive vocal timbre?

Were you in control? Were you too much in control? Have you begun to develop a method for rehearsal? Did memorization intrude? Ought memorization to have been used?

Were your muscles remembering the bodies you created in rehearsal? Did you make clear why each character remains onstage?

Did you pick up your cues?

Did you place the action of the scene directly out front? Did you keep the characters distinct?

If you used a lectern, was it part of the performance or part of the woodwork? Did you make your physical text part of the performance?

Did you cut your scene internally? Was it living when you finished?

These questions can also focus your responses to the performances of others in your class. Keeping in mind that your chief responsibility is to be descriptive, try to make sure that you say *precisely* what you saw and heard and, most important, that what you say is precisely what you mean. If there is some possibility of misunderstanding, take the time to clarify before proceeding. For example, if you say, "I thought the performer seemed out of breath, gasping and choking," when in fact you mean you thought a *character* in the scene demonstrated this behavior, do not be surprised if the interpreter is puzzled. Using clear, shared language includes understanding shared goals: in laboratory sessions a performer might work on a special problem (dialect, for example, or physical debility in a character) and, in his or her attention to this concern, might slight other responsibilities (character placement or volume). Know what the performer is working on; if you don't know or it isn't apparent, ask. As you know, performers like very much to talk about what they do.

Acknowledging that there are many responsibilities for a performer, as well as fulfilling each of these responsibilities with equal distinction, is a rare — a very rare — achievement. But because something remains to be done does not mean that nothing has been done. Much may have been omitted from a performance in which much else has been included.

Finally, discussing performance can become an enormously humanizing concern, if performer and audience are both primarily concerned with understanding. For criticism to be useful, it must be humane. This doesn't mean it cannot be specific or sharp or blunt, as the case warrants. It means that the goal for the critic ought to be the goal for the performer: the fullest possible communication of a work of literature. Whatever diverts attention from that goal isn't really worth our time.

Selections for Analysis and Oral Interpretation

Stephen Sondheim won a Pulitzer Prize for *Sunday in the Park with George,* a musical exploring the responsibilities of artists by examining the life of the French pointillist painter Georges Seurat. George's girlfriend has left him because he has been obsessed with his work and has neglected their relationship. Now she is looking for him. In this song George makes clear that what caused the problem will always remain. Sondheim also composed particularly ravishing music for these lyrics, but everything you need for performing is in the words he wrote. Show us how George thinks. Trust Sondheim's line length.

FROM *Sunday in the Park with George*
STEPHEN SONDHEIM

Finishing the Hat

Yes, she looks for me — good.
Let her look for me to tell me why she left me —

As I always knew she would.
I had thought she understood
They have never understood,
And no reason that they should.
But if anybody could . . .

Finishing the hat,
How you have to finish the hat.
How you watch the rest of the world
From a window
While you finish the hat.

Mapping out a sky,
What you feel like, planning a sky.
What you feel when voices that come
Through the window
Go
Until they distance and die,
Until there's nothing but sky.

And how you're always turning back too late
From the grass or the stick
Or the dog or the light,
How the kind of woman willing to wait's
Not the kind that you want to find waiting
To return you to the night,
Dizzy from the height,
Coming from the hat,
Studying the hat,
Entering the world of the hat,
Reaching through the world of the hat
Like a window,
Back to this one from that.

Studying a face,
Stepping back to look at a face
Leaves a little space in the way like a window,
But to see —
It's the only way to see.

And when the woman that you wanted goes,
You can say to yourself, "Well, I give what I give."
But the woman who won't wait for you knows
That, however you live,

There's a part of you always standing by,
Mapping out the sky,
Finishing a hat . . .
Starting on a hat . . .
Finishing a hat . . .
Look, I made a hat . . .
Where there never was a hat . . .

▌ Did you find the fulcrum of George's speech? Did your audience see it?
▌ What do the last five lines mean?

The beginning of this famous scene, with its entrances and exits, requires some care to keep the abrupt stage directions from interrupting the dialogue. Juliet's speech, with its problem of properties and her loss of consciousness at the end, has been discussed within this chapter. Watch the build-up of hysteria toward the end of the speech and the resultant problem of balancing the climactic "This do I drink to thee." Juliet is always *thinking*.

FROM *Romeo and Juliet*
WILLIAM SHAKESPEARE

ACT IV, SCENE 3

(*Enter* JULIET *and* NURSE.)

JULIET: Ay, those attires are best; but, gentle nurse,
I pray thee, leave me to myself to-night;
For I have need of many orisons
To move the heavens to smile upon my state,
Which, well thou know'st, is cross and full of sin.

(*Enter* LADY CAPULET.)

LADY CAPULET: What, are you busy, ho? Need you my help?
JULIET: No, Madame; we have cull'd such necessaries
As are behoveful for our state to-morrow.
So please you, let me now be left alone,
And let the nurse this night sit up with you;
For, I am sure, you have your hands full all,
In this so sudden business.
LADY CAPULET: Good-night.
Get thee to bed, and rest; for thou hast need.

(*Exeunt* LADY CAPULET *and* NURSE.)

JULIET: Farewell! God knows when we shall meet again.
I have a faint cold fear thrills through my veins,
That almost freezes up the heat of life.
I'll call them back again to comfort me.
Nurse! What should she do there?
My dismal scene I needs must act alone.
Come, vial.
What if this mixture do not work at all?
Shall I be married then to-morrow morning?
No, no; this shall forbid it. Lie thou there. (*Laying down her dagger.*)
What if it be poison, which the friar
Subtly hath minist'red to have me dead,
Lest in this marriage he should be dishonour'd
Because he married me before to Romeo?
I fear it is; and yet, methinks, it should not,
For he hath still been tried a holy man.
How if, when I am laid into the tomb,
I wake before the time that Romeo
Come to redeem me? There's a fearful point!
Shall I not then be stifled in the vault,
To whose foul mouth no healthsome air breathes in,
And there die strangled ere my Romeo comes?
Or, if I live, is it not very like
The horrible conceit of death and night,
Together with the terror of the place, —
As in a vault, an ancient receptacle,
Where, for this many hundred years, the bones
Of all my buried ancestors are pack'd;

Where bloody Tybalt, yet but green in earth,
Lies fest'ring in his shroud; where, as they say,
At some hours in the night spirits resort; —
Alack, alack, is it not like I,
So early waking, — what with loathsome smells,
And shrieks like mandrakes' torn out of the earth,
That living mortals, hearing them, run mad; —
O, if I wake, shall I not be distraught,
Environed with all these hideous fears,
And madly play with my forefathers' joints,
And pluck the mangled Tybalt from his shroud,
And, in this rage, with some great kindsman's bone
As with a club, dash out my desperate brains?
O, look! methinks I see my cousin's ghost
Seeking out Romeo, that did spit his body
Upon a rapier's point. Stay, Tybalt, stay!
Romeo, I come! This do I drink to thee.

(*She falls upon her bed, within the curtains.*)

▌ What kind of a mother was your Lady Capulet?
▌ What caused Juliet finally to drink the potion? Did your audience see that, too?

This play explores the slow denouement of at least three relationships in a
complex series of nine scenes that begin in 1977 and recede in time to 1968.
Midway through the play Robert and Emma — husband and wife — vacation
in Venice, but their sojourn cannot be relaxing for either. Pinter uses "*Pause*"
and "*Silence*" more eloquently than other modern dramatists, and you must
scrupulously follow his directions. Be sure, however, that these pauses are
filled with concentration.

FROM ***Betrayal,*** *Scene Five*
HAROLD PINTER

HOTEL ROOM. VENICE. 1973. SUMMER.

EMMA: *on bed reading.* ROBERT *at window looking out. She looks up at him,
then back at the book.*

EMMA: It's Torcello tomorrow, isn't it?
ROBERT: What?
EMMA: We're going to Torcello tomorrow, aren't we?
ROBERT: Yes. That's right.
EMMA: That'll be lovely.

ROBERT: Mmn.
EMMA: I can't wait.

Pause

ROBERT: Book good?
EMMA: Mmn. Yes.
ROBERT: What is it?
EMMA: This new book. This man Spinks.
ROBERT: Oh that. Jerry was telling me about it.
EMMA: Jerry? Was he?
ROBERT: He was telling me about it at lunch last week.
EMMA: Really? Does he like it?
ROBERT: Spinks is his boy. He discovered him.
EMMA: Oh. I didn't know that.
ROBERT: Unsolicited manuscript.

Pause

You think it's good, do you?
EMMA: Yes, I do. I'm enjoying it.
ROBERT: Jerry thinks it's good too. You should have lunch with us
one day and chat about it.
EMMA: Is that absolutely necessary?

Pause

It's not as good as all that.
ROBERT: You mean it's not good enough for you to have lunch with
Jerry and me and chat about it?
EMMA: What the hell are you talking about?
ROBERT: I must read it again myself, now it's in hard covers.
EMMA: Again?
ROBERT: Jerry wanted us to publish it.
EMMA: Oh, really?
ROBERT: Well, naturally. Anyway, I turned it down.
EMMA: Why?
ROBERT: Oh . . . not much more to say on that subject, really, is
there?
EMMA: What do you consider the subject to be?
ROBERT: Betrayal.
EMMA: No, it isn't.
ROBERT: Isn't it? What is it then?
EMMA: I haven't finished it yet. I'll let you know.
ROBERT: Well, do let me know.

Pause

Of course, I could be thinking of the wrong book.

Silence

By the way, I went into American Express yesterday.

She looks up.

EMMA: Oh?

ROBERT: Yes. I went to cash some travellers cheques. You get a much better rate there, you see, than you do in an hotel.

EMMA: Oh, do you?

ROBERT: Oh yes. Anyway, there was a letter there for you. They asked me if you were any relation and I said yes. So they asked me if I wanted to take it. I mean, they gave it to me. But I said no, I would leave it. Did you get it?

EMMA: Yes.

ROBERT: I suppose you popped in when you were out shopping yesterday evening?

EMMA: That's right.

ROBERT: Oh well, I'm glad you got it.

Pause

To be honest, I was amazed that they suggested I take it. It could never happen in England. But these Italians . . . so free and easy. I mean, just because my name is Downs and your name is Downs doesn't mean that we're the Mr and Mrs Downs that they, in their laughing Mediterranean way, assume we are. We could be, and in fact are vastly more likely to be, total strangers. So let's say I, whom they laughingly assume to be your husband, had taken the letter, having declared myself to be your husband but in truth being a total stranger, and opened it, and read it, out of nothing more than idle curiosity, and then thrown it in a canal, you would never have received it and would have been deprived of your legal right to open your own mail, and all this because of Venetian *je m'en foutisme*. I've a good mind to write to the Doge of Venice about it.

Pause

That's what stopped me taking it, by the way, and bringing it to you, the thought that I could very easily be a total stranger.

Pause

What they of course did not know, and had no way of knowing, was that I am your husband.

EMMA: Pretty inefficient bunch.
ROBERT: Only in a laughing Mediterranean way.

Pause

EMMA: It was from Jerry.
ROBERT: Yes, I recognised the handwriting.

Pause

How is he?
EMMA: Okay.
ROBERT: Good. And Judith?
EMMA: Fine.

Pause

ROBERT: What about the kids?
EMMA: I don't think he mentioned them.
ROBERT: They're probably all right, then. If they were ill or something he'd have probably mentioned it.

Pause

Any other news?
EMMA: No.

Silence

ROBERT: Are you looking forward to Torcello?

Pause

How many times have we been to Torcello? Twice. I remember how you loved it, the first time I took you there. You fell in love with it. That was about ten years ago, wasn't it? About . . . six months after we were married. Yes. Do you remember? I wonder if you'll like it as much tomorrow.

Pause

What do you think of Jerry as a letter writer?

She laughs shortly.

You're trembling. Are you cold?
EMMA: No.
ROBERT: He used to write to me at one time. Long letters about Ford Madox Ford. I used to write to him too, come to think of it. Long letters about . . . oh, W. B. Yeats, I suppose. That was the time when we were both editors of poetry magazines. Him at Cambridge, me at Oxford. Did you know that? We were bright

young men. And close friends. Well, we still are close friends. All that was long before I met you. Long before he met you. I've been trying to remember when I introduced him to you. I simply can't remember. I take it I *did* introduce him to you? Yes. But when? Can you remember?

EMMA: No.

ROBERT: You can't?

EMMA: No.

ROBERT: How odd.

Pause

He wasn't best man at our wedding, was he?

EMMA: You know he was.

ROBERT: Ah, yes. Well, that's probably when I introduced him to you.

Pause

Was there any message for me, in his letter?

Pause

I mean in the line of business, to do with the world of publishing. Has he discovered any new and original talent? He's quite talented at uncovering talent, old Jerry.

EMMA: No message.

ROBERT: No message. Not even his love?

Silence

EMMA: We're lovers.

ROBERT: Ah. Yes. I thought it might be something like that, something along those lines.

EMMA: When?

ROBERT: What?

EMMA: When did you think?

ROBERT: Yesterday. Only yesterday. When I saw his handwriting on the letter. Before yesterday I was quite ignorant.

EMMA: Ah.

Pause

I'm sorry.

ROBERT: *Sorry?*

Silence

Where does it . . . take place? Must be a bit awkward. I mean we've got two kids, he's got two kids, not to mention a wife . . .

EMMA: We have a flat.
ROBERT: Ah. I see.

Pause

Nice?

Pause

A flat. It's quite well established then, your . . . uh . . . affair?
EMMA: Yes.
ROBERT: How long?
EMMA: Some time.
ROBERT: Yes, but how long exactly?
EMMA: Five years.
ROBERT: *Five years?*

Pause

Ned is one year old.

Pause

Did you hear what I said?
EMMA: Yes. He's your son. Jerry was in America. For two months.

Silence

ROBERT: Did he write to you from America?
EMMA: Of course. And I wrote to him.
ROBERT: Did you tell him that Ned had been conceived?
EMMA: Not by letter.
ROBERT: But when you did tell him, was he happy to know I was
     to be a father?

Pause

I've always liked Jerry. To be honest, I've always liked him rather
more than I've liked you. Maybe I should have had an affair with
him myself.

Silence

Tell me, are you looking forward to our trip to Torcello?

▎ How did you demonstrate that Robert knows of the affair as the
   scene begins?
▎ How did you prepare your audience for Emma's confession?

Oedipus, king of Thebes, who once answered the riddle of the Sphinx and thus destroyed its power, has been visited by the elders and townsmen begging him to deliver them once again from famine and pestilence. He tells them that he has sent his brother-in-law, Creon, to the oracle to find out what he might do to save the state. When Creon returns, he reveals that the oracle has said the curse will not be lifted until the murderer of King Laius, who held the throne before Oedipus, is found and driven from Thebes. Oedipus has issued a proclamation to carry out this task. Moreover, he has sent for the blind prophet Tiresias in the hope that he can help identify the murderer through his powers of divination. Oedipus stands on the steps of his palace surrounded by his citizens, waiting for the arrival of the revered man.

FROM *Oedipus the King*

SOPHOCLES

(*Enter* TIRESIAS, *led by a* BOY.)

OEDIPUS: You know all things in heaven and earth, Tiresias:
Things you may speak of openly, and secrets
Holy and not to be revealed. You know,
Blind though you are, the plague that ruins Thebes.
And you, great prophet, you alone can save us.
Phoebus has sent an answer to our question,
An answer that the messengers may have told you,
Saying there is no cure for our condition
Until we found the killers of King Laius
And banished them or had them put to death.
Therefore, Tiresias, do not begrudge your skill
In the voice of birds or other prophecy,
But save yourself, save me, save the whole city,
Save everything that the pestilence defiles.
We are at your mercy, and man's noblest task
Is to use all his powers in helping others.
TIRESIAS: How dreadful a thing, how dreadful a thing is wisdom,
When to be wise is useless! This I knew
But I forgot, or else I would never have come.
OEDIPUS: What is the matter? Why are you so troubled?
TIRESIAS: Oedipus, let me go home. Then you will bear
Your burden, and I mine, more easily.
OEDIPUS: Custom entitles us to hear your message.
By being silent you harm your native land.
TIRESIAS: You do not know when, and when not to speak.
Silence will save me from the same misfortune.

OEDIPUS: If you can be of help, then all of us
Kneel and implore you not to turn away.
TIRESIAS: None of you know the truth, but I will never
Reveal my sorrow — not to call it yours.
OEDIPUS: What are you saying? You know and will not speak?
You mean to betray us and destroy the city?
TIRESIAS: I refuse to pain you. I refuse to pain myself.
It is useless to ask me. I tell you nothing.
OEDIPUS: You utter scoundrel! You would enrage a stone!
Is there no limit to your stubbornness?
TIRESIAS: You blame my anger and forget your own.
OEDIPUS: No one could help being angry when he heard
How you dishonor and ignore the state.
TIRESIAS: What is to come will come, though I keep silent.
OEDIPUS: If it must come, your duty is to speak.
TIRESIAS: I will say no more. Rage to your heart's content.
OEDIPUS: Rage? Yes, I will rage! I will spare you nothing.
In the plot against King Laius, I have no doubt
That you were an accomplice, yes, almost
The actual killer. If you had not been blind,
I would have said that you alone were guilty.
TIRESIAS: Then listen to my command! Obey the edict
That you yourself proclaimed and never speak,
From this day on, to me or any Theban.
You are the sinner who pollutes our land.
OEDIPUS: Have you no shame? How do you hope to escape
the consequence of such an accusation?
TIRESIAS: I have escaped. My strength is the living truth.
OEDIPUS: This is no prophecy. Who taught you this?
TIRESIAS: You did. You forced me to speak against my will.
OEDIPUS: Repeat your slander. Let me learn it better.
TIRESIAS: Are you trying to tempt me into saying more?
I have spoken already. Have you not understood?
OEDIPUS: No, not entirely. Give your speech again.
TIRESIAS: I say you are the killer, you yourself.
OEDIPUS: Twice the same insult! You will pay for it.
TIRESIAS: Shall I say more to make you still more angry?
OEDIPUS: Say what you want to. It will make no sense.
TIRESIAS: You are living in shame with those most dear to you,
As yet in ignorance of your dreadful fate.
OEDIPUS: Do you suppose that you can always use
Language like that and not be punished for it?
TIRESIAS: Yes. I am safe, if truth has any strength.

OEDIPUS: Truth can save anyone excepting you,
You with no eyes, no hearing, and no brains!
TIRESIAS: Poor fool! You taunt me, but you soon will hear
The self-same insults heaped upon your head.
OEDIPUS: You live in endless night. What can you do
To me or anyone else who sees the day?
TIRESIAS: Nothing. I have no hand in your destruction.
For that, Apollo needs no help from me.
OEDIPUS: Apollo! Is this your trick, or is it Creon's?
TIRESIAS: Creon is guiltless. The evil is in you.
OEDIPUS: How great is the envy roused by wealth, by kingship,
By the subtle skill that triumphs over others
In life's hard struggle! Creon, who has been
For years my trusted friend, has stealthily
Crept in upon me to seize my power,
The unsought gift the city freely gave me.
Anxious to overthrow me, he has bribed
This scheming mountebank, this fraud, this trickster,
Blind in his art and in everything but money!
Your art of prophecy! When have you shown it?
Not when the watch-dog of the gods was here,
Chanting her riddle. Why did you say nothing,
When you might have saved the city? Yet her puzzle
Could not be solved by the first passer-by.
A prophet's skill was needed, and you proved
That you had no such skill, either in birds
Or any other means the gods have given.
But I came, I, the ignorant Oedipus,
And silenced her. I had no birds to help me.
I used my brains. And it is I you now
Are trying to destroy in the hope of standing
Close beside Creon's throne. You will regret
This zeal of yours to purify the land,
You and your fellow-plotter. You seem old;
Otherwise you would pay for your presumption.
CHORUS: Sir, it appears to us that both of you
Have spoken in anger. Anger serves no purpose.
Rather we should consider in what way
We best can carry out the god's command.
TIRESIAS: Kind though you are, I have a right to answer
Equal to yours. In that I too am king.
I serve Apollo. I do not acknowledge
You as my lord or Creon as my patron.

You have seen fit to taunt me with my blindness.
Therefore I tell you this: you have your eyesight
And cannot see the sin of your existence,
Cannot see where you live or whom you live with,
Are ignorant of your parents, bring disgrace
Upon your kindred in the world below
And here on earth. And soon the double lash
Of your mother's and father's curse will drive you headlong
Out of the country, blinded, with your cries
Heard everywhere, echoed by every hill
In all Cithaeron. Then you will have learned
The meaning of your marriage, learned in what harbor,
After so fair a voyage, you were shipwrecked.
And other horrors you could never dream of
Will teach you who you are, will drag you down
To the level of your children. Heap your insults
On Creon and my message if you choose to.
Still no one ever will endure the weight
Of greater misery than will fall on you.

OEDIPUS: Am I supposed to endure such talk as this,
Such talk from him? Go, curse you, go! Be quick!

TIRESIAS: Except for your summons I would never have come.

OEDIPUS: And I would never have sent for you so soon
If I had known you would prove to be a fool.

TIRESIAS: Yes. I have proved a fool — in your opinion,
And yet your parents thought that I was wise.

OEDIPUS: What parents? Wait! Who was my father? Tell me!

TIRESIAS: Today you will see your birth and your destruction.

OEDIPUS: You cannot speak unless you speak in riddles!

TIRESIAS: And yet how brilliant you are in solving them!

OEDIPUS: You sneer at me for what has made me great.

TIRESIAS: The same good fortune that has ruined you.

OEDIPUS: If I have saved the city, nothing else matters.

TIRESIAS: In that case I will go. Boy, take me home.

OEDIPUS: Yes, let him take you. Here, you are in the way.
Once you are gone, you will give no further trouble.

TIRESIAS: I will not go before I have said my say,
Indifferent to your black looks. You cannot harm me.
And I say this: the man whom you have sought,
Whom you have threatened, whom you have proclaimed
The killer of King Laius — he is here.
Now thought an alien, he shall prove to be
A native Theban, to his deep dismay.
Now he has eyesight, now his wealth is great;

But he shall make his way to foreign soil
Blinded, in beggary, groping with a stick.
In his own household he shall be shown to be
The father of his children — and their brother,
Son to the woman who bore him — and her husband,
The killer and the bedfellow of his father.
Go and consider this; and if you find
That I have been mistaken, you can say
That I have lost my skill in prophecy.

(*Exeunt* OEDIPUS *and* TIRESIAS.)

▌ When did your Oedipus get seriously worried? What happened
to him during Tiresias' final speech? How did your audience
see that in Tiresias' face and body?

Bibliography

Berry, Cicely. *The Actor and His Text.* London: Harrap, Ltd., 1987.
> A useful study of the voice in Shakespeare and other dramatic texts by
> the Voice Director of the Royal Shakespeare Company.

Bentley, Eric. *The Playwright as Thinker: A Study of Drama in Modern
Times.* New York: Reynal and Hitchcock, 1946.
> A classic in dramatic criticism that has influenced the thinking of critics
> and dramatists for nearly half a century.

———. *The Brecht Memoir.* Evanston: Northwestern Press, 1991.
> A personal Remembrance of Brecht by his pioneer translator and chief
> American champion.

———. *The Life of the Drama.* New York: Atheneum, 1965.
> A brilliant and readable survey of the drama from Aeschylus to Shake-
> speare, and from Moliere to Samuel Beckett. This is an interesting and
> valuable collection of essays.

Boleslavsky, Richard. *Acting: The First Six Lessons.* New York: Theatre
Arts Books, 1949.
> A delightful, sound book on the basic principles of observation and
> character analysis.

Cohen, Robert. *Acting Power.* Palo Alto, Calif.: Mayfield Publishing
Company, 1978.
> A serviceable book that focuses primarily on training the actor's mind
> rather than the voice and body, with an emphasis on aligning the actor's
> consciousness of situation, character, style, and theatricality. Includes
> helpful exercises.

Dukore, B. F. *Dramatic Theory and Criticism: The Greeks to Grotowski.* New York: Holt, Rinehart and Winston, 1974.
Collects the major documents in dramatic theory.

Freytag, Gustav. *Technique of the Drama.* Trans. E. J. MacEwan. Chicago: Griggs, 1895. Reprinted by the Scholarly Press, 1972.
A useful constructionist approach to the analysis of drama; dated but still substantial.

George, Kathleen. *Rhythm in Drama.* Pittsburgh: University of Pittsburgh Press, 1980.
Defining rhythm as the processes through which perceivers are moved by drama, the author explores the ways in which rhythm is manifested in language, attitude, gesture, interaction among characters, staging, and set design. Her discussions are illustrated with the plays of Sophocles, Shakespeare, Chekhov, Ibsen, Beckett, Albee, and Pinter.

Granville-Barker, Harley. *Preface to Shakespeare.* 4 volumes, Princeton: Princeton University Press, 1946.
Among the earliest—and still the savviest—discussion of Shakespeare's impact on performance. Volume 3, pages 69–81 explore the complexities of *Cleopatra*; volume 4, pages 81–87 offer telling insights into Juliet's character and the dilemma she confronts. Unfailingly readable and useful.

Grotowski, Jerzy. *Towards a Poor Theatre.* New York: Simon and Schuster, 1970.
The author is the founder of the Polish Laboratory Theatre and for more than a decade has been a leader in the contemporary theatre movement around the world. Novel theories and methods.

McGaw, Charles. *Acting Is Believing: A Basic Method for Beginners.* 2nd ed. New York: Holt, Rinehart and Winston, 1966.
Clear, practical statement on basic theories and techniques of acting. Exercises from well-known plays and two complete plays for analysis and practice.

Nicoll, Allardyce. *The Theatre and Dramatic Theory.* New York: Barnes and Noble, 1962.
Succinct discussion of the practical implications of the theoretical debates about the theatre, its function, and its form.

Styan, J. L. *Chekhov in Performance.* Cambridge: Cambridge University Press, 1971.
A moment-by-moment discursive analysis of the four great Chekhov plays in performance, by a masterful critic who understands literature and performance.

———. *The Elements of the Drama.* Cambridge: Cambridge University Press, 1960.
An introduction to the drama with a very strong emphasis on performance. The book includes close textual analysis of works of Shakespeare,

Ibsen, Chekhov, Wilde, Shaw, Strindberg, Pirandello, Anouilh, Sartre, Eliot, and others.

——. *Restoration Comedy in Performance.* Cambridge: Cambridge University Press, 1986.
Another stimulating study by a critic committed to performance as the fullest way of knowing. Here he dissects the unique interplay between stage and audience in some of the wittiest and bawdiest dramatic literature.

Wiles, Timothy J. *The Theatre Event: Modern Theories of Performance.* Chicago: University of Chicago Press, 1980.
Explication and comparison of the theories of Stanislavsky, Grotowski, Brecht, and Artaud, particularly with regard to the relationship between actors, director, and audience in the theatre event.

IV

The Interpretation
of Poetry

If I read a book and it makes my whole body so cold no fire can ever warm me, I know that it is poetry. If I feel physically as if the top of my head were taken off, I know that it is poetry. Is there any other way?

Emily Dickinson

THE LANGUAGE OF POETRY

9

Broadly speaking, poetry differs from prose in its compactness, in the emotional weight of its content, and in the importance of its sound pattern. In poetry, perhaps more than in any other kind of literature, the content and the form are inseparable elements and intensify each other. A poet's ear is attuned to the sounds of words as a composer's is to tone and to the effect of tone sequences; the poet tests words for sound as well as for denotation and connotation. Because poetry is so condensed, an audience profits considerably from the trained interpreter's knowledge and control of vocal quality, inflection, force, and timing that help clarify the meaning and add richness to the associational values of the words.

The structure of poetry, examined in detail in Chapter 10, has its traditionally required rhythm, which is based on an effective combination of sounds and silences and of lighter and heavier stresses. This pattern of sound and stress can be fully realized and appreciated only when it strikes the ear. Poetry demands the utmost vocal flexibility and control, and it is your responsibility to keep the content and the sound pattern in harmonious balance so that neither obscures the other. The audience's response to a poem is influenced by this harmony, and the total effect of the poem is achieved only when content and structure are perfectly coordinated. Nevertheless, both content and structure present some individual problems that should be considered separately during the process of objective analysis.

Poetic Content

In previous chapters, logical content (what a piece of writing *says*) and emotive content (what causes the reader's pleasure or pain, relaxation or tension) often have been considered separately, although they actually can never be divorced in either prose or poetry. As we note in earlier chapters, emotive content may be found even in predominantly factual prose, where it is not an end in itself but rather a means of reinforcing or making more vivid the idea being developed. Descriptive prose has an accompanying emotive response that intensifies and adds effectiveness to the actual description. In drama, a high degree of emotive response may grow out of conflict and character reactions.

In poetry, the logical content and the emotive content are blended so completely that it is nearly impossible to tell where one ends and the other begins. Poetry leaves much unsaid. Because poets must give readers enough clues to guide their responses, they select every word with utmost care. Selectivity operates, of course, in other forms of writing, but in poetry each word must carry specific denotative and rich connotative meanings and make a harmonious contribution to the sound pattern as well. Careful selectivity leads to condensation, which in turn, sharpens the emotional impact and allows the poem to move on several levels simultaneously.

It may be necessary, therefore, to reconsider the established concept of content, or what the author has said. Obviously, a poet must say something that the audience understands. This does not mean that a poem must be as immediately clear and factual as an essay or a newspaper article. If the poet had wished simply to inform, he or she would have put the idea into a prose essay or article — that is, a form that lends itself more easily to developing a purely logical idea. But a poet intends to communicate something beyond fact or opinion. Indeed, much poetry does not require an opinion at all; it asks the reader merely to accept an attitude. One does not have to accept this attitude as a philosophy of life, but merely to grant the poet the right to hold it.

Some people distrust poetry because they think it does not say anything. They would insist that all literature must present information, an answer to some problem of living, or a logical explanation of some phenomenon. They are so accustomed to reading for information that they fall into the trap of message hunting.

Poetry is a record of *experience to be shared*. This does not mean that the experience needs to be explained, nor does it always mean totality of experience. A poem may give us only a segment of an experience. Poets may certainly write of facts, but they interpret these facts in the wider areas of human life. A poem may be motivated by an idea, but if the idea were the whole concern, the poet would not need the additional suggestion and richness of sound characteristic of poetry. Rather, poetry is usually concerned with an emotional or aesthetic response to an idea. Even in didactic poetry, where the idea may be of first importance, provoking emotive response is the force behind the idea. In any case, poetry goes beyond the confines of strictly logical content. The success of a poem should be judged in terms of what the poet has chosen to do, not what the reader thinks should have been done.

Archibald MacLeish says in his "Ars Poetica":

A poem should not mean
But be.

This statement implies that a poem must be a complete, harmonious entity — that it not *only* "means" something, but also has an existence beyond purely logical meaning. When you accept the fact that poetry is not only *what* it means but *how* it means (to borrow a phrase from John Ciardi), you are ready to let the poet and the poem begin their communication with you.

The first step in understanding and evaluating a poem is to read the entire work to get a general idea of what it says. This first step may be less objective, less purely "intellectual" with poetry than it is with much prose or drama. Your initial response to a poem may not be in terms of idea or logical content at all, but rather in terms of pleasure or pain, excitement or repose — in short, of emotive content. Read the poem aloud several times and permit yourself the luxury of a completely subjective response before beginning an objective analysis. Give full play to the sound. Instead of working on the poem, let the poem work on you. Enjoyment is a good starting point for appreciation, even if the reason for liking the poem cannot be put into words immediately.

Do not be discouraged if you find only a very simple, obvious meaning in a poem and someone else finds a great deal of implication. As your experience with life and poetry increases, you will be better able to enrich the core of meaning with appropriate associations. Above all, be careful not to get so preoccupied with reading between the lines that you lose sight of the lines themselves.

Classification of Poetry

Poetry has been classified by types according to innumerable systems. Some are based on content, some on structure, and some on combinations of both elements. Many of the classifications overlap, and you will find differences of opinion about the proper category in which certain poems should be placed. The interpreter is not concerned with technical names and categories, except as they provide handles for grasping the material.

We broadly classify poetry under three major headings: narrative, lyric, and dramatic. These distinctions are based largely on a consideration of the persona — the speaker in the poem. This consideration is important to you as a guide to your relation to the audience. As with stories and plays, you should know who is speaking in the poem, to whom the person is speaking, and whether the experience is being revealed directly (as in a narrative poem), is overheard (as in a dramatic poem), or is the personal utterance of a single speaker (as in a lyric poem). You may want to review the discussion of persona and locus in Chapter 2.

Narrative Poetry

Narrative poetry tells a story or relates a series of events that lead up to a climax. In this respect, narrative poetry resembles narrative prose, and many of the steps of analysis we discussed in Chapter 6 are applicable here. Discover the key situations, their focal points, and their relationship to the main climax. You should give attention to the establishment of time and place, the development of characters, and the relationships between characters, as these elements further the plot of the narrative. Setting, situation, and physical and psychological traits of character — and the interdependence of these factors — must also be considered. The persona is the narrator. Narrative poetry often includes dialogue, and, from your experience with dialogue in narrative prose, you should already know how to handle this element. Also, as in narrative prose, descriptive passages reinforce setting or effect transitions between key situations.

When you elect to present a narrative poem, you accept a twofold responsibility. You should, first of all, take the role of a storyteller; that is, the progression of events should be your primary concern. Analyze the content carefully to become thoroughly aware of all the aspects of organization. Remember that you are telling a story in poetry: use the aspects of poetry to implement the story and enhance its movement and emotional impact.

If it is necessary to cut a long narrative poem, you may follow the same procedure used in cutting narrative prose, but you should be very careful not to violate the poem's structural pattern. That is, if absolutely necessary, you may cut complete sections but not lines or parts of lines within stanzas. For example, the tag "he said" might be eliminated from a sentence of prose, but cutting it out of a line of poetry would destroy the pulse of the line and break the sound pattern.

One of the oldest types of narrative poetry is the *popular ballad*, a form that began before the advent of printing. It is a folk product, and its author is always anonymous. Over the centuries, many poets have adopted some of the characteristics of the popular ballad, which is a short, swift, stark narrative, simple in plot and metrical structure. The language is unadorned, and the characters are basically types rather than individuals. The ballad should have an easy flow of sound, but it also should tell a fast-moving and exciting story.

Ballads usually have refrains, which may help implement the plot but which often are primarily rhythmic. Refrains should be handled carefully so that they do not break the progress of the story but still serve their purpose of repetition. The narrator is usually objective and interjects little, if any, comment on the events being related. The modern interpreter needs a strong sense of performance to give these stark and often bloody stories the gusto to make them convincing.

The second important type of narrative poetry is the *metrical tale*, which is like a full-length novel or short story in verse. It may be a medieval tale such as Chaucer's *Canterbury Tales* or a more modern product like Keats's "The Eve of St. Agnes," Masefield's "Dauber," Frost's "The Death of the Hired Man," or Vikram Seth's *The Golden Gate*. In any case, the process of analyzing its content and organization is comparable to that used for the short story. As in "The Eve of St. Agnes," the characters may be romanticized types who exhibit little complexity; or they may be completely realized individuals, like Mary, Warren, and Silas in "The Death of the Hired Man." Descriptions of setting are likely to be fairly explicit, and the relationship between the characters and the setting is important. Moreover, the narrative persona expresses personal attitudes and sympathies from time to time, while still retaining the position of observer.

The third type of narrative poetry is the *epic*. An epic is characterized by its extreme length, by its elevated tone, and especially by the type of events it relates. An epic centers on a hero of superhuman proportions, both morally and physically, whose exploits are of great significance to a tribe, race, or nation. *The Aeneid*, an art epic, and *Beowulf*, a folk epic, are examples of this type of narrative poetry. Another kind of epic concerns humanity's battle with the forces of evil and the struggle for a divine victory; John Milton's *Paradise Lost* is a prime example. The mock epic, exemplified by Alexander Pope's "The Rape of the Lock," applies the grand epic scope and manner to the trivial circumstances of a haircut with amusing, satirical effect.

The style of an epic is lofty, the language is highly poetic and exalted, and the sentences are usually complex and elaborate, with numerous clauses and inversions. You can use these aspects of style to help suggest the scope of the episodes and the heroic proportions of the participants. Epics are not written about common people in everyday situations. They involve whole nations and heroes who are larger than life, and they should be given their proper dimension in performance.

Lyric Poetry

The *lyric* is most typically a short poem, although it may be a long, sustained emotional utterance. It is a strongly unified form of poetry, for all aspects of content are shaped toward the emotional focal point. A lyric poem has been compared to a flash of lightning that illuminates some object with a moment of vividness, in this case emotional vividness. Lyric poets usually give little, if any, account of what leads up to or follows the emotional experience, since their concern is with *sharing* the experience, not *explaining* it. You, however, may find that sketching in some relevant background in your own mind enhances appreciation and helps set the appropriate mood. The high degree of association and the intensity of emotion make it imperative for an interpreter to be in complete control of techniques before even beginning to read the poem to an audience, because the extreme condensation of a lyric poem allows no time to warm up or to find an equilibrium. Thus, the introduction is exceptionally important.

The persona in a lyric poem is usually a single speaker whose primary purpose is to share an emotional experience. Whether the speaker and the poet are the same is a matter of debate among contemporary critics. The differences of opinion grow in part out of a semantic problem. For our purposes, we assume that the poet is speaking in a "pure" lyric, remembering that poets, like the rest of us, have varying moods and attitudes and complex and many-sided personalities. When we discuss the dramatic lyric, we address the problem of someone who thinks and feels like the poet but who is a clearly distinguishable character. However, we are not concerned in a lyric with the physical being of the poet, his eyes or hair, her voice or gait. Rather, we are dealing with the *emotional* and *psychological personality* as it is revealed in the particular poem.

Most lyric poetry must be read more slowly than other forms of writing, partly because it contains much imagery, which is less easy to assimilate than a story line, and partly because a swiftly paced reading does not permit the sound pattern to make its full contribution to both music and emotion. The audience should have time to hear the words, re-create the images, and set up the response. Lyric poetry requires less directness in presentation than narrative writing: be careful, however, not to read as though you are lost in the clouds. The happy mean is to adopt an attitude of *sharing* the experience. You know that your listeners' emotions cannot be compelled. Your goal is to bring the audience into the poem, not to thrust the poem at them. Share — don't explain.

The emotion that characterizes lyric poetry is often expressed in terms of reflection or description. Thus, the *reflective lyric,* as its name suggests, is the persona's emotional response through recall and reflection or contemplation. This element of an emotional experience remembered is important to the interpreter, because it gives a clue to the degree of activity — or, more precisely, the absence of physical activity — in the poem. Mary Stewart Hammond's "Saving Memory" (Chapter 9) exemplifies a reflective lyric.

The *elegy* is a lyric that expresses grief, usually at someone's death. In Greek verse, the elegy had a definite structural form, but it was brought over into English poetry not as a form but as a type of emotional expression. Thus, an elegy may assume any conventional metrical pattern or may even be written in free verse. Usually, formality of language and structure lends dignity to the expression of grief and harmonizes with the solemn mystery of death and the sense of personal loss. W. H. Auden's "In Memory of W. B. Yeats" is an elegy that uses a combination of structural patterns that change as the tones of the separate sections change.

An *ode* is a dignified, relatively long lyric poem, which is formal in language and formal, though not necessarily strictly regular, in structure. Like the elegy, the ode was a recognized lyrical form in Greek verse. Designed to be accompanied by music and a highly stylized dance, it consisted of three movements, two of which had identical music and dance patterns. But although these Greek structures have been imitated in English verse, the term *ode* has come to be applied to any sustained lyric utterance of exalted theme, often in commemoration of some important event or experience. In general tone, the ode is more contemplative than active and suggests a restraint of movement similar to that expressed by a reflective lyric. By no means does it suggest complete passivity, for a sense of movement in the particularly strong kinesthetic imagery accompanies response to an exalted theme.

Perhaps the most familiar type of lyric is the *sonnet.* This poetic form is interesting to the interpreter for several reasons. In the first place, its form is widely used, and the greatest challenge it presents to both poet and interpreter lies in this fixed form.

A sonnet is a fourteen-line poem, written predominantly in iambic meter, with five feet — or ten syllables — to the line. It has, moreover, a prescribed rhyme scheme. The two most common types of sonnet are the Petrarchan and the Shakespearean, which differ primarily in the arrangement of their rhyming sounds. The distinction between them is important, but it need not concern the interpreter except as it gives certain guides to the organization of content and to the intricacy of the sound pattern.

Both in content and in structure, the Petrarchan sonnet is very strictly organized. The first four lines introduce the subject, and the next four develop it. In a true Petrarchan sonnet, each of these quatrains completes a unit of thought, and the sentences are *not* allowed to run on past the line ends. The next three lines introduce a new but related theme, and the last three lines bring the observation to its conclusion. The rhyme scheme, which is *abba, abba, cdc, cdc,* or *cdcdcd,* reinforces the division of content. A true Petrarchan sonnet is somewhat rare in English, however, as most poets have chosen to vary the strict form.

The Shakespearean sonnet follows the same principle of organization through the first eight lines; it departs from this pattern by devoting the last six lines to the conclusion, with the focal point occurring in the final two lines or the couplet. There is also greater flexibility in the rhyme scheme of the Shakespearean sonnet: *abab, cdcd, efef, gg.* This variation in rhyme pattern corresponds to the divisions of the content and helps bring the poem to a firm close by introducing a rhyming couplet for the last two lines.

When analyzing poetry that follows such traditional restrictions of organization and structure, be sure to pay particular attention to the way the sonnet form augments the emotion being expressed. The sonnet's prescribed principles organize the content; in analyzing this type of poem, be sure to preserve the sonnet's balance and proportion.

If a lyric is to achieve its purpose, you must respond to it completely. This does not mean that you should become carried away by emotions. In the earliest phases of preparation, you may indulge in complete subjectivity, but in performance your task is to *share* the *experience* in the poem — not to display personal sensitivity. This sharing requires intelligent control of techniques. The more your listeners focus on the material and are unaware of your presence, the more successful your performance will be.

Dramatic Poetry

Many contemporary critics take the position that all poetry is dramatic because it, in itself, is an action concerning a person or persons and because it contains a distinct development or revelation. This approach to analysis can prove helpful. Nevertheless, in line with our early classifications of literature, our discussion of dramatic poetry concerns works that center on a character who is in conflict with internal or external forces, whose development is revealed without a third-person narrator. There are four types of dramatic poetry: *dramatic narrative, dramatic lyric, dramatic monologue,* and *soliloquy.* Although these terms are often used interchangeably, the four types vary slightly in emphasis on character and situation. Knowing the differences among them helps in deciding on the degree of characterization that is necessary for performance. In each case, the persona is an identifiable character who speaks directly to an audience, thinks aloud, or talks to other characters involved in a dramatic situation. Physical setting and historical period are often important considerations.

A *dramatic narrative* is a poem in which the incidents or series of incidents are related by a participant who is affected by the events described. Lord Byron's "The Prisoner of Chillon" is a dramatic narrative. It opens with Bonivard's brief description of his present physical state. The purposes of this unit are to establish the flashback technique that reveals the plot and to indicate the point of view that gives the incidents greater vividness. After the introductory statement, Bonivard begins to draw the story out of the past. His attention is on the story, and his own reactions to events are used primarily as transitions from one key situation to the next. Thus, you may assume that the personality of Bonivard is in reality a device for revealing the plot and is not a motivating force for the plot's progression. Therefore, one need suggest only enough of the prisoner's broken health and spirit to make the plot credible and prepare for the closing phrase:

> — even I
> Regain'd my freedom with a sigh.

The *dramatic lyric,* like any other type of lyric poetry, reflects the poet's subjective responses, thoughts, and aspirations. It is dramatic because the poet reveals these thoughts and emotions through the words of an appropriate character, so that there is added force and vividness to the expression. Tennyson's "Ulysses" (Chapter 4) falls into the general classification of dramatic lyric, although it also shares some of the characteristics of a dramatic monologue. You need to emphasize in your suggestion of character those qualities that make the speaker an appropriate exponent of the philosophy being expressed. Ulysses' essential qualities, for instance, are his mental vigor, maturity, and wisdom and his authority and leadership. It is unwise to take too literally his phrase "you and I are old," because he turns immediately to the belief that

> Old age hath yet his honor and his toil,

which he reinforces with

> . . . but something ere the end,
> Some work of noble note, may yet be done,
> Not unbecoming men that strove with Gods.

The poem closes on the positive note that Ulysses is still

> . . . strong in will
> To strive, to seek, to find, and not to yield.

The *dramatic monologue* is spoken by a single character who is not the poet. The persona directly addresses other characters, who are also affected by the incidents taking place and who help motivate the persona's reactions and train of thought. The other characters do not speak, but they are developed as personalities, or at least as forces that act on the speaker. Browning's "My Last Duchess" (Chapter 10) is an excellent example of this type of dramatic poetry. The Duke's ideas reflect his time and his attitude toward himself and others. He is not a mouthpiece for Browning; he speaks for himself. In your performance, you should give the audience a clear, three-dimensional picture of the Duke so that they understand his thoughts and feelings.

The *soliloquy* is also spoken by a single character. The unique aspect of this form is that no other characters are being addressed. Since the speaker in a soliloquy is alone, the degree of directness is likely to be less pronounced. However, as in Browning's "Soliloquy of the Spanish Cloister" at the end of this chapter, the speaker may receive direct and immediate motivations from some exterior source. Although the monk is speaking only to himself, Brother Lawrence's actions direct his thoughts.

Figurative Language

Poetry is, as we have said, a highly condensed form of expression. Although poetry may seem to communicate less directly than prose, it actually makes a *more* direct appeal; it does not talk *about* something but attempts, rather, to present the essence of that something by reaching readers at as many points of contact as possible — striking at them through senses, emotions, intellect, and imagination, and calling forth a blended response that gives new insight into experience. Hence, the poet uses exact words that carry with them not only precise denotations but, perhaps more important, the right connotations as well.

The words the poet uses do not define a concept so much as they *expand* it in the reader's consciousness, as a pebble tossed into a pool sends ever-widening circles rippling out from the point of surface contact. The implications of the words take the reader beyond the narrow confines of exact definition into the area of suggested meaning. In examining a poet's choice of words, then, remember that just as a poem not only means something but *is* something beyond meaning, so the words that compose it go beyond fact and information. Indeed, words in poetry mean many things simultaneously.

In spite of good intentions, many people never learn to read poetry so that it has meaning for them or for others. This failure often stems from the reader's inability to untangle certain complexities that are present in all but the most direct poetic expression. One of the most common of these complexities is the use of figurative language.

Allusions

A poet often achieves condensation and emotional impact by using references, or *allusions*, that embody a wealth of implication. These allusions may contribute materially to the logical meaning of the poem, but they are likely to be most valuable for the associations they set up by implied comparison. Very often they are references to mythical or historical persons or places, although with the passing of the classical tradition, their associational value may be lessened for the reader today. Still, a reader can recognize them easily as allusions and knows that they are explained in an encyclopedia or other appropriate reference book.

In some poetry, however, connotative literary allusions may prove more difficult because they may involve the deliberate echo of a phrase or line from another poem or literary work to reinforce

mood or emotion by inviting comparison or ironic contrast. A poem
that uses implied reference to other works is Joanne Gilbert's "Upon
Learning That a Junior High School Acquaintance Has Been Nomi-
nated for an Academy Award" (Chapter 2). Can you point out two
or three of its most obvious allusions? Some of its lines even allude
to other than literary works, but a literary allusion says something
directly, in its context. Hearing literary echoes brings an added level
of understanding and a more complex response — it strengthens the
poem's impact.

How does an interpreter deal with allusions? Obviously, you are
not going to explain the references to the audience, to stand between
poem and audience as a sort of collection of footnotes. However, you
are concerned with the quality of your own understanding and response, for you cannot share the poem with your audience if you
have not assimilated it first yourself. The more thoroughly you understand the allusions, the more fully you will appreciate the poet's
purpose in using them — and the more intelligently you can use
them in communicating the whole intent of the poem to others. You
must, therefore, be familiar enough with the allusions to understand
the type of response they are intended to arouse or reinforce. By
integrating them into the poem as it stands, as a self-contained
whole, you can use them as a means of drawing the proper empathic
response from the audience.

Figures of Speech

Three of the most common figures of speech — *simile, metaphor,* and
analogy — are all based on comparing one thing to another. These
comparisons appeal to our senses and our motor responses. Therefore, they depend on sense imagery, which we discussed at some
length in chapters 4 and 5.

A *simile* is easily recognized, because it makes an explicit comparison, generally using the words *like* or *as.* It compares two objects
of common nature or the particular qualities of one thing to the
general qualities of another. Keats uses simile to compare Autumn's
activity to that of a gleaner:

> And sometimes like a gleaner thou dost keep
> Steady thy laden head across a brook.

A *metaphor* states that something *is* something else; the comparison is based on some related but not identical factor. It establishes
a relationship between two elements that may be dissimilar in their
basic components and yet have attributes in common, such as "Your

eyes are stars." Sometimes a metaphor expresses a synthesis of thought and feeling so subtle and complex that it becomes an organic or structural part of an entire poem. Indeed, critics often use the term *metaphor* or *metaphorical* to describe writing that goes beyond fact and obvious relationships.

An *analogy* is an extended metaphor and may serve to implement an entire poem. Sharon Olds's "The Race" (Chapter 4) compares the speaker's desperate striving to make a plane departure with her father's struggle to live and, as well, is especially rich in similes and metaphors within the analogy.

These three types of figurative language, all means of making comparisons, are important for several reasons. First, of course, you should understand what they are and how they function in order to find the total meaning of the poem. More particularly, you need to be aware not only of the objects being compared but of the attributes of those objects that make their comparison acceptable. Finally, you should use your knowledge of sense imagery and empathy to make the comparisons work effectively for the audience.

Two other figures of speech — *metonymy* and *synecdoche* — carry associational values that are somewhat different from similes, metaphors, and analogies. *Metonymy* is the use of one word for another that it suggests, such as "a good table" for "good food." *Synecdoche* is the use of a part for a whole, such as "sail" for "boat." The technical difference between these two figures is of minor importance for our discussion, and they are not likely to present you with any real difficulties once you are aware of their function. Metonymy and synecdoche are useful whenever they suggest certain characteristics emphasized by the part that is chosen for the whole. For example, "sail" is a more picturesque word than "boat" and could be used to imply majesty; you then might wish to make use of the visual and kinesthetic imagery that would be called up by tall sails against the sky rather than by a tugboat or a coal barge.

But your major concern is not with putting a name to what the poet did or classifying a figure of speech. You are always concerned with understanding why that figure was used, what it is intended to convey, and what it demands when the material is presented to an audience. The poet achieves concreteness and vividness of suggestion by using figures that indicate or imply a comparison or an association. They must be understood for what they are and for the purpose they serve before you can proceed with the job of doing justice to the poetry.

In addition to these five figures of speech, there are two others that directly affect the interpreter's communication: personification and apostrophe.

Personification is the attribution of human qualities to an abstract or inanimate object. This figure of speech is closely related to simile, metaphor, and analogy — the "comparison" figures — because the poet treats an inanimate object or abstraction as if it were a person, thus giving it definite human characteristics. Keats, for example, uses personification throughout "To Autumn" (see page 355). In the second line, he calls Autumn the "close bosom-friend of the maturing sun." In the second stanza, the personification is most vivid, where Autumn is depicted as "sitting careless on a granary floor," and "on a half-reaped furrow sound asleep," and "by a cider-press" watching "the last oozings hours by hours."

You will find personification a great aid in visualizing poetry because it is easier to re-create a person than an abstraction. Moreover, this device allows for more kinetic and kinesthetic imagery. You should not overlook the animate quality this figure of speech provides.

Frequently, personification is combined with the figure of speech known as *apostrophe* — direct address to an abstraction or to an absent or inanimate object. "To Autumn" consistently uses a combination of personification and apostrophe. The opening line, "Season of mists and mellow fruitfulness," might be taken merely as a reflective thought about the season, if considered by itself. On close examination, however, it is evident that the poet becomes more direct in his approach to the season as the poem progresses, and there can be no doubt about the directness of address in the opening lines of the final stanza:

Where are the songs of Spring? Ay, where are they?
Think not of them, thou hast thy music too . . .

Thus, figurative language enables a writer to express an abstract idea in concrete terms, to make it more vivid and more readily grasped by comparing it or relating it to a concrete object or a specific quality. Through figures of speech, poets may bring together things that are not ordinarily seen in relation to one another and thus open the way to new insights. Clearly, then, sense imagery and figurative language, or literary imagery, are interdependent, and the motor responses to literary and sensory imagery are inseparably tied to emotional response and empathy.

Imagery is discussed in Chapter 4 in terms of the primary and secondary strength of the appeals and its contribution to the intrinsic factors. The primary appeal was fairly easy to isolate in the excerpts used as examples of descriptive prose. In poetry, however, the appeals are often so blended and many sided that this separation is not possible. Even when the primary appeal in individual units is immediately identifiable, the secondary appeals assume an almost equal importance in the total effect. Frequently a particular type of imagery, such as kinesthetic, or a combination of types, is used in a secondary position throughout a poem and provides an important clue to unity and empathy.

Sensory Appeals

When poems depend strongly on sensory appeals, you should accept and use all the clues the writer has provided. Keats's "To Autumn" involves many sensory appeals. One of the characteristics of Keats's writing is its strong sensory quality, and his skill in blending and even combining words to intensify the appeal to the senses makes this poem one of his most famous.

The chief purpose of "To Autumn" is to record the sights, sounds, smells, and rich textures of the season. This poem makes no other important comment about life, except perhaps to imply that satisfaction can be found in inevitable change:

> Where are the songs of Spring? Ay, where are they?
> Think not of them, thou hast thy music too . . .

The poet devotes his entire attention to a series of descriptions of autumn, and the poem (which follows in its entirety) lays claim to emotional response through the pleasure this season gives to the senses.

To Autumn
JOHN KEATS

Season of mists and mellow fruitfulness,
   Close bosom-friend of the maturing sun;
Conspiring with him how to load and bless
   With fruit the vines that round the thatch-eaves run;
To bend with apples the mossed cottage-trees,
   And fill all fruit with ripeness to the core;
     To swell the gourd, and plump the hazel shells
   With a sweet kernel; to set budding more,
And still more, later flowers for the bees,
Until they think warm days will never cease,
     For Summer has o'er-brimmed their clammy cells.

Who hath not seen thee oft amid thy store?
   Sometimes whoever seeks abroad may find

Thee sitting careless on a granary floor,
    Thy hair soft-lifted by the winnowing wind;
Or on a half-reaped furrow sound asleep,
    Drowsed with the fume of poppies, while thy hook
        Spares the next swath and all its twinèd flowers:
And sometimes like a gleaner thou dost keep
    Steady thy laden head across a brook;
    Or by a cider-press, with patient look,
        Thou watchest the last oozings hours by hours.

Where are the songs of Spring? Ay, where are they?
    Think not of them, thou hast thy music too, —
While barrèd clouds bloom the soft-dying day,
    And touch the stubble-plains with rosy hue;
Then in a wailful choir the small gnats mourn
    Among the river sallows, borne aloft
        Or sinking as the light wind lives or dies;
And full-grown lambs loud bleat from hilly bourn;
    Hedge-crickets sing; and now with treble soft
    The red-breast whistles from a garden-croft
        And gathering swallows twitter in the skies.

The opening lines have a characteristic complexity of appeals. Since the title is "To Autumn," the "season of mists" has a strong thermal appeal that combines at once the warmth of the sun and the coolness of the mists. "Mellow fruitfulness" carries with it olfactory, gustatory, visual, and kinesthetic appeal, as well as a continuation of thermal and a possibility of tactual appeal. The second line brings in a still stronger thermal appeal. The effect is one of warmth, and it enhances the feeling of drowsiness and almost static heaviness that recurs in each stanza. The next three lines contain all of these previous appeals to sensory perception, but with kinetic appeals added — in fact, with special appeal to kinetic and kinesthetic response: "load and bless with fruit," "vines that run," "to bend with apples."

Because the appeals are so complex and so closely interwoven, it is almost impossible, and probably unnecessary, to decide which is the primary appeal within a unit of thought. The strength of the appeals shifts from one type to another almost within a single word. Indeed, the first five lines include every type of imagery except auditory, and even that is suggested later in the stanza by "the bees."

As the poem progresses, the visual and auditory appeals become increasingly important. The second stanza indicates the poet's concern with the visual by its opening question, "Who hath not seen thee . . . ?" The third stanza is strongly auditory, with its references to "songs" and "music." Within this framework the sensory appeals remain complex. You will find that the imagery acts not only as a guide to making the descriptions vivid, but also contributes significantly to the unity, harmony, and variety of the poem. Attention to the kinesthetic imagery and the kinetic imagery, both of which are made more vivid through personification, will help keep this poem from becoming merely a lush combination of beautiful sounds. Awareness of the shift to visual and then to auditory imagery in the second and third stanzas will help unravel the complicated sentences and keep the poem moving.

Stanzas

Paragraphs are the major organizational signposts in the progress of thought in prose writing. A stanza often serves the same purpose in poetry. Properly speaking, stanzas must all be the same length, but blank verse and free verse stanzas or unit divisions (if they exist) are often of irregular length. They are dictated by the amount of attention the author wishes to devote to each unit of content, and work as prose paragraphs as far as progression of content is concerned. In other types of poetry, however, the poet usually limits the stanzas to a specific length and condenses or expands each unit of thought to coincide with this structural restriction. Nevertheless, even in the most tightly structured poetry, a stanza usually operates as a major thought unit, and this entity is intensified if a formal rhyme scheme is used.

Stanley Kunitz's poem "Open the Gates" (at the end of this chapter) progresses chronologically and in giant steps from one four-line stanza to the next. John Ciardi, on the other hand, allows his two seventeen-line stanzas to move smoothly and flowingly on either side of the two-line fulcrum stanza in "As I Would Wish You Birds" (Chapter 10). Theodore Roethke uses a similar method of setting off the persona's flash of intense anger in "Old Lady's Winter Words" (Chapter 4), although his other stanzas are not as regular in length as Ciardi's. Do not assume that these poets just forgot to follow the form they started out with.

You will find considerable help in achieving variety as well as rhythm of content if you carefully consider stanzaic divisions. These separate units of thought should not be allowed to break off from each other, and the transitions from stanza to stanza should be kept clear so that the audience receives a unified experience. Transitions in poetry are often abrupt and implied rather than stated explicitly. They may be transitions of time or place, of course; but often, as in "To Autumn," they simply move us into another aspect of the same subject or provide a subtle shift in mood. In any case, the order of the stanzas is not an accident, and the stanza breaks are in reality links. In "Soliloquy of the Spanish Cloister," for example, some of the stanzas are linked by the monk's observations of some action by Brother Lawrence as he moves about in his garden, while others are connected only by the monk's stream of consciousness as he muses on his "heart's abhorrence" and his daily contacts with Brother Lawrence.

Poetic Syntax

The stanzas of a poem provide the main divisions of organization and content. Within the stanzas, sentences are minor units of thought progression. In poetry the syntax of the sentence is sometimes more complicated than it is in prose. This is due in part to the weight of suggestion within the condensation that is characteristic of poetry.

Poets often achieve this condensation by using long, involved sentences that contain numerous dependent clauses and descriptive phrases. These clauses and phrases are not always adjacent to the words they modify. Consequently some care in analysis and in performance may be required to keep the thread of thought from becoming hopelessly entangled and the poem from seeming to consist merely of unrelated sets of words.

Perhaps the first approach to an involved sentence is simply to recast it in normal order, identifying the subject, the verb, and the object, if any, and arranging the clauses and phrases to modify the appropriate parts of the sentence. You should not, however, insist that poetry display the same clarity and syntactical precision as factual prose. Often parts of speech are omitted, and references are implied rather than stated. Normal word order is frequently changed for emotional effect, for heightening of sound qualities, or both.

The opening sentence of Hopkins's "The Windhover" (which is completely reprinted at the end of this chapter) is an excellent example of this ellipsis or omission of words.

> I CAUGHT this morning morning's minion, kingdom of daylight's
>   dauphin, dapple-dawn-drawn Falcon, in his riding
>   Of the rolling level underneath him steady air, and striding
> High there, how he rung upon the rein of a wimpling wing

In his ecstasy! then off, off forth on swing,
As a skate's heel sweeps smooth on a bow-bend: the hurl and gliding
Rebuffed the big wind.

The sentence, which whirls on for five and one-half lines, begins reasonably enough with the simple "I caught" (meaning "caught sight of" rather than "captured"). The capitalization of "caught" is the poet's and adds a sense of surprise and wonder to the sight. The adverbial phrase "this morning" tells us when the event took place. After this comes the object of the sentence, the windhover, which the poet calls "minion," "dauphin," and "Falcon," and we are told what the bird was doing. He was riding and striding, and "he rung upon the rein of wimpling wing" — that is, he flew upward in spirals by folding or "pleating" or tipping one wing. And then he was off as smoothly as an ice skate cuts a curve, and "the hurl and gliding rebuffed" (snubbed, refused to consider) "the big wind." This, then, is the syntactical skeleton of the sentence.

The next step is to attempt to find the proper relationship of the rest of the words that modify and flesh out this syntactical skeleton in our own minds. We need to add some connectives and phrases to compensate for Hopkins's elliptical quality. In the process we obviously destroy much of the beauty of the sound, but that, too, may help prove our point. The sentence might now read: This morning I caught (sight of) morning's minion (in his) kingdom of (which he is) daylight's dauphin (and) dapple-dawn-drawn Falcon, in his riding of the rolling level (which was) underneath him (and which was) steady air and (when he was) striding high there (you should have seen) how he rung upon the rein of a wimpling wing in his ecstasy (and) then (he was) off, off forth on a swing as (smoothly as) a skate's heel sweeps on a bow-bend (and) the hurl and gliding rebuffed the big wind.

Admittedly, this is an extremely awkward sentence, plodding heavily from one detail to the next. We have lost all the "hurl and gliding," the sense of lift and freedom, and much of the beauty of the sound combinations. Harmony has almost completely disappeared. The insertion of "and" after the exclamation point defeats the poet's own breathless ecstasy at the sight. The substitution of "and" for the colon before the last clause robs it of its conclusive value by making it just one more item rather than a culmination of several. Now that you understand where the thought is going and how it gets there, you must go back to the sentence the poet wrote. With your control of pace and pauses, and the poet's remarkable imagery and tone color, your audience will have no difficulty in catching the totality of the poem's experience.

Tone Color

In addition to connotative values and sensory appeals, another important factor in poetry is the choice and arrangement of words. A poet strives for the perfect union of sense and sound and is acutely aware of the contribution that each makes to the other. This attention to the sounds of words separately and in combination is called *tone color*, which we discussed briefly in Chapter 5 in the section on prose style. It is so basic to the sound pattern of poetry, however, that we give it some added consideration here.

Tone color is the combination of vowels and consonants to help achieve a particular effect. Clearly, poets do not simply scramble together assorted vowels and consonants. They must, of course, use words. But the choice of a word and its position in relation to other words is partially dictated by the way the sounds go together. Cummings's poem "Spring is like a perhaps hand" (Chapter 10) owes part of its effectiveness to tone color. The two words "perhaps hand" are characteristic of his remarkable freedom with syntax, using "perhaps" as an adjective to modify "hand." The connotation is helped, however, by juxtaposing "haps" and "hand," both of which must be said carefully to pronounce the aspirate /h/ and the vowel /æ/. The /p/ and /s/ of "haps" slow the rate, and a slight pause is necessary before the /h/ of "hand." The effect is subtle, but to be aware of its importance one need only consider what a difference it would make if the line read, "Spring is perhaps like a hand" or "Perhaps spring is like a hand." This arrangement drastically changes (and even destroys) the meaning, rhythm, and sound values.

The general term *tone color* embraces onomatopoeia and alliteration, assonance and consonance.

Onomatopoeia is the use of words whose sounds suggest or reinforce their meaning: for example, "hiss," "thud," "crack," and "bubble." *Alliteration* is the repetition of identical or nearly identical sounds at the beginnings of two or more words in a line or phrase. The phrase "*morning morning's minion*" in "The Windhover" is a classic example, and there are many other alliterative combinations in the poem. Many poets use alliteration that is more widely spaced and operates throughout a large unit or even through an entire brief poem. Dylan Thomas does this most effectively in "In My Craft or Sullen Art" (at the end of this chapter), for example.

The use of identical or closely approximated vowels within words is called *assonance;* the close repetition of identical or approximate consonants within or at the ends of words is called *consonance.* These two techniques are also found throughout "The Windhover": assonance in the repeated /ɔ/'s and consonance very strong in the /n/ sounds of "morning morning's minion," and both assonance and consonance in "minion," "dauphin," and "Falcon" in the long first line.

Tone color performs several functions in poetry. The amount and richness of it vary with the poem's purpose. The more marked the aesthetic and emotional effect desired, the richer and more complex the tone color is likely to be. One of the most important uses of tone color is to enrich the emotional content. Most authorities agree that it is nearly impossible to divorce the connotation of a word from its sound. Even in everyday conversation, words are colored and their meanings intensified or depreciated by the elongation or shortening of the vowel sounds and by the softening or sharpening of the consonants. This coloring or intensification through sound is even more marked in poetry, when a word is used with others to strengthen the associational values. Thus, tone color makes an important contribution to suggestion.

Tone color is also important in implementing sense imagery and intensifying empathy. "To Autumn" offers a particularly good example. The opening lines, or indeed any lines chosen at random, provide unmistakable proof of Keats's concern with sounds:

> *Season* of *mists* and *mellow fruitfulness,*
> *Close* bos*om-friend* of the *maturing sun.*

Within these lines, the consonants /s/, /m/, /n/, and /l/ predominate, skillfully combined with rich /u/ and /ə/ sounds, while the lighter vowels in "mists," "mell," "ness," and "friend" keep the effect from becoming monotonous. With such a strong hint from the poet in the opening lines, the interpreter should pay particular attention to the combination of sounds in the rest of the poem. It will become clear that they vary as the content varies, but in every case, sound, connotation, and sense imagery reinforce each other.

Another extremely important function of tone color is to provide for change of tempo and give clues to variation in vocal quality. Certain combinations of vowels and consonants allow and even encourage the reader to speak more rapidly or slowly than other combinations do. A skilled poet is aware of variety of tempo and may have used it. You should look for it and use it, too. Of course, variations in tempo also depend on the content, both emotional and logical, and on the type of imagery they augment.

The last stanza of "To Autumn" contains an excellent example of the use of tone color to provide variety of tempo and vocal quality. The short speech phrases in the form of the questions

Where are the songs of Spring? Ay, where are they?

help achieve needed variety after the rich, slow sounds of

Thou watchest the last oozings hours by hours.

that close the preceding stanza. "Think not of them" is likewise light and almost crisp in its sound and its implication of dismissal. Immediately, however, the tempo slows again with "thou hast thy music too," and even more in the next line with "barrèd clouds bloom." The pace picks up slightly on "touched the stubble-plains" but immediately slows again on "rosy hue." This alternation continues throughout the entire stanza. The contrast between "lambs loud bleat from hilly bourn" and the following "hedge-crickets sing" is particularly effective. Attention to subtle changes indicated by the sounds will allow you to make the most of the needed variety. And certainly ease or difficulty in articulating any specific series of words is a factor in control and variety of pace and vocal quality.

Tone color usually does not make a major contribution to unity except within small units or stanzas. An entire poem that is richly laden with the same sound combinations would be extremely difficult to handle. But tone color is certainly basic to harmony and is valuable in achieving variety and contrast. Its primary function is supportive, and it should be used in its proper relationship with all the other elements you discover in analysis.

Tone color is another of the elements that make poetry so satisfying to and, in turn, so dependent on the artist-interpreter. Obviously, there is no way to appreciate tone color or permit it to achieve its purpose except to give the words their sounds. To use tone color fully, you should be sure to enunciate clearly but not self-consciously and to form all sounds properly. The poet purposefully combined sounds, and you should accept the responsibility of reproducing them accurately as they were written.

Titles

An important but sometimes overlooked clue to the meaning of a poem is found in its title. Hopkins identifies his "morning's minion" in the title "The Windhover" and thus helps us untangle the analogy. Browning tells us that his monk is alone and speaking in a soliloquy. Roethke clearly identifies the persona in "Old Lady's Winter Words." Poets choose their titles with great care to help us to decide what a poem is about as well as guide us in the way we are to take it.

Sometimes poets give us even more help by introducing the poem with an epigraph, as Hopkins does with the words "To Christ Our Lord" just beneath the title of "The Windhover." These brief quotations, frequently from literature or folk sayings, may establish the theme of the poem. Do not ignore them, even if you must translate them from a foreign language.

Admittedly, some poets (like Emily Dickinson) do not use titles. Then the elements of style within the poem itself reveal the meaning. The poet's choice of words and figures of speech and the way these elements are combined into phrases, line units, sentences, and stanzas should be carefully considered. Method of organization and the resultant balance and proportion give valuable clues to the weight attached to the various phases of thought development. The sound pattern supporting the content often indicates the degree of seriousness and dignity inherent in the attitude. We give this aspect more attention in Chapter 10.

What, then, is the secret of a poem's effectiveness? It is impossible to answer that question satisfactorily. We know only that the poet has somehow expressed and lifted out of time a transient moment — a universal moment — that may not, cannot be prolonged. The blending of logical and emotional qualities is certainly one of the important factors, but it is not the whole answer. Nor will we find the *whole* answer even after the most careful analysis. An objective study of the component parts enables you to let the poet's technique guide your performance. But the essence of a poem is not quantitative; its whole is more than the sum of its parts. The poem must be put back together after each step in analysis so that it will finally emerge as a complete entity — from its title or first words to its conclusion.

Let the poet lead the way. You must examine every word of the poem in its relationship to every other word and let each operate as it must within the whole — not as you wish it did. If there is a line or phrase that does not fit into your concept of the poem, you should reconsider your analysis. You should share with your audience the poet's or persona's attitudes toward love, death, childhood, or the passing years — not your own attitude. If you do not like the philosophy being expressed, you should find another selection. You are responsible for the totality of the poem as the poet has written it.

Selections for Analysis and Oral Interpretation

Let the full richness of the sounds come through to increase the lift and sweep of this poem. The dedication will help you understand the poet's attitude. The two stresses in the eleventh line were put there by the poet, as were the two words in capital letters. The poem shifts to direct address to Christ ("my chevalier") in the second stanza. We have been prepared for this by the epigraph.

The Windhover

GERARD MANLEY HOPKINS

To Christ our Lord

I CAUGHT this morning morning's minion, kingdom of daylight's
     dauphin, dapple-dawn-drawn Falcon, in his riding
  Of the rolling level underneath him steady air, and striding
High there, how he rung upon the rein of a wimpling wing
In his ecstasy! then off, off forth on swing,
  As a skate's heel sweeps smooth on a bow-bend: the hurl and
     gliding
  Rebuffed the big wind. My heart in hiding
Stirred for a bird, — the achieve of, the mastery of the thing!

Brute beauty and valour and act, oh, air, pride, plume, here
  Buckle! AND the fire that breaks from thee then, a billion
Times told lovelier, more dangerous, O my chevalier!

  No wonder of it: sheér plód makes plough down sillion
Shine, and blue-bleak embers, ah my dear,
  Fall, gall themselves, and gash gold-vermilion.

❚ What does "Buckle!" in the ninth line mean? How did you demonstrate all those levels to your audience?

This serene poem achieves its distinction as calmly and quietly as the scene it describes. Pay careful attention to the cadences, and give the repetition in the last two couplets your full concentration.

The House Was Quiet and the World Was Calm

WALLACE STEVENS

The house was quiet and the world was calm.
The reader became the book; and summer night

Was like the conscious being of the book.
The house was quiet and the world was calm.

The words were spoken as if there was no book,
Except that the reader leaned above the page,

Wanted to lean, wanted much most to be
The scholar to whom his book is true, to whom

The summer night is like a perfection of thought.
The house was quiet because it had to be.

The quiet was part of the meaning, part of the mind:
The access of perfection to the page.

And the world was calm. The truth in a calm world,
In which there is no other meaning, itself

Is calm, itself is summer and night, itself
Is the reader leaning late and reading there.

▌ Where in your performance did the book, the reader, and the
  house merge?
▌ How did your voice evoke the poem's progress?

The strength of the words and images, combined with the starkness and
near-brutality of syntax, help keep this brief poem moving fiercely and
swiftly to its conclusion.

Open the Gates
STANLEY KUNITZ

Within the city of the burning cloud,
Dragging my life behind me in a sack,
Naked I prowl, scourged by the black
Temptation of the blood grown proud.

Here at the monumental door,
Carved with the curious legend of my youth,

I brandish the great bone of my death,
Beat once therewith and beat no more.

The hinges groan: a rush of forms
Shivers my name, wrenched out of me.
I stand on the terrible threshold, and I see
The end and the beginning in each other's arms.

❚ Did your audience see the persona's discovery? How?

The reversed organization of content in the second stanza of this poem should be coordinated carefully with the opening stanza to allow this "credo" to come full circle. Pay close attention to the kinesthetic imagery, the slight alteration of the repeated lines, and the parallel grammatical structure.

In My Craft or Sullen Art
DYLAN THOMAS

In my craft or sullen art
Exercised in the still night
When only the moon rages
And the lovers lie abed
With all their griefs in their arms,
I labour by singing light
Not for ambition or bread
Or the strut and trade of charms
On the ivory stages
But for the common wages
Of their most secret heart.

Not for the proud man apart
From the raging moon I write
On these spindrift pages
Nor for the towering dead
With their nightingales and psalms
But for the lovers, their arms
Round the griefs of the ages,
Who pay no praise or wages
Nor heed my craft or art.

▌ Why did your speaker write for "lovers" who pay him no heed?

Don't be deceived by the simplicity of vocabulary and structure in this poem. Use the line lengths exactly as the poet has. The short sentences in the first and last stanzas set off the climaxes. Use them to stop the rush of the action, but remember that they relate strongly to the speaker, her brother, and/or "the man." Decide who is the major character, but don't neglect the others.

Power
CORRINE HALES

No one we knew had ever stopped a train.
Hardly daring to breathe, I waited
Belly-down with my brother

In a dry ditch.
Watching through the green thickness
Of grass and willows.
Stuffed with crumpled newspapers,
The shirt and pants looked real enough
Stretched out across the rails. I felt my heart
Beating against the cool ground,
And the terrible long screech of the train's
Braking began. We had done it.

Then it was in front of us —
A hundred iron wheels tearing like time
Into red flannel and denim, shredding the child
We had made — until it finally stopped.

My brother jabbed at me,
Pointed down the tracks. A man
Had climbed out of the engine, was running
In our direction, waving his arms,
Screaming that he would kill us —
Whoever we were.
Then, very close to the spot
Where we hid, he stomped and cursed
As the rags and papers scattered
Over the gravel from our joke.

I tried to remember which of us
That red shirt had belonged to,
But morning seemed too long ago, and the man
Was falling, sobbing, to his knees.
I couldn't stop watching.
My brother lay next to me,
His hands covering his ears,
His face pressed tight to the ground.

▌ Did your audience see and hear why the persona "couldn't stop
watching" while her brother's face was "pressed tight to the
ground"?

Here is another poem of children and trains, but these mischief makers have quite different intentions. Nevertheless, by the poem's conclusion we see the urge "to hold such power" in the palm is not unlike the attractions Hales described. Keep the memory of the experiment — and its results — vivid and tangible.

Saving Memory
MARY STEWART HAMMOND

Summer nights we put pennies on the track.
Even the station was quiet enough for crickets.
Mountains surrounded us, middling high and purple.
No matter where we stood they protected us
with perspective. People call them gentle mountains
but you can die in there; they're thick
with creeper and laurel. Like voodoo,
I drew pictures with a sparkler. A curved line
arced across the night. Rooted in its slope,
one laurel tree big as the mountain holding it.

You can hear the train in the rails,
They're round, not flat, as you'd expect,
and slick. We'd walk the sound, one step, two,
slip, on purpose, in the ballast, hopscotch
and waltz on the ties, watching the big round eye
enter the curve and grow like God out of the purple,
the tracks turning mean, molten silver blazing
dead at us. We'd hula. Tango. And the first
white plume would shoot up screaming long, lonely,
vain as Mamma shooing starlings from her latticed pies.

Sing Mickey Mouse, the second scream rising long, again,
up and up. Stick our right hip out, the third
wailing. Give it a hot-cha wiggle, the fourth
surrounding us. And bidding each other fond adieux,
we'd count to three, turn our backs, flash it a moon,
and materialize, fantastic, run over with light,
the train shrieking to pieces, scared, meaning it,
short, short, short, short, pushing a noise
bigger than the valley. It sent us flying,
flattened, light as ideas, back on the platform,
the Y6B Mallet compound rolling through
southbound, steamborne, out of Roanoke.

It wasn't to make the train jump the track
but to hold the breath-edged piece of copper
grown hot with dying, thin with birth,
wiped smooth of origin and homilies
To hold such power. As big as the eye
of the train, as big as the moon burning
like the sun. All the perspective
curved and gone.

   ❚ Is there a pun in the title? How did you embody it?
   ❚ What does your body remember during the third stanza?

This long, loosely constructed sentence requires careful attention to progression as you move through the numerous *ands* into new but closely related minor thought units. The fulcrum begins seven lines from the end, so an awareness of balance and proportion is important.

Nikki-Rosa
NIKKI GIOVANNI

childhood remembrances are always a drag
if you're Black
you always remember things like living in Woodlawn
with no inside toilet

and if you become famous or something
they never talk about how happy you were to have
your mother
all to yourself and
how good the water felt when you got your bath
from one of those
big tubs that folk in chicago barbecue in
and somehow when you talk about home
it never gets across how much you
understood their feelings
as the whole family attended meetings about Hollydale
and even though you remember
your biographers never understand
your father's pain as he sells his stock
and another dream goes
And though you're poor it isn't poverty that
concerns you
and though they fought a lot
it isn't your father's drinking that makes any difference
but only that everybody is together and you
and your sister have happy birthdays and very good
Christmasses
and I really hope no white person ever has cause
to write about me
because they never understand
Black love is Black wealth and they'll
probably talk about my hard childhood
and never understand that
all the while I was quite happy.

▌ What prompted your persona to speak? Did your audience see
   those memories?

This elegy for a little girl contains some interesting problems of balance and
proportion. Look carefully at the structure of the three middle stanzas. Keep
the speaker and his attitude clear.

Bells for John Whiteside's Daughter
JOHN CROWE RANSOM

There was such speed in her little body,
And such lightness in her footfall,

It is no wonder her brown study
Astonishes us all.

Her wars were bruited in our high window.
We looked among orchard trees and beyond,
Where she took arms against her shadow,
Or harried unto the pond

The lazy geese, like a snow cloud
Dripping their snow on the green grass,
Tricking and stopping, sleepy and proud,
Who cried in goose, Alas,

For the tireless heart within the little
Lady with rod that made them rise
From their noon apple-dreams, and scuttle
Goose-fashion under the skies!

But now go the bells, and we are ready;
In one house we are sternly stopped
To say we are vexed at her brown study,
Lying so primly propped.

■ Do the memories dispel the gloom of the setting? Why? Where
did you leave your audience?

The speaker in this tender poem changes his position in the world by the
last line. Although he knows what has happened to his brother from the
first line, the speaker comes to a special understanding by the last line. Let
the rhyme work.

Mid-Term Break
SEAMUS HEANEY

I sat all morning in the college sick bay
Counting bells knelling classes to a close.
At two o'clock our neighbors drove me home.

In the porch I met my father crying —
He had always taken funerals in his stride —
And Big Jim Evans saying it was a hard blow.

The baby cooed and laughed and rocked the pram
When I came in, and I was embarrassed
By old men standing up to shake my hand

And tell me they were "sorry for my trouble."
Whispers informed strangers I was the eldest,
Away at school, as my mother held my hand

In hers and coughed out angry tearless sighs.
At ten o'clock the ambulance arrived
With the corpse, stanched and bandaged by the nurses.

Next morning I went up into the room. Snowdrops
And candles soothed the bedside; I saw him
For the first time in six weeks. Paler now,

Wearing a poppy bruise on his left temple,
He lay in the four foot box as in his cot.
No gaudy scars, the bumper knocked him clear.

A four foot box, a foot for every year.

> ▐ How did you demonstrate the speaker's dawning awareness to
> what happened?

This poem presents a character study not only of the monk who is speaking,
but of Brother Lawrence as well. Remember that the poem is a soliloquy,
which indicates that the speaker is alone. Evidently, however, Brother Lawrence is moving within sight of the speaker, and his actions provide the
motivations for the swift changes of thought. Notice how spiteful the monk
who follows the letter of the law feels toward the man who lives by the
spirit. The structure of the poem helps underscore this feeling.

Soliloquy of the Spanish Cloister
ROBERT BROWNING

Gr-r-r — there go, my heart's abhorrence!
    Water your damned flower-pots, do!
If hate killed men, Brother Lawrence,
    God's blood, would not mine kill you!
What? Your myrtle-bush wants trimming?
    Oh, that rose has prior claims —
Needs its leaden vase filled brimming?
    Hell dry you up with its flames!

At the meal we sit together:
10   *Salve tibi.* I must hear
Wise talk of the kind of weather,
   Sort of season, time of year:
Not a plenteous cork-crop: scarcely
   Dare we hope oak-galls, I doubt:
What's the Latin name for "parsley"?
   What's the Greek name for Swine's Snout?

Whew! We'll have our platter burnished,
   Laid with care on our own shelf!
With a fire-new spoon we're furnished,
20   And a goblet for ourself,
Rinsed like something sacrificial
   Ere 'tis fit to touch our chaps —
Marked with L for our initial
   (He-he! There his lily snaps!)

Saint, forsooth! while brown Dolores
   Squats outside the Convent bank
With Sanchicha, telling stories,
   Steeping tresses in the tank,
Blue-black, lustrous, thick like horse-hairs,
30   —Can't I see his dead eye glow,
Bright as 'twere a Barbary corsair's?
   (That is, if he'd let it show!)

When he finishes refection,
   Knife and fork he never lays
Cross-wise, to my recollection,
   As do I, in Jesu's praise.
I the Trinity illustrate,
   Drinking watered orange-pulp
In three sips the Arian frustrate;
40   While he drains his at one gulp.

Oh, those melons! If he's able
   We're to have a feast! so nice!

10 *Salve tibi:* Hail.
39 *Arian:* The Arian heresy held that Christ was created by God, and was inferior to Him in nature and dignity.

One goes to the Abbot's table,
    All of us get each a slice.
How go on your flowers? None double?
    Not one fruit-sort can you spy?
Strange! — And I, too, at such trouble
    Keep them close-nipped on the sky!

There's a great text in Galatians,
50   Once you trip on it, entails
Twenty-nine distinct damnations,
    One sure, if another fails:
If I trip him just a-dying,
    Sure of heaven as sure can be,
Spin him round and send him flying
    Off to hell, a Manichee!

Or, my scrofulous French novel
    On gray paper with blunt type!
Simply glance at it, you grovel
60   Hand and foot in Belial's gripe:
If I double down its pages
    At the woeful sixteenth print,
When he waters his greengages,
    Ope a sieve and slip it in't?

Or there's Satan! One might venture
    Pledge one's soul to him, yet leave
Such a flaw in the indenture
    As he'd miss till, past retrieve,
Blasted lay that rose-acacia
70   We're so proud of! *Hy, Zy, Hine* . . .
'St, there's Vespers! *Plena gratia,*
    Ave, Virgo! G-r-r-r — you swine!

    ❚ How did locus and reflexive physical activity operate in your
    performance?

---

56 *Manichee:* A sect that combined Persian and Christian beliefs.
70 *Hy, Zy, Hine:* This series of sounds has caused considerable dissension among critics. It may
be the beginning of a curse on Brother Lawrence.
71–72 *Plena gratia, Ave, Virgo!:* Full of grace, Hail, Virgin!

James Dickey captures the sterility and chill of the hospital remarkably well as he underscores the isolation that it imposes on those who leave a loved one there and return to the outdoor world. (You might want to compare this poem with Sharon Olds's "The Race" in Chapter 4.) The word choice is excellent, even when it seems, deliberately, not poetic. Don't neglect the subtle tone color. The kinetic, kinesthetic, and auditory imagery make an excellent contrast to the hospital room. Watch the stanza divisions.

The Hospital Window

JAMES DICKEY

I have just come down from my father.
Higher and higher he lies
Above me in a blue light
Shed by a tinted window.
I drop through six white floors
And then step out onto pavement.

Still feeling my father ascend,
I start to cross the firm street,
My shoulder blades shining with all
The glass the huge building can raise.
Now I must turn round and face it,
And know his one pane from the others.

Each window possesses the sun
As though it burned there on a wick.
I wave, like a man catching fire.
All the deep-dyed windowpanes flash,
And, behind them, all the white rooms
They turn to the color of Heaven.

Ceremoniously, gravely, and weakly,
Dozens of pale hands are waving
Back, from inside their flames.
Yet one pure pane among these
Is the bright, erased blankness of nothing.
I know that my father is there,

In the shape of his death still living.
The traffic increases around me
Like a madness called down on my head.
The horns blast at me like shotguns,

And drivers lean out, driven crazy —
But now my propped-up father

Lifts his arm out of stillness at last.
The light from the window strikes me
And I turn as blue as a soul,
As the moment when I was born.
I am not afraid for my father —
Look! He is grinning; he is not

Afraid for my life, either,
As the wild engines stand at my knees
Shredding their gears and roaring,
And I hold each car in its place
For miles, inciting its horn
To blow down the walls of the world

That the dying may float without fear
In the bold blue gaze of my father.
Slowly I move to the sidewalk
With my pin-tingling hand half-dead
At the end of my bloodless arm.
I carry it off in amazement,

High, still higher, still waving,
My recognized face fully mortal,
Yet not; not at all, in the pale,
Drained, otherworldly, stricken,
Created hue of stained glass.
I have just come down from my father.

❚ How did you make your audience see and hear what caused
your persona to stop the traffic?

Much of the richness of this distinctive poem arises from the densely mixed
responses the speaker suggests. Make that scene absolutely vivid to your
audience.

Filling Station
ELIZABETH BISHOP

Oh, but it is dirty!
— this little filling station,

oil-soaked, oil-permeated
to a disturbing, over-all
black translucency.
Be careful with that match!

Father wears a dirty,
oil-soaked monkey suit
that cuts him under the arms,
and several quick and saucy
and greasy sons assist him
(it's a family filling station),
all quite thoroughly dirty.

Do they live in the station?
It has a cement porch
behind the pumps, and on it
a set of crushed and grease-
impregnated wickerwork;
on the wicker sofa
a dirty dog, quite comfy.

Some comic books provide
the only note of color —
of certain color. They lie
upon a big dim doily
draping a taboret
(part of the set), beside
a big hirsute begonia.

Why the extraneous plant?
Why the taboret?
Why, oh why, the doily?
(Embroidered in daisy stitch
with marguerites, I think,
and heavy with gray crochet.)

Somebody embroidered the doily.
Somebody waters the plant,
or oils it, maybe. Somebody
arranges the rows of cans
so that they softly say:
ESSO — SO — SO — SO
to high-strung automobiles.
Somebody loves us all.

▌ Where does the fulcrum occur in this poem? Why?
▌ What enables the speaker to say that "somebody loves us all"?

This soft-spoken poem is completely devoid of sentimentality. The negation is underscored by the simple word choice and by the conversational relationship of thought units and line lengths in the first four stanzas. Pay particular attention to the single-line stanzas.

Preface to a Twenty Volume Suicide Note
IMAMU AMIRI BARAKA

Lately, I've become accustomed to the way
The ground opens up and envelops me
Each time I go out to walk the dog.
Or the broad edged silly music the wind
Makes when I run for a bus —

Things have come to that.

And now, each night I count the stars,
And each night I get the same number,
And when they will not come to be counted
I count the holes they leave.

Nobody sings anymore.

And then last night, I tiptoed up
To my daughter's room and heard her
Talking to someone, and when I opened
The door, there was no one there . . .
Only she on her knees,
Peeking into her own cupped hands.

▌ How did your persona feel when he glimpsed his daughter?
▌ How did you demonstrate this attitude to your audience?

Bibliography

Consult the bibliography at the end of Chapter 10 for several sources on the structure and other technical aspects of poetry.

What I like to do is to treat words as a craftsman
does his wood or stone or what-have-you, to hew,
carve, mould, coil, polish and plane them into
patterns, sequences, sculptures, fugues of sound . . .

Dylan Thomas

THE STRUCTURE OF POETRY

10

LANGUAGE IN POETRY IS CARRIED to the highest degree of order. This order is apparent in the condensation and organization of the content and in the close interaction of content and form. It is even more apparent in the discipline that poetic structure places on the writer and, consequently, on the interpreter. In successful poetry, structure and content are in perfect harmony, and in an evaluation of the whole, neither may be considered without the other. Poetry depends for its full meaning on the perfect blend of sound and sense.

The study of the structure of poetry is called *prosody*. The term *structure* is used in different ways by different critics, but it is generally taken to mean the way the component parts of a piece of literature are formed into a whole. Structure includes all of the elements of the language of poetry that we have been discussing: sense imagery, paradoxes, allusions, and other literary imagery. In this chapter, however, we use the term to apply specifically to devices that produce the sound pattern in a poem. Obviously, this includes a careful consideration of tone color, which we discussed in Chapter 9, because this element is part style, or language, and part sound patterning.

In this chapter we focus on stanzaic form — composition and length of lines, rhythm as established by both stress and flow of sound, and rhyme. These are the bases of the sound pattern on which much of a poem's effectiveness depends. These component parts of the sound pattern depend in a special way on the skill of the interpreter because they fulfill their function only when the poem is read aloud.

Since the late nineteenth century, critics have found it convenient to make a distinction between conventional or traditional types of poetry such as the sonnet and free verse. The structure of *conventional poetry* is based on a clearly discernible pattern of light and heavier stresses, grouped into a traditional system of metrical feet, and on a fixed pattern of stanza and line length. The same pattern, with only slight variation, usually recurs from stanza to stanza, in both length of lines and arrangement of stresses within those lines. Moreover, the number of lines per stanza is usually consistent. Within this fixed structural framework, however, there may be numerous variations both in stress pattern and in the location of pauses in a line to keep the fall of the words from becoming monotonous. Finally, conventional poetry — with the notable exception of blank verse — has the added element of rhyme, with the corresponding sounds in the line-end positions arranged in an easily perceived pattern called the *rhyme scheme*.

Blank verse is a special type of conventional poetry. It is unrhymed and has no recurring stanza pattern because the stanzas are divided according to the development of the thought and are of varying length. Blank verse does have a definitely prescribed line length of five metrical feet, and a prescribed prevailing foot — the *iamb*. Blank verse is of particular interest to interpreters because it is so often used in material that is inherently attractive to an audience. Because of the absence of rhyme and the lack of restriction on stanzaic structure in blank verse, skillful poets use this form effectively with narrative and dramatic materials. Shakespeare, an acknowledged master of blank verse in poetic drama, used it to wed nobility of utterance to acceptable rhythms of speech. Poets as diverse as Robert Browning and Robert Frost have used it to sustain the dramatic quality of long poems and to achieve the difficult feats of making poetry sound like conversation and conversation like poetry.

Free verse is often considered to be a recent addition to the realm of poetry. The term is modern, and the genre has developed during the last hundred years or so, though it is possible to find earlier examples of free verse. Free verse is a term adopted from the French *vers libre*. *Vers* in French refers to a "line" of poetry; hence, *vers libre* actually means a "free line." It is the varying lengths of the lines and the arrangement of stresses within them that gives the surest indication that a poem is in free verse.

Free verse differs in many ways from traditional poetry. If a free-verse poem is divided into units at all, they are often irregular in length, although a free-verse poem *may* have quite regular stanzaic division. The free-verse line may vary in length from a single syllable to fifty or more — if the poet needs to use such a long line and can bring it off successfully. Free verse often is not rhymed, though the poet may choose to introduce rhyme to achieve some special effect, as T. S. Eliot frequently does. Free verse exhibits no significant pattern of metrical feet, and its rhythm is based on cadence rather than meter.

Successful free verse is not, as the term might suggest, completely lacking in form and discipline. A discoverable rhythmic basis must exist. Sometimes it can be found in the number of syllables in the speech phrases within the lines, or in the number of heavier stresses within those speech phrases. Sometimes it can be discovered by analyzing the number of heavier stresses per line regardless of their relative positioning with lighter stresses. The important point is to find out what the poet has done and then see how it works with the content to produce a successful whole.

The strict dichotomy between conventional verse and free verse is becoming much less important in contemporary poetry. Most poets today work *from* rather than *within* strict metrical patterns, so that we often find an interesting combination of the two modes within a single poem. The traditional lines establish a certain expectation for us; when, a few lines later, we find the insertion of free verse, and that expectation is denied, variety and contrast are underscored. Or, on the other hand, a strictly regular line may surprise us with its steady beat and help point to a climax. Stanley Kunitz's poem "Open the Gates" (Chapter 9) contains an interesting example of this effect. William Van O'Connor, speaking of T. S. Eliot's prosody, quotes the poet when he says, "Even in the 'freest' of free verse there should lurk the ghost of some simple meter 'which should advance menacingly as we doze, and withdraw as we arouse.'"[1] And Robert Frost once remarked that writing what some people called free verse was like playing tennis with the net down. Thus, contemporary free verse could more accurately be labeled "freed verse." You should make a careful study to find out how freed it is from traditional patterns and how this freedom is coordinated with the content to produce the total effect of the poem.

---

1. William Van O'Connor, *Sense and Sensibility in Modern Poetry* (Chicago: University of Chicago Press, 1948), p. 58.

The Stanza

In Chapter 9 we learned that a stanza of poetry is roughly comparable to a paragraph in prose in that it is often a major unit of thought. As such, it is an important factor in the organization. But a stanza also may be a unit of sound, just as a line of poetry is not only a line of print but also a unit of sound, and a word is not only a symbol for meaning but a sound or combination of sounds as well. The stanzaic structure may contribute significantly to the poem's pattern of sound. The recurrence of the same stanza pattern throughout, together with the poet's skill in making thought units coincide with the stanzas, may divide the poem into nearly identical units of sound when the poem is read aloud. We tend to separate major divisions in thought by appropriate use of pause and to establish terminations by both pause and vocal inflection.

How stanzaic length contributes to the sound pattern of a poem varies considerably in importance from one selection to another. In general, shorter stanzas and a tighter rhyme scheme produce a more apparent sound effect. For example, a poem written entirely in two-line stanzas sets up an extremely close pattern of sounds and silences, especially if each pair of lines completes a thought division. This is an important aspect of structural unity but might seriously threaten the variety unless the poet has been very skillful. In blank verse, on the other hand, the contribution of stanzaic structure to sound pattern is almost negligible, partly because of the absence of rhyme, but primarily because the stanzas are of unequal length and may run to a hundred lines or more.

In contemporary poetry with a regular stanzaic pattern, the thought units are frequently not identical with the stanzas but run on from one to another. There may be a comma or another punctuation mark that does not indicate a full stop — or, indeed, there may be no punctuation at all — at the end of the last line of a stanza. This pattern appears throughout Cruz's poem "Today Is a Day of Great Joy" at the end of this chapter. This type of punctuation serves as a warning that the thought is unfinished and that the break imposed by the stanza pattern is a suspended break. The poet has chosen the stanzaic pattern as a discipline but has reserved the right to take liberties within it whenever it seems justified by the over-all purpose.

Stanza length and composition can be strong factors in the unity, harmony, and rhythm of both content and structure. Variety and contrast are also served by this aspect of structure. A change in stanzaic pattern is sometimes used to emphasize the fulcrum or the climax, as it does in Ciardi's "As I Would Wish You Birds" and in Alice Walker's untitled poem, both at the end of this chapter.

You should be aware of whatever contribution the stanza length makes to the sound pattern adopted by the poet. In evaluating the importance of stanza length, you must take your cue from the poet. When the poet has made a point of adhering to brief, regular stanzas, or has emphasized stanza divisions by repetition, you should assume that this strict discipline serves a definite purpose. On the other hand, when the stanzas are long or irregular in length, you may assume that the stanzas function primarily as a means of organizing the logical or emotional content.

The Line

The three main types of prosody, which all are based on the composition of the individual lines within stanzas, are usually designated as *metrical* or *foot prosody, stress prosody,* and *syllabic prosody.* We discuss metrical or foot prosody first because it is the most familiar and, at least until the last few decades, has been the most commonly used in poetry written in English.

Foot Prosody

Poetry is generally characterized in part by a high degree of regularity in the pattern of structural rhythm. The structural rhythm of conventional poetry is based on meter. *Meter* is the pattern set up by a reasonably regular recurrence of an identifiable combination of light and heavier stresses within a line. This pattern is discovered through *scansion,* the division of the poetic line into metrical feet. A *metrical foot* is a grouping of light and heavier stresses into a unit. The groupings, which were named centuries ago, are useful primarily for making the metrical pattern graphic, as the stresses are marked and grouped within the poetic lines. The most common feet in English poetry are the following:

1. *Iamb* — an unstressed syllable followed by a stressed syllable ($\smile$ $/$)[2]:

       ˘ /   ˘   /   ˘ /   ˘   /   ˘ /
    When I / have fears / that I / may cease / to be

2. ($/$) indicates a stressed syllable; ($\smile$) is an unstressed syllable. A line ($/$) is used here to mark off the feet.

2. *Anapest* — two unstressed syllables followed by a stressed syllable
(˘ ˘ ´):

˘ ˘ ´   ˘   ˘ ´ ˘   ˘ ´   ˘   ˘   ´
Of my dar / ling — my dar / ling — my life / and my bride

3. *Trochee* — a stressed syllable followed by an unstressed syllable
(´ ˘):

´   ˘   ´ ˘   ´   ˘   ´   ˘
Tell me / not in / mournful / numbers

4. *Dactyl* — a stressed syllable followed by two unstressed syllables
(´ ˘ ˘):

´   ˘   ˘   ´   ˘   ˘
Cannon to / right of them

5. *Spondee* — two heavy stresses (´ ´), usually used in combination
with other types of feet:

´   ´   ˘   ´   ˘   ´   ˘   ´
Beat once / therewith / and beat / no more.

6. *Pyrrhic* — two light stresses (˘ ˘), also usually found within another basic pattern:

˘   ´   ˘   ˘   ˘ ´   ˘   ˘   ˘   ´   ˘   ´
The end / and the / begin / ning in / each oth / er's arms.

There are some other combinations, such as the *amphibrach* (˘ ´ ˘)
and the *amphimacer* (´ ˘ ´), but these six types are the most common.

A line is classified according to its prevalent foot as *iambic, an-
apestic, trochaic,* or *dactylic;* and according to the number of feet it
contains as a *monometer* (one foot), *dimeter* (two), *trimeter* (three),
tetrameter (four), *pentameter* (five), *hexameter* (six), and so on. Thus, a
line of five iambic feet is spoken of as an *iambic pentameter.*

In almost all conventional poetry, one type of metrical foot pre-
vails. In English poetry, the iamb (˘ ´) is the most common foot, due
in part to our pronunciation. It is often varied by the trochee (´ ˘),
its reversed counterpart. The next most common is probably the
anapest (˘ ˘ ´), and then the dactyl (´ ˘ ˘). The spondee (´ ´) and
pyrrhic (˘ ˘) are used primarily for variation within a framework of
the other more common patterns. Certain harmonies are sometimes
achieved most successfully by strict consistency in meter, or by ap-

proximate consistency (as in the combination of iamb and anapest), but most poets make effective use of variations in the prevalent measure, since variety in unity is the keystone of all art.

A detail that may clarify the process of scanning a conventional poem is relative stress. Not all stressed syllables receive the same degree or value of stress when the poem is read aloud. The following line might be scanned as a regular iambic pentameter:

> ˘ ′ ˘ ′ ˘ ′ ˘ ′ ˘ ′
> Not mar / ble, nor / the gild / ed mon / uments

However, in an oral reading, the relative values of the stresses would be something like this, where (′) indicates a heavy stress, (`) a lighter one, and (˘) little discernible stress:

> ` ′ ˘ ` ˘ ′ ˘ ′ ˘ `
> Not mar / ble, nor / the gild / ed mon / uments

A most interesting study can be made of the relative values of stresses, but for our purposes we use only two degrees, lighter and heavier; that is, a syllable receives a lighter or heavier stress than the syllables on either side of it.

How do you begin to scan a poem? Stress in poetry, as in prose, results from the demands of proper pronunciation and of the total meaning, mood, and purpose of the literature. It is simplest to start with the words of more than one syllable, putting the stress where it must fall for pronunciation. *Marble* is of course pronounced *már-ble*, not *mărble*. If unsure of syllabication, the interpreter should check a dictionary. When scanning a poem, account for every syllable.

The next step cannot be undertaken until the poem has been at least partially analyzed and you are familiar not only with what it says but how it means what it says. You should note key words that must be emphasized for clarity and general comprehension. The attitude of the speaker is an important consideration here. This step is followed by a careful look at words that create mood or contribute sharply to needed variety and contrast. For instance, when a new type of sense imagery is introduced, it may need to be emphasized slightly so it will serve its purpose for later lines. The purpose of scanning is to find what the poet has actually done, not to make the lines fit a preconceived pattern.

After these first two steps, you may discover that a *fairly* regular pattern of light and heavier stresses in traditional feet is beginning to emerge. Complete the pattern by filling in whatever syllables have not yet been assigned a degree of stress to conform as nearly as is practical to the predominant type of foot. If no such pattern emerges, examine the poem further to determine if you are dealing with stress prosody. Perhaps the poet has used syllabic prosody. This will be easy to determine because you have already marked the stresses. You should look to line lengths, speech phrases, and the number of stresses within them for structural unity.

The relative degree of stress is a matter you must work out for yourself from an understanding of the poem, for there is no one "right" way of reading a poem that can be imposed. Not to submerge meaning in meter and not to lose sight of pattern in an attempt to communicate expressively: these are the twin channel markers you should watch in steering your course. The poet always leads the way. Find out what the poet has done with meter, if that is the basis of rhythm in the poem, but be sure to allow the necessary variations. If poets can best achieve the rhythmic effects they want by following a regular meter closely, they will keep to that meter; if they can achieve them by departing from a regular meter, they will do that.

Stress Prosody

Stress prosody finds its rhythmic base in the number of stresses *per line*, regardless of their position in relation to each other. Thus, it is often impossible, or at least impractical, to try to group the lighter and heavier stresses into traditional metrical feet. The number of syllables in a line may vary widely, but the number of stresses per line remains consistent or varies only occasionally for a specific effect. This concept of rhythm is important in understanding cadences of poetry and in determining the effectiveness of stresses within flows of sound. Dylan Thomas makes excellent use of a nearly consistent number of stresses per line in "In My Craft or Sullen Art" (Chapter 9).

Syllabic Prosody

Syllabic prosody is somewhat less common in English, although it is the basis of French prosody. Since the turn of this century, many poets have used syllabic prosody most effectively in combination with foot or stress prosody. Syllabic prosody measures flow of sound rather than stresses and depends quite simply on the number of syllables per line. Thomas combines this technique with a consistency of stresses in "In My Craft or Sullen Art," and all but three lines contain seven syllables. Incidentally, two of those three lines are used to terminate stanzas.

Stanley Kunitz's lyric "Open the Gates" is an excellent example

of how at least two of the three systems work within a single contemporary poem.

Open the Gates
STANLEY KUNITZ

1   Within / the ci / ty of / the burn / ing cloud,

2   Dragging / my life / behind / me in / a sack,

3   Naked / I prowl, / scourged by / the black

4   Tempta / tion of / the blood / grown proud.

5   Here at / the mon / ument / al door,

6   Carved with the / curious / legend of / my youth,

7   I brand / ish the great / bone of / my death,

8   Beat once / therewith / and beat / no more.

9   The hing / es groan: / a rush / of forms

10 Shivers / my name, / wrenched out / of me.

11 I stand / on the ter / rible thresh / old, and / I see

12 The end / and the / beginning / in each oth / er's arms.

Admittedly, there is more than one way to group the light
and heavy stresses into traditional feet, particularly in lines 6, 11,
and 12. This is a problem that may plague a prosodist, but our
concern is basically with the relative positioning of the stresses within
the line.

For us, the grouping of stresses into traditional feet is largely a
convenient way of clarifying the pattern. The scansion reveals that
the meter is *basically* iambic with a great many variations. As a matter
of fact, Kunitz uses each of the other five common types of feet at
least twice. The only purely iambic line is line 9, which immediately
follows the fulcrum.

From our preliminary marking, then, we discover that the first two lines and the last two lines of "Open the Gates" have five feet; the others have four feet. The four pentameter lines all have a pyrrhic foot, however, so that the stresses per line are consistently four, except for line 8, which is the fulcrum, and line 10, which contains the emotional climax; in these lines, spondees add a fifth stress. Thus, despite the greater length of the opening and closing lines, unity of stress is carefully preserved.

Some interesting details immediately become apparent. For instance, line 6 contains eleven syllables and yet contains only four heavier stresses, as does the nine-syllable line that follows it. These two lines immediately preceding the fulcrum are the only ones with an uneven number of syllables.

An examination of the scansion of this brief poem ensures us that there is more to poetic rhythm than a "da-dá da-dá" alternation of light and heavy stresses. Stanley Kunitz has achieved remarkable variety within unity. See also the chart of this poem later in this chapter.

The Interpreter's Use of Line Lengths

Early in our discussion of the three types of prosody, we mention the importance of the line as a structural unit. A line of poetry, it should be remembered, is not just a line of print. It is a unit of sound as well as a minor unit of thought. Because it functions as both sound and sense, it is important to consider in some detail the twofold discipline that poets have imposed on themselves — and consequently on their interpreters — with specific line lengths.

Poets who write conventional poetry consistently divide the stanzas into lines whose length is appropriate to the form of stanza they are using. They combine this measure with a more or less regular arrangement of stresses, and perhaps with rhyme at the line ends, to achieve the pattern of sound. Obviously, then, the line units should not be ignored. After all, poets had some reason for selecting this particular line length, or at least that, having selected it, they made some effort to fit their thought units — which also become sound units when the poem is read aloud — into that pattern.

Blank verse presents us with the greatest temptation to ignore line length, partly because the line ends do not have the added reinforcement of rhyme. Yet one of the accepted requisites of the best blank verse is that there must be an opportunity to establish the line length when the poem is read aloud. The degree or value of the pause will vary, but the line length should be given special consideration since it is one of the components of the rhythmic pattern. The extent to which the poet is able to conform to this

discipline, while achieving variety within it, is one standard for mea-
suring excellence of achievement. On the other hand, you should
remember that verse is written in sentences as well as in lines, and
that the line should not be emphasized at the expense of sentences
and overall sense. Not only would a drop of the voice or a distinct
pause at the end of every line produce monotony; it also would
distort the sense (because we are accustomed to consider a marked
pause as signifying the completion of a thought) and would cancel
out one of the chief advantages of the blank verse line — its approx-
imation of the rhythms of conversational speech.

A writer of free verse often uses long sentences, so that the flow
of sense may be technically uninterrupted for an entire unit (T. S.
Eliot does this in most of his poems). One may certainly assume,
then, that since the poet may arrange these sentences in lines as long
or as short as desired, there is a reason for the line division used.
Some critics contend that a line of free verse ends where it is convenient to take a breath — that it is written with the scope of a breath
in mind. We may invert this statement and say that for the interpreter's practical purposes, it is convenient to take a breath where
the free verse line ends. It is logical, too, because the breath comes
at a division of the thought, or at a point where the poet wishes to
reinforce feeling or establish a relationship or progression. There is
an excellent example of such subtle progression in Eliot's "Journey
of the Magi" (at the end of this chapter). In the last stanza we find
these lines:

> All this was a long time ago, I remember,
> And I would do it again, but set down
> This set down
> This: . . .

When the lines are read aloud, their arrangement gives a far
different effect from what it would be if the words were arranged as
follows:

> All this was a long time ago,
> I remember, and I would do it again,
> But set down this, set down this:

To realize the full contribution of line length to rhythm and to
content, then, you must make a pause *of some kind* at the end of each
line of poetry.

It should be remembered that pauses vary greatly in duration.
The line end as a line end (that is, apart from punctuation, sentence

construction, and overall meaning) does not require a terminal pause of the kind used to end a sentence. Indeed, if the sentence or speech phrase runs over into the next line — a device technically known as *enjambment*[3] — there is no *obvious* hesitation. Nevertheless, the line length imposes a sense of the boundaries or "shape" of the poem; this shape is marked by the eye in silent reading and is carried over into the voice in oral interpretation, though not to the point where the physical pattern of the poem obtrudes into the listener's consciousness at the expense of meaning, sound, and feeling.

Thus, the length, force, and terminal effect of the line-end pauses vary — from a barely perceptible pause, or a slight drawing out or suspension of the terminal vowel sound, to a semistop or "breath pause," to a full pause at the end of the sentence or thought unit. Accordingly, you should be alert to make the most of these opportunities for variety in treating line lengths by the use of pauses and voice inflections at the line ends. In a caution to poets, Ezra Pound once wrote: "Don't make each line stop dead at the end, and then begin every next line with a heave. Let the beginning of the next line catch the rise of the rhythm wave, unless you want a definite longish pause." Interpreters, too, can apply this advice to their own art.

Line length, especially in free verse, is considered further in the following discussion of cadence. And a thorough understanding of the contributions of line length will help your performance of verse drama and narrative verse, as well as many contemporary musical works (see Stephen Sondheim's "Finishing the Hat" at the end of Chapter 8). For the moment, however, give poets credit for being able to fit their thoughts into whatever restrictions of structure they have set for themselves. Obviously, the audience should not be made aware of the length of each line, any more than of any other single aspect of the material. Each element makes its contribution to the whole and should be blended with and properly related to all of the other elements.

Cadences

Analyzing cadences is a way of making graphic the length and stress composition of the separate flows of sound within a poem. This process brings together considerations of syllabic prosody (the num-

---

3. From the French *enjambement*, meaning "straddling": that is to say, one leg of the thought on either side of the line end.

ber of syllables in each line) and stress prosody (the number rather than location of stresses in each line).

A *cadence*, as the term is used here, is simply an uninterrupted flow of sound. Pauses of varying duration and prominence break the flow and thus establish new cadences. Because the syllable is the smallest functional unit of sound, cadences are measured by the number of syllables they contain.

When we mentioned syllabic and stress prosody earlier, we were concerned only with the line as a unit of measure. In analyzing cadences, we are concerned again with the line, but we also give attention to the way the individual lines may be divided into speech phrases when the poem is read aloud and to the length of entire sentences, whether or not they continue past the line end.

We touched on these matters of sentence length and speech phrases within sentences in our examination of prose style in Chapter 5. Here we apply the same approach to poetic style. Analyzing the length and composition of speech phrases and sentences is important in studying prose rhythm, and it is absolutely essential in examining poetic rhythm. This is partly because of the importance of line lengths in poetic structure. It is also because cadences are part of the essential sound pattern on which all poetry depends and because they should be coordinated with all the other sound factors.

A *primary cadence* is the number of syllables in an entire sentence. *Secondary cadences* refer both to line lengths and to the speech phrases within the lines. It is, of course, immediately obvious that merely counting syllables does not give us the total picture. This is simply a way of getting at one of the basic elements of poetic rhythm, especially in contemporary poetry. Cadences should always be considered in relation to two other elements that exist within them. The first of these is the number and arrangement of stresses, especially within lines. This consideration, of course, overlaps scansion in conventional poetry, and it is considerably important in free verse even when a clear, consistent metrical pattern cannot be established. The second element is partly a matter of tone color and has to do with the length or duration of the sounds within syllables. Thus, a duration pattern as well as a stress pattern is at work within the syllables in secondary cadence. We do not go into detail here on the aspect of duration because you are already familiar with tone color and its effect on tempo and quality.

There can be no question about the length of the primary cadences in a given poem. A primary cadence is the number of syllables in the sentence, from its beginning to its end as marked by terminal punctuation. The number of syllables in each line is also immediately evident. The lengths of the speech phrases, however, are somewhat more subjectively determined since not all interpreters pause at precisely the same places. Sometimes there can be no doubt about the need for a pause, and hence for establishing a cadence — for example, when the poet has inserted appropriate punctuation. Beyond these restrictions, however, you may make your own decisions about pauses, as you are guided by the requirements of content (both logical and emotive), by the relationship of phrases and clauses to the terms they modify and to the complete sentence, and by opportunities for conveying variety and contrast within unity and for communicating imagery and tone color. These pauses, however slight, will break the line into speech phrases.

Meter is, of course, the basis of the rhythmic structure in foot prosody, but a consideration of the cadences as well may open up unsuspected possibilities for variety and harmony. Frequently, poets achieve a large part of their rhythm by manipulating the cadences within a strict pattern of scansion. This is one of the important attributes of successful blank verse. Tennyson uses cadences most effectively, for instance, in "Ulysses" (Chapter 4), in which many of the lines are broken near the middle either by terminal punctuation or by a colon or semicolon. This provides variety, of course, without breaking the unity of the iambic pentameter line. Such a significant pause within a line is called a *caesura*. In numerous other lines, a balanced syntax or the need to point a comparative phrase may cause the interpreter to insert a somewhat less distinct pause, which nevertheless interrupts the flow of sound within the line as a unit.

The line-length cadences are probably the most fundamental in poetry, since all types of prosody take the line as a basic measure. Keeping this in mind, we can look at speech phrases *within* the separate lines, knowing that even an enjambment line has some kind of pause, however unobtrusive, at its end. In extremely long lines (as in Walt Whitman's poems), these speech phrases often provide the surest basis for the rhythm.

Since analyzing cadences brings together syllabic prosody and stress prosody, you also should be aware of any consistency in the number of stresses per secondary cadence. The number of stresses in the primary cadences is not likely to help much if the sentences are long and overflow the line.

In Kunitz's "Open the Gates," which is an interesting example of carefully controlled variation from traditional metrics, the cadences contribute to unity and harmony as well as to variety and contrast. Counting the syllables and major stresses within lines and speech phrases and noting the sentence lengths, we discover the following pattern:

| | Secondary Cadences | | | | Syllables per Primary Cadence |
Line No.	Syllables per Line	Stresses per Line	Syllables per Speech Phrase	Stresses per Speech Phrase	
1	10	4	10	4	36
2	10	4	7-3	3-1	
3	8	4	4-1-3	2-1-1	
4	8	4	3-3-2	1-1-2	
5	8	4	1-7	1-3	36
6	11	4	1-7-3	1-2-1	
7	9	4	9	4	
8	8	5	4-4	3-2	FULCRUM
9	8	4	4-4	2-2	16
10	8	5	4-4	2-3	CLIMAX
11	12	4	9-3	3-1	24
12	12	4	2-5-5	1-1-2	

As usual, the primary cadences tell us less by their specific length than they do by their relation to each other. Although they are of minor significance in this poem, the primary cadences are obviously a unifying factor in the first two stanzas. Furthermore, the change from the established thirty-six syllables to sixteen syllables helps set off the climax.

Looking at the secondary cadences, we notice that lines of identical length are used in pairs or in threes, except for the two center lines. These two are neatly bracketed by eight-syllable lines and serve as a steadying force in the middle of the poem. The stresses per line are a strong unifying force, with the added stress in lines 8 and 10 providing contrast to reinforce the fulcrum and the climax.

The speech phrases provide needed variety within this unity. They too, however, tend to cluster; three predominate near the opening, varied by units of seven, four, one, and two. The one-and-seven combination is apparent in line 5, and one and seven and three in line 6. The even four-and-four division in lines 8, 9, and 10, mentioned in relation to scansion, helps reinforce the emotional weight of the content.

Further analysis reveals even more subtle effects in this remarkable poem. Perhaps we have proved well enough that the line-length and speech-phrase cadences and their stresses are important in the pattern of a successful poem — and that such analysis is basic in discovering the rhythmic elements of free verse.

Why have we bothered to make a chart of it? Because this is the simplest way to clarify what you have to work with. A careful analysis of the cadences and stresses in a poem will convince you that conventional poetry does not need to be read like a nursery rhyme, and that the discipline inherent in free verse is a safeguard against the danger of reading this type of poetry as if it were prose. Free verse, properly written, is probably the most demanding type of poetry to read aloud, and interpreters who choose it should be prepared to analyze its structure painstakingly. Such analysis will greatly increase your own artistic ability as well as your appreciation of the poet's artistic achievement.

Clearly, no audience could be expected to appreciate the subtlety of this rhythmic pattern for itself when the poem is read aloud. Indeed, it would be most unfortunate if you called attention to the pattern. Nevertheless, you should understand what the poet has done to communicate the total effect.

Rhyme

Rhyme is closely allied with line length because it most commonly occurs at the line ends. The lines may contain internal rhymes as well. Rhyme, unlike rhythm and cadence, is not an essential element of poetry. But when it is used, it is important because it reinforces rhythm, cadence, pattern, and tone color.

Although corresponding sounds strike the mind's ear in a silent reading, they emerge for complete appreciation only when a poem is read aloud. Like a chime of music, rhyme is satisfying and pleasing to hear; it gives intellectual pleasure through the delights of repetition and anticipation. But the purpose of rhyme is not to decorate a poem but rather to bind it more closely together. For one thing, it unifies the pattern of sound. Consider rhyme's power and continuing popularity in rap music, where the texts derive much of their potency from the satisfied expectations rhyme creates. In more traditional poetry, rhyme reinforces the stanza pattern by establishing a recurring rhyme scheme. It emphasizes the line lengths by creating an expectation of repeated sounds at regular intervals. On the other hand, experienced poets and interpreters know that rhyme, if used unwisely, can shatter rather than intensify the unity of a poem. Therefore, when they use rhyme, they exhibit great care and variety in handling it. An interpreter who bears down hard on every rhyme makes the physical shape of the poem block out all of its other qualities. If a poem is read in this way, the audience will have the sensation of being taken for a ride on a rocking horse, instead of on a winged Pegasus.

Rhyme is the exact correspondence of both final vowel and consonant sounds (*love – dove*); *assonance* is the correspondence of vowel sounds only, regardless of the final consonant sounds (*place – brave*). There are many kinds of rhyme. In *half rhymes* (*pavement – gravely, river – weather*) only half of a two-syllable word rhymes with another. In *double rhymes*, the two final syllables correspond (*crying – flying, arrayed – afraid*). There are even *triple rhymes* (*din – afore – pinafore*), though these are usually too jingling and ingenious for anything but humorous verse. And there is *approximate rhyme* or *rhyme by consonance:* most commonly, the final consonant sounds are identical, but the vowel sounds are not (*rock – luck*). If used carefully, rhyme can be a strong way to reinforce tone color.

A rhyme scheme is indicated in prosodic analysis by letters that stand for the terminal rhyme sounds; *a* represents the sound of the first line and of every line corresponding to it; *b* stands for the next terminal sound and its corresponding lines; and so on. The rhyme scheme in this stanza from Percy Bysshe Shelley's "Adonais" would be marked as follows:

Most musical of mourners, weep anew!	*a*
Not all to that bright station dared to climb;	*b*
And happier they their happiness who knew,	*a*
Whose tapers yet burn through that night of time	*b*
In which suns perished; others more sublime,	*b*
Struck by the envious wrath of man or God,	*c*
Have sunk, extinct in their refulgent prime;	*b*
And some yet live, treading the thorny road,	*c*
Which leads, through toil and hate, to Fame's serene abode.	*c*

This gives a rhyme scheme designated by the letters *ababbcbcc*.

Rhyme can cause some trouble for an interpreter, especially if the pattern is very strict and the form the poet has adopted is too rigid for effective oral reading. When this is true, you should attempt to compensate by giving close attention to every opportunity for variety in using pauses and inflection at line ends. Particular attention to tone color within lines can bring some of the interior words to a prominence that challenges the strength of the rhyming words. Emphasis on imagery also adds variety.

As we have said, the problem of rhyme does not arise in blank verse. But its very absence here affects interpreters. On one hand, you are released from one of the disciplines you often should consider in interpreting poetry; on the other hand, you are deprived of a significant means of communicating structural unity. For these reasons, you should pay particular attention to other elements in the sound pattern of blank verse: alliteration, harsh or euphonious vowel and consonant combinations, the echoing of mood or sense in sound. The surest guide to structural unity in blank verse is found in the prevalent iambic meter and in the consistent line length.

Writers of free verse may or may not use rhyme. They may use it consistently throughout a poem, but this technique is unusual. Sometimes rhyme appears, if it appears at all, only in brief units of the poem. When these units appear, you should carefully examine their contribution to content, for the poet will have used rhyme consciously. It will not be part of a conventional pattern, but will come out of a subjective decision to use rhyme at that particular point. The sounds of the rhymes and the length of the lines containing the rhymes are very important for intensifying certain aspects of the content.

Contemporary poets are very sophisticated in their use of rhymes and near-rhymes. "Open the Gates" provides us with an excellent example of this use. On reading the poem aloud, one finds rhyming sounds woven intricately throughout the poem. The terminal rhymes are identical and are therefore satisfying; the only exceptions are the paradoxical rhyme of "youth" and "death" immediately preceding the fulcrum, and the slight variance between "forms" and "arms" in the last stanza. Moreover, the identity of the rhymes is emphasized because all but three of the lines are wholly or partially end-stopped by punctuation. Of the three enjambment lines, the first is the inescapable, harsh rhyme of "black" and "sack." The other two are found in the last stanza, one the softening "forms," the other the softening "see."

An additional aspect of line-end sounds, which is not strictly a matter of rhyme but is worthy of the interpreter's attention, is the use of masculine and feminine line endings. A *masculine* line ending has a discernible stress. All of the line endings in "Open the Gates," for example, are masculine. A *feminine* line end terminates on a lighter stress. Sometimes feminine endings are used to weaken or soften the line end, especially when they are combined with enjambment. Modern poets, like T. S. Eliot, frequently use feminine line ends to reinforce a feeling of instability. They are effective psychologically, because the added light stress negates our expectations.

Careful, detailed analysis of the structure of a poem gives you a sure basis for understanding the poet's techniques. Poetry is an art, but it is also a kind of science, and the intricacies of a successful poem are amazing. Once you have discovered the aspects of structure that the poet has used, you should carefully relate them to content. You should then evaluate both content and structure in the light of the touchstones for judging every piece of literature: the extrinsic factors of universality, individuality, and suggestion; the intrinsic factors of unity and harmony, variety and contrast, balance and proportion, and rhythm. Finally, when you present a selection, remember that no single aspect of structure should be exhibited for its own sake; it should be skillfully blended with every other aspect to communicate the aesthetic wholeness of the poem.

Analyzing the Performance

Poetry's condensation provides special challenges to interpreters, and your understanding of the language and structure of poetry is constantly tested in rehearsal and performance. Of course, we do not mean that we are no longer interested in the basic problems of every kind of performance: efficient management of the vocal and physical resources and careful attention to communicating the intellectual, emotional, and aesthetic entirety of the work. But poetry brings more complex uses of sound and sense than do many kinds of narration or drama. The interpreter must be particularly careful not to allow concentration to lapse and the communicative thrust of the performance to fade. Poetry performances in which the interpreter seems chiefly interested in musing over the lines for himself or herself and the people seated closest are really still in rehearsal.

With the information you have obtained from chapters 9 and 10, then, and an informed and observant perspective, use the following questions to analyze the performance you gave. As before, any questions you ask of yourself can as well be asked of other performances you see. Keep the poem at the center of your discussion and analysis and treat it with respect. Remember, it was alive before you met it and will be around long after all of us have gone.

Did you let the poet lead the way?

Was your audience responsive to what the poet meant and especially to *how* it was meant?

Did you use your empathic response fully so that the audience responded empathically as well?

Did you carefully preserve the unity of the poem? Did you keep all the other instrinsic factors working fully within it?

Was the persona clear? Was the locus clear?

Did you take full advantage of all of the sound patterns? Did you use the poem's rhythm, or did it use you? Did you clarify the relationship between the lines and the cadences? Did you demonstrate the interaction of rhyme and tone color?

Did your brief introduction prepare the audience for the mood and attitude of the poem? Did you spend more time introducing than performing?

Were you able to blend aspects from the previous chapters applicable to this selection and keep them in their proper relationship to create the "whole" poem?

Did your audience hear the poem as a totality? Were they primarily interested in and aware of you as performer?

How did the poem change for you after your analysis? How has it changed for you after your rehearsals and performance?

What problems still plague you as a performer? What progress have you made in defining them? In solving them? In eliminating them?

For the performances you saw, how did the interpreter suggest the complex language and structure of poetry? Specifically, how did the poem you saw and heard compare with the one you read on the page?

Selections for Analysis and Oral Interpretation

It is interesting to compare the structure and syntax of these two Roethke poems. They offer sharply contrasting physical responses. This first poem is held at a fairly steady level and builds to the final triumph a child would feel at having undivided attention. Keep the poem unified without sacrificing the excitement of the separate thought units within the single primary cadence.

Child on Top of a Greenhouse
THEODORE ROETHKE

The wind billowing out the seat of my britches,
My feet crackling splinters of glass and dried putty,

The half-grown chrysanthemums staring up like accusers,
Up through the streaked glass, flashing with sunlight,
A few white clouds all rushing eastward,
A line of elms plunging and tossing like horses,
And everyone, everyone pointing up and shouting.

▐ How did you use reflexive physical activity in your performance?

This villanelle uses a highly restrictive structure. Let the stanzaic structure help keep the cadences from becoming abrupt. Make full use of the remarkable tone color, especially the assonance.

For Roethke all of life was a waking toward the sleep of death. His affirmation of life is reminiscent of Dylan Thomas's.

The Waking
THEODORE ROETHKE

I wake to sleep, and take my waking slow.
I feel my fate in what I cannot fear.
I learn by going where I have to go.

We think by feeling. What is there to know?
I hear my being dance from ear to ear.
I wake to sleep, and take my waking slow.

Of those so close beside me, which are you?
God bless the Ground! I shall walk softly there,
And learn by going where I have to go.

Light takes the Tree; but who can tell us how?
The lowly worm climbs up a winding stair;
I wake to sleep, and take my waking slow.

Great Nature has another thing to do
To you and me; so take the lively air,
And, lovely, learn by going where to go.

This shaking keeps me steady. I should know.
What falls away is always. And is near.
I wake to sleep, and take my waking slow.
I learn by going where I have to go.

▐ How did you distinguish among the different levels of meaning in
the repeated lines?

Posture is crucial to performing this poem because we will not understand the impact of the last stanza if it hasn't been prepared. Let the memory of the two men be distinctively different.

Two Men Loved Me Once
JUDITH BAUMEL

Two men loved me once
for my long long knee-long hair.
One would sing and tell me
of an old religious man
who had declared
that only God my dear
could love Anne Gregory
for herself alone
and not her yellow hair.
The other knew a life so hard
he never shed a prayer
nor murmured out his tears
but wept, or said he wept,
to see me shorn beyond repair.
And like the foolish Anne
in front of young men in despair
I believed nothing simple or sincere.

Now and then I move my small, bare
head and feel the heft
of what's not there.

> ▌ How did you distinguish between the memory and the present?
> Why?

The stanzaic structure is interesting here, as is the author's use of dashes. Be sure you understand the seemingly simple allusions as they are used to reflect attitude. The line lengths as units of thought are particularly important; use them as the poet has.

As I Would Wish You Birds
JOHN CIARDI

Today — because I must not lie to you —
there are no birds but such as I wish
for. There is only my wish to wish you

birds. Catbirds with spatula tails up
jaunty. Jays, gawky as dressed-up toughs.
Humming birds, their toy engines going.
Turkeys with Savonarola heads. Bitchy
Peacocks. The rabble of Hens in their
stinking harems — these three (and
Ostriches and Dodos) a sadness to think
about. But then Gulls — ultimate bird
everywhere everything pure wing and wind
are, there over every strut, flutter, cheep,
coo. At Dover over the pigeon-cliffs.
At Boston over the sparrows. Off tropics
where the lyre-tails and the green-
irridescent heads flash. And gone again.

You never see Gulls in aviaries. Gulls are
distance. Who can put distance in a cage?

Today — and I could never lie to you —
there is no distance equal to what I wish
for. There is only my wish to wish you
a distance full of birds, a thronged air
lifting above us far, lifting us, the sun
bursting in cloud chambers, a choir there
pouring light years of song, its wings
flashing. See this with me. Close your eyes
and see what air can do with more birds in it
than anything but imagination can put there.
There are not enough birds in the eyes we
open. There are too many hens, turkeys, and
that peacock seen always on someone else's
lawn, the air above it wasted unused, songless.
Birds cannot be seen in fact. Not enough
of them at once, not now nor any day. But think
with me what might be, but close your eyes and see.

▮ How did you show *your* audience the persona's audience?
▮ Does the relationship between persona and audience change?
   How?

In this poem the line-length cadences are not only important for structural rhythm but provide clues to emotional content and connotations. The first five lines are quoted from a famous sermon. Notice how skillfully Eliot moves into his own comment. The quote should not be set off too obviously from the rest of the stanza. Eliot uses capital letters for spiritual birth and death as opposed to physical birth and death.

Journey of the Magi

T. S. ELIOT

'A cold coming we had of it,
Just the worst time of the year
For a journey, and such a long journey:
The ways deep and the weather sharp,
The very dead of winter.'
And the camels galled, sore-footed, refractory,
Lying down in the melting snow.
There were times we regretted
The summer palaces on slopes, the terraces,
And the silken girls bringing sherbet.
Then the camel men cursing and grumbling
And running away, and wanting their liquor and women,
And the night-fires going out, and the lack of shelters,
And the cities hostile and the towns unfriendly
And the villages dirty and charging high prices:
A hard time we had of it.
At the end we preferred to travel all night,
Sleeping in snatches,
With the voices singing in our ears, saying
That this was all folly.

   Then at dawn we came down to a temperate valley,
Wet, below the snow line, smelling of vegetation;
With a running stream and a water-mill beating the darkness,
And three trees on a low sky,
And an old white horse galloped away in the meadow.
Then we came to a tavern with vine-leaves over the lintel,
Six hands at an open door dicing for pieces of silver,
And feet kicking the empty wine-skins.
But there was no information, and so we continued
And arrived at evening, not a moment too soon
Finding the place; it was (you may say) satisfactory.

   All this was a long time ago, I remember,
And I would do it again, but set down

This set down
This: were we led all that way for
Birth or Death? There was a Birth, certainly,
We had evidence and no doubt. I had seen birth and death,
But had thought they were different; this Birth was
Hard and bitter agony for us, like Death, our death.
We returned to our places, these Kingdoms,
But no longer at ease here, in the old dispensation,
With an alien people clutching their gods.
I should be glad of another death.

> ❚ Was your persona "glad of another death" as the poem began?
> How did your audience know?

> Here is another and very different poem about the same people. Here,
> however, the speaker observes the Magi with mixed emotions. Be sure we
> see how carefully Glück establishes the scene she wants us to remember.

The Magi
LOUISE GLÜCK

Toward world's end, through the bare
beginnings of winter, they are traveling again.
How many winters have we seen it happen,
watched the same sign come forward as they pass
cities sprung around this route their gold
engraved on the desert, and yet
held our peace, these
being the Wise, come to see at the accustomed hour
nothing changed: roofs, the barn
blazing in darkness, all they wish to see.

> ❚ How does this speaker's attitude differ from Eliot's?

> James Wright's gift for simple eloquence is unmatched among contemporary
> American poets. Restraint and sincerity characterize the achievement in this
> lyric.

A Blessing
JAMES WRIGHT

Just off the highway to Rochester, Minnesota,
Twilight bounds softly forth on the grass.
And the eyes of those two Indian ponies

Darken with kindness.
They have come gladly out of the willows
To welcome my friend and me.
We step over the barbed wire into the pasture
Where they have been grazing all day, alone.
They ripple tensely, they can hardly contain their happiness
That we have come.
They bow shyly as wet swans. They love each other.
There is no loneliness like theirs.
At home once more,
They begin munching the young tufts of spring in the darkness.
I would like to hold the slenderer one in my arms,
For she has walked over to me
And nuzzled my left hand.
She is black and white,
Her mane falls wild on her forehead,
And the light breeze moves me to caress her long ear
That is delicate as the skin over a girl's wrist.
Suddenly I realize
That if I stepped out of my body I would break
Into blossom.

■ What happened to your body and voice four lines from the
end? Why?

Trust this poet completely, and use his line lengths exactly as he has put them down. He uses capital letters for a shade of emphasis. Keep the thought suspended across the parentheses, which make a sort of "subpoem" in themselves. The kinesthetic imagery is important.

Spring is like a perhaps hand
E. E. CUMMINGS

Spring is like a perhaps hand
(which comes carefully
out of Nowhere)arranging
a window,into which people look(while
people stare
arranging and changing placing
carefully there a strange
thing and a known thing here)and

changing everything carefully

spring is like a perhaps
Hand in a window
(carefully to
and fro moving New and
Old things,while
people stare carefully
moving a perhaps
fraction of flower here placing
an inch of air there)and

without breaking anything.

▌ How did your body and voice capture the *perhaps*es? Were they all the same?

This poem is a feast of images; each contributes mightily to the flavor and richness of this sensual banquet. Miss no opportunity for tone color.

Who Among You Knows the Essence of Garlic?
GARRETT KAORU HONGO

Can your foreigner's nose smell mullets
roasting in a glaze of brown bean paste
and sprinkled with novas of sea salt?

Can you hear my grandmother
chant the mushroom's sutra?

Can you hear the papayas crying
as they bleed in porcelain plates?

I'm telling you that the bamboo
slips the long pliant shoots
of its myriad soft tongues
into your mouth that is full of oranges.

I'm saying that the silver waterfalls
of bean threads will burst in hot oil
and stain your lips like zinc.

The marbled skin of the blue mackerel
works good for men. The purple oils
from its flesh perfume the tongues of women.

If you swallow them whole, the rice cakes
soaking in a broth of coconut milk and brown sugar
will never leave the bottom of your stomach.

Flukes of giant black mushrooms
leap from their murky tubs
and strangle the toes of young carrots.

Broiling chickens ooze grease,
yellow tears of fat collect
and spatter in the smoking pot.

Soft ripe pears, blushing
on the kitchen window sill,
kneel like plump women
taking a long, luxurious shampoo,
and invite you to bite their hips.

Why not grab basketfuls of steaming noodles,
lush and slick as the hair of a fine lady,
and squeeze?

The shrimps, big as Portuguese thumbs,
stew among cut guavas, red onions,
ginger root, and rosemary in lemon juice,

the palm oil bubbling to the top,
breaking through layers and layers
of shredded coconut and sliced cashews.

Who among you knows the essence
of garlic and black lotus root,
of red and green peppers sizzling
among squads of oysters in the skillet,
of crushed ginger, fresh green onions,
and pale-blue rice wine simmering
in the stomach of a big red fish?

❚ How did you separate the distinct flavors and smells?
❚ How hungry was your audience when your performance was
over?

This famous sonnet uses a different but equally conventional rhyme scheme
and division of content.

On His Blindness
JOHN MILTON

When I consider how my light is spent
Ere half my days, in this dark world and wide,
And that one talent which is death to hide
Lodged with me useless, though my soul more bent
To serve therewith my Maker, and present
My true account, lest he returning chide,
"Doth God exact day-labor, light denied?"
I fondly ask. But Patience, to prevent
That murmur, soon replies: "God doth not need
Either man's work or his own gifts: who best
Bears his mild yoke, they serve him best. His state
Is kingly: thousands at his bidding speed,
And post o'er land and ocean without rest;
They also serve who only stand and wait."

❚ How did your body and voice convey the persona's certainty?

Be sure you embody the Duke's character. He is moved alternately by guilt and regret and admiration and contempt. And don't ignore the poem's tight structure — those rhymed couplets are not simply accidental and suggest some of the restrictions inherent in the Ferrara of the poem.

My Last Duchess
ROBERT BROWNING

Ferrara

That's my last Duchess painted on the wall,
Looking as if she were alive. I call
That piece a wonder, now: Frà Pandolf's hands
Worked busily a day, and there she stands.
Will't please you sit and look at her? I said
"Frà Pandolf" by design, for never read
Strangers like you that pictured countenance,
The depth and passion of its earnest glance,
But to myself they turned (since none puts by
The curtain I have drawn for you, but I)
And seemed as they would ask me, if they durst,
How such a glance came there; so, not the first
Are you to turn and ask thus. Sir, 'twas not
Her husband's presence only, called that spot
Of joy into the Duchess' cheek: perhaps
Frà Pandolf chanced to say, "Her mantle laps
Over my lady's wrist too much," or "Paint
Must never hope to reproduce the faint
Half-flush that dies along her throat:" such stuff
Was courtesy, she thought, and cause enough
For calling up that spot of joy. She had
A heart — how shall I say? — too soon made glad,
too easily impressed: she liked whate'er
She looked on, and her looks went everywhere.
Sir, 'twas all one! My favour at her breast,
The dropping of the daylight in the West,
The bough of cherries some officious fool
Broke in the orchard for her, the white mule
She rode with round the terrace — all and each
Would draw from her alike the approving speech.
Or blush, at least. She thanked men, — good! but thanked
Somehow — I know not how — as if she ranked
My gift of a nine-hundred-years-old name
With anybody's gift. Who'd stoop to blame

This sort of trifling? Even had you skill
In speech — (which I have not) — to make your will
Quite clear to such an one, and say, "Just this
Or that in you disgusts me; here you miss,
Or there exceed the mark" — and if she let
Herself be lessoned so, nor plainly set
Her wits to yours, forsooth, and made excuse,
— E'en then would be some stooping; and I choose
Never to stoop. Oh sir, she smiled, no doubt,
Whene'er I passed her; but who passed without
Much the same smile? This grew; I gave commands;
Then all smiles stopped together. There she stands
As if alive. Will't please you rise? We'll meet
The company below, then. I repeat,
The Count your master's known munificence
Is ample warrant that no just pretence
Of mine for dowry will be disallowed;
Though his fair daughter's self, as I avowed
At starting, is my object. Nay, we'll go
Together down, sir. Notice Neptune, though,
Taming a sea-horse, thought a rarity,
Which Claus of Innsbruck cast in bronze for me!

▌ How did you sketch the world of the Duke's palace?
▌ How did you keep the Count's emissary present and lively?

This resilient speaker knows herself and admits her shortcomings with sometimes astonishing accuracy. She never feels sorry for herself, either. Can we
see her recall her experiences as vividly as she describes Billielou?

The Kilgore Rangerette Whose Life Was Ruined
CYNTHIA MACDONALD

There we were that beautiful line, synchronized as
A row of pistons in an Eldorado, except
There are only eight of them and there were a hundred of us
(Flowers weeded out of flowers, the cream of the crop).
There we were in the Cotton Bowl, the world-famous
Kilgore Rangerettes, kicking to "The Eyes of Texas Are Upon You"
And they were. In our white cowhide skirts and white felt hats
And red satin shirts and vests with silver stars and
I kicked with the wrong leg and the heel of
My white patent boot got caught in Marybelle's heel on the right

And we both fell and knocked into
The girls on either side of us who sprawled into
Others and half the line went down
Like a keyboard in a demo derby whacked by an axe.

Maybe I should have known — there had been
Problems of appearances before:

Hugging Grandma too tight after she'd had her surgery.
She held the empty place and cried.
Grandpa said she loves you; be more careful.
He bought me a grey suede bag to keep things in.

Giggling in my Hark the Herald Angels Sing duet,
Infecting my partner, too.
The principal said we ruined the Christmas Concert.
My father gave me a garnet and emerald
Synthastone pin in the shape of a clef.

Having a nosebleed when I was shaking hands with
The head of Pan American who came for dinner.
A drop fell on his tan pants.
My father didn't get promoted
But he said that wasn't why.
My mother gave me a box of linen handkerchiefs
Embroidered Monday, Tuesday, Wednesday . . .

Not only did I have to leave the Rangerettes
I left Kilgore, too, even though my roommate,
Who'd been the Maid of Cotton, told me she still loved me.
My intended said the same and gave me
A satin slip, but I don't know . . .
I felt he shouldn't have a ruined wife.
It was that way with any good job, too.
How could I work in the fine crystal section at Neiman's?
All those long-stemmed goblets. Cascades of glass chimes
Woke me every night. I asked to be transferred to
Sterling and Gems. But the tines, the blades, the facets
Menaced me. I learned you break or are broken.
And then a Texaco receptionist, Jack-In-The-Box waitress . . .
No need to spell the perils out.

They know me in Dallas — the only bag lady — lots in NYC —
But all of them are old and I am not. I saw them

On a Kilgore trip to catch the Rockettes and the Balanchine
Swan Lake. (We all agreed those swans would be
Hissed off the field at any Southwest half-time show.)
It's not a bad life. No one expects grace or precision.

Outdoors scavenging the city's trash — presents for yourself —
You collect what you can, what you want, what you need.
Last night I found a Lilly Daché hat and three foam mats.
Street life has its dangers: cold, jail, insults.
But no humiliation. A year ago I got knocked up.
Rape, yes, but no mutilation.
It wasn't bad. I don't feel much these days.
I keep the baby, Billielou, in my bag, snug
In a nest of rags, a Dallas kangaroo.
If Beebeelou — that's what I call her — wants
To be a Rangerette . . . Well, I don't know . . .
Her fingers curl around my thumb like little tongues.
She'll have to have her chance to kick her boots to the sky,
To slice it with her legs, the perfect blue
Deep in the heart of Texas.

> ▌ How did you capture the speaker's unique "grace and preci-
> sion" of recall and description?

The two long sentences in this poem must not be allowed to become repetitious in their tight syntax. The fulcrum begins in the ninth line and moves
slowly to the climax in the last half line. Use the two short cadences in the
last line with enough strength to balance the "negative" aspects of the other
thirteen lines.

FROM *Fatal Interview*
EDNA ST. VINCENT MILLAY

Sonnet XXX

Love is not all: it is not meat nor drink
Nor slumber nor a roof against the rain;
Nor yet a floating spar to men that sink
And rise and sink and rise and sink again;
Love can not fill the thickened lung with breath,
Nor clean the blood, nor set the fractured bone;
Yet many a man is making friends with death
Even as I speak, for lack of love alone.
It well may be that in a difficult hour,

Pinned down by pain and moaning for release,
Or nagged by want past resolution's power,
I might be driven to sell your love for peace,
Or trade the memory of this night for food.
It well may be. I do not think I would.

▌ How did you demonstrate the thought processes of the
persona?
▌ What was happening in the pause between the two sentences
in the last line?

This poem both describes and reconsiders the small facts of a poet's world.
It uses Dickinson's own language to bring us an image of the poet that
blends both the speaker and Dickinson. Keep the locus clear in the performance; we need to see both worlds.

The Upper Story
MARY JO SALTER

As Emily Dickinson
would not come down, I'm
sorry, but I've felt the need to climb
the worn steps to her room,
winding up the stair
as if into her inner ear.

Art, as she once said,
is *a House that tries to be haunted,*
and as I stand
on the landing where she curled in shadow
to follow the piano
and soprano voice of Mabel Todd

(her editor years later —
who now graciously accepted
a poem and glass of sherry in place
of having seen her face),
this would become that House.
No trespass can erase

what she once made of it —
that gate she opened, resolute
to escape, and just as quickly shut:
I think I was held in check by some

invisible agent . . . And when she wrote
Again — his voice is at the door —
here is the door she meant.
Her room, probably Spartan
even when lived in, now holds but few
fabled artifacts: a snow-white
coverlet; a "sleigh bed," narrow
like a wooden shoe; a snipped

lily of a dress, limp in the closet;
a wilted hatbox; a woven basket
she'd lower, something like Rapunzel,
full of gingerbread.
Or so our guide has said. Yet
devoted to the genuine

as she was — first jasmine of the season,
hummingbird and snake —
I doubt she would have taken umbrage
when learned men in Cambridge
spirited off her writing table
to higher education. A double

(its surface little more
than two feet square, and where
poems commensurately small
were scrawled on backs of envelopes)
sits convincingly beneath the tall
window onto Main Street.

To shut our eyes is Travel,
and that table may as well
be anywhere as here.
She'd have held close whatever house
she was born in, as a squirrel
palms its acorn; but with a need

not wholly fed by fear.
At twenty-four, moving back
to her birthplace, she'd lived the thought
transposed: To travel, shut the eyes.
I supposed we were
going to make a "transit,"
as heavenly bodies did . . .

She was truly half-
astonished at those carriages
and cartons — almost as if
she'd lived only in that other life,
unseen, in her upper story.
Touch Shakespeare for me,
she wrote to Mabel in Europe,
thinking her close enough.
Why had anyone expressed the hope
to see Emily, who'd compare in letters
her unmet friends to Peter's
Christ: "whom having not seen, ye love"?

Finding nothing and no time
impalpable, she'd call
attention to the Biblical
"house not made with hands" for all
who'd listen. Wasn't that her home
as much as this was? Fame,

a lower form of Immortality,
in the intervening century
has unpacked her cradle to restore
its place, steps from her deathbed.
There is no first, or last, in Forever . . .
To the West, across the field

from another window, lives the family
at The Evergreens, whom Emily
saw little more than I can: Austin
and dark sister-in-law Sue.
I would have come out of Eden
to open the Door for you . . .

but she hadn't had to.
Drumming down the stair,
my ears fill with the spirals of a fly
a poem let in and won't be shown the way:
as if that buzzing, when she died,
were here still amplified.

▌ Who spoke the italicized lines? Why?
▌ On how many levels is the title operating?

The long suspended sentence that makes up this poem must be carefully sustained without allowing the variety to break the build. Notice how skillfully the one-line stanzas are used as fulcrum and climax. The poem is full of energy and empathy, especially after the fulcrum. Remember what we have said about poets breaking their lines where they want to achieve subtle effects. Allow Cruz his privilege.

Today Is a Day of Great Joy
VICTOR HERNANDEZ CRUZ

when they stop poems
in the mail & clap
their hands & dance to
them
when women become pregnant
by the side of poems
the strongest sounds making
the river go along

it is a great day

as poems fall down to
movie crowds in restaurants
in bars

when poems start to
knock down walls to
choke politicians
when poems scream &
begin to break the air

that is the time of
true poets that is
the time of greatness

a true poet aiming
poems & watching things
fall to the ground

it is a great day.

▌ How vivid was your persona's desire?
▌ How poignant are the repeated lines?

The single long sentence of the first two stanzas makes the background of the persona remarkably clear. Make full use of the change of style at the fulcrum. Be meticulous about the punctuation and line lengths. Don't slight the faint suggestions of rhyme. Keep the repetitions well within the unity of each stanza as they build to the final single word. Don't overlook the change from "your" to "our" in the last stanza. Although the poem requires superb aesthetic control, it rewards you accordingly.

FROM *Horses Make a Landscape Look More Beautiful*

ALICE WALKER

for two who
slipped away
almost
entirely:
my "part" Cherokee
great-grandmother
Tallulah
(Grandmama Lula)
on my mother's side
about whom
only one
agreed-upon
thing
is known:
her hair was so long
she could sit on it;

and my white (Anglo-Irish?)
great-great-grandfather
on my father's side;
nameless
(Walker, perhaps?),
whose only remembered act
is that he raped
a child:
my great-great-grandmother,
who bore his son,
my great-grandfather,
when she was eleven.

Rest in peace.
The meaning of your lives

is still
unfolding.

Rest in peace.
In me
the meaning of your lives
is still
unfolding.

Rest in peace, in me.
The meaning of your lives
is still
unfolding.

Rest. In me
the meaning of your lives
is still
unfolding.

Rest. In Peace
in me
the meaning
of our lives
is still
unfolding.

Rest.

❚ How did you chart the prayer's progress for your audience?

Bibliography

Bodkin, Maud. *Archetypal Patterns in Poetry*. New York: Oxford University Press, 1963.
   Poetry analyzed in terms of Jung's theory of the collective unconscious. Psychological studies in imagination.

Brooks, Cleanth. *The Well Wrought Urn*. New York: Harcourt, Brace and World, 1947.
   Based on the theory of poetry as dramatic discourse and on the organic relationship of art and meaning in poetry. Essays on specific poems.

Brooks, Cleanth, and Robert Penn Warren. *Understanding Poetry.* 4th ed. New York: Holt, Rinehart and Winston, 1973.
A good introductory book. An anthology with critical discussions and commentaries on representative poems.

Ciardi, John. *How Does a Poem Mean?* Boston: Houghton Mifflin Company, 1959.
An excellent discussion of reading poetry, with particularly good examples. Covers many aspects of content and structure.

Crane, R. S. *The Languages of Criticism and the Structure of Poetry.* Toronto: University of Toronto Press, 1953.
A scholarly discussion on the complexities of poetic criticism.

Davie, Donald. *Articulate Energy: An Enquiry into the Syntax of English Poetry.* London: Routledge and Kegan Paul, 1955.
A somewhat specialized but stimulating examination of syntactical manipulations in a variety of poems.

Deutsch, Babette. *Poetry Handbook: A Dictionary of Terms.* New York: Funk and Wagnalls, 1957.
A complete, concise sourcebook of poetic terminology.

Eliot, T. S. *On Poetry and Poets.* New ed. New York: Farrar, Straus and Company, 1957.
Essays on poetry, poetic drama, and poetic criticism, with chapters on specific poets from Virgil to Yeats.

Empson, William. *Seven Types of Ambiguity.* 3rd ed. London: Chatto and Windus, 1956.
A scholarly consideration of imaginative language as it functions to convey several meanings simultaneously.

Frye, Northrop. *The Well-Tempered Critic.* Bloomington: Indiana University Press, 1963.
A refreshing re-evaluation of some traditional and contemporary modes of criticism.

Fussell, Paul, Jr. *Poetic Meter and Poetic Form.* New York: Random House, 1965.
A clear discussion of the elements of prosody.

Geiger, Don. *The Dramatic Impulse in Modern Poetics.* Baton Rouge: Louisiana State University Press, 1967.
An important book for its intelligent and readable consideration of the problem of persona, written by a poet and teacher of interpretation.

Gibbons, Reginald, ed. *The Poet's Work.* Boston: Houghton Mifflin Company, 1979.
Twenty poets, including Lorca, Stevens, Schwartz, Moore, Thomas, Williams, Auden, and Levertov, have written separate chapters on their methods and aims. Includes a selective bibliography on poets (such as Eliot) who have extensively written elsewhere on this subject.

Hackleman, Wauneta, ed. *The Study and Writing of Poetry: American Women Poets Discuss Their Craft.* Troy, N.Y.: Whitson Publishing Company, 1983.

Brief, readable essays by fifty women poets discussing abstract and organic forms of poetry and poetic technique, illustrated with examples from their own work and with poetry of their contemporaries.

Nemerov, Howard, ed. *Poets on Poetry.* New York: Basic Books, 1966.

Nineteen essays by poets on their own work. Contributors include Conrad Aiken, Marianne Moore, Richard Eberhart, John Berryman, May Swenson, Richard Wilbur, and James Dickey.

Preminger, Alex, Frank J. Warnke, and O. B. Hardison, Jr., eds. *Princeton Encyclopedia of Poetry and Poetics.* Enl. ed. Princeton, N.J.: Princeton University Press, 1974.

Comprehensive yet lucid treatment of all aspects of poetry by noted scholars. A bibliography of primary sources for further study accompanies each entry. A valuable reference tool.

Ransom, John Crowe. *The World's Body.* Baton Rouge: Louisiana State University Press, 1963.

A fine collection of fifteen essays, primarily on Ransom's own theory of poetry. The book offers a lucid explanation of the obscurity of contemporary verse.

Shapiro, Karl. *A Bibliography of Modern Prosody.* Baltimore: Johns Hopkins University Press, 1948.

A valuable sourcebook for detailed study of critical and practical discussions of poetic techniques.

Smith, Barbara Herrnstein. *Poetic Closure: A Study of How Poems End.* Chicago: University of Chicago Press, 1968.

A superb and lucid study of the behavior of poems. The book sees closure as "a function of the perception of structure." It draws on illustrations from all of the related arts.

Wimsatt, W. K., Jr. *The Verbal Icon: Studies in the Meaning of Poetry.* New York: Farrar, Straus and Company, 1954.

One of the classics of modern criticism, with particular attention to some of the fallacies of poetic criticism.

V

Group Performance

You must habit yourself to the dazzle of the light
      and of every moment in your life.

Long have you timidly waded holding a plank by the shore
Now I will you to be a bold swimmer
To jump off in the midst of the sea, rise again, nod to
      me, shout, and laughingly dash with your hair.

Walt Whitman, "Song of Myself"

THE GROUP PERFORMANCE OF LITERATURE

11

CLEARLY, THIS BOOK HAS BEEN written primarily for the solo interpreter. Nevertheless, group performance methods often help individuals to solve performance problems. Although there are fundamental differences between solo and group performances, there is a great deal of common ground. Unfortunately, in the past group performance too often meant that a collection of relatively like-minded solo interpreters agreed to attack the same text at the same time and place, although not necessarily in the same manner. Today, happily, groups successfully tackle everything from *Paradise Lost* to the wits of the Algonquin round table, or the literature of AIDS.

Some form of group performance of literature has existed since the rhapsodists read plays in relays in ancient Greece. In the past forty years — and particularly in the last two decades — this area of oral interpretation has flourished. Many reasons for the popularity of group performance undoubtedly exist. Known now as *Readers Theatre* (or *reader's theater*), *Chamber Theatre, mixed-media, compiled scripts*, or simply *group performance*, this exciting part of the experience of oral interpretation benefits from the professional theatre's concurrent interest in plays that feature presentational techniques. Contemporary plays freely range through several levels of consciousness, stop time to examine character motivation, frankly admit the illusion of the theatre, present a single character performed by several different performers to demonstrate the facets or sides of the character, or assign one performer many characters to portray with little outward differentiation. Such innovative techniques born in interpretation productions, transplanted and refined in theatrical settings, flourish and produce dramatic events centering on the staging of narrative (such as The Steppenwolf Company's *The Grapes of Wrath* or the Royal Shakespeare Company's monumental *Nicholas Nickelby*) or on collections of poems, letters, and memoirs (such as *Belle of Amherst*, a program celebrating Emily Dickinson).

Such crossbreeding has obliterated whatever line formerly separated "theatre performances" and "interp performances" and has encouraged many of the innovative developments that make group performance so attractive. Just as theatre events began to feature interpretation's experimental techniques, interpreters discovered that groups could solve literary problems with theatrical techniques. And as more interpreters explored group performance, scenography and staging became more elaborate, greater flexibility arose in developing performance analogues for literary devices, and the range of texts selected for performance broadened. The presence of several performers permitted — even demanded — greater physical and vocal variety. Frankly presentational performances capitalized on localized settings. More bodies and voices meant more opportunities (and more potential pitfalls) for interpreters to take on those texts a solo performer might understandably avoid — such as large group scenes, multiple attitudes, several scenes occurring simultaneously at the same or different locales, scenes with many characters, entire novellas, carefully abridged longer works, nonfiction works, experimental plays, concrete poetry, and texts that demand multiple media or that were not conceived with performance in mind.

The foundations remain the same: a group's analysis and rehearsal begin with, and return to, the embodying of the text. A group performance requires the same kind of technical facility as that needed by an individual performance. The interpreter's respect for the audience's proper function in the creation of the work never changes.

Understandably, with the changes that group performance underwent came dangers: an urge to provide a "good show" might sacrifice the intricacies of the text. Sometimes a director might channel a group's energies into exploring one aspect of the literature at the expense of others. Like any other kind of performance, group performance should present the text through the bodies and voices of the performers to an audience that joins with the performers to create the whole of the literary selection.

Readers Theatre

Readers Theatre and *Chamber Theatre* are two terms used to describe group performance events. For some they have relatively unrestricted meanings; for others *Readers Theatre* is an umbrella term referring to any group interpretation event, and *Chamber Theatre* refers specifically to the staging of narrative. In its broadest and simplest definition, Readers Theatre is a performance by a group of interpreters seeking to explore, to embody, and in special ways, to *feature* a given literary text. This convention of performance, with a long history rooted in the presentational modes of the ancient Greeks, is used today as an exciting and flexible method to explore drama, fiction, nonfiction, and poetry.

There is no recipe for a Readers Theatre production any more than there is a recipe for solo performance. Readers Theatre — like any group performance of literature — has developed because people have tried different ways to achieve the same goal. Because contemporary notions about Readers Theatre are flexible and accommodating, the future for Readers Theatre is particularly exciting.

Readers Theatre does have certain characteristics and criteria. One of the most obvious conventions of the Greek theatre, for example, figures prominently in most contemporary productions of Readers Theatre: the presentational, rather than the representational, reality of the performance. For the Greeks, the role of the actor was similar to the role of the priest — the actor symbolized the actions of the gods and the great mortals. During the ritual of the performance, the audience believed in the *re-enactment* of the story or play, rather than in its immediate illusion of reality. No Greek actually endured the travails of Oedipus; Medea was not meant to be like the woman next door. Telling the tale became the central focus: how beautifully the dance embodied the emotional dilemma of those colossal characters, how richly the cadences of the verse, with the delicate harmonies of the music, suggested the experiences of those great beings.

Suppose you attended a play about the last days of Abraham Lincoln. Your major concern would not be to know how things turn out, although you may become fearful and excited when Lincoln decides to attend the theatre one night in April. Rather, you would be interested in the character of the man himself. You would, perhaps, admire his efforts, regret his follies, pity his mistakes, understand his limitations; but in the end your attention would focus on how the story is told rather than on any of its events. Just as you might be curious about the way a playwright would tell the story of

Lincoln, the Greeks were interested in how that young playwright Euripides handled a tale previously told by Aeschylus.

This interest in presentation, in the manner of the telling and hence in the text itself, still primarily influences contemporary experiments in Readers Theatre. For one thing, there is no "fourth wall," or illusion of eavesdropping, in Readers Theatre, as there is in most realistic drama. The action is all turned outward because the performers frankly admit that the audience has come to see and hear a text. The performing space is a playing space from which you project the text, not unlike the space you silently describe for yourself when you begin a solo performance.

In the Greek theatre this space was called the *orkastra* and was often occupied by the chorus, since they were the ones who interpreted and reflected on the action by commenting about it to the audience. Because the Greek theatres were enormous and had no amplifiers, the actors wore masks with enormous features that not only revealed to even the most distant spectators the inner states of the characters but also projected their voices.

Shakespeare also used the stage as a projection space. Many of his characters talk in soliloquy directly to the playgoers, thus allowing them to participate in the characters' inner workings and motivations. Hamlet tells the audience what he's thinking and, quite openly in front of them, upbraids himself for what he sees as his cowardice.

These presentational conventions have also been used by many modern dramatists, including Sam Shephard, Bertolt Brecht, and Thornton Wilder. (See the Singer's interpretation of the internal life of Grusha and Simon in Brecht's *Caucasian Chalk Circle* at the end of this chapter.) The Readers Theatre would open up and project frankly out front a scene that a traditional theatrical convention might play as closed or onstage. When two characters (for example, George and Martha in Albee's *Who's Afraid of Virginia Woolf?*) talk to each other, traditional staging allows them to play to and with one another. The audience observes them. The line representing their tension is perpendicular to the sight lines of the audience. George moves toward Martha with a drink, facing her and expecting her to reach for the drink. Compare this with a Readers Theatre presentation of the same scene, in which George and Martha stand several feet apart and "look at" each other out front: that is, each sees the other directly in front, above, and slightly beyond the audience, as shown on page 429.

When George approaches Martha, he steps directly toward the audience. Martha sees him approaching as if he were entering from the audience and would reach out there for the drink he carries. Thus, audience members examine the play's multiple levels by sitting literally in the middle of the activity, participating intimately in what is going on between the characters. Furthermore, this form reveals secrets that a staged performance simply cannot disclose. When George approaches Martha with the drink, he offers to continue her inebriation, perpetuating her way of life. As she reaches for this

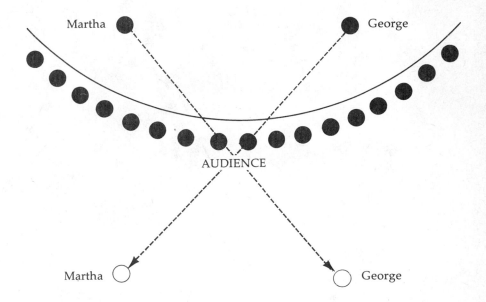

sustenance, we see how their codependence perpetuated "this sewer of a marriage." The image in front of us — Martha reaching out for help, George offering the alcoholic solution — is an icon of the play itself, foreshadowing what will happen and symbolizing what is wrong with George and Martha. Readers Theatre features this element of the text by frankly placing it out front.

Some technical problems arise in this form of performance, but these can be solved by careful thinking. George and Martha cannot be so close together on stage that it seems odd for them not to address each other. They cannot enter the same physical relationship that they would display in a staged production; nor can they intimately relate to a background of props and scenery as they might in a staged production. The formality of the convention prohibits such kinds of behavior, even as it allows other kinds. George advances forward rather than sideways. If he and Martha were close together, they might legitimately be expected to turn and talk to each other. If addressing another character out front instead of directly seems uncomfortable to you, think about the last time you had your hair cut. When the barber or stylist asked you about length and shaping, you probably looked at yourself in the mirror, responding to the reflected

questioner, who answered your questions by looking at your *reflection*, not at you.

The scene should be projected from a *playing space* or a *performance
area* neutral enough to suggest a locale that belongs neither to audience nor to characters. For us to accept the convention, the angles
of vision need to intersect. If George and Martha were to see one
another like this

they would not appear to be in the same scene; they would not
intersect. Moreover, this point of intersection must occur within the
audience, for there the action clashes. If the intersection of each angle
were to occur onstage, as in

AUDIENCE

the scene would still be closed, and it would seem extremely odd for the characters not to turn toward one another and play the scene in that closed space they both obviously occupy.

For the convention to be accepted, the tension of each character reaching for the other must pierce the "wall" that separates audience from character. Only then can the audience participate in the internal processes of each of the characters.

Readers Theatre enables a selection of literature to be presented so that performers — and the audience — share new insights into the text. To do this, the interpreter should keep responsibly and responsively in touch with the literature. In opening up the work, we must remain open to it.

Chamber Theatre

Chamber Theatre is a rewarding method to perform narrative fiction. Robert Breen, the scholar who was most responsible for the innovation and development of Chamber Theatre, defined it as "a technique for dramatizing the point of view of narrative fiction." We have discussed how, in narrative fiction, point of view manifests the relationships among the narrator and the characters and events of the story. Simply discovering the point of view does not solve all performance problems, of course, but it does provide the center of focus for a group wishing to demonstrate to an audience how a *specific* tale is related by a *specific* narrator. Moreover, Chamber Theatre embodies in concrete form the relationships between *that* narrator and *those* characters in *that* setting. Because the action of the novel unfolds with the immediacy of drama, the audience can see and hear the impact of the events on the characters; and because the narrator is retained, the governing central intelligence of the fiction so conditions the audience's view of the world that they listen to and watch exactly what — and *only* what — the narrator wants them to hear and see at the same time they see and hear what the performers embody.

A Chamber Theatre production of a novel or a story may boast all of the scenographic resources of a staged production of a play. Performers may be costumed, may appear without scripts of any kind, may represent one or several characters at one time, and may even focus on each other rather than out front. In all cases, narrators are present and highly visible onstage, *at the center of the action*. The narrators are not on the periphery watching the activity, unless they have momentarily stepped aside to let a scene between the characters play uninterrupted. Staged narrators participate in the action, organize it, unify it, just as they do in the novel. The heart of Chamber Theatre remains a careful and intelligent demonstration of the narrator. The narrator governs the selectivity of the story by directing the audience's attention and by conditioning the listeners' responses to the characters and the action.

The intriguing theoretical and aesthetic values of Chamber Theatre can best be understood after you look at a segment of a story from a practical point of view. One of the first elements to consider in the development of a Chamber Theatre production for the stage is the preparation of the script. Numerous choices are presented to the director/adapter. In grappling with the problems these choices present, we can examine some important features of this technique.

Read the following scene from Nathaniel West's *Miss Lonelyhearts*, a novel about a man in his middle thirties who is the author of an advice column in the New York *Post-Dispatch*. He is haunted by his troubled correspondents and plagued by moral and religious doubts. Miss Lonelyhearts (he is never given any other name in the novel) takes Mary Shrike, the wife of his editor, out for dinner. Although they share considerable intimacy, they are not having an affair.

She came out of the closet wearing a black lace slip and began to fix her hair in front of the dressing table. Miss Lonelyhearts bent down to kiss the back of her neck.

"Now, now," she said, acting kittenish, "you'll muss me."

He took a drink from the whiskey bottle, then made her a highball. When he brought it to her, she gave him a kiss, a little peck of reward.

"Where'll we eat?" she asked. "Let's go where we can dance. I want to be gay."

They took a cab to a place called El Gaucho. When they entered, the orchestra was playing a Cuban rhumba. A waiter dressed as a South-American cowboy led them to a table. Mary immediately went Spanish and her movements became languorous and full of abandon.

But the romantic atmosphere only heightened his feeling of icy fatness. He tried to fight it by telling himself that it was childish. What had happened to his great understanding heart? Guitars, bright shawls, exotic foods, outlandish costumes — all these things were part of the business of dreams. He had learned not to laugh at the advertisements offering to teach writing, cartooning, engineering, to add inches to the biceps and to develop the bust. He should therefore realize that the people who came to El Gaucho were the same as those who wanted to write and live the life of an artist, wanted to be an engineer and wear leather puttees, wanted to develop a grip that would impress the boss, wanted to cushion Raoul's head on their swollen breasts. They were the same people as those who wrote to Miss Lonelyhearts for help.

But his irritation was too profound for him to soothe it in this way.

For the time being, dreams left him cold, no matter how humble they were.

"I like this place," Mary said. "It's a little fakey, I know, but it's gay and I so want to be gay."

She thanked him by offering herself in a series of formal, impersonal gestures. She was wearing a tight, shiny dress that was like glass-covered steel and there was something cleanly mechanical in her pantomime.

"Why do you want to be gay?"

"Every one wants to be gay — unless they're sick."

Was he sick? In a great cold wave, the readers of his column crashed over the music, over the bright shawls and picturesque waiters, over her shining body. To save himself, he asked to see the medal. Like a little girl helping an old man to cross the street, she leaned over for him to look into the neck of her dress. But before he had a chance to see anything, a waiter came up to the table.

"The way to be gay is to make other people gay," Miss Lonelyhearts said. "Sleep with me and I'll be one gay dog."

The defeat in his voice made it easy for her to ignore his request and her mind sagged with his: "I've had a tough time," she said. "From the beginning, I've had a tough time. When I was a child, I saw my mother die. She had cancer of the breast and the pain was terrible. She died leaning over a table."

"Sleep with me," he said.

"No, let's dance."

"I don't want to. Tell me about your mother."

"She died leaning over a table. The pain was so terrible that she climbed out of bed to die."

Mary leaned over to show how her mother had died and he made another attempt to see the medal. He saw that there was a runner on it, but was unable to read the inscription.

"My father was very cruel to her," she continued. "He was a portrait painter, a man of genius, but . . ."

He stopped listening and tried to bring his great understanding heart into action again. Parents are also part of the business of dreams. My father was a Russian prince, my father was a Piute Indian chief, my father was an Australian sheep baron, my father lost all his money in Wall Street, my father was a portrait painter. People like Mary were unable to do without such tales. They told them because they wanted to talk about something besides clothing or business or the movies, because they wanted to talk about something poetic.

When she had finished her story, he said, "You poor kid," and leaned over for another look at the medal. She bent to help him and pulled out the neck of her dress with her fingers. This time he was able to read the inscription: "Awarded by the Boston Latin School for first place in the 100 yd. dash."

It was a small victory, yet it greatly increased his fatigue and he was glad when she suggested leaving.

The first "character" to consider is the narrator, who governs all our responses to Miss Lonelyhearts, the hero of the story. Many of Nathaniel West's narrators have characteristic and complex ways of telling their stories: the language of *Miss Lonelyhearts*, for example, is often as vivid and brutal as are its characters. Full of human misery presented in relentless progression, the novel moves swiftly and painfully to its final moments. The narrator does not spare us from suffering or unpleasantness. His metaphors throughout the novel are blunt, nightmarish, and disturbing, even though they are based on the everyday objects that swarm about the characters. Miss Lonelyhearts receives letters that are "stamped from the dough of suffering with a heart-shaped cookie knife," and we can see the pathetic, funny, and painfully mundane worlds their writers inhabit. The air in a little park smells "as though it had been artificially heated," and we detect the rancid oil and dense closeness of cheap rooms. The shadow of a lamppost pierced him "like a spear," and "the gray sky looked as if it had been rubbed with a soiled eraser." We see how ineffectual Miss Lonelyhearts is in relieving the pain suffered by the people who expect aid from him and how their expectations smudge even the daylight.

So, at the center of this novel is a narrator who speaks strong and vivid poetry. To eliminate such a person from the drama and let only the characters occupy the stage would render only part of the work, and an interpreter is interested in the fullest possible performance of the literature. The narrator points us carefully into the interior life of Miss Lonelyhearts himself; through the narrator we are privy to the tortured mind and spirit that seek to counsel the troubled world.

Let's get back to the scene itself: "She came out of the closet wearing a black lace slip and began to fix her hair in front of the dressing table." This stage direction describes simply and directly what Mary Shrike is doing, and yet the description itself indicates a deliberate move on her part. She is wearing *only* a slip. Why would a woman enter like that? Let us assign the line to the narrator, who is sure to point up that detail; perhaps he will even speak to both the audience and Miss Lonelyhearts, who needs to know that he is deliberately being tempted by Mary Shrike's display. Perhaps Miss Lonelyhearts does not know quite how to respond. He is, in a sense, impotent and is caught over and over again in the web of other people's problems. Since Miss Lonelyhearts is unsure, let the narrator tell him what to do: the line "Miss Lonelyhearts bent down to kiss the back of her neck" is spoken directly to Miss Lonelyhearts so that he knows what to do and so that the audience will not miss the closeness of his relationship with Mary.

"Now, now . . . you'll muss me" is obviously Mary's response to the kiss. She is, as you recall, at her dressing table, preening and admiring herself. Since "acting kittenish" is a conscious decision by Mary as well as another effort to tantalize Miss Lonelyhearts, Mary could take the entire line: " 'Now, now,' she said, acting kittenish, 'you'll muss me.' " Thus, she has a second level in the performance: there is a Mary who is in the scene, reacting and responding on the surface in the public way Miss Lonelyhearts sees; and there is a Mary who is inside watching herself, describing her own motivation. The next short paragraph gives another simple stage direction. There might be some value, though, in providing for the audience both the action that is performed by the characters and the narrator's description of it. "When he brought it to her, she gave him a kiss, a little peck of reward." But isn't "a little peck of reward" Miss Lonelyheart's attitude toward the kiss? If we allow him to say so, we can see the part of him that corresponds to the second, interior side of Mary. In revealing these various aspects, the director and adapter of a Chamber Theatre production can amplify and expand on the numerous levels of the text, clarifying the author's artistry.

There is even a further possibility in the exchange between Mary and Miss Lonelyhearts. Because scenes in the novel shift fluently from speakeasy to bedroom, from Shrike's apartment to the office, to the little park, even from wakefulness to sleep, the staging requires a mobility that realistic or detailed scenography would prohibit. The space of the novel itself is more psychological than physical. Miss Lonelyhearts moves about his world as through a void, caught here or there by the disturbing troubles of his correspondents. If there are only a few set pieces and specific scenes are suggested by neutral properties, then the void of Miss Lonelyhearts's world can be demonstrated without the problems of sixteen full sets with attendant decorations.

Such flexibility itself leads to some tantalizing possibilities, since it becomes the physical or performance analogue for the literary construction that is our imagined world of Miss Lonelyhearts. Throughout the novel we read the letters — full texts of pleas from "Sick-of-it-all" or "Desperate" or "Harold S." or "Broad Shoulders" — but Miss Lonelyhearts actually meets only one of the correspondents during the story. Still, since he doesn't have real bodies for them, his tortured consciousness creates real people. He *sees* them everywhere; they have a palpable reality for him. How can he be sure that the woman he passes on the street is not the woman who left her husband because he had contracted tuberculosis and she couldn't stand the smell of death?

Marvelously, Chamber Theatre creates these ghosts: the interpreter playing Miss Lonelyhearts confronts *living* letters — real people who pursue him and invade his consciousness at strategic points throughout the action. One may haunt him during the scene with Mary Shrike. The set is minimal, so why not let "Sick-of-it-all" or "Disillusioned-with-Tubercular-Husband" hold Mary's mirror for her? And do you even need an actual glass? Try using just the empty oval mirror frame, so that when Miss Lonelyhearts crosses the room to hand Mary her drink, as he bends over to kiss her neck, he sees into the mirror, and there, where there ought to be the face of Mary Shrike, he sees the haunting face of one of the correspondents he cannot escape. Staring at that face and thinking, "Will I never be free?" he could hear Mary Shrike's words — echoed by the face in the glass — "Where'll we eat? Let's go where we can dance. I want to be gay."

The novel has begun to become as immediate as a play: you have given it the simultaneity of drama, since more than one thing is happening at once. Of course the serial perception of the novel is not lost because the narrator sustains the importance of the progress through the fiction; but in Chamber Theatre we see both the question and the answer at the same time. Miss Lonelyhearts is caught vividly between the forces that will destroy him: the decadence and emptiness of Mary Shrike and her world and the pain and privation of the world of "Sick-of-it-all." What an irony it is for Miss Lonelyhearts to seek escape in Mary Shrike's mirror, only to find there the face of the very specter he most wants to avoid!

After Mary says, "I want to be gay," the action speeds up and, as if in a film, we jump to the cab and then to the entrance of El Gaucho. Such a rapid transition requires the stage to be as flexible and dynamic as the screen. There is no scenery to move around, happily; at the center there is the one who describes the setting — the narrator, who can cross-fade or dissolve a scene by saying a few words, or by merely walking in front of it. You can let the narrator suspend or protract time; and using this person's special relationship with the audience, you can have the narrator cross down toward the audience, summarizing with the line, "They took a cab to a place called El Gaucho." Mary and Miss Lonelyhearts need do no more than get up and turn arm-in-arm to face what has now become the entrance to the restaurant. If the narrator slips a white towel over an arm and prepares to function as one of the minor service characters, Miss Lonelyhearts himself can observe, after he hears the music, "When they entered, the orchestra was playing a Cuban rhumba." Then the narrator could lead the two characters around the stage back to the seats center, saying, "A waiter dressed as a South-American cowboy led them to a table." Mary, caught up in the atmosphere and again conscious of the effect of her actions, could say, "Mary immediately went Spanish and her movements became languorous and full of abandon."

Mary's comment, spoken about herself, might sound awkward to a beginning performer. You might be troubled by characters' speaking about themselves in the third person or in the past tense, but you should remember that all of the performers on the stage are telling and showing the story to the audience. A slight alienation effect — much like the one created in the Epic Theatre of Brecht or in the Japanese Noh drama — is created when characters are allowed to perceive themselves as participants in a scene. This distancing can have aesthetic value as well: it may serve to bring us even closer to the characters, since it reminds us that they lead only fictional lives. And such third-person talk is really not so foreign to everyday lives. Perhaps you have heard a woman cautioning her child, "Mommy doesn't want her little girl to get too near the hot stove."

As Mary plunges into the ambience of El Gaucho, Miss Lonely-hearts becomes troubled and pulls into himself. Although this internalization would be hidden from an audience at a play, the narrator (who has dropped the waiter persona), privy to the workings of Miss Lonelyhearts's heart, reports what an audience needs to know: "But the romantic atmosphere only heightened his feeling of icy fatness." It would be ludicrous to stage this moment with the narrator and characters far apart physically. The closer they are to each other temperamentally, the closer their placement on the stage should be, and the more they will share in the same experience. In this way too, you can achieve on stage the performance analogue of West's fiction.

Have the narrator speak the line "But the romantic . . . fatness" directly to Miss Lonelyhearts, who, in turn, can respond directly to the narrator with, "He tried to fight it by telling himself that it was childish." This interchange is a good opportunity for Miss Lonely-hearts to tell his response physically *to himself* as if he were the narrator, who functions throughout the novel as Miss Lonelyhearts's alter ego. The result is really a dialogue scene. It takes place on the stage, which for the moment becomes Miss Lonelyhearts's mind. Both performers should play to each other, listening and responding to each other.

NARRATOR: What had happened to his great understanding heart?
MISS L.: Guitars, bright shawls, exotic foods, outlandish costumes — all these things were part of the business of dreams.

NARRATOR: He had learned not to laugh at the advertisements offering to teach writing, cartooning, engineering, to add inches to the biceps and to develop the bust.

MISS L.: He should therefore realize that the people who came to El Gaucho were the same as those who wanted to write and live the life of an artist,

NARRATOR: wanted to be an engineer and wear leather puttees,

MISS L.: wanted to develop a grip that would impress the boss,

NARRATOR: wanted to cushion Raoul's head on their swollen breasts.

MISS L.: They were the same people as those who wrote to Miss Lonelyhearts for help.

NARRATOR: But his irritation was too profound for him to soothe it in this way.

MISS L.: For the time being, dreams left him cold, no matter how humble they were.

At this point, Mary stops this internal scene by intruding the external world of the nightclub, "I like this place." Now try to adapt the rest of the scene. When does the narrator step in to advance the action? Is there more internal dialogue? ("Was he sick?") What happens when you get to the paragraph in which suffering voices seem to invade Miss Lonelyhearts's heart with "My father was a Russian prince," "my father lost all his money in Wall Street," and so on? Can you use those other specters again?

Each of the narrative forms we examined in Chapter 6 — a third-person narrator who is objective, a second-person narrator who addresses a character within the tale, or a first-person narrator who is a character in a story — has its own opportunities for demonstration. Any narration — prose or verse, fiction or nonfiction — can benefit from the scrutiny that Chamber Theatre affords.

What Chamber Theatre tells us about the nature of the relationships in narration should not be separated from its entertainment or performance value. Like all forms of interpretation, Chamber Theatre should be based on a clear understanding of the principles involved in the mode of presentation, a careful analysis of the author's achievement, and a high degree of artistic integrity and flexibility. Chamber Theatre does not make plays out of stories. It presents fiction *as it was written*, with the narration making point of view as vividly physical as it is focal. Summary, scene, and description all perform their usual functions; and performers physically embody literary style. For Chamber Theatre to serve the narrative, the interpreter undertakes all of these responsibilities in the spirit of experiment and inquiry, attempting at all times to stage what the author has conceived. The transformation of the story thus becomes an endless process of discovery in which all of the skills you have learned contribute to the fullest performance of the text.

Group Performance of Compiled Scripts

With an increasing interest in the group performance of nonfiction texts came experiments to combine fiction and nonfiction in full-length programs. Essays, reportage, impressions, memoirs, travel literature, diaries, oral histories, and testimony all offer interesting opportunities for group performance and can be approached by a group using the methods of Chamber Theatre or Readers Theatre. By supplementing material with slides, film, television, tapes, or other media, interpreters use tools of the electronic era to examine the various levels of life in a text.

The techniques used in Readers Theatre and Chamber Theatre are flexible enough to be adapted to the performance of such compiled scripts, but the interpreter should keep several key responsibilities in mind. First, the shape of the entire program should reflect the intention of the works involved; too often the performer can lose sight of the whole when closely engaged with each segment. Second, whatever nonliterary material is used should contribute to the entire program, rather than appearing for its own sake. Film and sound effects can be very enriching, but the goal should not simply be a slide show with words. The works of literature should illuminate each other, and their relationship should be clear to the audience. Third, compiled scripts should be constructed with a clear beginning, middle, and end. Their components should be cohesive, and although they may not be of the same mode or genre, they should still contribute in some apparent way to the progress of the entire program. Combining a series of smaller pieces can lead to either coalescence or diffusion — to a totality that is greater than the sum of the parts, or to simply a string of parts. The possibilities of multimedia presentations are tempting. Remember that it is better to examine *some* of the levels of a text clearly and precisely than all the levels (or even most of the levels) muddily or incompletely.

Suggestions for program possibilities are endless. The requirements of each performance opportunity will restrict your choices and suggest new and sometimes widely different concepts. If the faithful communication of text always remains your guideline, with each selection you will begin an exciting and thoroughly uncharted experiment.

Current interest in nonfiction, journals, letters, diaries, maga-

zines, and newspapers as sources for group performance has probably resulted from a desire for new types of material and from the
flexibility of these texts. To celebrate a particular date, such as the
founding of a town or a school, a group of performers could combine
audio, visual, or physical representations with selections from several
area or national newspapers and magazines, thereby suggesting what
was happening in the rest of the world at that particular time. A
group also could celebrate the variety and impact of a particular
publication by presenting selections that represent the publication's
characteristic quality or attitude. (Appendix A discusses a production
of the *New York Times*.) Groups have commonly celebrated events or
anniversaries by combining original documents, diaries, letters, and
dispatches with journal accounts that have appeared in various places
and relate to the commemorated event.

There are great opportunities for research in such programs,
apart from the obvious searches through archives and back issues of
serial publications. Consider obtaining oral histories from people who
recall the events, who knew the chief agents, or who felt the events'
impact directly. Don't stop with "literary" texts: popular music, art,
advertisements, and architecture all can contribute to understanding
and embodying this different culture. Such presentations also encourage nonperformers to experience the rewards of performing and
can lead to powerful converts to oral interpretation.

Commercial art often characterizes a time or an event: posters,
handbills, advertisements, and catalogs give an excellent impression
of what life was like during a particular time. If you select an event
in the not-too-distant past, you can also use audio and video recordings. A production about Chautauqua, New York (see Appendix B),
might feature the advertisements and announcements that heralded
the annual opening; typical speeches and performances; photographs
or sketches (published and private); songs from original presentations; and descriptions of people who used Chautauqua as a base for
their national activities. Through costume, slide, film, sound, and
performance, a group can evoke the earnest yet brash approach of
the era in its attempt to popularize and democratize "culture."

Fanny Burney's late eighteenth-century diaries and letters can tie
together an examination of the world in which she traveled and of
the people she knew. In depicting that rare woman who was accepted
as an equal in exclusively male circles, a performance could examine
her peculiar impact on the literary and political titans of her day,
giving as well substantial attention to her characteristic contributions
to English literature, to the curious London of the late 1700s, to its
fashions and its colorful underworld.

Joan Didion's extended essay "Slouching Towards Bethlehem,"

which describes in a cinematic series of sixty-three incidents and scenes the social atmosphere of San Francisco's Haight-Ashbury district in 1967, could be supplemented with contemporaneous videotape, film, slides, newspaper accounts, political speeches, music, and commercial advertisements. Such material, if arranged as carefully as her essay is, could further demonstrate Didion's view of the atomization of American culture in the late sixties and her pervading sense that, as Yeats said in "The Second Coming" (Chapter 4), "the centre cannot hold."

Or comb the several works about the American experience in Vietnam. Any of the several oral histories of the soldiers who served there (such as Al Santoli's *Everything We Had* — see the excerpt at the end of this chapter — or Wallace Terry's *Bloods*), or the histories of the people who made the decisions about involving American personnel (such as Stanley Karnow's *Vietnam*), or the reportage filed on the scene (such as Michael Herr's *Dispatches*), or the attitudes about U.S. involvement offered by an articulate officer (such as Philip Caputo's *A Rumor of War*), or the effects of the war at home (as in C. D. B. Bryan's *Friendly Fire*) offer numerous powerful passages for performance. Combined with video and film clips from television news reports or press conferences, with newspaper headlines and music of the period, and perhaps with clips from films that examine the experience (such as Francis Ford Coppola's *Apocalypse Now*) and the testimony of the many Vietnamese who now live in America, an interpreter could shape a stirring and powerful production. Indeed, any major historical event, for example, the Holocaust, the civil rights struggles, or the Depression, offers countless opportunities to examine and understand. Ken Burns's monumental video exploration of the Civil War displays how tellingly image and sound, word and picture can touch the reaches of our national consciousness. Terrible events, when carefully scrutinized, reveal human beings in the very acts of heroism and cowardice that are the stuff of great literature. To share such truth with an audience can be both ennobling and entertaining.

The most valuable tools for the director-adapter to use in this form of script composition are imagination and tact when drawing relationships between events and texts. Keep your mind open to possible inclusions and remember that an artfully structured program that allows the greatest flexibility and achieves the maximum impact has at its center substantial literature that is worth performing. Perform the literature as fully as possible, while simultaneously suggesting what the event, time, or publication was like. Performing the individual components does not differ significantly in responsibility from any other type of group performance. Chamber Theatre techniques work just as richly with nonfiction narrative as they do with fiction; bodies and voices can suggest the nonverbal and visual elements as well as they do in Readers Theatre or Chamber Theatre productions.

Other Kinds of Literature

We have described some of the techniques that are used in Readers Theatre and Chamber Theatre and have discussed some of the ways in which compiled scripts are prepared. The current interest in the group performance of literature is not limited to these methods, however, and a great deal of excitement and many discoveries can be generated when a group attempts to perform materials that are not usually associated with performance, such as concrete poetry or filmscripts, to name only two of the countless possibilities. Naturally, these sources should conform to the original criteria for selecting performance material; but the new challenges each form creates offer experienced students new ways to understand literature.

Concrete poetry can be defined broadly as a verbal work in which visual, tactile, or iconographic representation carries at least as much weight as any of the denotative and connotative meanings of the words. Sometimes concrete poems are printed in patterns, which themselves tell stories about the "text" of the poem; sometimes they are not reproducible as print on paper but rather appear as pictures or forms or sculpture or even, appropriately enough, castings in concrete. Once again, *form* is tangible, realizable in three dimensions.

When you decide to perform a sonnet, you consider that the poem is composed of fourteen lines of iambic pentameter that follow a particular rhyme scheme and obey certain formal strictures regarding octave and sestet. All of these elements are parts of the poem's *form*, and your performance corresponds to that form, insofar as your body and your voice are able. Of course, all poetry — all literature — has form. Concrete poetry asks you to present in your performance, as fully as your bodies and voices can, a form that corresponds to the form of the work. Because group performance allows much greater flexibility in the creation of that form, concrete poetry allows groups to experiment with the sounds and attitudes of the work by using the combined voices and bodies to suggest — in three dimensions — the full size and shape of the poem. Mary Ellen Solt's "Forsythia" and Reinhard Döhl's "Apfel" (both at the end of this chapter) are both enormously challenging and a great deal of fun. Your experience thus far probably will not have prepared you for this kind of experimentation; we encourage you to stretch your understanding of performance. The interpreter who attempts that stretch will perform more traditional literatures in a much broader world. Not everyone masters every form instantly, but all responsible artists try to discover ways to refine their art and techniques.

Initially it would seem that to perform a filmscript would come easily to interpreters. Filmscripts are, after all, plays put on film; and interpreters perform plays all the time. Even a cursory study of literate scripts, however, indicates how very different a good film is from a play, although the outward similarities of dialogue remain obvious (see Penelope Gilliatt's fine screenplay for *Sunday, Bloody Sunday* at the end of this chapter). Rather, a better analogy can be made between fiction and film — that of a narrator and the eye of a camera. If you are particularly impressed by a filmscript, why not perform it by casting a performer as the camera and allowing that interpreter to perform all of the camera directions? The performer would operate much as a narrator would in a work of narrative fiction. You could develop the cinematic sense by continuing the analogy when the camera, in its role as eye, displays carefully to the audience what it wants them to see. Since characters in film exist only insofar as the camera sees or hears them, why not show them similarly in the production? The camera can show characters, indicating carefully what the audience is to see; perhaps the camera could even assist a character in performing actions an audience should see, and then, as it turns its eye to someone else, let the *performer* resume normal behavior. The tension that is created between the illusion of what the camera shows and what is seen after the camera leaves can demonstrate still another level of the tale. Or you can continue the tension of the scene among the characters until the scene concludes.

Directing the Group Performance of Literature

Whatever form of the group performance of literature that you choose to explore, you will face problems that always confront groups, specifically the usual limitations of time, talent, cooperation, and technical demands. The following discussion will not answer all the questions you are likely to encounter, but it can give you an idea of the kinds of problems that most often plague group performances.

Group performance demands a substantial commitment in terms of analysis, rehearsal, spectacle, and staging. The potential rewards are considerable and, make no mistake, very different from the rewards of solo performance. As you develop expertise and begin to trust yourself and your choice of literature, you will undoubtedly acquire your own method of proceeding. Use the following suggestions as a source of good advice, not as recipes or rigid regulations.

The director's first responsibility is to prepare the script for performance. Allow for innovation during rehearsal, but provide the individual performers with the foundation to begin their explorations. Use the touchstones for selecting literature with which you are by now familiar, and which you can present fully in terms of cast, staging, scenography, and rehearsal time.

Suppose you choose Bernard Malamud's "The Prison" (Chapter 6). Now, you begin a series of questions for yourself that do not end until well after the final performance. Do you fully understand everything that is going on in the story? Read it again, and then again, to be sure. Look at other stories by Malamud. How can you cast the story with the available performers? (If yours is a group of eleven nine-year-olds, you probably can't.) Do you have enough time to prepare the story? Will you be able to suggest the atmosphere of the candy store, its inhabitants, and their lives?

Reread the story. What interests you? Do you visualize any particular image that suggest what the audience might see? Have you any ideas — even vague ones — of how a specific scene or a sentence or even a phrase may sound or look to an audience? Reread the story again. Do you still want to spend all the time and effort on this work? If you are still convinced of your choice at this point, prepare a *working* script.

Next you must solve the issue of permissions. Performance outside of class — whether for public audiences or other classmates, regardless of whether an admission fee is charged — requires permission from the copyright holder. Although the work you select may be in the public domain, even older works (such as the plays of Shakespeare) exist in several different editions, each the product of an editor who holds the copyright on the work. Rather than risk any legal unpleasantness, write a letter well ahead of time to the publisher(s) of the work(s) you are presenting, stating performance dates and the nature of your production plans for each work you are using. You may wish to enclose a copy of the script you have prepared. Only when you receive the permission of the copyright holder are you legally (and ethically) free to show your work to the public. Because you have chosen Malamud's "The Prison," contact the copyright holder, Farrar, Strauss and Giroux, Inc.

Since this story features a narrator who is sympathetic toward the central character, you will use the technique of Chamber Theatre for your presentation. Examine the story from the perspectives of the audience and of the director, using the analytical principles we discussed in chapters 2, 5, and 6 as well as the technical suggestions given earlier in this chapter. Many of your decisions will be adjusted or even discarded when rehearsal comes, and some things that you think ought to work stupendously will have to be changed.

What of the playing space and its configuration? At this point, you should make some firm decisions about the visual statement you expect the performance to make. Typically, this decision will be based on the amount of time and money you budget and on the degree to which crucial action, properties, and scenes must be enacted. Don't waste time, money, and effort trying to dress an army battalion in complete costumes when helmets alone might suffice admirably. Audiences can create finer settings than any designer if given the proper clues. Slides and filmclips can suggest a Boeing 747 in flight; one period chair can suggest an entire English great house library. The settings need to be available soon into the rehearsal period because the longer the performers work with them, the more confident they will appear to the audience.

Several business problems re-emerge. Has the publisher responded to your request for permission? If not, write again. Programs, tickets, ushers, advertising, house management, and other similar details can quickly grow into major dilemmas if ignored. Can you count on someone reliable to assist in any of this? Enlist that person now.

Even though you have not even begun to audition potential performers, you have made tremendous progress toward your goal. Avoid performing and directing simultaneously, since both tasks are difficult enough alone. When you audition performers for your production, you will doubtless have ideas about how each of the characters should behave; possibly you will have a specific person in mind for a particular part. Allow each auditioning performer sufficient time to make an impression but do not waste that person's — and your own — time. If there is no possible way for the seven-foot-tall basketball player to play a little girl, don't expect him or ask him to try. Generally, you should cast the strongest performer as the narrator because, as we read in Chapter 6, the narrator carries the heaviest burden by being responsible for moving along the action of the story. Be sure that the performers whom you have tentatively selected look and sound appropriate together; unless you wish to achieve some comic or outlandish effect, be sure that they are able to operate as an ensemble. For many directors, casting a production is the most difficult job, but if you have done your homework, you know what you need. Take the time you need to make sure you have what you want, but make the choice as soon as you can.

Now put cast and *tentative* script together. See what the story does under the close pressure of the group's attention to it. Watch what happens as the performers begin to feel their bodies and their voices. Be patient, attentive, and clearsighted: respond to the performers with suggestions. Answer their questions frankly. A performer needs to understand the perspective of the director, but also wants room to create. Don't crowd the performers with too many details too soon. They need a little freedom to get used to new ways of walking, talking, seeing, and thinking. Give them time.

Slowly the story will begin to come alive, sometimes through only a sentence or a phrase, in brief moments. Work out a rehearsal schedule that uses each performer's time economically. Does the distribution of lines exactly demonstrate the relationship between narrator and character? Serious and responsible interpreters will begin by asking questions and end by helping. In this process of creating, everyone involved comes to know the story at its fullest.

The production should be on its feet now; if you will not be using books, they should be disappearing at this point. Certain moments should be emerging as clear and stable, but do not allow the story to become glib or easy. Inexperienced performers might want now to simply say the words without remembering what the words carry. Be patient. At this point in rehearsal, no performer wants (or needs) to hear, "Something's wrong with that line; try it another way." Specify what you expect; be prepared to let the performer work on it, too.

As the performance date approaches, integrate the technical elements as soon as they are available. Sound and film cues should be rehearsed as often as possible to enable the people responsible for their operation to understand how their contribution enhances the entire presentation. Also, the performers have to know what is going on around and behind them so that they can cooperate with it. In performance the flexibility of people must accommodate the inflexibility of the machines. It frequently makes sense to rehearse only the technical elements, including lights, tapes, film, and set or property changes. Don't cut corners or time at this point in the rehearsal period: be sure that every item that must be obtained or action that must be performed is clear and set and ready.

The scenography is ready; the performers are rehearsed; the script probably looks somewhat different from what you originally intended, but somehow more accurate than you imagined. Run-throughs before an audience of sympathetic friends alert performers to how an audience may respond, and where to expect a laugh. Follow each rehearsal with brief discussions with performers and technical people to solve new problems as well as to improve the production.

Each performance ought to be a learning experience for you: take notes and discover the story under the pressure of performance with an audience. This production probably will not capture everything you know to be in the story; nor will it represent everything this group of people is capable of doing. But you have begun.

Some Concluding Cautions

The suggestions we give are not the only ways to perform these materials or direct group performance. Many difficulties attend the group performance of literature. Everything printed — and even that which is not printed — is fair game for the sensitive, serious, and tactful interpreter. If you have understood and followed the touchstones we present at the beginning of the book, you will be able to present literature and performances that interest your audiences.

We are convinced that the students who enjoy and learn from solo performance can develop deeper, richer, and special kinds of knowledge from working with each other in group performances. If the texts remain the center of your attention and interest, the kinds of knowledge you derive from group performance will enormously expand the limits of the literature. No one method of performance is always best for all kinds of literature with all casts. Most good literature responds in different ways to the pressure put on it by different performance techniques, yielding quite diverse and surprising discoveries under each different test. Only the potential rewards are limitless.

Analyzing the Performance

Admitting that a group performance differs from a solo performance suggests that the criteria for evaluating the two kinds of performance must be different. This suggestion is both true and insufficient. Group performances are made up of individual performers, and many of their responsibilities are not radically different from those we have discussed thus far. Each performer must understand the language of the text; must carefully attend to the tone, color, and imagery of the text; and must be able to be seen and heard without difficulty. In short, each performer must suggest the intellectual, emotional, and aesthetic entirety of that segment of the whole work that is his or her specific charge.

In a group performance, however, each individual executes these responsibilities in concert with other interpreters, under the direction of still another interpreter whose general vision and principal concern remains the work as a whole. The audience responds to the contributions of several individuals. Analyzing such performances often requires a preliminary sorting out of responsibilities and an attempt to understand, first of all, what was *conceived* before judging what was *achieved*.

This procedure does not greatly differ from the familiar process of analysis we have examined throughout this book — describing what was seen and heard and comparing that description with the text itself. In analyzing a group performance, however, some special questions arise that can apply to performances of narration, lyric poetry, dramatic prose, or any combination of these types. First, however, be sure that you are familiar with the specific kinds of questions that the efficient management of body and voice bring to mind (see chapters 2 and 4). If you are unsure about problems in performing narration, consult Chapter 6; if the performance analysis of drama still puzzles you, see Chapter 8; techniques for discussing the performance of poetry appear in Chapter 10. These questions all provide the foundation on which we can build some questions for group performance.

How did the presentational nature of the Readers Theatre display the text? Was the literature the center of the production?

Did the various interpreters vocally and physically demonstrate significantly different aspects of the literature?

How did the individual performers contribute to the total impression of the event? Did they detract from the aesthetic entirety? How?

What dimensions of the text(s) seemed most fully demonstrated in performance? What dimensions needed to be clearer? Give specific examples.

How well did the individual performers project themselves into the audience? Was there sufficient opportunity for the audience to participate in the creation of the work?

Was the overall concept both clear and responsive to the text(s) performed?

In a Chamber Theatre performance of a story (or stories), was the narrator central or incidental to the action? How was the narrative presence demonstrated in performance? What dimensions were emphasized by the group? What dimensions were ignored or lost?

Was the distribution of dialogue lines appropriate to the characters? What was demonstrated when the characters spoke narrative lines? Were there clear and apparent reasons in the story?

How did the scenography clarify and refine the goals of the story? What functions did members of the group serve in making these goals clear during performance?

How did this adaptation of the story explore dimensions or levels a solo performer could not?

In a compiled script, did the components individually and collectively advance the progress and intention of the entire program? Did each component clearly and significantly contribute to a newer, fuller understanding of the topic? Was the beginning concise? Did the development cover all the major aspects? Was the climax clearly presented? Did the conclusion permit the audience to understand the full implications of the works and the topic?

Did nonliterary material clearly serve the texts? Were the media used effectively? How did the media used clarify those dimensions of the work(s) inaccessible to the performers?

Was there sufficient variety in the selections and modes of performance to sustain the audience's interest? Did the components appropriately contrast tempo, rhythm, attitude, and persona?

Finally, what did you see and hear from the group that you could not have seen and heard from an individual? How did this enrich your understanding and appreciation of the material performed? How did the vividness of collected bodies and voices demonstrate the intentions of the literature?

Obviously, you can develop further questions that respond more accurately to any specific presentation. Remember that as the number of performers increases, the number of potential problems a director can face increases geometrically. The realms of literature open to group performance almost always make the possibility of staging an attractive option. In that "almost" is all of the attraction and danger of the experience.

Selections for Analysis and Oral Interpretation

This tale — familiar although told in quite a startling way — is drawn from Anne Sexton's *Transformations*. Once again, the audience in the work occupies a central position. Be sure to personify the curiously contemporary narrator. Can you determine the fulcrum? Why is it where it is?

Cinderella
ANNE SEXTON

You always read about it:
the plumber with twelve children
who wins the Irish Sweepstakes.

From toilets to riches.
That story.

Or the nursemaid,
some luscious sweet from Denmark
who captures the oldest son's heart.
From diapers to Dior.
That story.

Or a milkman who serves the wealthy,
eggs, cream, butter, yogurt, milk,
the white truck like an ambulance
who goes into real estate
and makes a pile.
From homogenized to martinis at lunch.

Or the charwoman
who is on the bus when it cracks up
and collects enough from the insurance.
From mops to Bonwit Teller.
That story.

Once
the wife of a rich man was on her deathbed
and she said to her daughter Cinderella:
Be devout. Be good. Then I will smile
down from heaven in the seam of a cloud.
The man took another wife who had
two daughters, pretty enough
but with hearts like blackjacks.
Cinderella was their maid.
She slept on the sooty hearth each night
and walked around looking like Al Jolson.
Her father brought presents home from town,
jewels and gowns for the other women
but the twig of a tree for Cinderella.
She planted that twig on her mother's grave
and it grew to a tree where a white dove sat.
Whenever she wished for anything the dove
would drop it like an egg upon the ground.
The bird is important, my dears, so heed him.

Next came the ball, as you all know.
It was a marriage market.

The prince was looking for a wife.
All but Cinderella were preparing
and gussying up for the big event.
Cinderella begged to go too.
Her stepmother threw a dish of lentils
into the cinders and said: Pick them
up in an hour and you shall go.
The white dove brought all his friends;
all the warm wings of the fatherland came,
and picked up the lentils in a jiffy.
No, Cinderella, said the stepmother,
you have no clothes and cannot dance.
That's the way with stepmothers.

Cinderella went to the tree at the grave
and cried forth like a gospel singer:
Mama! Mama! My turtledove,
send me to the prince's ball!
The bird dropped down a golden dress
and delicate little gold slippers.
Rather a large package for a simple bird.
So she went. Which is no surprise.
Her stepmother and sisters didn't
recognize her without her cinder face
and the prince took her hand on the spot
and danced with no other the whole day.

As nightfall came she thought she'd better
get home. The prince walked her home
and she disappeared into the pigeon house
and although the prince took an axe and broke
it open she was gone. Back to her cinders.
These events repeated themselves for three days.
However on the third day the prince
covered the palace steps with cobbler's wax
and Cinderella's gold shoe stuck upon it.
Now he would find whom the shoe fit
and find his strange dancing girl for keeps.
He went to their house and the two sisters
were delighted because they had lovely feet.
The eldest went into a room to try the slipper on
but her big toe got in the way so she simply
sliced it off and put on the slipper.
The prince rode away with her until the white dove

told him to look at the blood pouring forth.
That is the way with amputations.
They don't just heal up like a wish.
The other sister cut off her heel
but the blood told as blood will.
The prince was getting tired.
He began to feel like a shoe salesman.
But he gave it one last try.
This time Cinderella fit into the shoe
like a love letter into its envelope.

At the wedding ceremony
the two sisters came to curry favor
and the white dove pecked their eyes out.
Two hollow spots were left
like soup spoons.

Cinderella and the prince
lived, they say, happily ever after,
like two dolls in a museum case
never bothered by diapers or dust,
never arguing over the timing of an egg,
never telling the same story twice,
never getting a middle-age spread,
their darling smiles pasted on for eternity.
Regular Bobbsey Twins.
That story.

▌ Is the narrator's body in the same world as the characters'
 bodies? Did your audience see that?

This excerpt suggests the torturous internal life of a soldier in Vietnam. It
seems as if several different forces are battling within James Bombard's mind.
Why not personify each of these agents and let them together demonstrate
the war within this soldier that mirrors the war surrounding him?

FROM *Everything We Had*
AL SANTOLI

James Bombard
Rifle Platoon Leader
101st Airborne Division
Phan Rang
December 1967 – February 1968

I can remember sitting at McCord Air Base before I went to Vietnam with a friend of mine, Hunter Shotwell, he and his wife. He was a West Pointer and had been to Vietnam before the build-up as an adviser. He was from Massachusetts. He had a beautiful wife and a little child, it was beautiful. I said to him, "Hunter, why are you going back? You're going to get out of the Army." He wanted to be a lawyer. He wanted to set his life in motion. And he said, "I'm going back because I am a soldier." I said, "But you're leaving the military." He said, "But I believe in the nation and I believe that this is my duty. I went to West Point. I am leaving, but I must shoulder the responsibility of leadership." Hunter was a patrician and from a good family. Hunter and I and his wife proceeded to have a few beers and we were pretty mellow when we left together that day. We had served together in the 82nd, we were very close. He had been a hockey player and I was a hockey player, and we had a lot to talk about. He represented everything that was good about the country, the future of the country — it was bright, he was bright, he was handsome. He was everything that our generation stood for.

Right after the Tet offensive I found out that Hunter Shotwell had been killed. And I couldn't help but feel that had been such a loss, such a waste. I had seen other people killed, I had experienced the loss of many friends closer than Hunter was to me, guys I was in the field with . . . But somehow his death to me was the most significant, the most moving. Somehow I saw that he had served, he had shouldered his responsibility and yet he had done it again. The nation shouldn't have asked him to do it again. He represented to me what was good and right in the nation. And he was destroyed. I thought of his little child and his wife, what that did to them. And with that death and many like his, with each death a little bit of the fiber of what was good in this country was being destroyed. That's what bothered me.

I didn't see Hunter Shotwell get killed, but I felt like I had. There were many people close to us in the field who were killed. Doc Brown. I remember Doc Brown was a medic who always read philosophy and never took a bath and would always tell everybody to clean up and wash for infection: "Do as I say, not as I do." He would read Saint Thomas and he was a confirmed atheist and he would philosophize. But in the field he was tremendously skilled as a medic and also very daring, and he was killed the day I was wounded. He was moving to a man and he was wounded and killed. Here was a man who was an intellectual, a philosopher, a thinker, and he was there. Probably not agreeing with what was happening. But somehow, again, the good was being destroyed.

I think we lost a lot more in Vietnam than the troops we lost. We really didn't lose too many battles. When we met the enemy we usually won. What did we win? We lost more than we won, especially the aftermath of the war. Having served in Vietnam, having served in the infantry, having been wounded, feeling the bullet rip into your flesh, the shrapnel tear the flesh from your bones and the blood run down your leg, and feeling like you're gonna piss in your pants and it's the blood running down your leg. To put your hand on your chest and to come away with your hand red with your own blood, and to feel it running out of your eyes and out of your mouth, and seeing it spurt out of your guts, realizing you were dying . . .

I had been hit the second time by a direct hit from a mortar. I was ripped open from the top of my head to the tip of my toes. I had forty-five holes in me and I was bleeding everywhere. I can remember saying to myself, "My God, I'm dying." And at that split second, I was calm. Completely, completely at peace with myself.

▌ Remember that this is the recounting of one human being. Did your group maintain his integrity?

Simon and Grusha pledged themselves to each other before Simon went to war. Grusha rescues the Governor's abandoned infant, Michael, and together they begin an uncertain, event-filled life. And now, of course, Simon returns. Keep the Singer close to the two — and don't forget the river that separates them. Their poignant formality increases the tension in the scene.

FROM *The Caucasian Chalk Circle*, Section III
BERTOLT BRECHT

MICHAEL *runs away. The children run after him.* GRUSHA *laughs, following them with her eyes. On looking back, she sees* SIMON SHASHAVA *standing on the opposite bank. He wears a shabby uniform.*

GRUSHA: Simon!
SIMON: Is that Grusha Vashnadze?
GRUSHA: Simon!
SIMON (*formally*): A good morning to the young lady. I hope she is well.
GRUSHA (*getting up gaily and bowing low*): A good morning to the soldier. God be thanked he has returned in good health.
SIMON: They found better fish, so they didn't eat me, said the haddock.
GRUSHA: Courage, said the kitchen boy. Good luck, said the hero.
SIMON: How are things here? Was the winter bearable? The neighbor considerate?

GRUSHA: The winter was a trifle rough, the neighbor as usual, Simon.

SIMON: May one ask if a certain person still dips her toes in the water when rinsing the linen?

GRUSHA: The answer is no. Because of the eyes in the bushes.

SIMON: The young lady is speaking of soldiers. Here stands a paymaster.

GRUSHA: A job worth twenty piasters?

SIMON: And lodgings.

GRUSHA (*with tears in her eyes*): Behind the barracks under the date trees.

SIMON: Yes, there. A certain person has kept her eyes open.

GRUSHA: She has, Simon.

SIMON: And has not forgotten? (GRUSHA *shakes her head.*) So the door is still on its hinges as they say? (GRUSHA *looks at him in silence and shakes her head again.*) What's this? Is anything not as it should be?

GRUSHA: Simon Shashava, I can never return to Nuka. Something has happened.

SIMON: What can have happened?

GRUSHA: For one thing, I knocked an Ironshirt down.

SIMON: Grusha Vashnadze must have had her reasons for that.

GRUSHA: Simon Shashava, I am no longer called what I used to be called.

SIMON (*after a pause*): I do not understand.

GRUSHA: When do women change their names, Simon? Let me explain. Nothing stands between us. Everything is just as it was. You must believe that.

SIMON: Nothing stands between us and yet there's something?

GRUSHA: How can I explain it so fast and with the stream between us? Couldn't you cross the bridge there?

SIMON: Maybe it's no longer necessary.

GRUSHA: It is very necessary. Come over on this side, Simon, Quick!

SIMON: Does the young lady wish to say someone has come too late?

GRUSHA *looks up at him in despair, her face streaming with tears.* SIMON *stares before him. He picks up a piece of wood and starts cutting it.*

SINGER:

So many words are said, so many left unsaid.
The soldier has come.
Where he comes from, he does not say.
Hear what he thought and did not say:

"The battle began, gray at dawn, grew bloody at noon.
The first man fell in front of me, the second behind me, the
    third at my side.
I trod on the first, left the second behind, the third was run
    through by the captain.
One of my brothers died by steel, the other by smoke.
My neck caught fire, my hands froze in my gloves, my toes in
    my socks.
I fed on aspen buds, I drank maple juice, I slept on stone, in
    water."

SIMON: I see a cap in the grass. Is there a little one already?

GRUSHA: There is, Simon. There's no keeping *that* from you. But
please don't worry, it is not mine.

SIMON: When the wind once starts to blow, they say, it blows
through every cranny. The wife need say no more. (GRUSHA *looks
into her lap and is silent.*)

SINGER:

There was yearning but there was no waiting.
The oath is broken. Neither could say why.
Hear what she thought but did not say:
"While you fought in the battle, soldier,
The bloody battle, the bitter battle
I found a helpless infant
I had not the heart to destroy him
I had to care for a creature that was lost
I had to stoop for breadcrumbs on the floor
I had to break myself for that which was not mine
That which was other people's.
Someone must help!
For the little tree needs water
The lamb loses its way when the shepherd is asleep
And its cry is unheard!"

SIMON: Give me back the cross I gave you. Better still, throw it in
the stream. (*He turns to go.*)

GRUSHA (*getting up*):   Simon Shashava, don't go away! He isn't mine!
He isn't mine! (*She hears the children calling.*) What's the matter,
children?

VOICES: Soldiers! And they're taking Michael away!

GRUSHA *stands aghast as two* IRONSHIRTS, *with* MICHAEL *between them,
come toward her.*

ONE OF THE IRONSHIRTS: Are you Grusha? (*She nods.*) Is this your child?

GRUSHA: Yes. (SIMON *goes.*) Simon!

IRONSHIRT: We have orders, in the name of the law, to take this child, found in your custody, back to the city. It is suspected that the child is Michael Abashwili, son and heir of the late Governor Georgi Abashwili, and his wife, Natella Abashwili. Here is the document and the seal. (*They lead the* CHILD *away.*)

GRUSHA (*running after them, shouting*):   Leave him here. Please! He's mine!

▌ How did your group underline the physical separation between the characters?
▌ Did your Singer sing?

The following three poems owe at least as much to their typographic layout as to their words. They require flexible bodies and voices. In Roger Mc-Gough's poem, be sure your group physically shows the line separating the couple. Play tennis with the words.

40 – Love
ROGER McGOUGH

middle	aged
couple	playing
ten	nis
when	the
game	ends
and	they
go	home
the	net
will	still
be	be
tween	them

▌ How did your group let the audience see the net and hear the rackets?

Note how the stems of the forsythia in this poem telegraph a kind of code.
Can a chorus of voices suggest that sound?

Forsythia

MARY ELLEN SOLT

▮ How did your bodies and voices suggest the delicacy of the forsythia? How can this delicacy also "insist action"?

Reinhard Döhl offers an elusive intruder in his apple. Consider the apple as
a symbol in Western mythology before you plan your group performance.

Apfel

REINHARD DÖHL

ApfelApfelApfelApfel
pfelApfelApfelApfelApfelA
felApfelApfelApfelApfelApfe
ApfelApfelApfelApfelApfelApf
pfelApfelApfelApfelApfelApfel
ApfelApfelApfelApfelApfelApfe
pfelApfelApfelApfelApfelApfelA
ApfelApfelApfelApfelApfelApfe
pfelApfelApfelApfelApfelApfel
pfelApfelApfelApfelApfelApf
elApfelApfelApfelWurmAp
felApfelApfelApfelApfel
pfelApfelApfelApfel
felApfelApfelA

▮ Did your audience meet the surprise visitor the way the silent
reader does? How?

The distinctive power of Ntozake Shange's verse arises from the flexibility of her language and the commitment of her experiences. If you take time to find the music the characters mention, you will see how, as in good jazz, the rhythms of the lines correspond to and take off from their musical models. Bodies inextricably linked to voices characterize this passage.

FROM *For Colored Girls Who Have Considered Suicide/When the Rainbow Is Enuf*

NTOZAKE SHANGE

The Dells singing "Stay" comes in and all of the ladies except the lady in blue join in and sing along.

LADY IN BLUE:
you gave it up in a buick?
LADY IN YELLOW:
yeh, and honey, it was wonderful.
LADY IN GREEN:
we used to do it all up in the dark
in the corners . . .
LADY IN BLUE:
some niggah sweating all over you.
LADY IN RED:
it was good!
LADY IN BLUE:
i never did like to grind.
LADY IN YELLOW:
what other kind of dances are there?
LADY IN BLUE:
mambo, bomba, merengue

when i waz sixteen i ran off to the south bronx
cuz i waz gonna meet up wit willie colon
& dance all the time
            mamba bomba merengue
LADY IN YELLOW:
do you speak spanish?
LADY IN BLUE:
olà
my papa thot he was puerto rican & we wda been
cept we waz just reglar niggahs wit hints of spanish
so off i made it to this 36 hour marathon dance
con salsa con ricardo
'suggggggggggar' ray on southern blvd

next door to this fotografi place
jammed wit burial weddin & communion relics
next door to la real ideal genuine spanish barber
            up up up up up stairs & stairs & lotsa hallway
wit my colored new jersey self
didn't know what anybody waz saying
cept if dancin waz proof of origin
                i was jibarita herself that nite
& the next day
i kept smilin & right on steppin
if he cd lead i waz ready to dance
if he cdnt lead
i caught this attitude
                i'd seen rosa do
& wd not be bothered
i waz twirlin hippin givin much quik feet
& bein a mute cute colored puerto rican
til saturday afternoon when the disc-jockey say
'SORRY FOLKS WILLIE COLON AINT GONNA MAKE IT TODAY'

& alla my niggah temper came outta control
& i wdnt dance wit nobody
& i talked english loud
& i love you more than i waz mad
un huh uh huh

more than more than
when i discovered archie shepp & subtle blues
doncha know i wore out the magic of juju
heroically resistin being possessed

ooooooooooooooh the sounds
sneakin in under age to slug's
to stare ata real 'artiste'
& every word outta imamu's mouth waz gospel
& if jesus cdnt play a horn like shepp
waznt no need for colored folks to bear no cross as all

& poem is my thank-you for music
& i love you more than poem
more than aureliano buendia loved macondo
more than hector lavoe loved himself
more than the lady loved gardenias
more than celia loves cuba or graciela loves el son
more than the flamingoes shoo-do-n-doo-wah love bein pretty

oyè négro
te amo mas que   te amo mas que
when you play
yr flute
EVERYONE (*very softly*):
te amo mas que   te amo mas que
LADY IN RED:
without any assistance or guidance from you
i have loved you assiduously for 8 months 2 wks & a day
i have been stood up four times
i've left 7 packages on yr doorstep
forty poems 2 plants & 3 handmade notecards i left
town so i cd send to you have been no help to me
on my job
you call at 3:00 in the mornin on weekdays
so i cd drive 27½ miles cross the bay before i go to work
charmin charmin
but you are of no assistance
i want you to know
this waz an experiment
to see how selfish i cd be
if i wd really carry on to snare a possible lover
if i waz capable of debasin my self for the love of another
if i cd stand not being wanted

when i wanted to be wanted
& i cannot
so
with no further assistance & no guidance from you
i am endin this affair

this note is attached to a plant
i've been waterin since the day i met you
you may water it
yr damn self
LADY IN ORANGE:
i dont wanna write
in english or spanish
i wanna sing   make you dance
like the bata   dance   scream
twitch hips wit me cuz
i done forgot all abt words
aint got no definitions
i wanna whirl
                    with you

Music starts, "Che Che Cole" by Willie Colon. Everyone starts to dance.

our whole body
wrapped like a ripe mango
ramblin whippin thru space
on the corner in the park
where the rug useta be
let willie colon take you out
swing your head
push your leg to the moon with me

i'm on the lower east side
in new york city
and i can't   i can't
talk witchu no more
LADY IN YELLOW:
we gotta dance to keep from crying
LADY IN BROWN:
we gotta dance to keep from dying
LADY IN RED:
so come on
LADY IN BROWN:
come on

LADY IN PURPLE:
come on
LADY IN ORANGE:
hold yr head like it was ruby sapphire
i'm a poet
who writes in english
come to share the worlds witchu
EVERYONE:
come to share our worlds witchu
we come here to be dancin
       to be dancin
     to be dancin
   baya

There is a sudden light change, all of the ladies react as if they had been struck in the face. The lady in green and the lady in yellow run out up left, the lady in orange runs out the left volm, the lady in brown runs out up right.

> ▌ How did your group permit interaction during individual speeches? Why did they do it the way they did?

Dr. Daniel Hirsh and Alexis Greville (known in the script as Alex) have shared the affections of young Bob Elkin for some time; although each knows about the other, they have never met. Alva and Bill Hodson, their daughter Lucy, and Professor Johns are friends of all three of the principals. Pauline Kael called *Sunday Bloody Sunday* "a novel written on film," and the precise, literate direction of the camera narrates for us the impact of this segment, the last minutes of the film.

FROM *Sunday Bloody Sunday*
PENELOPE GILLIATT

SUNDAY

Daniel's consulting room and garden. Dawn.
   "Sunday" title on shot.
   DANIEL *is playing Italian language-records, wearing a polo-necked sweater and grey flannels. He opens the French windows.*

   He walks out to his pool and crouches down to look at the goldfish. The sound of the recorded voice comes out into the cold garden. Time passes.

Daniel's stairs. Dawn.
   BOB *is coming quietly down the stairs in a raincoat. He leaves the front door key on the kitchen table.*

DANIEL is still crouched by the pool. He has his head bent and the sight of BOB going out of the house is not visible to him.

Street outside Daniel's house. Dawn.
  Long shot of BOB letting himself out of DANIEL'S house.

Answering service. Early morning.

ANSWERING SERVICE WOMAN: We'll be sorry, Mr. Elkin. But you'll be back, will you? Well, I can't say I blame you. The dollar's where the future is. I'll give that message to Miss Greville, yes. And to Dr. . . . ? Well, very well. (*She unplugs, and smirks a bit and nods to herself, and opens a packet of fruit pastilles.*)

Bob's pad. Sunday morning.
    He comes downstairs with rubbish and leaves it outside his front door. A VOICE *from the area yells up.*

VOICE FROM AREA: Rubbish belongs down here, Mr. Elkin. (*He slams the front door behind him and goes away.*)

The Hodsons'. Sunday morning.
    ALEX *drives up in her car, looking at the* HODSON FAMILY *having lunch inside the house.* DANIEL *is with the* FAMILY *and* PROFESSOR JOHNS.

ALVA: When are you off to Italy?
DANIEL: The twenty-first, God willing.
ALVA: Are you going with Bob?
DANIEL: I don't think so.

ALVA *makes commiserating sound, checked by* BILL.

BILL: We've always thought we should try to be a bit more grown-up ourselves about having holidays on our own. Separately, I mean. Have you ever thought of one of those Scholars' Cruises? Alva nearly went on one.
DANIEL: It isn't what I'd have chosen.

ALVA *makes her own married warning gesture to* BILL *and speaks to* DANIEL, *meaning what she says, in her own way.*

ALVA: I'm terribly sorry.

Sprightly snigger from LUCY. DANIEL *looks at them coldly.*

DANIEL: No need.

There is a view of the scene from the outside of the house, from ALEX'S *point of view, and a long snatch of "Così."* DANIEL *comes out of the house.*
    ALEX *gets out of her car and sits on the wing of his. They shake hands, absurdly. He sits down in his own driving seat.*

ALEX: I didn't know you were going to be here. I'm sorry. You know who I am.
DANIEL: Thank you for not coming in. You must have been out here a long time. (*awkward*) Have you had lunch?
ALEX: It's the sort of thing we say, isn't it? (*pause*) I'm ravenous. (*pause*) He's all right, is he?
DANIEL: I think so. (*pause*) This isn't very easy, is it?

She shakes her head.

ALEX: I thought he'd be with you today.

They light cigarettes.

DANIEL: He's gone away, yes?

ALEX: I don't know.

DANIEL: It's all right to tell me.

ALEX: I'm sorry. I only had it from the answering service.

They make wry faces at each other. As she goes up the path to the HODSONS', *DANIEL raises his voice at her.*

DANIEL: You're welcome to them today.

London airport. Sunday afternoon.
     BOB *buys American magazines and walks to the Pan Am counter.*

Alex's studio. Sunday afternoon.
     She comes in and finds an envelope with her name on it facing her on the floor, and a key like the one in her hand wrapped up in a piece of paper with a note: Could you look after the toucan for a bit? The TOUCAN *stares at her from the window sill. She stares it out.*

Daniel's consulting room. Sunday afternoon.
     DANIEL *is in his patient's chair, with his back to camera. His own seat behind the desk is empty because he is managing a Hi-Fi nearer his grasp from this position. The Italian language-record is going.*

RECORD: I prefer my scampi without garlic and my wife would like a steak if the meat is first class.

Record repeats phrase in Italian.

RECORD: Preferisco i miei scampi senz' aglio e mia moglie desidera una bistecca purchè la carne sia buonissima.

Pause for the student to repeat the Italian. DANIEL *says the phrase, in a shorter time than the record allows. Pause.*
     Camera starts to move round very slowly. We see DANIEL'S *profile.*

RECORD: You have used the present tense and the conditional. Now we will repeat the phrases in the past tense as if telling a story. "I said that I preferred my scampi without garlic and my wife would have liked a steak provided that the meat was first class."

The record repeats the phrase in Italian. DANIEL *speaks simultaneously with the record.*

RECORD AND DANIEL: Ho detto che volevo i miei scampi senz' aglio e mia moglie avrebbe preferito la bistecca se la carne era buonissima.

RECORD: Molto bene. Arrivederci.

The gramophone switches itself off. By this time the camera movement has brought us to a view of DANIEL *in full face, looking at the book on his knee. It is as if he is the patient now, talking to himself: or to us, it begins to be clear.*

DANIEL: We went to hear "Aida" in the open air and it was not first class but we enjoyed the music and the landscape.

He repeats the phrase in Italian, lifting his head and staring straight at us.

DANIEL: Siamo andati a vedere l'Aida all'aria aperta. Saremmo andati a vedere l'Aida. (*pause*) — Bugger the conditional. (*pause*) When you're at school and want to quit, people say you're going to hate being out in the world. Well, I didn't believe them and I was right. When I was a kid I couldn't wait to be grown up and they said childhood was the best time of my life and it wasn't. Now I want his company and people say, what's half a loaf, you're well shot of him; and I say, I know that, I miss him, that's all. They say he'd never have made me happy and I say, I am happy, apart from missing him. You might throw me a pill or two for my cough. (*pause*) All my life I've been looking for someone courageous and resourceful, not like myself, and he's not it. (*pause*) But something. We were something. You've no right to call me to account. (*pause*) I've only come about my cough.

He, too, stares us out. Fade to black. Full credits.

▮ How sympathetic to Daniel was *your* camera?
▮ If the narrator also takes the lines of the record, what is the impact on Daniel's last scene? Why?

This selection easily lends itself to being excerpted. You may wish to follow the thread of Miss Lizzie's encounters with Mr. Pitcher, her business transactions, her first taste of freedom, or her experiences in California.

We have here an amusing blend of affection and humor. Notice how the narrator often reflects Miss Lizzie's attitude even when she is not using direct discourse, as in the Anderson Girls' feeling about Uncle's advice not to sell the land. Be careful not to make Miss Lizzie a caricature. She is unsophisticated, but she is not senile. Let the narrator step aside often enough to permit the group to enjoy the scene.

Miss Lizzie
CLAIRE MORRILL

That morning, when Lizzie crossed the road to see Mr. Pitcher, he had a big new gadget hanging down from the ceiling in front of his livingroom window. It seemed to be made of thin rods of different lengths, some wire, and a number of crystal balls.

"What is it?" she asked.

"Why, it's a mobile, Lizzie," Otto said.

"What does it do?"

"It doesn't do anything," he told her. "It just hangs there."

"Oh," she said.

The next time Miss Lizzie came, she surveyed the mobile again with a thoughtful eye.

"When do you light it up?" she asked.

Mr. Pitcher shook his head. "It doesn't light up. It doesn't do anything. It's an ornament."

On her third try a few days later Miss Lizzie took still a different tack.

"I expect it makes music," she said craftily.

"No," said Otto, "it doesn't make music; it doesn't light up. It doesn't do anything. It just hangs there."

Not long afterward, on the street in Taos, Otto ran into Mrs. John Dunn.

"I understand from Lizzie Anderson," she said slyly, "that you've got the only indoor lightning rod in Taos."

Otto was devoted to Miss Lizzie. Her sister Miss Jennie was another matter. But he saw quite a lot of both of them during those several years when he served as neighbor, chauffeur, advisor, and general troubleshooter for the Anderson Girls on their farm across the road from his house.

His volunteer unpaid services were often called upon at extremely short notice. For if the Andersons took no thought for the morrow, it was because the morrow seemed too far away. When they needed feed for their 120 chickens, they needed it *now*. When Miss Lizzie summoned Mr. Pitcher to drive her to town for chicken feed, he knew the hens were facing immediate famine and that he must hastily drop any of his own concerns and do something about it.

In willingly spending so much time with Miss Lizzie, Otto was admittedly motivated by more than his affection for her and a humanitarian concern for the state of affairs in the henhouse. As an old pro actor, he was enormously diverted by his role of straight man in the deadpan, inadvertently comic routines Miss Lizzie continually provided.

Though Miss Jennie was in her eighties and her sister coming along only five years behind, they carried their water, winter and summer, from a spring three or four hundred feet from their dilapidated Victorian frame house. But when he was not home, they accepted his neighborly offer to get it from Otto's house instead. After the first of these periods, Miss Lizzie approached him in a state of bright-eyed wonderment.

"Do you know, Mr. Pitcher," she asked, "that if you turn on that *other* tap, *hot* water comes out?"

Uncle Alex Anderson, when he had died forty years ago, had left the girls a hundred acres including some of the best land in Taos County, plus a few more acres and a small mine in Arroyo Seco, not far away. But Uncle had told them never to sell any of it. And he had known all about such matters.

Uncle had been a businessman and a man of property. He had owned the grist mill, with its sluice and waterwheel and its grain storage building, an establishment part of which has now become Otto's house. Besides this and the mine, with its showing of copper and a few other ores, he had thirty beehives and sold the honey. He had raised prize Dahlias and marketed them wholesale.

Furthermore, Uncle was much more than a memory. They were still grateful to him and loved him. They had first lived in Embudo, twenty-five miles south of Taos, where their father had worked in a little mine and had to be away from home a lot of the time. And when their mother had had a mental break and had to be taken away, Uncle had brought the two little girls home with him to Taos and given them solicitous care. So when he told them never to sell the land, they knew he was right. No matter how scarce cash got over the years, they hung on grimly.

For years they prepared dinners in the old house in Los Cordovas, three or four miles from Taos, for the town's elite. There would be chicken, potatoes cooked in two to seven ways at the same meal, three kinds of salad or slaw, two or three kinds of pie, and cake with ice cream.

Of course, no matter what time the guests arrived, dinner was never ready, for there were still the dishes to do from previous meals, and one of the gentlemen had to be detailed to turn the ice cream freezer. Nor could you, in contemporary Taos fashion, fill in the wait with a sociable highball. The girls didn't hold with any such sinfulness, which had to be carried on, if at all, surreptitiously among the lilacs at the side of the house. So strongly did they feel on this subject that in later years, when Miss Lizzie saw a bottle of rum with which Otto was mellowing a Christmas cake, she sadly reported to Elsie Weimer, "Mr. Pitcher has taken to drink."

As age began to catch up with the Anderson Girls and more and fancier restaurants opened in Taos, they gave up serving dinners and settled for selling eggs, the cream from their four cows, and the angelfood cakes which they still liked to bake. Miss Lizzie brought these to town on weekly trips.

I don't think I ever laid eyes on Miss Jennie. She couldn't, she felt, leave the property unprotected. This was the reason why, after the road commission had ripped out Uncle's old wooden bridge, replaced it with a culvert, and piled the old timbers up at the side of the road, Miss Jennie broke out her shotgun and sat by the pile through all of one chilly autumn night. If she hadn't you never could tell who would have stolen her timber.

But while Miss Jennie seldom left the old homestead, I saw Miss Lizzie about every week, though, since we bought only eggs, we never saw her during those periods when the hens were moulting. It was, it appeared, impossible for them to lay when they were moulting or else to moult when they were laying. Whichever it was, these physiological phenomena never occurred simultaneously, the fact interrupting Miss Lizzie's visits to us.

Her spare New Englandish figure was garbed in winter in a long dogskin coat; in spring and fall in a long fitted black one of cloth. In summer she came in her countrywoman's dress of cotton. Her wide-brimmed hats, felt in winter and black straw in summer, were anchored in place with a scarf that tied under her chin and produced a sunbonnet effect.

Her speech, coming out in a high, thin voice, was brisk and chipper. But it was hard for me to keep my mind on what she was saying because of the interruptions that happened once or twice in each sentence when her upper dentures began to slip from their proper place. When this happened, she was, of course, forced to arrest their fall by a brisk upward movement of her lower jaw, and so had her choice of muttering through clenched teeth or waiting until things settled down and she could reopen her mouth to finish her sentence. This had to be accomplished with all possible speed before the same thing began to happen again.

The procedure, fascinating to see, caused Miss Lizzie no concern or embarrassment. And if, after she had brought out the eggs from one of the two pasteboard cartons she carried by their rope fastenings, her visits were always short, it was only because she had to hurry to the Safeway to meet Mr. Pitcher and get a ride home.

At the Safeway she would buy an Eskimo Pie, an addiction she had learned to finance by raising the price of eggs to a few cents above the figure she would report to Miss Jennie. Then on the way home, Mr. Pitcher would have to stop the car under a friendly shade tree, while she ate the delicacy with leisurely relish.

When Miss Jennie finally slipped on an icy spot and died as an indirect result of a broken hip, everyone worried about Miss Lizzie. What would she do now, all by herself in that old rattletrap of a house? Miss Jennie had always taken the lead; what would Miss Lizzie do without her?

But Otto was not apprehensive. He knew Miss Lizzie had only been scared to death of her sister.

He was out of town when Miss Jennie died, and got home a few days after the funeral. When Miss Lizzie asked him to drive her over to the cemetery, he complied with more than his usual alacrity. There was something he was curious about.

He knew there was room for five graves in the Anderson family plot. Father and Mother and Uncle Alex had long been there, side by side in a neat row. There was one more prized spot, right next to Uncle. But the fifth Anderson would have to settle for a crosswise place at the foot of the row.

As he and Miss Lizzie reached the plot and stood looking down, she nudged Otto's elbow and a slow grin spread over her face.

"See where Jennie is," she said. "Across the feet."

Now after more than eighty years, Miss Lizzie discovered freedom. For one thing, she sold some land. Though this radical move was rather forced upon her by the staggering size of the bills attending Miss Jennie's passing, she decided to use what money was left over to pay back the loans that had been made to them over the years by some of their longtime friends. She was touched when most of them refused the payments; they'd written those loans off years ago. Miss Lizzie was pleased, too, with the new checkbook she took around to use in paying the debts.

It was during this period that somebody paid her a check that bounced.

"Well, Mr. Pitcher," she said, "I see the bank's run out of money."

"Oh, I don't think so," Otto replied. "How do you know?"

"Well," said Miss Lizzie, "I took in this check and they didn't give me the money. They said they didn't have any more."

Soon she made another bold move — she went up in the attic. Miss Jennie had never allowed her to go up there; she might fall down the stairs and break a hip. But now in the attic she came upon Uncle's old wind-up phonograph and a bunch of cylinder records. There was one, though, that she didn't find that she wanted to hear again. She was especially fond of "Birmingham Jail." Mr. Pitcher, when she asked him about it, didn't have this record either, but he did have a tape recording. Miss Lizzie watched his contraption with interest.

"That's the funniest phonograph I ever saw," she declared. "It eats up the record as it goes along."

Now she decided to fix up an old radio that Mabel Luhan had once given them for Christmas. You could run it with batteries or you could plug it into the wall. Miss Lizzie tried to find batteries but the model was obsolete, so she had the kitchen wired for electricity and put in just one outlet where she could plug in the radio. Otto discovered her there one evening, blissfully listening in a dim room still lighted by an old kerosene lamp.

"What, no electric light?" he inquired.

"Oh, that's too expensive," Miss Lizzie said. Unless it cost too much, nobody who had electricity in his house would eat his dinner by candlelight, as she had often seen Mr. Pitcher doing. But after he had explained that he just thought it was nicer to have candles at dinner, she agreed to have an electric light, so Otto went to a rummage sale, found an old lamp, and hitched it up with a double plug to the radio outlet.

Thus reassured on the question of expense, she soon afterward bought an electric refrigerator. And the first thing she got to go into it was a hundred Eskimo Pies.

But her pleasure in what you could do by plugging things into the wall was dashed one day when she overloaded the line and blew out a fuse. Again she repaired to Otto's house, this time at seven o'clock in the morning.

"Mr. Pitcher," she asked, "have you used up all *your* electricity yet?"

"I don't think so," he said, flipping a switch.

"Well, I guess I've used all of mine," she said. "The radio hasn't said a word since six o'clock."

Now she settled down to enjoy life. She sold some more land and drilled a well. In fact, life was improving so much that she didn't accept when her cousin in California wrote and asked her to come and live with him and his wife. He'd visited her once and he liked her. He worried about her there all alone in the winters in that old, cold house with its woodburning stoves. But she was not yet ready to go.

Nor did she get ready until it finally happened — Miss Lizzie fell and struck her head against the cast-iron oven door of the kitchen stove. The door broke, and while her own injuries were, comparatively speaking, less serious, the neighbors took her off to the hospital, where she stayed for three weeks.

When the time came to go home, she found she couldn't face that cold house. In the hospital the heat sort of came out of the walls; hot water came out of the other tap there, too; and somebody cooked your meals and brought them right to you.

She went home only long enough to sell her house and the rest of her land. They brought enough money to live on the rest of her life. When her cousin came to take her to California, she walked out of the house with only two suitcases and scarcely a backward glance. Miss Lizzie knew she had had it.

And California was wonderful. Her cousins lived in Concord, just outside San Francisco. Their house was warm and pretty, and they were pleasantly attentive. Not too attentive, either. She could come and go as she liked. And Miss Lizzie, who had been known to get lost in Taos, found she could get around out there with no trouble at all. The thing was, there were so many policemen.

She did slide into things gradually. At first she just went to the supermarket, which was only a block or two away. Then she saw she could range farther afield on the bus that stopped right in front of the supermarket and stopped there again on its way back. And if you got off downtown and didn't know how to get home again, you could just ask one of those nice policemen. He wouldn't just tell you how to get home; he'd *take* you there in his car.

Things got more and more interesting. If you wanted to you could just stay on the bus and ride for two hours for twenty-five cents, up through Lafayette and Walnut Grove and back again, and get off at the supermarket. Her cousins got so they didn't even worry about her much. There seemed to be lots of policemen.

Emboldened by these successes, she remembered some other cousins in Glendale and went off to visit them, an all-day trip on the train. There were some relatives in Vancouver, too, and Miss Lizzie even went up there, two or three times, to help them pick strawberries.

These trips she made by herself, though of course when she took in the World's Fair in New York, she went with her cousins.

A while ago she jetted in from San Francisco to Albuquerque to visit an old friend, and came up to Taos for a day. Otto said he missed seeing her, but Pat McCarthy saw her.

"Just as full of juice as ever," was the way Pat put it.

And, of course, why not? She was only eighty-seven.

Here in Taos she is still the subject of amused and affectionate remembrance. At least, every time a few people gather at Otto's somebody is sure to ask, "Now just what was it Miss Lizzie said about the mobile?"

And I will say, Otto always tells it the same way.

▌ What physical and vocal characteristics did your group use to convey Miss Lizzie's toughness and Otto's respect for her?
▌ How did you show her different solutions to the mystery of the mobile? How did Otto maintain his concentration?

Bibliography

Breen, Robert S. *Chamber Theatre*. Evanston, Ill.: William Caxton, 1986.
> Provocative and illuminating discussions of the scope and practice of staging prose fiction written by the scholar who is most responsible for its success.

Coger, Leslie Irene, and Melvin R. White. *Readers Theatre Handbook: A Dramatic Approach to Literature*. Rev. ed. Glenview, Ill.: Scott, Foresman and Company, 1973.
> Readers Theatre as a "theatre of the mind." Among the earliest works, this pioneering book features scripts, discussions, and illustrations of practical solutions to problems.

Hollander, John. *Types of Shape*, 2nd ed. New York: Oxford University Press, 1991.
> Contemporary patterned poems, with a lively introduction on shaped verse and explanatory discussion of each poem.

Kleinau, Marion L., and Janet Larsen McHughes. *Theatres for Literature*. Sherman Oaks, Calif.: Alfred Publishing Company, 1980.
> A substantial discussion of the theory and practice of Readers Theatre, Chamber Theatre, and other group performance events, featuring practical advice and stimulating theoretical questions. An excellent all-round book.

Long, Beverly Whitaker, Lee Hudson, and Phillis Rienstra Jeffrey. *Group Performance of Literature*. Englewood Cliffs, N.J.: Prentice-Hall, 1977.
> Some theoretical discussion precedes a substantial collection of script suggestions, fragments, and reports of productions, which are illustrated and amplified by their original directors.

Maclay, Joanna H. *Readers Theatre: Toward a Grammar of Practice*. New York: Random House, 1971.
> Among the earliest efforts to develop a theoretical foundation for staging literature, this book asks provocative questions and supplies substantial practical suggestions.

McHughes, J. L. "The Poesis of Space: Prosodic Structures in Concrete Poetry." *Quarterly Journal of Speech*, 63 (1977), 168–179.
> A discussion arguing that space is the axis from which the poem emerges. This and the article by Francine Merritt have provided considerable support to the growing interest in the performance of concrete poetry.

Merritt, Francine. "Concrete Poetry — Verbivocovisual." *Speech Teacher*, 18 (1969), 109–114.
> Chiefly a series of definitions and examples of ten different kinds of concrete poems.

APPENDIX A

Building and Presenting a Program

A SUSTAINED AND WELL-INTEGRATED PROGRAM focuses the audience *equally* on texts and on performance. This discussion of program building assumes that the interpreter has thoroughly analyzed the literature and that physical and vocal techniques are under control.

Although we have not focused on training the professional recitalist, there can be considerable pleasure and satisfaction gained from presenting a program or lecture recital to an audience outside the classroom. Much of the discussion that follows can also be applied to the longer class performance, such as a final reading, or to the increasingly popular reading hours being offered on many campuses. After all, the techniques used in performance are dictated by the demands of the *material* rather than by the length or circumstances of the presentation.

The difference between a program and a lecture recital is primarily one of proportion and degree. A *program* uses a minimum of transitional material and focuses almost entirely on the various works of literature themselves. A *lecture recital*, by contrast, has a strong central unity; critics' opinions, historical data, and, even video and audio media devices are used as transitions. The selections illustrate whatever technical or thematic development the speaker has chosen. The lecture recital emphasizes evaluation as much as appreciation, but it should not simply use the literature to endorse a position or assume a posture that is inconsistent with the integrity of the writing.

In this appendix, because the lecture recital appeals to a more specialized audience and is much less practical for the beginning interpreter, we build programs of varied selections, referring to material in the text as well as to selections you can find in your library, and featuring group performances of both fiction and poetry and nonfiction.

Selecting Material

The first consideration in selecting the material you will present is its literary worth. Do not read something you consider to be inferior because you think your audience will not accept anything more difficult to understand. It is your job to present the selection so well that it does not seem difficult. The second consideration is permission to use the material. Reread the advice about copyright in Chapter 11 if you are in doubt (see page 444).

You might be asked to do a special program for a particular group or occasion. Perhaps the group is following a particular course of study — contemporary theatre, the Old Testament, human relations, ecology, or any one of a number of areas of interest — and they want you to add a new dimension or an introductory or concluding unit. The time of year may influence your selection. For a Christmas program, for example, you might want to include both an old favorite (Truman Capote's *A Christmas Memory*) and a less well-known piece (say, Ogden Nash's witty "Epstein, Spare That Yule Log"). A spring luncheon could feature Eudora Welty's "Lily Daw and the Three Ladies." February offers the opportunity to read love poems, love letters, and love scenes from plays. Since February also celebrates the birthdays of two famous Americans, it offers the opportunity to present historical material or patriotic selections. Perhaps a scene from Gore Vidal's *Lincoln* and selections from Walt Whitman's journals and his poem "When Lilacs Last in the Dooryard Bloom'd" could be used in a program on Lincoln. Any topic of human interest can become the focal point of a program. The range of possibilities is limited only by the interpreter's skill and imagination.

Unifying the Program: A Traditional Method

Whatever the occasion, your program should have a unifying theme that is dictated by many factors including what you know about your audience, the time of year, and the purpose of the organization for which you are reading. The program itself should demonstrate the intrinsic factors of unity and harmony, variety and contrast, balance and proportion, rhythm of emotional impact, and focus of interest.

Although a unified program is important, often it is more practical to begin planning with what you like to read and can get ready in time. Then, see what thematic unity your preferences offer. For example, suppose you already have prepared Robert Frost's "Wild Grapes." This poem is about many things, all operating within a harmonious unity: memory of childhood, a young girl and her brother, an experience with nature, wisdom, letting go with the hands but not with the heart, and so on. Any one of these topics could unify your program. If you choose memories of childhood for your program topic, you might wish to include Theodore Roethke's "Child on Top of a Greenhouse," a selection from Eudora Welty's *One Writer's Beginnings*, a selection from Garrison Keillor's *Lake Wobegon Days*, Cynthia Macdonald's "The Kilgore Rangerette Whose Life Was Ruined," Corinne Hales' "Power," and Mary Stewart Hammond's "Saving Memory." Mark Twain's writing evokes warm memories for many people. Gwendolyn Brooks's *Annie Allen* and *A Street in Bronzeville* contain many examples of a black girl's memories, as do the poems of Nikki Giovanni, and Sonia Sanchez, or Toni Cade Bambara's story, "The Lesson." Walt Whitman's "A Child Went Forth" and A. E. Housman's "When I Was One-and-twenty" could be used, as could selections from the poetry of William Wordsworth. Look also at the scene from Lanford Wilson's *5th of July* at the end of Chapter 7. The list of available material is practically endless; the interpreter needs only time and interest.

You might decide to set the theme with Jaques's speech from Shakespeare's *As You Like It*, moving from infancy and childhood to maturity and old age. You could close with Roethke's "Old Lady's Winter Words" and use Stanley Kunitz's "I Dreamed that I Was Old" and Tennyson's "Ulysses." Edith Sitwell's poem "Colonel Fantock" and D. H. Lawrence's short story "The Lovely Lady" would add interesting variety, as would units from Edgar Lee Masters's *Spoon River Anthology*, or scenes from such widely divergent plays as Henrik Ibsen's *A Doll's House*, George Bernard Shaw's *Caesar and Cleopatra*, or Shakespeare's *King Lear*. There are innumerable variations on the theme of youth and age. The readings might have a strongly humorous tone or a rhythm that combines the gently humorous and the deeply moving.

Interesting programs can be arranged around people and places, rural and urban life, regional American literature, descriptive and dramatic writing about foreign places, or the letters, travel accounts, and diaries of famous people.

The works of one particular author may unify a program. Concentrate on the treatment of a theme, such as Shakespeare's kings; or on a method of revealing character, as through Browning's monologues or Ann Beattie's short stories. You could suggest a developmental trend by beginning with an author's early works and concluding with the later ones.

Following is a description of a unified, well-illustrated performance treating the works of D. H. Lawrence. The program which was presented at a D. H. Lawrence festival combined Lawrence's fiction and nonfiction with books and letters that were written about him by other people. The eight readers held their manuscripts and sat on stools of various heights; a general wash of warm light illuminated the stage. The four women wore simple white blouses and long, full denim skirts in vivid colors; the four men wore khaki trousers, solid color sports shirts, and corduroy jackets.

To begin, an introductory montage was followed by autobiographical material and selections from *Sons and Lovers*. The next section included some of Lawrence's letters dealing with his mother's illness and death and closed with two short poems he wrote in her memory.

A short biographical paragraph formed a bridge to Lawrence's meeting with Frieda Weekley. His poem "Fröhleichnam," followed by four excerpts from letters, led to "The Song of the Man Who Has Come Through." The next section took up the couple's travels that eventually took them to Sicily. Lawrence's letters introduced his famous poem "Snake" and a section from *Sea and Sardinia*, and one of Frieda's letters led into Mabel Dodge's account of her invitation for the Lawrences to visit New Mexico. The first act of the performance ended with the Lawrences' acceptance and their later postponement of the trip.

The second act began with the Lawrences' arrival in Taos and included some humor — from Frieda's and Lawrence's letters to friends, from Mabel Dodge's comments, and from the poet Dorothy Brett. A fragment of the play *Altitude* was used; because much of this work's humor depends on the pointless, amusing activity of breakfast preparations when the cook fails to appear, the group decided to stage, rather than read, this segment. The performers simply put down their books, moved their stools to suggest a stove and a grouping around a table, and began the play. When the play ends abruptly, since Mabel Dodge never finished it, the readers moved rapidly to replace the stools and retrieve their books, resuming with the Lawrences' move to Lobo Ranch and the long winter that followed. Dorothy Brett's account, Lawrence's poem, "Mountain Lion," his letters, and his essays "Taos," "New Mexico," and "Indians and an Englishman" followed. A segment from one of Lawrence's letters told enough about his declining health to form a bridge to Frieda's letter about his death, which was interspersed with brief sections from Lawrence's "The Ship of Death." The program concluded with the poem "Bavarian Gentians."

This program's unity and variety — both in type of writing and in range of mood and feeling — suggest how rhythms of the emotional impact should be carefully considered to make the entire performance move smoothly and without monotony. Don't be afraid of variety: use materials from various sources, interspersing them for contrast and illumination. Different texts talk to each other. Often, throughout this text we have juxtaposed works on the same topic (stars, the death of a pet, childhood mischief) to suggest that each work viewed next to another creates special access to the texts' richnesses.

Using Multiple Readers, Different Types of Literature, and Multimedia

Using more than one reader for a program often helps solve the problems of short preparation time and inexperience. Moreover, two or more interpreters add variety and thus increase the program's audience appeal. We do not suggest that several people can simply read whatever they happen to have handy. There must be some central unity. The several readers should rehearse together so that transitions are clear and the material is arranged to provide variety and contrast, rhythm of emotional impact, and effective use of climactic selections.

There are great opportunities for experimentation in program building with groups. Much literature combines well with dance and music, which either can accompany the reading or can be inserted at various places in the program to underscore, sustain, or alter mood. Electronic media strike instant and effective responses in an audience; be sure to eliminate any potential technical glitches. Visual art can also be used. For example, William Blake and E. E. Cummings were both artists of some distinction as well as poets, and some of their drawings and paintings might well be combined with their writing for an interesting program. Hundreds of poems have been written about specific paintings. Why not stage a "gallery" of such poems using slides of the art they illumine?[1] The drawings and prose writings in Gerard Manley Hopkins's *Notebooks* might be skillfully combined with his poetry to provide an unusual and enlightening program. Or you could combine Vaslav Nijinsky's intriguing diaries with dance, adding film clips of Nureyev or Baryshnikov performing some of the ballets that Nijinsky created and enriching the entire presentation with excerpts from Igor Stravinsky's music, Charles Rosen's essays, and slides of the stage designs.

There are practically endless possibilities for combining readers and other art forms with all types of literature. Combine Readers Theatre and Chamber Theatre with the performance of single readers when the material seems suitable for the techniques. You should be careful, however, not to let variety overpower unity. Also, be sure that the literature itself is not obscured by too many sound effects or visual distractions. The audience wants text *and* performers.

Suppose you decide to work with the *New York Times*.[2] After examining several issues, you detect the newspaper's characteristic attitudes towards advertisements, politics, presentation, and news. Remember, any publication frankly seeks readership. The performance analogue for such frankness is an equally frank frontal placement and focus — bodies and voices creating the presentational equivalent to the newspaper. Such placement frees the bodies and voices to suggest the pictures, drawings, and graphics. In rehearsal, try to achieve an ensemble that can display all the levels of the work as well as its impact as a whole.

What does the *New York Times* represent? It holds a position as the "paper of record" in the United States, offering pre-eminent news reporting, widely respected editorials, broadly distributed features, an immediately recognizable logo, a particular style of presentation, and a certain kind of straightforward seriousness.

What should a performance represent? Since there is no need to limit oneself to any single issue of the paper, select from among the finest of the editorials, op-ed articles, obituaries, sports stories, fashion news reports, lifestyle and social information, the television-film-theatre-dance-music reviews, the Sunday *New York Times Magazine* articles and crossword puzzles, the book reviews and interviews with authors, the advertisements, the personal columns, and the job offerings. Your selection, of course, will be based on the needs and interests of the audience, so you may wish to slant your presentation

1. Beverly Whitaker Long created a powerful program in this manner, with the performers serving as "docents" in front of rear-projected slides of the artworks.

2. Julian Kaufman ingeniously devised many ideas about staging the *Times*.

toward a particular period or event, if you maintain an accurate reflection of the typical components of an issue. Should you include selections from works written about the *Times* (Gay Talese's *The Power and the Glory*, Harrison Salisbury's *Without Fear or Favor*, David Halberstam's *The Powers That Be*, or even a collection of the wicked gossip about the *Times* that appears in the "Naked City" column of *Spy* magazine)? It all depends on what you intend this performance to demonstrate.

Look at the visual responsibilities. What are the characteristic graphic elements used in the *Times*? How can these be suggested in performance by bodies and voices? Your rehearsals will begin in experimentation, so don't restrict yourself in terms of the visual elements. Sometimes the group can represent the visual element better than slides or set pieces could.

Consider what could happen with the front page in a group production. The front page of the *Times* is characterized by several different but related factors. First, the chief stories of the day all begin (but never end) on the front page. On occasion, a feature story or a research story also begins on the front page — but it, too, never ends there. The front page also includes — in extremely small print — one- or two-line advertisements at the bottom of some columns, the weather forecast, and price and publication information. Usually there is one large three- or four-column photograph, often illustrating the major story of the day. Sometimes a small chart or a symbol tied to the text of a story that appears elsewhere appears above the fold to the left of center. The most important stories appear in the columns that begin at the top of the page; stories of lesser importance begin below the fold. Several stories about the same event are clustered, usually to the upper right or the upper left. The front page also features variations in print size, from the most prominent headline to the smallest classified advertisement. The largest print on the page is always the Gothic type masthead — *The New York Times*.

How can the bodies and voices of the performers suggest the world of that page? Obviously, if the news stories are going to be performed, they will require all the attention normally given the performance of nonfiction. But since the stories are separate, why not give one story to each performer? When a news figure is quoted, let the performer suggest the figure as fully as possible, and let the stories continue simultaneously. At first everyone talking at once may seem cacophonous, but the blurt of all the news is one of the distinctive features of the paper's front page. And, before the stories begin, the group can suggest the elaborate archaic type of the masthead by singing the words *The New York Times* like a madrigal. Perhaps the large picture could be frozen into space by three or four of the performers; or a slide of the performers in an identical posture could be projected on a screen in back. Although the performers start together with the stories skipping along, they will stop at random, as their contents are continued elsewhere and new stories take their place. How can you suggest the newer, less important news? Could those tiny want ads be whispered?

Similar questions need to be answered for all the parts of the paper you intend to perform. The attitudes of the editorials tend to be dignified, except for an occasional whimsical salute to a change of season, but the attitudes of the letters and op-ed page offer real potential for characterization, and the masthead can be elaborate, stately, and refined. Photos can duplicate fashion news, but might not bodies and voices better suggest fashion's attitudes? Try to achieve the peculiar attitude of the recipes: knowledgeable, clear-sighted, with an extraordinarily well-equipped kitchen that could be the domain of the chef of a great French restaurant. Can you convey the intriguing, sometimes cryptic, world that lies behind the terse abbreviations of want ads or personal advertisements? Surely there are several opportunities for characterization among these. Capture the appeal each advertisement makes, through postures and voice. Plan each of the components carefully.

When compiling the parts — putting the paper together, as it were — be careful to watch the amount of time you spend on each "page." Work for balance and continuity by trying to achieve the feeling of the page turning. The arrangement of the pieces depends on changes of tempo in the stories, on the sizes of the advertisements you encounter, on how "thick" a paper you want to present, and on the degree to which you want to embody pictorial elements or to represent them with slides.

Whatever choices you make, the performance should build to a climax — something that the paper never does, but that an audience must see. Your decision to perform a newspaper imposes a structure that the paper itself does not necessarily follow. But it always moves along. Your performance should convey to the audience all that is involved in reading the *New York Times*.

Of course, a newspaper is not the only kind of publication that would benefit from such an effort. The *New York Review of Books*, for example, offers interesting reviews and articles, distinctive advertisements and David Levine graphics, and irrepressible personal announcements. The *Dial*, a magazine of poetry, fiction, and criticism, which was published during the twenties and provided an early forum for many outstanding contemporary authors, would be an equally interesting publication to perform, since its visual statement deftly supported the verbal substances of the work.

Perhaps the most obvious choice among magazines would be the *New Yorker*: its unsurpassed collection of nonfiction, poetry, light fiction, articles, and humor, with renowned cartoons and the unmistakably bemused hauteur of Eustace Tilley, the magazine's monocled symbol, provide a wonderfully varied forum for a performance. This program might include other works from typical *New Yorker* writers, or passages about the magazine from Brendan Gill's *Here at the New Yorker*, or segments from the memoirs and autobiographies of some of its most famous staffers. A collection of *New Yorker* pieces, including Janet Flanner's "Letter from Paris" (collected as *Paris Was Yesterday*), might provide the foundation for another program. Whatever you choose, you should determine the attitude that makes the publication unique, and you should develop the corresponding physical and vocal behaviors.

Just as literature demonstrates social consciousness, so can performers planning programs respond to important concerns and issues by selecting texts (literary, visual, aural) that explore reactions to events and, even, lead to action. Consider the anguish and anger surrounding AIDS. Poets, novelists, essayists, painters, composers, choreographers, and playwrights have all contributed to the growing canon that speaks to AIDS. One of the most powerful works to examine the impact of the disease is Susan Sontag's "The Way We Live Now." This story, narrated by all the friends of a person with AIDS, can provide the site for interpolating others' works that address the issue from other perspectives: poems such as Michael Lassell's "How To Watch Your Brother Die" or Mark Doty's "Tiara"; fiction such as John Weir's *The Irreversible Decline of Eddie Socket* or Paul Monette's *Afterlife*; plays such as William Hoffman's *As Is* or Larry Kramer's polemic *The Normal Heart*. Add to these opportunities the works of essayists, filmmakers, and composers and you are confronted with a broad array of possibilities with which to construct a program that can enlighten at the same time it empowers.[3]

The important thing to remember is that the performances as a whole should have both unity and variety. It should have an introductory unit, a climax (usually the longest selection and the one that most clearly exemplifies your theme), and a conclusion. When you have selected and arranged your material, look at the whole program and check it against each of the intrinsic factors. Keep the introduction short. The audience came to hear the program, not a long preamble. Your introductory remarks bridge the mood and train of thought you wish to establish. The transitions between selections

---

3. Annette Martin directed a production using many of these works.

should allow the listeners a few seconds to complete their emotional response to the preceding selection and should lead them economically into the mood of the one that follows.

Adapting to the Audience

It is impossible to know exactly what the interests of your audience are, unless the group has a special purpose. It is possible, however, to make some generalizations. Gender makes less difference than age, which is probably the most important factor to consider in audience adaptation. In general, a young audience of either sex is more open to experimental material and to a wider range of subject matter. An audience of elderly people usually wants to see and hear traditional, familiar material. While you might understandably avoid material about old age, illness, or death, do not ignore Maryann Hartman's work. In a group with a wide age spread, there should be something for everyone; but if you are in doubt about the suitability of a selection for even a segment of the audience, it is better to omit that selection than to risk offending anyone.

Children make a wonderful audience. They like material about people, animals, nature, and anything they can visualize, whether real or imaginary. They like poetry with a clear rhythm and a rhyme. You should choose selections that are short, and you should handle the transitions carefully to connect what the children know with what the literature says. Stories, of course, are great favorites, and children enjoy having the characters made vivid by more explicit vocal and physical characterization than would be appropriate for a mature audience. Don't limit yourself to children's literature exclusively. Children are young in experience but they are sensitive and intelligent; they might enjoy the sounds and basic references in Hopkins's "The Starlight Night" or "Pied Beauty," Lewis Carroll's "Jabberwocky," and Walter de la Mare's "The Listeners."

You should in no way sacrifice your own standards of literary value to audience expectation. There are dozens of ways to write about any subject. Your audience is interested in the substance of your material and in how that material is presented; second-rate material can only result in second-rate performance.

You should be aware of the audience's image of you. An audience that has asked you to present a program expects you to be skilled and intelligent and to have something interesting to say. They expect you to be well prepared, and they have a right to be critical if your performance is not polished. They have invited you because they think of you as an artist.

Timing

You should be careful not to let your program run past its allotted time by more than one or two minutes. Listeners often become ill at ease and distracted if the program runs long. It is better to leave an audience wishing for more than to risk their sigh of relief and hurried exit.

Time your selections and transitions frequently during your preparation. You will find that you consume more time as you progress. It is probably safe to add at least ten minutes per hour to your early reading time; audience response and your own increased control of the selections will tend to slow your pace in final performance. If you are sharing a program with other readers or with musicians, find out how much time you have been allotted and stick to it *precisely*.

A program of varied selections is particularly difficult to time, because it may be lengthened by laughter within or applause between selections. This is, of course, a phenomenon no performer wishes to prevent. Nevertheless, enthusiastic applause can add ten minutes or more to a fifty-minute program of fairly short selections. Be sure to consider this in your planning. In general, applause permits the audience to complete their response to what you have just given them. Accept it graciously and with poise.

In some instances, applause is inappropriate. If you sense that this is the situation, a moment's pause after each selection and before the next transition can be helpful. Do not prolong the pause so that your audience thinks you are waiting for applause. This sense of timing will develop as your experience increases. Applause might break a mood that you are trying to establish, especially if you are using a number of short selections. In this case, you might indicate in your transition that you will be using a group of short poems that touch on one aspect of your theme. Hold your performance dimension for a brief pause after each piece, and then move directly into the next selection or brief transition. When you finish the group of poems, drop your directness slightly and allow the audience to show its appreciation before you move into the next unit. Your audience will be sensitive to your wishes and will take your cues easily.

Whenever you do a program, remember that in your role of interpreter it is your duty and privilege to *share* a piece of interesting literature with your audience. Remember that your art and your technique should serve the author's intentions. Planning and preparing a performance takes time and energy. Even so, the experience of sharing good literature with an audience is always rewarding and exciting.

APPENDIX B

A Brief History of Theories of Interpretation

FROM EARLIEST TIMES, THE SPOKEN WORD has attracted audiences and influenced their thinking. The history of public speaking has been traced by numerous authorities, who have shown that its thread has been unbroken from the fourth century B.C. to the present. The theatre enjoys a similarly clear history. Oral interpretation, too, even though its genesis and growth as a distinct art may be less easy to define, has a long lineage of its own.

The art of interpretation probably had its beginnings with the rhapsodies of ancient Greece, when poets gathered to read their works in public competition. However, the emergence of interpretation as a field of study in its own right was delayed, because for a long time it was subsumed into oratory and rhetoric. In the eighteenth and nineteenth centuries, actors and ministers were given extensive training in what was, in reality, interpretation. It is enough to sketch the outlines briefly here to note the development of certain theories and to see where we now stand in relation to those theories.

American colleges were already giving some attention to the oral interpretation of literature at the beginning of the nineteenth century. As early as 1806, when John Quincy Adams assumed the chair of Rhetoric and Oratory, Harvard, which from its founding had carried on the medieval tradition of "declamations" and "disputations," was offering a few courses that included the interpretative approach to literary materials. As the century progressed, more and more colleges offered specific courses in spoken English — courses that carried such titles as "Declamation and Composition," "Declamation," "Elements of Orthoepy and Elocution," or simply "Elocution."

The word *elocutio* (Latin *eloqui, elocutus,* "to speak out") originally referred to effective literary or oratorical style. Between 1650 and 1750, however, a shift in connotation took place, and the term *elocution* was applied to the manner of oral delivery rather than to the written style of a composition. *Pronuntiatio,* which had meant primarily the management of voice and body, gradually took on our modern meaning of pronunciation as the correct phonation of individual words. By 1750, then, these shifts in meaning had taken place, and the term *elocution* had come to connote a considerable degree of emphasis on delivery. By this time, also, a renewed interest in reading aloud and in oratory had developed, especially in England, where an important group of writer-speakers known as the English Elocutionists had come into being. Outstanding among them were Thomas Sheridan (1719–1788) and John Walker (1732–1807), whose books and lectures had great bearing on the development in America of what we now call interpretation.

Thomas Sheridan, father of the famous dramatist Richard Brinsley Sheridan and himself an actor, published his *Course of Lectures on Elocution* in 1763. This book came out strongly against artificialities and stressed the method of natural conversation in the oral presentation of literature. Sheridan thus became known as the leader of the "natural school." His thesis was that elocution should follow the laws of nature. He held that body and voice are natural phenomena and are therefore subject to the laws of nature. He pointed out that nature gives to the passions and emotions certain tones, looks, and gestures that are perceived through the ear and the eye. Therefore, he contended, the elocutionist should reproduce these tones, looks, and gestures as nearly as possible in presenting literature orally to an audience.

As often happens in the application of a theory, however, Sheridan became trapped in his efforts to be specific, and he began to evolve a system of markings and cues for the discovery and reproduction of these "natural" tones and gestures. By the end of his career, he had become the exponent of a method that, judged by modern standards, was much more mechanical than natural. Nevertheless, the term "natural school" has persisted to the present day.

The other famous eighteenth-century English Elocutionist, John Walker, published his *Elements of Elocution* in 1781. He, too, professed to take his cues from nature. However, he could not (or at least did not) resist the urge to set down specific rules and markings for the slightest variations of vocal tempo, inflection, and force, and for the various aspects of gesture. These markings caught the public fancy because they were more concrete than anything that had been offered before. (It is always so much easier to be told exactly how to do something than to put one's own intelligence to work to solve each individual problem as it arises!) Walker must be given credit for stating clearly that these markings were intended as aids toward the satisfactory projection of the material at hand; and perhaps he is not to be held wholly responsible for the fact that future generations placed more emphasis on the markings and other mechanical devices than on the projection of material. Walker and his imitators, then, established what has been called the "mechanical school" — in seeming opposition to Sheridan's "natural school." Thus began a schism that occupied minds for one hundred fifty years.

Two other names must be mentioned in connection with the English Elocutionists of the eighteenth century. Although they were less prolific and influential than Sheridan and Walker, John Mason (1706–1763) and James Burgh (1714–1775) both wrote books that enjoyed considerable popularity. Mason's *An Essay on Elocution or Pronunciation* (1748), the first book to include the word *elocution* in its title, put heavy emphasis on the "right" management of the voice.

James Burgh was primarily a political philosopher whose interest in speech probably grew out of his political activities. In his book *The Art of Speaking* (1762), he discussed with some vehemence the rules for expressing "the principal Passions and Humors." This volume, which contained an anthology of readings, with the passions and humors carefully documented, was based on the theory that nature had given every passion its proper physical expression and that only by careful attention to the physical features, such as the eye, can the proper passion be projected.

To summarize, the closing years of the eighteenth century saw an increased interest in the use of voice and body in the oral presentation of literature. Sheridan had set up a "natural school," purportedly based on the "laws of nature"; Walker had established a "mechanical school," based in fact on the same premises but more preoccupied with markings and charts. It is understandable that the followers of these men tended to emphasize their differences rather than their similarities, and that some degree of confusion and dissension resulted.

In the nineteenth century, two names stand out above all others in the history of interpretation. The first is that of an American, James Rush (1786–1869), a medical doctor turned speech teacher and lecturer. Rush confined himself almost entirely to the study of vocal projection. He believed that the management of the voice is in reality not an art but a science, and he went to great lengths to develop an appropriate vocabulary for that science. Indeed, much of his terminology became standard among teachers of speech. He also went to great lengths in the title of his book, published in 1827: *The Philosophy of the Human Voice: Embracing its Physiological History: Together with a System of Principles by Which Criticism in the Art of Elocution May be Rendered Intelligible, and Instruction, Definite and Comprehensive, to Which Is Added a Brief Analysis of Song and Recitative.*

Rush developed elaborate charts and markings for pitch, force, abruptness, quality, and time. He was convinced that rules could be developed to govern the analysis of vocal technique, although he was careful to point out that the practice of these rules must be accompanied by concentration on the literature being read. This last bit of advice, however, was often forgotten by his more zealous and less discriminating followers; as a result, attention was focused even more sharply on markings and symbols. Nevertheless, Rush's use of appropriate scientific method and vocabulary and his studies of the mechanisms of the human voice were valuable contributions to the field of speech.

The second significant name in nineteenth-century interpretation is François Delsarte (1811–1871). About the time Rush's method was making its way in America, Delsarte was delivering lectures in France on elocution and calisthenics. He left no writings, but so strong was his influence that many of his students recorded his philosophy and system in great detail. The Delsarte system concerned itself entirely with bodily action, and it became an accepted complement to Dr. Rush's treatises on vocal management. Delsarte based his system on a philosophy of the interrelation of the human soul, mind, and body, and on a complicated and highly mystical concept of a corresponding triune relationship throughout the entire universe. Despite this philosophical premise, the system became mechanical in the extreme.

Delsarte, like Sheridan, Walker, and Rush, suffered somewhat at the hands of his followers. One example of the perversion of a basically sound but inadequately expressed theory — that gestures must spring from the heart — was the notion that all gestures must start from the breastbone and sweep out in a graceful curve. This misconception persisted for generations. Although Delsarte's system in practice took on mechanical aspects that had some unfortunate results, modern teachers of speech have been greatly influenced by his concept of mind, soul (heart or emotions), and body working together.

Thus, almost simultaneously, Rush in America was setting up a scientific approach to vocal technique and Delsarte in France was teaching a philosophical approach to bodily action. Although both men were originally concerned with the artistic projection of materials, the people they influenced often concentrated on the *application* of techniques rather than on the *reasons* for the techniques. In this way, the mechanical school, well established under the aegis of Walker's disciples, became even more firmly entrenched.

Near the close of the nineteenth century, the natural school received new impetus under the leadership of Samuel Silas Curry (1847–1921). His first book, *The Province of Expression*, published in Boston in 1891, was based on the major premise that the mind, to express an idea, must actively hold that idea and thus dictate the appropriate means of expression. This theory he summed up in the admonition "Think the thought!" It is understandable that such a phrase would catch the fancy of those who read his books and heard of his teachings — and equally understandable that it would lead to oversimplification, to the extent that Curry's fundamentally sound theory came to be popularized as "Think the thought and all things else will be added unto you." As a result, many teachers began to assert that the training of voice and body were wholly artificial and mechanical procedures, and that comprehension of thought and active concentration on that thought will alone ensure adequate projection of any material to an audience.

Admittedly, this idea came as a relief to those who had become weary of the exhibitionism that prevailed among the second- and third-generation advocates of the mechanical method. In an attempt to break more completely with the earlier artificialities, teachers even began to shy away from the term *elocution*, with all its connotations, and to adopt instead Curry's term *expression*. Thus, lessons in "elocution" became lessons in "expression."

One of the most interesting and influential teachers in America at the close of the century was Charles Wesley Emerson (1837–1908), founder of the Emerson College of Oratory, now Emerson College in Boston. His *Evolution of Expression* (1905) stressed vocal technique and gymnastics for their therapeutic value as well as for their contribution to the techniques of communicating literature.

By the end of the nineteenth century, then, three distinct groups had emerged: one militantly carried on the traditions of the mechanical school; another, distrustful of mechanics, relied on the natural method, and developed in the direction of "think-the-thought"; and a third was composed of a few independents who found some values in each camp and attempted to blend the two approaches.

During the same time, Victorian interest in earnest self-improvement and edification gave rise to emporiums for the dispersal of culture: for example, the Lyceum Movement, and, more prominently, the Chautauqua Institution. The latter was begun in the mid-nineteenth century as a Sunday-school teachers' summer camp and still thrives as a lively cultural center. At its most influential time, Chautauqua established nationwide book clubs and correspondence schools; great readers, speakers, and artists performed on its lecture platforms. Chautauqua was not an isolated phenomenon. From across the country came the call for performers and a full complement of touring guest artists and readers, who covered the country with uplifting readings and speeches, lectures, and programs. Famous readers or lecturers — Charles Dickens, for example, and Wendell Phillips — were paid considerable sums for their personal appearances. These professionals catered to the call for living performers. Periodicals and publications like *The Voice* and *Werner's Magazine* carried testimonials for products like voice balm, scripts with appropriate and elaborate markings, annotated transcriptions of how famous performers read famous speeches — all responding to the needs of amateur elocutionists in remote towns and villages.

By the beginning of the twentieth century, a number of colleges were offering courses in elocution or expression, but most students did not include speech in their program of studies unless they were preparing themselves for the ministry, politics, or law. Most of those who wished to do "platform work" as "readers" enrolled in private schools or studios. There they worked under teachers often three or four times removed from the originators of basically sound theories, and received instruction that, having filtered through several personalities, was strongly flavored by the individual teacher's own taste and understanding.

The first three decades of the twentieth century were the era of the private, highly specialized school or studio of speech. Each had its own staff of teachers, most of whom had been trained by the head of that particular school. Each had its own course of study and its own special emphasis. And each prided itself on its independence and its difference from the others. Consequently, there was no common philosophy or methodology. Each school emphasized its individuality, rather than working with the others toward solidarity and a unity of purpose among all teachers in the field.

Many people who studied at these schools returned to their homes, framed their certificates and hung them on their walls, and opened their own studios, where they taught to the best of their ability what they had learned. Their students, in turn, acquired certificates and went out to spread the gospel as they understood it. Thus, of the thousands of teachers who were conducting classes and giving private lessons, very few had had an opportunity to receive sound training under the great leaders. As a result, the original principles and practices were continually watered down. Not only were teachers often imperfectly prepared, but they worked in comparative isolation, without professional associations and strong university departments of speech to serve as centers for the exchange of ideas. The better informed and more progressive teachers who studied under Curry and his contemporaries grew with the entire educational system to become the outstanding men and women in the field of speech as a whole and in the more specialized area of interpretation. Others, however, continued to teach specific gesture, highly obtrusive vocal technique, and the use of materials of questionable literary merit, thus perpetuating not only the more regrettable excesses and misconceptions in vogue in the early years of the century but also a confusion in terminology and in standards of performance.

An important link between the theorists and teachers of the nineteenth century and the present is *Principles of Vocal Expression* (1897), by William B. Chamberlain (1847–1903) and Solomon H. Clark (1861–1927). This book, acknowledging a deep indebtedness to Curry, stressed the interaction of mind and body and the control of "instincts" by reason. Clark made a more important contribution in his *Interpretation of the Printed Page* (1913), which helped turn the attention of teachers and students from the mechanical techniques to the appreciation and analysis of the literature itself. His concept of "impression" as distinct from and prerequisite to "expression" became the basis of *The Art of Interpretative Speech*, by Charles H. Woolbert and Severina E. Nelson, published in 1929.

Another popular book of the early twentieth century was *Natural Drills in Expression with Selections* (1909). The author, Arthur Edward Phillips (1867–1932), reflects much of Chamberlain's interest in paraphrase and tone drills, and the book was used extensively for many years in schools and colleges.

With the advance of the twentieth century, departments of speech grew in stature in colleges and universities and became fully accepted members of the academic family. Speech training, freed from the cultist studio, flourished under the stimulating crosswinds of professional associations and the spur of more commonly shared standards. Ideas were pooled, theories argued, heritages re-evaluated. Interpretation emerged from the strait jacket of the "reading" (which was not a reading at all, but a virtuoso exhibition of memory and technique), and reoriented itself to the printed page.

The fourth decade of this century was one of transition and stabilization. Interest in history and research increased, as described by Mary Margaret Robb in *Oral Interpretation of Literature in American Colleges and Universities* (1947) and the establishment of doctoral programs in the field.

Cornelius Carman Cunningham, Gertrude Johnson, Wayland

Maxwell Parrish, Solomon Henry Clark, and Maud May Babcock published texts that had an important effect on the whole area of study. Although these books differ somewhat in emphasis, all firmly insist on the primacy of the literature and the importance of the demands it makes. These authors' ability to come to grips with critical and aesthetic principles and to formulate standards that apply to both analysis and performance contributed mightily to the field at mid-century.

In the 1950s and 1960s, the academic study of interpretation centered on the original and powerful rewards performance offered the literary study of texts. It followed, then, that during this period several analytical studies of individual texts, authors, and genres influenced the development of theory. These studies all emphasized in some way the unique kinds of information obtained through performance. At the same time, other theorists continued to view interpretation from a communication perspective: interpreter derives information from a text and then communicates this information to an audience. Still another group of theorists — smaller, but no less energetic or informed — believed that interpretation was essentially a method for developing the performance techniques of students while exposing them to good literature. Obviously, all of these theories have value. Since its first edition, this book has drawn on aspects of each of them, although we have consistently prized the value of performance as a way of knowing a literary work of art, recognizing that technical skills enhance and refine the act of performance both for audiences and interpreters themselves.

During the 1970s, changing ideas about the social responsibilities of literature outside the field and changing perspectives on the nature of performance outside the academic establishment began to affect the three prevalent theories of interpretation. Literary study continued to influence interpretation theory but, as literary theory began to reflect the insights obtained through deconstruction, post-structuralism and the de-centering of the *literary* text, contemporary interpretation theory had to confront new concepts of "text." In this respect — and in others — phenomenologists and speech act theorists greatly influenced the philosophical and theoretical foundations of the field.

If the nature of a "text" was expanding, so, too, was the nature, variety, function, and extent of "performance." The pervasive influences of performance in everyday life suggested other areas of study, other modes of research, and other avenues of discourse. Interpreters became interested in the ways that performance could derive from, and contribute to, political and social causes; thus, for example, theory needed to reflect Marxist or feminist perspectives on texts in performance. Interpreters saw more clearly how performance could alter the performer, and thus theory had to recognize the psychological and healing powers of the act of performance. As interpreters looked at their roots, at a heritage of one-person shows and monologists such as Ruth Draper, theory needed to account for the ways in which popular culture affected the art. Indeed, because performance is central to how we acquire knowledge of cultures, ethnographers contributed their insights to theory. The contributions of such diverse areas of interest (and there are many others, with vigorous adherents and important assistance to offer) obviously resulted in changes in theory and in the shape of the field, in the kinds of questions being asked, and in the ways traditional answers are being reconsidered. Some of this healthy ferment has been reflected in the emergence of the popular term *performance studies* as a way to describe the expanded scope of interest.

In the flux of these heady times, we must remember that social consciousness, political awareness, philosophical acumen, anthropological sensitivity, and responsiveness to developing literary theory need not be mutually exclusive interests. Each contributes to a fuller understanding of how inclusive "performance" has become in our — and indeed, in every — culture. Among the paths to Eden are many graveled walks. Access to the rewards of our field may be through any number of avenues, not the least of which remains the performance of literature. Careful scrutiny and thorough analysis of a "text" best permits the interpreter with a flexible, articulate instrument to "perform" that work for and with an audience.

Happily, the different paths of research pursued today are relatively free of the "thou-shalt-nots" that characterized interpretation in the early part of this century — and that is how it should be. With a mind open to the rich and startling insights offered by aestheticians, literary theorists, linguists, philosophers, ethnographers, folklorists, and performance theorists, today's interpreter realizes that the opportunities offered by performance and text are more numerous, attractive, and empowering now than at any time in our history.

Bibliography

The following works explore various aspects of the history of oral interpretation and suggest avenues for future development.

Pelias, R. J., and VanOosting, J. "A Paradigm for Performance Studies." In *Quarterly Journal of Speech*, 73 (1987), 219–231.

One of the earliest and most articulate rationales for changing the name of the field to reflect broadening research interests.

Strine, M. S., B. W. Long, and M. F. HopKins. "Research in Interpretation and Performance Studies: Trends, Issues, Priorities." In G. Phillips and J. Wood (eds.), *Speech Communication: Essays to Commemorate the 75th Anniversary of the Speech Communication Association*. Carbondale, Ill.: Southern Illinois University Press, 1989.
A magisterial discussion of how the development of the field has opened new territory to contemporary researchers, with potent suggestions for the kinds of research the field needs.

Taft-Kaufman, J. "Oral Interpretation: Twentieth-century Theory and Practice." In T. W. Benson (ed.), *Speech Communication in the 20th Century*. Carbondale, Ill.: Southern Illinois University Press, 1985.
A readable and clear-headed discussion of the development of oral interpretation in this century.

Thompson, D. W. (ed.). *Performance of Literature in Historical Perspectives*. Landham, Md.: University Press of America, 1983.
The product of eight years of research by six editors and thirty-three prominent scholars, this compendium explores "five continuing concerns of the field of interpretation, namely language, culture, teaching, theory, and entertainment."

Text and Performance Quarterly, formerly *Literature in Performance*, is a journal sponsored by the Speech Communication Association, "concerned with the whole process from creation and criticism of text through the creation and criticism of performance, together with the history and theory of both ends of the spectrum."

ACKNOWLEDGMENTS

Ackerman, Diane. "Still Life." Diane Ackerman, a poet and naturalist, is the author of ten books, the most recent of which are *A Natural History of the Senses* (prose), *Jaguar of Sweet Laughter* (poetry), and *The Moon by Whale Light*.

Albee, Edward. Reprinted with permission of Atheneum Publishers, an imprint of Macmillan Publishing Company, from *Who's Afraid of Virginia Woolf?* by Edward Albee. Copyright © 1962 by Edward Albee.

Allison, Jay. "Back at the Ranch." Copyright © 1990 by The New York Times Company. Reprinted by permission.

American Heritage Dictionary. © 1980 by Houghton Mifflin Company. Reprinted by permission from *The American Heritage Dictionary of the English Language, New College Edition*.

Angelou, Maya. From *I Know Why the Caged Bird Sings* by Maya Angelou. Copyright © 1969 by Maya Angelou. Reprinted by permission of Random House, Inc.

Auden, W. H. "Leap Before You Look" from *W. H. Auden: Collected Poems* by W. H. Auden, ed. by Edward Mendelson. Copyright 1945 by W. H. Auden. Reprinted by permission of Random House, Inc., and Faber and Faber Ltd.

Bambara, Toni Cade. "The Lesson" from *Gorilla, My Love* by Toni Cade Bambara. Copyright © 1972 by Toni Cade Bambara. Reprinted by permission of Random House, Inc.

Baraka, Imamu Amiri. "Preface to a Twenty Volume Suicide Note." Reprinted by permission of Sterling Lord Literistic, Inc. Copyright © 1961 Imamu Amiri Baraka.

Baumel, Judith. "Two Men Loved Me Once" © 1988 by Judith Baumel. Reprinted from *The Weight of Numbers* by permission of Wesleyan University Press and University Press of New England.

Beattie, Ann. "Snow" reprinted by permission of International Creative Management, Inc. Copyright © 1983 by Ann Beattie.

Bierhorst, John. From "The Night Chant," Navajo Ceremonial Chant, translated by Washington Matthews from *Four Masterworks of American Indian Literature*, edited by John Bierhorst, University of Arizona Press, 1984. Reprinted by permission of John Bierhorst.

Bishop, Elizabeth. "Filling Station" from THE COMPLETE POEMS, 1927–1979 by Elizabeth Bishop. Copyright © 1955 by Elizabeth Bishop. Copyright © 1979, 1983 by Alice Helen Methfessel. Reprinted by permission of Farrar, Straus and Giroux, Inc.

Bissinger, H. G. H. G. Bissinger, *Friday Night Lights*. © 1990 by H. G. Bissinger. Reprinted with permission of Addison-Wesley Publishing Company.

Bowen, Elizabeth. From THE LITTLE GIRLS by Elizabeth Bowen. Copyright © 1963 by Elizabeth Bowen. Reprinted by permission of Alfred A. Knopf, Inc.

Brecht, Bertolt. From *The Caucasian Chalk Circle* by Bertolt Brecht. Reprinted by permission of the University of Minnesota Press.

From *The House on Marshland*, first published by The Ecco Press in 1975. Reprinted by permission.

Hales, Corrine. "Power," by Corrine Hales, in *New Voices 1979–1983*, ed. May Swenson. Reprinted by permission of the Academy of American Poets.

Hamilton, Virginia. From THE PEOPLE COULD FLY by Virginia Hamilton. Text copyright © 1985 by Virginia Hamilton. Reprinted by permission of Alfred Knopf, Inc.

Hammond, Mary Stewart. "Saving Memory" is reprinted from OUT OF CANAAN, Poems by Mary Stewart Hammond, by permission of W.W. Norton & Company, Inc. Copyright © 1991 by Mary Stewart Hammond.

Handke, Peter. From *Offending the Audience*. Excerpt from KASPAR AND OTHER PLAYS by Peter Handke. Translation copyright © 1969 by Farrar, Straus and Giroux, Inc. Reprinted by permission of Farrar, Straus and Giroux, Inc.

Hardy, Thomas. "In Church" from THE COMPLETE POEMS OF THOMAS HARDY, edited by James Gibson (New York: Macmillan, 1978).

Heaney, Seamus. "Mid-Term Break." From *Death of a Naturalist* by Seamus Heaney. Copyright 1985. Reprinted by permission of Faber and Faber Limited.

Hongo, Garrett Kaoru. "Who Among You Knows the Essence of Garlic?" © 1980 by Garrett Kaoru Hongo. Reprinted from *Yellow Light* by permission of Wesleyan University Press and University Press of New England.

Hoyt, Helen. "The Sense of Death" from *The Home Book of Modern Verse*, edited by Burton E. Stevenson. Reprinted by permission of the Trustee for the Burton E. Stevenson Endowment for Children.

Hughes, Langston. "The Negro Speaks Rivers." From SELECTED POEMS OF LANGSTON HUGHES by Langston Hughes. Copyright 1926 by Alfred A. Knopf, Inc. and renewed 1954 by Langston Hughes. Reprinted by permission of the publisher.

James, Henry. "Letter to Grace Norton." Reprinted with permission of Charles Scribner's Sons, an imprint of Macmillan Publishing Company from THE LETTERS OF HENRY JAMES edited by Percy Lubbock. Copyright 1920 Charles Scribner's Sons; copyright renewed 1948 William James and Margaret James Porter.

Joans, Ted. "The .38." From BLACK POW-POW by Ted Joans. Copyright © 1969 by Ted Joans. All rights reserved. Reprinted by permission of the Author's Representative, Gunther Stuhlmann.

Joyce, James. From FINNEGAN'S WAKE by James Joyce. Copyright 1939 by James Joyce. Copyright renewed © 1967 by George Joyce and Lucia Joyce. Used by permission of Viking Penguin, a division of Penguin Books USA Inc.

Keillor, Garrison. From LAKE WOBEGON DAYS by Garrison Keillor. Copyright © 1985 by Garrison Keillor. Used by permission of Viking Penguin, a division of Penguin Books USA Inc.

Kunitz, Stanley. "Open the Gates." From *Selected Poems 1928–1958* by Stanley Kunitz. Copyright 1929, 1930, 1944, 1951, 1953, 1954, © 1956, 1957, 1958 by Stanley Kunitz. By permission of Little, Brown and Company.

Larkin, Philip. "Home Is So Sad" reprinted with permission of the author.

Lassell, Michael. "How to Watch Your Brother Die" is from *Poems for Lost & Unlost Boys*, Poems by Michael Lassell, AMELIA Press, 1985.

Leavitt, David. From THE LOST LANGUAGE OF CRANES by David Leavitt. Copyright © 1986 by David Leavitt. Reprinted by permission of Alfred A. Knopf, Inc.

Macdonald, Cynthia. "The Kilgore Rangerette Whose Life Was Ruined." From (W)HOLES by Cynthia Macdonald. Copyright © 1980 by Cynthia Macdonald. Reprinted by permission of Alfred A. Knopf, Inc.

MacLeish, Archibald. "Ars Poetica" from NEW AND COLLECTED POEMS 1917–1982 by Archibald MacLeish. Copyright © 1985 by the Estate of Archibald MacLeish. Reprinted by permission of Houghton Mifflin Co.

Madgett, Naomi Long. "Her Story" from *Star by Star* by Naomi Long Madgett, Detroit. Harlo, 1965, Evenill, 1970. With permission of the author.

Malamud, Bernard. "The Prison" from THE MAGIC BARREL by Bernard Malamud. Copyright © 1950, 1958, 1977 by Bernard Malamud. Reprinted by permission of Farrar, Straus and Giroux, Inc.

Marshall, Archibald. "The Detective" from *Simple Stories [for Children and Grownups]* by Archibald Marshall. Copyright 1927. Reprinted by permission of Tessa Sayle Agency.

McGough, Roger. "40–Love." From *After the Merrymaking* by Roger McGough. Reprinted by permission of Jonathan Cape, Publishers, and Peters Frasers & Dunlop.

Millay, Edna St. Vincent. Sonnet XXX of FATAL INTERVIEW by Edna St. Vincent Millay. From COLLECTED SONNETS, Revised and Expanded Edition, Harper & Row, 1988. Copyright © 1931, 1958 by Edna St. Vincent Millay and Norma Millay Ellis. Reprinted by permission of Elizabeth Barnett, Literary Executor.

Moon, William Least Heat. From *BLUE HIGHWAYS: A JOURNEY INTO AMERICA* by William Least Heat Moon. Copyright © 1982 by William Least Heat Moon. By permission of Little, Brown and Company.

Morrill, Claire. "Miss Lizzie." From *A Taos Mosaic, Portrait of a New Mexico Village*. Albuquerque: University of New Mexico Press, 1973. Copyright held by author. Used by permission of the author.

Morrison, Toni. From *Sula*, by Toni Morrison. Copyright © 1973 by Toni Morrison. Reprinted by permission of Toni Morrison.

The New Testament. From *The Holy Bible, King James Version*. Copyright 1974 by New American Library, a division of Penguin Books USA Inc.

Olds, Sharon. "The Race." Reprinted by permission; © 1985 Sharon Olds. Originally in The New Yorker.

Ovid. "The Story of Baucis and Philomen" from *The Metamorphoses* by Ovid, translated by Rolfe Humphries. Copyright 1955. Reprinted by permission of Indiana University Press.

Pinter, Harold. From *Betrayal* by Harold Pinter. Copyright © 1978 by H. Pinter Limited. Used by permission of Grove Press, Inc., and Faber and Faber Ltd.

Pound, Ezra. From *Writers at Work: The Paris Review Interviews*, Second Series, edited by George Plimpton. Copyright 1963. Reprinted by permission of Penguin USA.

Proust, Michael. From *Within a Budding Grove* by Michael Proust, translated by C. Scott Moncrieff. Copyright 1970 by Random House, Inc.

Ransom, John Crowe. "Bells for John Whiteside's Daughter." From SELECTED POEMS, 3RD ED., REVISED & ENLARGED by John Crowe Ransom. Copyright 1924 by Alfred A. Knopf, Inc. and renewed 1952 by John Crowe Ransom. Reprinted by permission of the publisher.

Read, Herbert. From *English Prose Style* by Herbert Read. Copyright 1952. Reprinted by permission of Pantheon Books, a Division of Random House, Inc.

Roethke, Theodore. "Child on Top of a Greenhouse" copyright 1946 by Editorial Publications, Inc. "The Waking" and "Old Lady's Winter Words" copyright 1948, 1952 by Theodore Roethke. All from *The Collected Poems of Theodore Roethke* and reprinted by permission of Doubleday & Company, Inc.

Rostand, Edmond. CYRANO DE BERGERAC by Edmond Rostand, translated by Brian Hooker. Copyright 1923, 1937 by Henry Holt and Company, Inc. Copyright 1951 by Doris C. Hooker. Reprinted by permission of Henry Holt and Company, Inc.

Roth, Philip. "The Conversion of the Jews" from GOODBYE COLUMBUS by Philip Roth. Copyright © 1959 by Philip Roth. Reprinted by permission of Houghton Mifflin Co.

Salter, Mary Jo. "The Upper Story." From UNFINISHED PAINTING by Mary Jo Salter. Copyright © 1989 by Mary Jo Salter. Reprinted by permission of Alfred A. Knopf, Inc.

Santoli, Al. From *Everything We Had* by Al Santoli. Copyright 1981 by Al Santoli and Vietnam Veterans of America. Reprinted by permission of Random House, Inc.

Schlissel, Lillian. From *Women's Diaries of the Westward Journey*, ed. Lillian Schlissel. Reprinted by permission of Gertrude Tortillot Bradley.

Sexton, Anne. "Ringing the Bells" from TO BEDLAM AND PART WAY BACK by Anne Sexton. Copyright © 1960 by Anne Sexton. Reprinted by permission of Houghton Mifflin Co. "Cinderella" from TRANSFORMATIONS by Anne Sexton. Copyright © 1971 by Anne Sexton. Reprinted by permission of Houghton Mifflin Co.

Shange, Ntozake. Reprinted with permission of Macmillan Publishing Company from

For Colored Girls Who Have Considered Suicide/When the Rainbow is Enuf by Ntozake Shange. Copyright © 1975, 1976, 1977 by Ntozake Shange.

Shakespeare, William. All selections from *Complete Plays and Poems of William Shakespeare*, edited by William Allan Neilson and Charles Jarvis Hill. Copyright © 1942 by Houghton Mifflin Company. Used with permission.

Shaw, George Bernard. Reprinted by permission of The Society of Authors on behalf of the Bernard Shaw Estate.

Sherman, Deborah. "Dulce." Reprinted by permission of the author.

Singer, Isaac Bashevis. Excerpt from "A Crown of Feathers" from A CROWN OF FEATHERS by Isaac Bashevis Singer. Copyright © 1974 by Isaac Bashevis Singer. Reprinted by permission of Farrar, Straus and Giroux, Inc.

Solt, Mary Ellen. "Forsythia" from *Concrete Poetry: A World View*, edited by Mary Ellen Solt. Copyright 1969. Reprinted by permission of Indiana University Press.

Sondheim, Stephen. Copyright © 1984 and 1987 by Revelation Music Publishing Corp. & Rilting Music, Inc. A Tommy Valando Publication, International Copyright Secured, Made in U.S.A., All Rights Reserved.

Sophocles. From *Three Theban Plays* by Sophocles, translated by Theodore Howard Banks. Copyright © 1956 by Theodore Howard Banks; renewed 1984 by Marian C. Banks. Reprinted by permission of Oxford University Press, Inc.

Stevens, Wallace. "The House Was Quiet and the World Was Calm." From THE COLLECTED POEMS OF WALLACE STEVENS by Wallace Stevens. Copyright 1947 by Wallace Stevens. Reprinted by permission of Alfred A. Knopf, Inc.

Terkel, Studs. From WORKING: PEOPLE TALK ABOUT WHAT THEY DO ALL DAY AND HOW THEY FEEL ABOUT WHAT THEY DO by Studs Terkel. Copyright © 1972, 1974 by Studs Terkel. Reprinted by permission of Pantheon Books, a division of Random House, Inc.

Thomas, Dylan. Reprinted by permission of Harold Ober Associates Inc. Copyright © 1961 by the Trustees for the Estate of Dylan Thomas.

Updike, John. "A & P." From PIGEON FEATHERS AND OTHER STORIES by John Updike. Copyright © 1962 by John Updike. Reprinted by permission of Alfred A. Knopf, Inc. Originally appeared in "The New Yorker."

Walker, Alice. Poem from Introduction in HORSES MAKE A LANDSCAPE LOOK MORE BEAUTIFUL, copyright © 1984 by Alice Walker, reprinted by permission of Harcourt Brace Jovanovich, Inc.

Welty, Eudora. From *One Writer's Beginnings*. Reprinted by permission of the publishers from ONE WRITER'S BEGINNINGS by Eudora Welty, Cambridge, Mass.: Harvard University Press, Copyright © 1983, 1984 by Eudora Welty. From *Losing Battles* by Eudora Welty. Copyright © 1970 by Eudora Welty. Reprinted by permission of Random House, Inc.

West, Nathaniel. Nathaniel West: *Miss Lonelyhearts*. Copyright © 1933 by Nathaniel West, 1960 by Laura Perelman. Reprinted by permission of New Directions Publishing Corporation.

Wilson, Lanford. Scene from 5th OF JULY by Lanford Wilson. Copyright © 1969 by Lanford Wilson. Reprinted by permission of Hill and Wang, a division of Farrar, Straus and Giroux, Inc.

Wright, James. "Autumn Begins in Martin's Ferry, Ohio" © 1971 by James Wright. Reprinted from *Collected Poems* by permission of Wesleyan University Press and University Press of New England.

"A Blessing" © 1961 by James Wright. Reprinted from *The Branch Will Not Break* by permission of Wesleyan University Press and University Press of New England.

Yeats, William Butler. "Among School Children." Reprinted with permission of Macmillan Publishing Company from *The Poems of W.B. Yeats: A New Edition*, edited by Richard J. Finneran. Copyright 1928 by Macmillan Publishing Company, renewed 1956 by Georgie Yeats.

"The Second Coming." Reprinted with permission of Macmillan Publishing Company from *The Poems of W.B. Yeats: A New Edition*, edited by Richard J. Finneran. Copyright 1924 by Macmillan Publishing Company, renewed 1952 by Bertha Georgie Yeats.

SUBJECT INDEX

SELECTIONS INDEX